Incidental Archaeologists

INCIDENTAL ARCHAEOLOGISTS

*French Officers and the Rediscovery
of Roman North Africa*

BONNIE EFFROS

CORNELL UNIVERSITY PRESS
ITHACA AND LONDON

First published 2018 by Cornell University Press

Printed in the United States of America

Library of Congress Cataloging-in-Publication Data

Names: Effros, Bonnie, 1965– author.
Title: Incidental archaeologists : French officers and the
   rediscovery of Roman North Africa / Bonnie Effros.
Description: Ithaca : Cornell University Press, 2018. |
   Includes bibliographical references and index.
Identifiers: LCCN 2017048068 (print) | LCCN 2017051402 (ebook) |
   ISBN 9781501718533 (epub/mobi) | ISBN 9781501718540 (pdf) |
   ISBN 9781501702105 | ISBN 9781501702105 (cloth)
Subjects: LCSH: Archaeology—Political aspects—Algeria—
   History—19th century. | Archaeology—Political aspects—
   France—History—19th century. | Archaeology and state—
   France—History—19th century. | France—Armed Forces—
   Algeria—Operations other than war—History—19th century. |
   Algeria—Antiquities, Roman. | Algeria—History—1830–1962.
Classification: LCC CC101.A4 (ebook) | LCC CC101.A4 E34 2018
   (print) | DDC 965/.03—dc23
LC record available at https://lccn.loc.gov/2017048068

To Max and Simon, in the fervent hope
that you will know only peace in your lifetimes

De patria meo uero, quod eam sitam Numidiae et Gaetuliae in ipso confinio meis scriptis ostendistis, quibus memet professus sum, cum Lolliano Auito c. u. praesente publice dissererem, Seminumidam et Semigaetulum, non uideo quid mihi sit in ea re pudendum, haud minus quam Cyro maiori, quod genere mixto fuit Semimedus ac Semipersa. Non enim ubi prognatus, sed ut moratus quisque sit spectandum, nec qua regione, sed qua ratione uitam uiuere inierit, considerandum est.

Apuleius, *Apologia*, ed. and trans. Paul Valette,
2nd ed. (Paris: Les Belles Lettres, 2002), 56–57

Car une ère nouvelle, une ère dévastrice va s'ouvrir pour cette contrée; peut-être serez-vous tenté de venir observer cette quatrième domination. N'en faites rien; épargnez-vous le déplaisir d'un cruel mécompte. Surtout si vous cherchez un aliment à l'admiration que vous professez pour la France, votre beau pays, restez, restez chez vous, et gardez-vous bien de la venir voir dans ses colonies.

Ernest Carette, *Précis historique et archéologique sur
Hippone et ses environs* (Paris: Imprimerie
Lange Lévy et Compagnie, 1838), 16

Les Romains se sont perpétués en Afrique; la race créole française, née sur place et fille des premiers immigrants, commence elle-même à y faire souche.

Gustave Boissière, *Esquisse d'une histoire de la conquête
et de l'administration romaines dans le nord de l'Afrique
et particulièrement dans la province de Numidie*
(Paris: Librairie Hachette et Cie, 1878), 81

CONTENTS

ACKNOWLEDGMENTS

Thinking initially that I would explore the impact of French excavations in North Africa on the professionalization of archaeology in late nineteenth-century France, I launched this book project without fully anticipating the violence I would see recorded in the documents conserved in the French overseas and military archives. With the pioneering work of Nabila Oulebsir as a guide to where I should begin, I commenced my research at the same time I accepted a position as the Rothman Chair and director of the Center for the Humanities and the Public Sphere at the University of Florida in August 2009. For his encouragement throughout this journey, I thank Peter Brown, who enthusiastically cheered along my initial and tentative exploration of the topic and provided helpful guidance as the research advanced. I am also grateful for the generosity of Éric Rebillard, who, even before I had actually begun this undertaking, gave enormously sound advice on how I might approach the topic of North African archaeology and where archival sources might be located. Nina Caputo's razor-sharp input came at a crucial moment as I debated how to move forward with the evolving project and encouraged me to make the most of the disparities between French metropolitan and colonial archaeological practice. I owe to Suzanne Marchand, whose writing continues to serve as a model for the history of antiquarianism and archaeology, a great debt for her firm encouragement of this undertaking from its earliest stages. Margarita Díaz-Andreu and Michael Kulikowski were likewise stalwart backers of the project from its earliest phases, and Peter Potter, then at Cornell University Press, paved the way for its publication.

This venture into a territory thoroughly unfamiliar to me before the start of my research would not have been possible had it not been for generous funding from the Robert and Margaret Rothman Endowment at the Center for the Humanities and the Public Sphere at the University of Florida, which I directed from 2009 to 2017. The Rothman Endowment made it possible for me to make repeated visits to archives and libraries in Paris and Aix-en-Provence between 2010 and 2016 and to acquire many of the photographs reproduced in this volume, and it provided a subvention that enabled me to illustrate the volume sufficiently. In 2013, a National Endowment for the Humanities (NEH) Summer Stipend (FT-60454-13) allowed me to travel for two months to archives in Paris and the Getty Research Institute, where I gained access to relevant photographic evidence and rare nineteenth-century printed works. In 2013–2014, a George Kennan Membership at the School of Historical Studies at the Institute for Advanced Study in Princeton, with additional funding provided by the Hetty Goldman Membership Fund, and support from the College of Liberal Arts and Sciences at the University of Florida, gave me eleven blissful months nearly free of teaching and administrative responsibilities. While there, I benefited from both the collections and the capable research staff of the History-Social Science Library and Princeton University's Firestone and Marquand Libraries, as well as the famous Institute Woods, a peaceful setting for mind and body. In this setting, I profited enormously from the expertise of Michael von Walt von Praag, Patrick Geary, and the members of their working groups on modern international relations and medieval history, respectively. In particular, I want to acknowledge the timely advice and assistance of Yücel Yanikdağ, Hennig Trupper, and the late Patricia Crone, who came to the rescue when I had questions about modern armies, nineteenth-century antiquaries, and Arab historians, respectively.

At Princeton University, both Matthew McCarty and Brent Shaw offered friendly encouragement and advice on the project.

In January 2015, a conference grant from the American Council of Learned Societies Comparative Perspectives on Chinese Culture and Society Program, funded by the Chiang Ching-kuo Foundation for International Scholarly Exchange, gave my colleague Guolong Lai and me the unparalleled opportunity to invite thirteen international scholars to the University of Florida for a comparative workshop with their counterparts in Gainesville on colonial archaeology in a global context, an event that proved incredibly inspiring and instructive for my thoughts on how to shape this book. In 2015–2016, I spent a year of funded research leave from the University of Florida at the Centre d'études supérieures de civilisation médiévale (CESCM) at the Université de Poitiers at the generous invitation of Cécile Treffort, then the director. My family and I were received with great warmth and hospitality by its new director, Martin Aurel, and members as I wrote the second half of this book in France. In addition, for the incredible impetus offered by their invitations to present or publish the ongoing work in progress, I am grateful to Leora Auslander and Tara Zahra (Chicago), Alexandra Chavarría (Padua), Michael Decker (Tampa), Margarita Díaz-Andreu (Barcelona), Sang-Hyun Kim (Seoul), the late Henrika Kucklick (Philadelphia), Richard McMahon (Portsmouth), Daniel Sherman (Chapel Hill), Alice Stephenson (London), Lillian Tseng (New York), and Philipp von Rummel (Berlin). As I have put the finishing touches on this volume, I want to express my great thanks to my new colleagues at the School of Histories, Languages, and Cultures at the University of Liverpool for the warm welcome they have given me and my family during our recent transatlantic move to the United Kingdom.

My debts at this point are many, and I hope that I have not inadvertently omitted the name of anyone to whom thanks are due. I acknowledge with gratitude Sophia Acord and Sean Adams, who backed me by generously agreeing to take on the leadership of the Center for the Humanities and the Public Sphere during my two year-long absences from Gainesville, and Barbara Mennel for taking on this role as I departed. Tim Blanton and Allison Millett helped in myriad ways, most of all scanning articles, helping look after our boys when our hands were full, and tending to our home when we were overseas. Successive College of Arts and Sciences (CLAS) deans at the University of Florida, Paul D'Anieri and David Richardson, supported me in my research endeavors at and away from the Center for the Humanities and the Public Sphere despite the administrative complications they involved, and Head of School Lin Foxhall and Head of History Elaine Chalus at the University of Liverpool have been a great support during my transition to life and work in northern England. To Matthew Delvaux, I owe an extraordinary debt for his generosity in sharing his expertise in military history and his patience in sifting through each chapter in progress with a fine-toothed comb for possible problems and lacunae while launching his own dissertation at Boston College. Nina Caputo, Alexandra Chavarría, Alice Conklin, Sarah Davies Cordova, Wendy Doyon, Corisande Fenwick, William Gallois, Mitch Hart, Ashley Jones, Michael Kulikowski, Matthew McCarty, Nabila Oulebsir, Fiona Rose-Greenland, Jaime Wadowiec, Yüçel Yanikdağ, and the anonymous readers for Cornell University Press offered helpful critiques, advice, and suggestions on parts of or all of the manuscript in progress. At Cornell University Press, Mahinder Kingra, Karen M. Laun, Julie F. Nemer, and Carolyn Pouncy all worked to tame the infelicities of my unruly prose, increase the consistency of my citations, and smooth the narrative of this book.

For their general encouragement on this project and life in general, I am grateful for the warmth of old and new friends, including Sophia Krzys Acord, Sharon Goss Bacharach, Stephanie Bohlmann, Courtney Booker, Ursula Brosseder, Nina Caputo, Wendy Brown Chapkis, Gary Condon, Sarah Davies Cordova, Marios Costambeys, Dianne Benveniste Golden, Guy Halsall, Susan Mason, Makeda Moore, Isabel Moreira, Hiral Parekh, Laura Sandy, and Cécile Treffort. My love and great thanks for their unwavering support through thick and thin go to my husband, David Laber; my parents, Richard and Gail Effros; my siblings Michelle Effros and Jim Effros; my brother-in-law John Murillo; and my extended family, especially Edward and Rita Effros, Steve and Suzanne Effros, Rachel Effros, Jane and Steven Hochman, and Marcia Katel Cohen. To David, especially, who has been a stalwart companion through extended travel, work, and recent illness, I would like to publicly express my gratitude for his cheerful willingness to look after the boys, make lunches, and cook untold meals so that I could meet the challenges that have unfolded while this project was underway. While it will be impossible to repay the enormous debt I have incurred during the past few years, I will try anyway. I am so glad that he has not yet regretted any of our adventures. Last, but far from least, I dedicate this book to Max and Simon, two mischievous fellows who think that their mom gets too much "screen time" on her computer but humor her with visits to lots of "broken buildings," despite their preference for things more modern. Although their heart is in the "pouma planet during the honey age" (where they imagine their origins lie), they have willingly accompanied me to far off destinations on this earth and adjusted to the new places we have embraced as home whether for brief sojourns or longer stays. As they continue to grow, I hope that they will understand someday how much I treasure their laughter, hugs, questions and insights, drawings, flowers, and stories, and how much lighter their presence has made the burden, while writing this book, of confronting the untold miseries that humans create for one another through greed, xenophobia, and historical amnesia.

Abbreviations

AD	Archives départmentales
AIBL	Académie des inscriptions et belles-lettres
A.G.M.Afr.	Archives de la Société des Missionaires d'Afrique
AN	Archives nationales
ANOM	Archives nationales d'Outre-Mer
BNF	Bibliothèque nationale de France
MAN	Musée d'archéologie nationale
SHAT	Service historique de l'Armée de Terre

Note on Spellings

In this volume, with a few exceptions such as Lambaesis and al-Jazā'er, I have privileged the French spelling of place names (with Arabic and Latin alternatives in parentheses on the first use) and institutions, because these were the names by which French officers knew and wrote about these locations. All translations, unless otherwise indicated, are my own.

INCIDENTAL ARCHAEOLOGISTS

Introduction

WAR AND THE DESTRUCTION OF ANTIQUITIES IN THE FORMER OTTOMAN EMPIRE

With reports of the obliteration of ancient archaeological sites in Syria and northern Iraq by Daesh regularly on the front page of the news, many in the West have reacted with disbelief and outrage to the fundamentalist theater of destruction.[1] They have blamed the pillage, looting, and purposeful demolition of monuments for destabilizing the moral economy that underlies the conservation of World Heritage sites.[2] Yet many commentators have neglected to mention that for more than a century Europeans argued that these antiquities, and the monuments of which they were a part, had little or no value to the Arab inhabitants of the lands from which they were purchased, stolen, received as gifts, or taken by force.[3] European imperial powers alleged the indifference or hostility of Indigenous peoples toward ancient remains and therefore invoked archaeological claims to assert their right not only to procure or "protect" artifacts but also to impinge on the jurisdiction of foreign powers, in this case the Sublime Porte.[4] Indeed, Ottoman authorities sought to curb this wholesale European appropriation, and in some cases theft, of antiquities from various parts of the empire as yet one more feature of European intransigence with regard to its territorial sovereignty.[5] Legislation passed in the 1870s and 1880s not only attempted to ban the export of ancient remains but also established antiquities museums in Istanbul and Tunis. Both measures enjoyed only limited success.[6] After the fall of the Ottoman Empire, the Muslim and Christian populations in the Middle East and North Africa continued to pay a high price for Western claims to the ancient patrimony located on their lands.[7]

The nearly two-hundred-year struggle over the rightful place of ancient monuments located in the former Ottoman Empire context is fundamental to understanding Daesh's recent destruction of classical remains. Although their rhetoric for the annihilation of these remains has included references to their pagan origins, most of the Roman monuments under attack did not share the anthropomorphic features central, for instance, to the Taliban's iconoclastic justification of the destruction of the Buddhas of Bamiyan in Afghanistan in 2001.[8] Roman architectural remains instead constitute potent symbols of European imperial power in ancient just as in modern times. The annihilation of symbols identified with Western civilization has become a powerful tool by which Daesh rejects Western hegemony and conveys its dismissal of de facto Western claims (via international bodies such as the United Nations Educational, Scientific and Cultural Organization [UNESCO]) to the universal value of these sites for humankind.[9] In fact, the designation of World Heritage status may even have made some Syrian monuments more desirable targets of the wrath of Daesh.[10] Efforts to save ancient monuments from destruction through exportation or replace them digitally, undertakings benefitting primarily Western audiences who have funded them, have contributed to the one-sidedness of the conservation narrative.[11] By rejecting Western narratives of the foundation of civilization and claims to the benefits of cultural internationalism and "encyclopedic museums" made by institutions such as the British Museum, the Louvre, the Getty Museum, and the Pergamon Museum, fundamentalist actors in the Middle East have staked a claim to a new world order, one just as, if not more, destructive than the last.[12]

Although the case of the active annihilation by Daesh of classical monuments, as at Palmyra and ancient monuments at Nineveh, is extreme, the negative perception of Roman and other pre-Islamic monuments that underlies its ideology is far from unique in the Middle East and North

Africa. The ambivalent legacy of nineteenth- and early twentieth-century archaeology has shaped the selective reception of classical and biblical-era remains in modern Israel and Egypt,[13] just as it has affected conservation policy in the post-colonial Maghreb, where suspicion of French narratives of history has led to the near erasure of events that do not fit with postcolonial discourse.[14] In the People's Democratic Republic of Algeria, the perception that Arabs and Berbers have little connection to the classical past (an argument first made by colonial authorities in the time of the French conquest) has contributed no doubt to the present shortfall of resources available for the preservation of ancient Roman sites like Tombeau de la Chrétienne.[15] In Tunisia, despite the peaceful symbiosis between the living populations and ancient remains for more than a millennium before the arrival of the French, the convergence of European archaeological research with colonial domination has left bitter memories among the Arab and Berber populations.[16] The legacy of Tunisians' complex relationship to ancient monuments has continued to be negotiated since the revolution in 2011.[17] It undoubtedly also contributed to terrorists' choice of the Bardo Museum in Tunis as the site of an attack in March 2015 that left twenty-two dead.[18]

These recent examples underline the intimate connection between the modern destruction of classical antiquities and the persistent legacy of European colonial and postcolonial violence to both the people and objects found in North Africa and the Middle East. Although in the past thirty years, the bloody history of the French conquest of Algeria (1830) has been studied with an increasingly critical eye and its connections to the archaeology of the Maghreb have been firmly established, the main focus of these publications, with few exceptions, has been on the period following 1871, when research in the Maghreb was first institutionalized under the colonial administration of the Third Republic.[19] By contrast, significantly less attention has been granted to the more poorly documented and frequently idiosyncratic contributions of the largely self-appointed imperial officer-archaeologists who explored ancient remains during the period from 1830 to 1870. These men, in an emergent and still amateur field, laid the groundwork for the more formal archaeological and anthropological investigations that began in the last third of the nineteenth century, when the decontextualization and commodification of archaeological objects became a dominant trope and opened the door to the more formal instrumentalization of archaeological ethics in the twentieth century.[20]

In an effort to fill this important lacuna, in this book I address the mostly unmanaged explorations of military (and a few civilian) archaeological enthusiasts in the context of the ongoing French onslaught on the former Ottoman principalities of al-Jazā'er and Constantine. Not only did their wartime explorations shape the mission and narrative of classical archaeology in North Africa for decades to come with a near exclusive focus on military remains, but the ideological implications of officers' claims to and appropriation or destruction of the unique historical heritage of ancient monuments also had a more direct impact on military strategy than heretofore expressed in the context of the tradition of imperial collecting. In an exceedingly violent and destructive colonial war that included a retributive massacre against the civilian population of the city of Blida (southwest of Algiers) in November 1830, an attack on the El-Ouffia tribe that nearly eliminated its entire membership in April 1832, and French military and economic policies that resulted in the loss of more than a third of the Indigenous population by the late 1860s, these military officers' activities underlay the conquest and pacification of what would become the French colony of Algeria.[21] As becomes clear in the chapters that follow, their involvement in archaeology, which may have been at times haphazard and often lacked the approval of their commanding officers, nonetheless had immediate utility in military strategy and tactics. As military officers, their archaeological activities differed in significant ways from traditional orientalist research and altered irrevocably the European antiquities rush from which many of their methods derived.[22]

The European Antiquities Rush

What were the origins of what Suzanne Marchand has characterized as the "antiquities rush"? Among European states, she points to the unregulated and competitive amassing of ancient monuments and artifacts by Napoleonic armies that raided Egypt and Rome at the turn of the nineteenth century.[23] The popularity of such enterprises at home helped normalize and legitimize this form of rapacious looting and collecting of antiquities.[24] During Napoleon I's Egyptian campaign and those that followed, prized monuments were wrenched from their original environs for transport to imperial museums in France, Great Britain, and elsewhere in Western Europe.[25] While alleging his intention to transform Egypt into a modern country, moreover, Napoleon directed French forces under his command not just to gather antiquities but also to document historical and geographical information for the metropole.[26] Indeed, his abbreviated campaign in Egypt coupled collecting with a new model of cartographic and scientific exploration directed at imperial military objectives. In the course of this "muscular" venture in North Africa, scholars such as Vivant Denon did not simply expropriate antiquities in the manner of wartime booty.[27] More important in the long term was how they used these "scientific" activities to promote the primacy of French culture and values.[28] Edward Said has noted that Napoleon's military-scientific mission brought about structural change, normalizing "foreign conquest within the cultural orbit of European existence."[29]

The medium by which Denon conveyed this information was lithography, a technology that he avidly promoted from 1809 due to the superior quality of the new process for multiplying art and text (despite its potential dangers for the Napoleonic regime from those who wished to disseminate subversive ideas).[30] The remarkably successful series collectively known as the *Description de l'Égypte* (1809–1829) not only popularized an idealized vision of ancient Egypt but also helped substantiate and circulate claims of French military and scientific prowess.[31] Although the authors of the lavishly illustrated expedition volumes of the Napoleonic mission gave great attention to antiquities, however, they largely turned their back on the modern inhabitants of the region (except to castigate them for allegedly damaging these same monuments). In the French missions that followed Napoleon I's venture to Egypt, particularly those to the Peloponnese and Algeria in the 1820s and late 1830s, respectively, military-scientific expeditions were honed as an instrument of imperial domination.[32] The garb of European military officers had become the de facto costume and vernacular for European scholarly exploration and subsequent expropriation. Symptoms of this change may be seen in the French and British search for the mythical city of Timbuctoo in this period, when explorers wore military uniforms as opposed to dressing in the less obtrusive fashion that had been the custom of European travelers to Africa and the Middle East in the eighteenth century.[33]

Despite the disastrous end of Napoleon's military campaign in Egypt, this landmark undertaking made the ancient past an integral feature of broadly defined scientific research, which in turn supported subsequent French efforts to identify, claim, order, and govern the patrimonial resources of the lands their forces dominated, conquered, or occupied. In the case of Egypt in the following decades, during and after the reign of Muhammad 'Ali (Mehmed 'Ali in Ottoman Turkish), scientific exploration was coupled with large-scale French projects such as the construction of the Suez Canal and British interest in commercial agricultural crops such as cotton. Mid-nineteenth-century excavations in Egypt took advantage of broad changes in labor practices that the European presence had helped usher in, namely the transition from corvée to largely unskilled wage labor.[34] There the search for antiquities (and later archaeological research) was entangled in a complex matrix of developments linked to European intervention in the Egyptian economy.[35]

As noted by Bruce Trigger, the practice of "imperial archaeology" allowed states to extract archaeological resources from other parts of the world and use them to exert political dominance.[36] To be certain, archaeological exploration in the early nineteenth century was an unsophisticated affair: it consisted mostly of disengaging stone structures and inscriptions from surrounding debris with little attention to context or stratigraphy. This approach was the result of archaeological science remaining largely subservient to the narrative of classical texts and inscriptions, which were the primary subjects of study.[37] French colonial activities in the decades that followed Napoleon's conquest of Egypt, and particularly in the context of the French occupation of the Maghreb, gave epigraphical and archaeological study, among other disciplines, significant impetus because they provided the raw materials needed to benefit cartographic studies and military planning.[38] The type of material collected focused on items that directly or indirectly supported the goal of imperial dominance and thus reflected metropolitan values and needs rather than those of the regions' Indigenous residents.[39] We should therefore not be surprised that the antiquities and monuments "discovered" in the Mediterranean basin acquired symbolism specifically linked to Western knowledge and offered historical justification for European control over subject populations.

French Military and Archaeological Intervention in al-Jazā'er

In 1827, French military intervention in the Maghreb began with a naval blockade of Algiers. This act of aggression followed the French consul's refusal to address Hussein Dey's demand that France pay the 8 million francs still owed to two Jewish merchant families for wheat that had been supplied to French revolutionaries between 1793 and 1798.[40] The consequent embargo, which created an economic crisis in the south of France, only worsened the political challenges faced by the Bourbon regime. In July 1830, on the pretext of combatting piracy and Christian slavery on the Barbary Coast, Charles X authorized the naval bombardment and invasion of the Regency of al-Jazā'er. Although the successful French landing at Sidi Ferruch (Arabic [A.]: Sidi Fredj), 30 kilometers to the west of Algiers, was also intended to bolster the French king's rapidly waning popularity, the French monarch was forced to abdicate within weeks of the landing and was replaced by his cousin Louis-Philippe.[41]

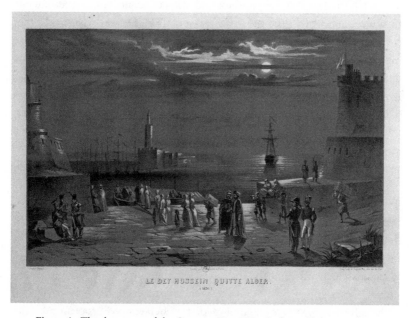

LE DEY HUSSEIN QUITTE ALGER.

Figure 1. The departure of the Ottoman Dey Hussein from Algiers in 1830. Reproduced by permission of the Bibliothèque nationale de France, Département des estampes et de la photographie.

In the initial assault, the landing of thirty-seven thousand armed soldiers quickly led to the dissolution and exile of the Ottoman administration, which had for centuries operated with significant autonomy from Istanbul.[42] During the early years of the July Monarchy, Louis-Philippe was forced to deal with the consequences of the poorly thought-out North African incursion into a territory inhabited at that time by somewhere between three and five million inhabitants.[43]

Although Louis-Philippe's reign was not otherwise shaped by ambitious military ventures, his eighteen-year tenure saw the rapid expansion of the armée d'Afrique (as the French army in North Africa was known) to nearly three times its initial size by the early 1840s.[44] Many of the military officers who led the costly campaign were graduates of the École polytechnique, and as disciples of social reformers such as Prosper Enfantin, they thought of themselves as bringing about the enlightenment and material improvement of the colonial territory (and, thereby, metropolitan France) through scientific and technological innovation.[45] But their idealism ran contrary the realities of a brutal military campaign, and they seemed, at least initially, wholly impervious to the consequences of the damage they wrought against the Indigenous population. Despite assurances that the French would respect the religion and property rights of the region's mainly Muslim inhabitants, the armée d'Afrique quickly resorted to using deadly measures against civilian residents.[46] As I discuss in chapter 1, from the start of the invasion, French forces confiscated homes, land, and places of worship from Arab and Kabyle (as the French called the Berbers) inhabitants.[47] They indiscriminately massacred any who resisted French authority in the former Regency, a nominal Ottoman possession on the fringes of the empire.[48]

In 1831 and 1832, the destruction of numerous buildings in the city center, including mosques, had already begun. Colonial authorities alleged that these measures were necessary to create an assembly place for the armée d'Afrique and convey in physical terms the imposition of a new order on the former Ottoman Regency of al-Jazā'er.[49] The French Government-General, which was quickly assembled for the purpose of ruling the conquered territory, oversaw what the French christened "Algeria" by 1838. Although there was an exception made for enclaves of European-majority populations, which from the mid-1840s were governed by civilian authorities, the military regime administered the expanding territory under French authority until the establishment of the Third Republic in 1870.

From the early years of this four-decade period of violent military rule, a substantial number of French officers stationed in the colony elected to engage in archaeological research on ancient sites they encountered during their campaigns. Because Roman monumental remains were among the most visible, and certainly the most familiar to officers steeped in classical military history, French officer-archaeologists in Algeria tended to devote their attention almost exclusively to this period rather than more recent epochs (or more ancient ones, whether prehistoric or Punic). For the most part, moreover, these efforts were self-directed rather than initiated at the command of metropolitan or military authorities. Their undertakings mainly involved identifying and drawing monuments, transcribing inscriptions, creating topographical maps with reference to ancient remains, and digging for the purpose of dislodging monuments hidden from full view so that they might be displayed. When they engaged with Roman monuments, officers personally identified with the conquerors who had built them in the second, third, and fourth centuries. This connection allowed them to justify a particularly brutal modern campaign by finding parallels in the ancient past.[50] The kinship that officers felt with the ancient Roman legions also allowed them to distance themselves from the Arab population of the region, whom they dismissed as comparative newcomers whose arrival dated to the seventh century.

In contrast to Napoleon's Egyptian campaign, the Ministry of War did not initially organize a scholarly expedition to Algeria, despite calls for

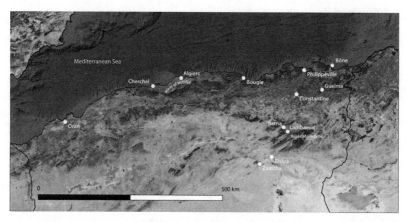

Figure 2. Some of the locations central to French archaeological exploration in mid-nineteenth-century Algeria.

them to do so by the Académie des inscriptions et belles-lettres. As I discuss in chapter 1, metropolitan officials did so only belatedly and hesitantly nearly ten years after the invasion, when a group of civilians and military officers vetted by the Académie des inscriptions et belles-lettres and the minister of war were permitted at last to launch a modest program for scientific exploration in the region. Begun in 1839, the project ended abruptly in 1842, when participants were ordered to depart from North Africa due to concerns for their safety.[51] Performed largely by or under the protection of the officers of the armée d'Afrique, their research, which included archaeological exploration, offered tacit if not enthusiastic ideological and practical support for the French imperial military operations of which it formed a part. Like a spider web or a root system, as vividly characterized by Margarita Díaz-Andreu, colonial discourse became not just an intrinsic part of administrative practice but also of contemporary academic research.[52]

The legacy of French colonialism in Algeria is still the subject of debate in contemporary French politics.[53] Nevertheless, imperial scientific exploration explicitly supported a regime that had few contemporary parallels in terms of its brutality.[54] In a discourse formed of European military chauvinism, a Saint-Simonian vision of modernization, and "irrefutable" scientific rationale, the disciplines of classical history, epigraphy, numismatics, and archaeology helped cement claims for the historical connections between the ancient Roman and modern French conquerors of the region. The French hailed themselves as a new Rome with authority over a defeated Africa, as commemorated in a nineteenth-century medallion celebrating French prowess.

Together with ethnographic surveys and interviews of the Indigenous population conducted by the Bureaux arabes (Office of Arab Affairs) from the 1860s onward, archaeological exploration also supported administrators' claims of continuity between the ancient Maures, subject peoples to the ancient Romans, and the contemporary Kabyles of Algeria.[55] The result, to which classical studies were an essential contributor, formed a narrative that helped the French legitimize their claim that their rule would bring the benefits of civilization to the Arab and Kabyle populations of the Maghreb.[56]

Ignoring the admonition of the second-century Algerian native son Apuleius that comportment and the values by which one lived were more

Figure 3. Medallion commemorating Charles V's conquest of Algiers in July 1830. The imagery incorporates a pastiche of iconographic elements borrowed from ancient Roman coinage. Marianne wears Minerva's helmet as Roma and sits atop a defeated lion, an emblem of North Africa from as early as Punic times. Reproduced by permission of the Bibliothèque nationale de France, Département de monnaies, médailles et antiques.

important than one's place of birth, the French imposed a rigid new order on the conquered territory and its largely illiterate population.[57] French authorities claimed that both the Arabs and Kabyles—especially the former, whom they characterized as more fanatical—had not evolved over time but had instead remained mired in a primitive stage of development. As noted by Homi Bhabha, French colonialism depended on "the concept of 'fixity' in the ideological construction of otherness."[58] It also had little room to accommodate "permanent outsiders."[59] By contrast, the French viewed themselves as having passed through this stage centuries earlier when they were under Roman rule. They therefore promoted the idea that French intervention in the Maghreb would allow the Maures to return to their former glory.[60]

Nevertheless, the outcome of colonization, as Aimé Césaire has argued, is not the alleged civilizing of the colonized but the dehumanization of the colonizers.[61] The colonial-historical perspective that reigned in French circles allowed many authorities to deny responsibility for their failed experiments in social engineering. To name one, in the late 1860s, when hundreds of thousands of Algerian Muslims died from largely human-induced famine, in addition to plague, typhus, and cholera epidemics, advocates of colonial expansion suggested that the poor outcome for the Indigenous residents was not the result of French policies. Rather than accept responsibility for the dire consequences of colonial practices implemented by first French military and then civilian officials in Algeria, these advocates alleged that natural selection was eliminating populations that were biologically and culturally inferior.[62]

Diplomatic Exploration of the Maghreb

In actual fact, the exploration and expropriation of Algerian antiquities during the first forty years of French military intervention in Algeria were exceptional; they marked a significant rupture with how European antiquaries had treated the Maghreb historically, because the region had not previously been understood to hold the material remains of the ancient European past. Indeed, compared to the long-standing French, German, and British activity in Ottoman Egypt, Greece, Asia Minor, and regions further to the east, the Maghreb was a relative backwater for the harvest of antiquities in the eighteenth and early nineteenth centuries.[63] This neglect stemmed in part from a widespread preference, well into the late 1870s, for Hellenic models of civilization and culture over what many British characterized as the degeneracy of Roman imperialism.[64] The oversight of North African antiquities also had much to do with a balance of power in which European travelers were still relatively vulnerable in the lands they visited, which in this case had a reputation mainly linked in the West with piracy and Christian slavery. This contrasted significantly with French confidence in the same territory decades later, when the exploration of Roman remains was applied directly to the objectives of conquest, domination, and settlement.[65]

Even so, the Roman ruins of the Maghreb were by no means completely unknown to those of an antiquarian bent. Travelers ventured to North Africa for a variety of reasons during the early modern period and took note of monuments and inscriptions and sometimes even succeeded in exporting them.[66] In the late seventeenth and eighteenth centuries, a handful of European antiquaries received authorization to undertake voyages of exploration in the Ottoman regencies based in Tunis and Algiers. Most of the men who enjoyed such opportunities and survived to relate them had come to North Africa as a result of official diplomatic or religious duties. Their responsibility as consuls or their support staff—dragomen (guides or translators), physicians, and clerics—included gathering a variety of information in the Ottoman provinces with the consent of their host dignitaries as well as seeing to the needs of the small communities of Europeans who lived in the Maghreb mainly for commercial purposes. These European enthusiasts and adventurous travelers typically benefited from either a background in the classics or a religious education that enabled them to appreciate the vestiges of the ancient civilizations they encountered.[67]

While at the Ottoman court at Tunis between April 1667 and April 1668, the Italian physician Giovanni Pagni corresponded with colleagues in Europe and made observations to them about what he saw during his visit, including references to ancient monuments. Between 1688 and 1690, Claude Le Maire, while serving as the French consul in Tripoli, exported twenty-nine marble columns to metropolitan France from the Roman site of Leptis Magna.[68] Shipped from Tripoli to Toulon, the spolia he gathered were reused in architectural contexts at Saint-Germain-des-Prés, Versailles, and the cathedral of Rouen.[69]

In the early eighteenth century, the Spanish priest Ximenes, administrator of a hospital of Christian slaves in Tunisia, also visited Roman monuments such as Sbeïtla and El Jem.[70] He was a contemporary of and knew the French physician and naturalist Jean-André Peyssonnel, who made more substantive contributions to the study of ancient monuments, along with his successors the British chaplain and antiquarian Thomas Shaw and the Scottish antiquarian James Bruce. Shaw, in particular, was trained at the University of Oxford and traveled extensively through North Africa between 1720 and 1732 before returning to Queens College, where he was elected a fellow. By contrast, Bruce, a minor aristocrat of Scottish descent, was in Algiers following his appointment as British consul by Lord Halifax.[71] During his stay in the Regency of al-Jazā'er, he improved his Arabic and prepared for an expedition to the African interior, where he planned to look for the source of the Nile.[72]

In the early nineteenth century, following Napoleon's venture to Egypt, European visitors to North Africa also counted among their numbers the Milanese Barnabite monk Caroni and Sir Grenville Temple, a lieutenant-colonel in the British cavalry.[73] While in the Maghreb, they collected everything from botanical specimens to climatological data, and they also drew maps and sketches of principal ancient sites and recorded some of the inscriptions they found in the region.[74] And, of course, travel to North Africa was not a prerequisite for writing about the Roman period. In 1816–1817, for instance, the Italian Jesuit epigrapher Stephano Antonio Morcelli compiled a history of early Christianity in the region working almost exclusively from ancient literary evidence and inscriptions that had already been published by earlier explorers.[75]

A good portion of antiquaries' attention was trained specifically on the ancient Punic capital of Carthage in the Regency of Tunis. The Dutch military engineer Jean-Émile Humbert (in 1817, 1822, and 1824), Count Camillo Borgia of Naples (1816), the Danish consul Christian Falbe and the British consul-general Thomas Reade (from 1824); and the Paris-based Society for the Exploration of Carthage, which sponsored Falbe and Temple in 1838, each received permission from the Bey of Tunis to conduct exploratory excavations.[76] Their objective was to export to their respective countries any obtainable objects of artistic and scientific value, regardless of the damage it caused to the location from which these items were harvested.[77] As a consequence of this activity, mostly classical artifacts from the Maghreb made their way to the Museum of Leiden, the National Museum of Copenhagen, the Louvre, and the British Museum. Others, such as the author and historian François René de Chateaubriand, who visited Carthage in 1807, were content to write of the glory of the ancient landscape and the death of Louis IX from dysentery near this location in 1270 while engaged in the eighth crusade.[78]

In addition, there were contemporary travelers, explorers, dragomen, and military officers active in archaeological exploration in what would become modern Libya, including the Italian physician Della Cella, in service to the Bey of Tripoli (1819); the British Royal Navy officer William Beechey and his half-brother Henry William (1821–1822); and Jean-Raymond Pacho (1824–1827).[79] Slightly later, but more in the style of these earlier ventures, were the excavations and collecting activities of the dragoman-chancellor of the French Consulate General of Tripoli, Joseph Vattier de Bourville. His explorations were based at Benghazi in the ancient Roman province of Cyrenaica.[80]

With the conquest of Algiers in July 1830, the French applied many of the lessons they had learned from Egypt. They initially established their monopoly over archaeological studies in the occupied territory because they required information about ancient ruins to supplement older maps and accounts in support of their military conquest and subordination of the region.[81] As their work became increasingly trained on its service to French national (as opposed to international scholarly) objectives, the focus of their interest shifted from traditional efforts to trace the origins of Western civilization to an uncritical celebration of Roman imperialism.[82] As was generally true of military practice in this period, French officers devoted their attention above all to geographical and epigraphical studies, as well as addressing any other topics that might allow them to learn Roman techniques for governing the North African territory. The military and antiquarian expertise gained on the Algerian front might then be taken elsewhere. For instance, after serving under General Bertrand Clauzel, commander of the armée d'Afrique in 1833, Arnauld d'Abbadie traveled to Ethiopia with his older brother Antoine. Some of his observations tended toward the mundane: he wrote of local apparel there as being not dissimilar from the Roman toga.[83] In such a context—as was also true, for instance, of the British in colonial India—the role of antiquarian, epigrapher, scientist, and officer were easily conflated.[84]

The French Officer Corps and Roman Archaeology

The officer corps of the French army was the source of most of the men who conducted archaeological exploration in the years that followed the

French invasion of the Regency of al-Jazā'er. The corps had faced significant decline during the Bourbon Restoration (1816–1830) because, following the final defeat of Napoleon I in 1815, many of his former commanders faced assassination or exile. In addition, these men were often replaced by returning aristocrats with little wartime experience.[85] Thus, between 1820 and 1848, the number of French military officers fluctuated only slightly between fifteen thousand and sixteen thousand, a figure that grew to twenty-two thousand by 1855 (excluding those who commanded troops specific to the war in Algeria, such as the Tirailleurs indigènes—light infantry recruited locally—and the Foreign Legion).[86] They commanded a reduced standing army of two hundred thousand men and a royal guard of eight regiments of infantry and cavalry. From 1824, the French army conscripted sixty thousand men annually to serve for a period of eight years, a requirement that was reduced to seven years in 1832.[87]

During the July Monarchy (1830–1848) and the Second Empire (1852–1870), most French officers in active service came directly from the technical and military schools created or reorganized by Napoleon I, including the École polytechnique, the École spéciale militaire de Saint-Cyr, the École de Saumur, and the École d'application de l'artillerie et du génie de Metz. Despite a series of decrees by Louis-Philippe reforming the training and promotion of officers, the factor of privilege never disappeared from these formerly aristocratic schools: the cutthroat entrance exams and cost of preparation for such institutions resulted in a distinct lack of democratization in the officer corps, and especially the cavalry, a situation that prevailed until the start of the Third Republic in 1871. By contrast, soldiers who became commissioned officers without the benefit of the military academies did so, to a large extent, on the basis of rank, meaning that they had already served in the army for eight years, at least four of them as noncommissioned officers. Preference for direct promotion was given to candidates from military or bourgeois families as opposed to those from the popular classes, who faced greater scrutiny to ascertain that they possessed the proper demeanor in addition to the ability to read, write, and calculate. Although they had significant field experience, the officers who bypassed the schools lacked the theoretical and administrative training received by their contemporaries and were liable to be slighted by their academy-trained colleagues.[88]

Founded in the late eighteenth century, the École polytechnique was considered the premier technical school in the West and sent its graduates into the army, navy, public works, mining, and industry. Although the institution was briefly under the authority of the Ministry of the Interior from 1816 to 1831, it was thereafter restored to the portfolio of the Ministry of War. The École polytechnique's entrance exams were highly competitive, with about one-sixth admitted of those who sat for them from the mid-1830s. School officials tested candidates' knowledge in arithmetic, plane and solid geometry, conic sections, algebra, trigonometry, statics (physics), drawing, Latin translation, and French composition.[89] Among the faculty of the institution, at least for a brief period of time, were some who had exhibited significant interest in classical antiquities. These included the cartographer Edme-François Jomard, editor of the *Description de l'Égypte*, and Karl Benedikt (Charles-Benoît) Hase, a German philologist who taught ancient history and numismatics.[90] The latter was known to have impressed on his students the importance of the ancient past in shaping the French vision of the future of North Africa.

By comparison with the École polytechnique, entrance exams at the École spéciale militaire de Saint-Cyr were somewhat less severe and consisted mainly of mathematics. Knowledge of Latin disappeared from the requirements, although it was reinstated in 1861. These prerequisites gave candidates from private institutions a distinct advantage over those from the popular classes who had received a lay public education, because they could not afford the approximately 2,000 francs it cost to attend a preparatory school. These conditions, in addition to the cost of attending a military school with few options available for stipends, reinforced the overwhelming number of students coming from well-to-do homes.[91] They also meant, however, that many men with ambitions of becoming officers arrived at these institutions with a knowledge of Latin and classical history, a background that meant that ancient monuments and inscriptions were a "reassuring point of reference" wherever they encountered them.[92]

Training at the École polytechnique and the École Saint-Cyr lasted typically two but sometimes as long as three years. At the former, students' time was dedicated to learning calculus, stereotomy (descriptive geometry of three-dimensional objects), general physics, chemistry, mechanics, astronomy, geodesy, topographical, landscape and figure drawing, military studies, French composition and literature, and German.[93] At Saint-Cyr, students enrolled in courses on mathematics, chemistry, physics, cartography, drawing, military history, administration, fortification, and offensive and defensive exercises (which were often practiced through elaborate field exercises).[94] Not all polytechniciens entered the military, however; some went into positions in state munitions manufacturing, the corps of engineers responsible for bridges and highways, a variety of industrial occupations, and so on. Nonetheless, the cartographic and drafting skills they acquired, as well as their knowledge of ancient battles and fortifications, meant that academy-trained officers who developed an interest in antiquities were better prepared to engage practically in archaeological study than their civilian contemporaries.

Many graduates, especially of the École polytechnique, moved from this program to further their training in more specialized applied schools. These included, among others, the École d'artillerie et du génie de Metz, the École d'état-major at Paris, the École des ponts et chaussées, the École des mines, and the École du génie maritime.[95] At Metz, in addition to learning the practical skills of operating and transporting artillery, offensive and defensive tactics, skills on horseback, and mapmaking, students were expected to continue their study of mathematics, physics, drawing, architecture, and military construction during their two-year stay.[96] From 1845, they benefited from access to spaces in which to conduct military exercises, a library, and laboratories in which to study geodesic calculations, chemistry, physics, and natural history. They learned topography from a collection of relief models, could use equipment for lithography, and of course trained with horses kept at the stables at Metz.[97] Although this educational background and such important skills were not acquired with the intention of engaging in the study of the ancient past, such pursuits became a logical preoccupation of many officers trained at Metz once they were stationed in distant regions in which Roman monuments were plentiful.

With the invasion of the Regency of al-Jazā'er in the summer of 1830, those who deplored the state of the military during the Bourbon Restoration saw a golden opportunity for the regeneration of the French army. Although the conquest force consisted of thirty-seven thousand troops, the size of the armée d'Afrique ballooned to one hundred and eighteen thousand men by the mid-1840s under Governor-General Bugeaud; the armée d'Afrique constituted of roughly one-third of a significantly expanded

Zouave d'Afrique.

Figure 4. Indigenous infantryman of the Zouaves, who often served alongside French soldiers under the command of French military officers in Algeria. Ferdinand-Désiré Quesnoy, *L'armée d'Afrique depuis la conquête d'Alger* (Paris: Librairie Furne Jouvet et Cie, 1888).

French standing army.[98] From an early date in the conquest, forces in North Africa included Indigenous troops who proved to be of great utility to French forces. In October 1830, General Clauzel sanctioned the creation of French-led battalions of Zouaves, composed in part of Indigenous soldiers recruited for their reputation for being exceedingly fierce in battle.

These men were integrated with Parisian volunteers who had fought in the July Revolution but had subsequently found their unit, Volontaires de la Charte, dissolved. The armée d'Afrique often cobbled such unruly units together in columns with the fragmented contingents of the recently created Foreign Legion, which was transferred in 1831 from Toulon on France's southern coast to Algiers.[99] Similar approaches were taken in recruiting cavalry. In November 1831, the French established two regiments of light cavalry known as the Chasseurs d'Afrique. Their squadrons included a mix of French volunteers, settlers, and Indigenous cavalrymen who were supplemented by less well-compensated Indigenous cavalrymen known as the Spahis (or Sipahis in Ottoman Turkish). Despite the lack of success in instilling discipline among such troops, French administrators favored their enlistment for service in the territory of Algiers because it enabled metropolitan authorities to rid French urban centers of potentially disruptive elements and allowed French military officials in North Africa to deprive Indigenous leaders of potential recruits.[100]

The rapid expansion of the armée d'Afrique to prosecute the war in the former Ottoman territory had an enormous impact on the entire French army, and the violence that resulted shocked even the most seasoned senior officers.[101] Despite the dangers, many military men were attracted to service in North Africa owing to the possibility of earning promotions twice as quickly as they could if they remained in continental Europe.[102] Due to the numbers of conscripted soldiers who served in Algeria, the poorly organized war in the Maghreb now became a practical training ground for French troops, a role it had never been intended to play.[103] The mix of metropolitan troops with Indigenous forces, the rush to put newly minted officers into the field, and the rapid deployment of fresh conscripts in battle had negative effects on both relations with the Muslim inhabitants and the army itself. Indeed, even those who supported the war complained that the officers and soldiers who trained under such conditions suffered from poor discipline, insufficient instruction, and their encounters with a human and geographical terrain that had little connection

ALGÉRIE.

SPAHIS.

Figure 5. Indigenous light cavalry known in the nineteenth century as the Spahis or Sipahis. HIP/Art Resource, NY.

with their European training.[104] In Algeria, newly minted officers learned harsh tactics to deal with civilian populations as a result of their inexperience, their troops' ramshackle origins, and the difficult situations they were called to face. They thus responded with a level of force that had heretofore been considered unacceptable in a noncolonial setting.[105] The result, perhaps not much different from the ancient Roman experience, was a rapidly growing army with little effective oversight, ambitious officers eager for conflicts that would further their quest for rapid promotion, and poorly disciplined and underprovisioned troops prone to violence. These obvious problems with the military infrastructure were reformed only after the Prussian defeat of France in 1870.[106]

French military officers serving in Algeria, most the product of the highest-level French schools, thus encountered, and in many cases provoked, the appalling violence that characterized the North African campaign. It was in this degraded environment of field operations that some of these same officers opted, in certain circumstances, to express sensitivity to or interest in ancient monuments as they prosecuted the war in the French colony. By contrast, French soldiers, unless given explicit orders to participate in these activities, were not typically involved in archaeological exploration due to their limited familiarity with classical history, inability to read Latin (and often French), and apparent lack of interest in such undertakings. They were more typically blamed for looting.[107] These contradictory, and often rapidly changing, conditions were the matrix of and shaped the practice of Roman archaeology in French Algeria between 1830 and 1870.

Colonial Archaeology in Algeria, the Formative Decades: 1830–1870

In French Algeria, the extent to which the ancient Roman legacy was exploited depended on who was involved in the enterprise and to what ends they applied it.[108] By the early twentieth century, for instance, French authors such as Pierre Hubac denied the relevance of Rome as a model for France.[109] Yet, although approaches to the ancient past were far from monolithic in their expression and application, and some scholars expressed a degree of empathy for the informants they encountered, archaeological research conducted in the first four decades of the French colony was almost without exception supportive of French national and imperial objectives.[110] It benefited from what Gary Wilder has characterized as the inherent structural contradictions of colonial modernity, including the "tension between coexisting policies to abstract and modernize or to differentiate and primitivize subject populations."[111] Nearly all studies were undertaken as a part of or inspired by French military operations financed by the Ministry of War, and nearly all engendered the marginalization or destruction of the populations researchers encountered in the course of their activities. And as this interpretation—or robbery—of the North African Roman past, accrued from historical sources, inscriptions, and monuments, and percolated deeply into the wider social consciousness, it accumulated scholarly weight.[112] Its public acceptance allowed administrators, officers, and scholars of the Third Republic to construct a unified and seemingly uncomplicated vision of the Mediterranean as "Latin."[113]

Because of the inconsistent and contradictory nature of early archaeological exploration in Algeria, many of the scholars who have explored the implications of scientific endeavors in the Maghreb have concentrated on the period in which institutionalization began, at the start of the Third Republic in 1870.[114] In particular, studies of archaeology have focused on the period following 1880, when the Service des monuments historiques en Algérie was established.[115] The last decades of the century were particularly important for the professionalization of the discipline, since it was then that greater efforts were made to regularize excavation procedures; institutionalize collecting, research activities, and publications; and formalize the existence of colonial archaeological museums and Roman tourist sites such as Thamugadis (French [F.]: Timgad) in Algeria and Tunisia.[116] This period also saw the emergence of physical anthropology and ethnography.[117] Myriam Bacha and Clémentine Gutron have painstakingly reconstructed the activities of military and civilian archaeological enthusiasts in the French Protectorate of Tunisia following its creation in May 1881.[118] The religiously motivated archaeological contributions of clerics such as Alfred-Louis Delattre of the White Fathers (Pères blancs) in the Maghreb during this period have likewise solicited important scholarly attention.[119]

By the end of the nineteenth century, there is no doubt that archaeological endeavors had become deeply engrained in the activities of the colonial state. Nevertheless, French colonial scholars' relationship to the antiquities of the Maghreb revealed the uneven valuation of the ancient monuments and the human beings who lived, worked, and died in their vicinity; in many ways, these matters were viewed no more critically in the early twentieth century than before. In the 1890s at Dougga (Latin [L.]: Thugga) in Tunisia, for example, when Louis Carton, a medical officer in the French army who became an active defender of ancient monuments and a promoter of tourism in Carthage and elsewhere in his adopted land, wished to proceed with excavations, French authorities forcibly removed the Indigenous residents from their homes built on the ancient site and subsequently destroyed them.[120] Although archaeological activities were cast in the language of science and the need to purify ruins of later accretions, Muslim inhabitants quickly learned from such incidents that ancient remains simply offered metropolitan authorities an additional excuse to disrupt their lives and confiscate their property.

In contrast to important studies by Gutron, Bacha, Jan Jansen, Alice Conklin, and others that focus on the period after 1870, in this book I concentrate on the first four decades of the French conquest and pacification of Algeria under the authority of the French military Government-General. Although it did not reach full flower until the late nineteenth century, the seeds for the discourse of the French "mission civilisatrice" were planted in the first four decades of the French conquest and sustained through the collection, consumption, and display of Roman antiquities.[121] During this poorly planned but rapidly evolving phase of the invasion and colonization of the former Ottoman regency, the initiative and persistence of individual military officers and occasional French civilians, rather than a directive from the Ministry of War or the governor-general, prepared the ground for French claims to be the rightful custodians of the Roman past. This ideological framework allowed French authorities, officers, and colonists to argue confidently in later decades that they were the legitimate and heroic heirs of the Romans.[122] Although it was not the motivation for the colonization of the region, French officers' belief that they possessed the right to control much of North Africa not only influenced military tactics in the region but also—which is more important—provided historical justification that helped sustain French officers through brutal military campaigns against both Indigenous armies and civilian populations.

During this initial phase of the conquest, self-styled archaeologists and epigraphers took independent and often idiosyncratic paths in their research that benefited from the entwined nature of republicanism and colonialism.[123] This less well-studied period, once called the "âge héroïque" of archaeology (as opposed to the "la période des réalisations" of the 1880s and 1890s), matched the most destructive phases of the conquest and colonization of the former Ottoman Regency of al-Jazā'er.[124] My focus on the period prior to 1870 also makes it imperative to restore to the history of archaeology the human tragedy that underlay what were once thought of as "heroic" archaeological interventions. Although this exploratory phase of archaeological endeavors in Algeria owed much to Napoleon's venture in Egypt, in which the Arab and nonwhite pasts were written over in favor of the classical past, it nonetheless represented a groundbreaking and formative enterprise.[125] The North African conquest offered self-appointed officer-archaeologists, and a small number of civilians, considerable intellectual latitude in shaping their own undertakings and interpreting their results. It is true that military officers could not control certain critical facets of their lives such as the location where they were stationed and the amount of time they had available for drawing ancient monuments and maps, copying ancient inscriptions, and collecting antiquities (issues that were typically controlled by the minister of war or their superior officers in response to contemporary military exigencies). Nevertheless, they shared, on the basis of their training in institutions such as the École polytechnique, a number of preconceived notions about France's place in history and on the world stage. Thus, despite the lack of directives from higher authorities and the relative freedom of officer-archaeologists to set the objectives and priorities of their explorations, their activities were fairly homogeneous. Their work, and its underlying assumptions, laid the foundation for more regular archaeological undertakings in subsequent decades, by which time many of the sites in the region studied by these initial colonial explorers had been destroyed or altered beyond recognition.

Despite the uneven archival terrain for this period, a substantial number of important studies of the military, political, and ideological implications of the initial French conquest and settlement of the former Ottoman territory have appeared in rapid succession.[126] Similarly, historians of archaeology and architecture inside and outside Algeria have given attention to this formative epoch. They have begun by filling in the critical outline of the developments proposed by Marcel Bénabou and Jacques Frémeaux[127] and laid out in greater detail by Paul-Albert Février in the 1980s.[128] Most notably, Monique Dondin-Payre, Nabila Oulebsir, Nadia Bayle, and Ève Gran-Aymerich have assessed the impact of central figures on Algerian monuments: Adrien Berbrugger, founder of the Bibliothèque et Musée d'Alger (1835); Captain Adolphe-Hedwige-Alphonse Delamare and Amable Ravoisié of the Commission d'exploration scientifique d'Algérie

(1839–1842); Colonel Jean-Luc Carbuccia at Lambaesis (1848–1850); Léon Renier and his epigraphical research in the vicinity of the Aurès Mountains (1850–1852); and the archaeological publications of more ephemeral participants during this period.[129]

The task remains, in large part, to link these tenacious archaeologists and their lesser-known contemporaries to more than the broader archaeological and epigraphical developments of which they were a part, including the widespread destruction that often served as the catalyst of their activities.[130] Indeed, officer-archaeologists made more than a practical contribution to the quotidian features and milestones of the military operation in which they were frequently intimately involved.[131] Taking inspiration from, among others, Gutron's critique of the aims and implications of archaeology in Tunisia under the French Protectorate, I underline the irresponsibility of creating pristine or romanticized narratives of classical archaeology in Algeria.[132] It is necessary to reassert the violence that was an integral part of archaeological exploration yet rarely figured in the official reports of excavation, the documentation of monuments, or the scholarly publications that celebrated the fruits of archaeological activities in Algeria.[133]

Yet the story that we can tell of this early phase of archaeological research is, like any other historical account, shaped to a significant degree by the original organizational principles of the imperial and colonial archives.[134] According to Oulebsir, what is preserved in the archives of the People's Democratic Republic of Algeria related to this project is negligible for the middle third of the nineteenth century.[135] And the Archives nationales d'Outre-Mer (ANOM) in Aix-en-Provence (Bouches-du-Rhône), as they are now known, are a relatively recent creation containing papers related to Algeria among a core of documents "repatriated" to metropolitan France in the 1960s. These holdings were consolidated at ANOM with items originally held at the Centre de recherches des archives nationales (CARAN) in Paris, which were moved to Aix, despite protest, following a 1979 fire that threatened the storage area of the overseas documents.[136] Most recently, as my own project was underway, some items of relevance to the study of archaeology of Algeria, such as correspondence between French ministries that remained at CARAN until the early 2010s, have been moved to the branch of the Archives nationales (AN) located at Pierrefitte-sur-Seine (Seine-Saint-Denis).

Whereas references to archaeological institutions and regulations during the Third Republic are fairly well documented in the organizational apparatus at ANOM, CARAN, and AN Pierrefitte-sur-Seine, documenting extant administrative correspondence and circulars of the Third Republic and afterward, the number of archival files related to the first forty-year phase of archaeological activity in Algeria is not substantial. The rarity of these documents is, in part, a reflection of the limited role of metropolitan authorities in shaping the objectives and implementation of research into Algeria's Roman past. It is nonetheless also clear from what survives that significant gaps existed between the wishes of the metropolitan-based minister of war and the activities of the Algerian-based governor-general with respect to the protection of antiquities. Likewise, regular disagreement between the minister of the interior and the minister of war over the earmarking of funding and resources for archaeological activities and the transport of antiquities to metropolitan France impeded both of these projects. These basic differences in outlook, visible in the repetitiousness of correspondence related to particular monuments and the apparent inability of authorities to resolve concerns over jurisdiction and finances, leave little doubt as to the contested relevance of antiquity to the French state at the highest echelons of power.

Moreover, what is striking about documents of the early period of French colonial rule preserved in the French national and colonial archives, just like those of Britain for India, is their contribution to a record of events and decisions in which the Indigenous inhabitants of the colony are largely absent from the narrative.[137] In the case of Algeria, as was also true of French missions to the Middle East, the administrators who authored reports on conquered territory shared basic assumptions of colonial discourse that affected their ability or desire to see the Muslim subject populations as at all relevant to their considerations.[138] Moreover, repositories of correspondence on archaeology as well as archaeological reports at institutions such as the Musée du Louvre (housed since 2015 at AN Pierrefitte-sur-Seine), the Académie des inscriptions et belles-lettres (AIBL; housed at the Bibliothèque de l'Institut de France), archives of the Cabinet des Médailles of the Bibliothèque nationale de France (BNF; housed since 2015 at the BNF Mitterrand), and the Commission des monuments historiques (housed at the Médiathèque de l'architecture et du patrimoine at Charenton-le-Pont) offer, first and foremost, documents pertaining to the augmentation of metropolitan collections and the production of scholarly publications. By contrast, they reveal few details about the political and military context in which these antiquities and observations were gathered. The relatively sparse documentation dating from before 1870 contrasts starkly with the expanding paper trail on antiquities assembled after the classification of numerous Roman monuments in Algeria in 1876.[139]

Given the military thrust of the many accounts of Algeria composed during the first four decades of French rule, the archives of the Service historique de l'armée de terre (SHAT) in Vincennes (Val-de-Marne) have played an important role in my research. Nevertheless, they, too, have been frustratingly opaque when it comes to the issue of archaeological activity. Namely, the dossiers of the careers of individual officers typically contain little information beyond a summary of their comportment in battle, promotions, and requests for sick leave or retirement. Because their archaeological activities were in most cases irrelevant to their career trajectories, few documents make any reference to antiquarian activities, even for officers who are known to have been engaged in archaeological research from their contemporary publications in learned society journals in Constantine and Algiers.[140] Additional series of documents in the archives of the armée d'Afrique related to military campaigns periodically mention sightings of Roman ruins but are nonetheless only marginally helpful regarding activities extraneous to military exercises, a category into which most archaeological endeavors in the French colony before 1870 fit.

Rather, beyond the relatively formulaic archaeological articles published by a great number of officers in the two main journals established for this purpose in Constantine and Algiers and the surprising number of monographs self-published by higher-ranking officers with an interest in archaeology, an important source of archaeological information from the military archives includes the regular topographical, historical, and ethnographic reports that lower-ranking officers were asked to produce when the army entered new territories.[141] As noted by Ann Laura Stoler, when one is looking for a particular kind of information that goes against the grain of what was intended by those who recorded events and nonevents, it becomes evident that private passions did have consequences.[142] In this instance, the enthusiastic attention given to copying inscriptions and sketching monuments suggests that French officers devoted far more time and energy to these tasks than their superiors demanded. This dedication was owed not just—as has been proposed—to the lack of sufficient leisure-time activities but, at least in part, to their belief in the relevance of the Roman past to the future of the French colony (and thus their own careers).[143] In particularly difficult periods of the French conquest, especially the expansionist regime of Governor-General Thomas-Robert Bugeaud in the 1840s, archaeological work offered officers a way to claim diachronic community with ancient Roman colonizers and thereby justify the historical significance of the brutal "fourth domination" of Algeria by foreign conquerors.[144]

Based on archival and published sources, this book challenges the triumphal narratives of the history of French officers' engagement with archaeology in Algeria, a genre that dates back to the earliest decades of the conquest but achieved new heights during the centennial celebrations of the same. By the early 1930s, recollections of the French archaeological intervention celebrated European discoveries in lands rich in antiquities at the same time that they claimed that the Indigenous population not only failed to appreciate these monuments but also had caused their degradation or destruction.[145] These one-sided narratives, which focused almost entirely on European developments, understood archaeological research within the framework of "professionalization" and "discovery" during the colonial period.[146] Without exception, they took the European perspective of these events while popularizing the premise that Arab and Kabyle residents had little interest in or engagement with Roman and other ancient remains before the French conquest because these monuments originated in the pre-Islamic epoch. Although this book does not go so far as to recover Arab and Kabyle responses to French archaeological interest, which appear to be scarce before ethnographic studies of the 1920s (and are, in any event, too late to chronicle the firsthand preconquest perspectives of Muslim residents), it does reassert their presence as entangled in French archaeological pursuits and subjugated by them.

In the Regency of Tunis, which likewise lay on the fringes of Ottoman possessions, an example typical of such one-sided narratives was composed by the French scholar Charles-Ernest Beulé, who excavated at Carthage in 1859. He argued that the Arabs could not identify with the pre-Islamic past of their country because they lacked blood ties to the ancient inhabitants. According to Beulé, this condition thus predisposed the local population to destroying ancient remains.[147] Likewise, Salomon

Reinach, whose experience with Tunisian archaeology dated from the mid-1880s, shortly after the establishment of the French Protectorate, argued that these alleged circumstances meant, in no uncertain terms, that Europeans were in a better position than local authorities to understand the antiquities, to which they had historical connections lacked by Indigenous peoples.[148] By pointing to close interactions with Indigenous witnesses by several officer-archaeologists in the 1830s, which allowed them to document ancient monuments in North Africa to which they had little or no access, in this monograph I expose the inaccuracies of later archaeologists' claims that Arabs and Kabyles were unfamiliar with or lacked valuable information about Roman sites.

By suggesting such indifference toward or rejection of antiquities among North African populations in the Maghreb, the French set themselves up as the saviors of these monuments' conservation and appreciation. Such claims were possible mainly because of their ignorance or neglect of Arabic sources such as the writings of Al-Bekri (d. 1094), the eleventh-century geographer who provided a detailed and admiring description of the ancient Roman theater of Carthage as a former center for entertainment and seemingly endless source of building materials in the region.[149] The twelfth-century geographer Al-Idrissi (d. 1165) wrote with praise of the same structure and noted that the Roman aqueduct, which had once brought water into the city and was now empty, had supported a population much larger than in his own day.[150] The medieval travelers Al-Abdari of Valencia in the late thirteenth century and Al-Tijāni in the early fourteenth century signaled their awareness of the presence of ancient monuments in Carthage and farther south, such as the remains of the amphitheater of El Jem.[151] In Morocco, sites such as the fourteenth-century Marinid necropolis of Chellah in Rabat, built atop (and in part with) the ruins of the Roman Sala Colonia, signal the attraction that Roman monuments in the region exercised on Muslim imaginations.[152]

This level of appreciation is not to suggest that all residents shared such understanding of the ancient ruins they found in their midst. Al-Tijāni, during a journey eastward from Tunis to Tripoli, remarked on mutilated marble columns he viewed at Zouar'a, which a local ruler had allegedly broken to find treasure.[153] Similarly, the fourteenth-century geographer and proto-sociologist Ibn Khaldûn was thoroughly familiar with the engineering feats of the Romans, such as the aqueducts bringing water to

Carthage and the monuments of Cherchel, suggesting that these ancient works were representative of the engineering skills and effective coordination of labor achieved by the ancient nation. He took time in the same passage, however, to dismiss what he described as the error of storytellers who claimed that such achievements were made by giants. Ibn Khaldûn instead argued more generally that monumental achievements of this nature were a measure of the social organization and cooperation of then-ruling dynasties.[154]

European approaches to the Maghreb in this sense were not exceptional. Motivated by their self-interest in controlling the interpretation of ancient Roman sites and the collecting of antiquities, Europeans resisted and even sought to undermine early legislative efforts in the Ottoman Empire and elsewhere to regulate archaeological practices and establish protections for ancient artifacts and monuments.[155] Because the colonization of Algeria began decades before the establishment of laws protecting antiquities, even in metropolitan France, the poor treatment of monuments was more extreme, since proponents were restricted by neither convention nor the kinds of policies that hindered their activities in Tunisia a half-century later. Indeed, officer-archaeologists in Algeria had the ability in many cases to determine which monuments should be saved and which might be destroyed.

From the 1860s, ideological disinheritance of the Indigenous population from any meaningful connection to ancient monuments received support from ethnographic research, in which European interpreters suggested that Arabs and Kabyles possessed only a primitive understanding of the significance of ancient sites of all genres.[156] Jocelyne Dakhlia, one of the few anthropologists in recent years to explore the collective Muslim understanding of the past in Tunisia, has relied too heavily on highly biased reports by early twentieth-century ethnographers working in the Maghreb.[157] Indeed, sources such as Edmond Doutté's reports of the superstitious beliefs of Moroccan natives, whom he claimed attributed prehistoric ruins to a race of giants, were tainted by the innate prejudices engrained in his study. Doutté's blunt admission that he viewed North Africa as having been plunged into barbarism by Islam and his professed distaste for Arab architectural styles, for instance, reveals the French ethnologist's predisposition to seeing his informants as backward or primitive.[158] Doutté's flawed approach throws into doubt the reliability of his contention that Indigenous peoples had little or no relevant knowledge of prehistoric and ancient Roman archaeological sites in the Maghreb.

In postcolonial histories of modern Tunisia, scholars have not sufficiently nuanced their understanding of Arab and Kabyle interactions with the ancient past. Ahmed Abdesselem, for instance, has asserted that from the seventeenth to the nineteenth centuries, the pre-Islamic past of the Maghreb was of little or no interest to Tunisian historians; he argues that they viewed this as an obscure and unimportant period in the history of North Africa. In his view, the arrival of the French, and the effectiveness of their exclusive claims to Roman remains, negatively affected perceptions of this period and its abundant antiquities still further.[159] The circumstances of the nineteenth-century French conquest and colonization of Algeria and the ideological use of ancient remains to support French claims to govern the region shaped its institutions.[160] They erased what were probably far more regular interactions with and reuse of ancient monuments.[161] In the present, the colonial period has been relegated to a long "parenthesis" in the social memory of Algerian history.[162] Consequently, a central thrust of the postcolonial historiography of the ancient period written in Algeria has been at pains to emphasize the Berber resistance to Roman colonial domination and exploitation.[163] In this context, it is easy to understand why interest in classical antiquities has waned among the Algerian authorities and public, and why this is unlikely to change any time soon.[164] A more nuanced understanding of the early decades of French archaeology in Algeria is thus critical to any effort to move forward productively with classical research and heritage concerns in North Africa.

In the five chapters and brief epilogue that follow this introduction, I examine French officers' exploration of Roman Algeria between 1830 and 1870. The chapters are organized roughly chronologically, according to the successive phases of the French conquest. Each opens with a brief narrative of the central events and structural developments in the establishment of the colony of Algiers and then turns to the place of the Roman past, seen from a historical or archaeological perspective, in the thinking and activities of French military officers and civilians. The themes of the chapters reflect prevailing sensibilities during overlapping periods of roughly ten years each. My discussion in chapter 1 opens with the military conquest of Algiers and Constantine, and the scientific assessment of the region's resources, including ancient monuments (1830–1842), that followed. Focusing on the second decade of the French colony, in chapter 2 I examine how competing visions of the colonial settlement of Algeria were impacted by the French understanding of the ancient Roman past (1837–1847). In chapter 3, I address French military officers' and civilian scholars' engagement with the exceptional archaeological site of Lambaesis, the former camps of the Third Augustan Legion located in the Aurès Mountains (1844–1854). Assessing the foundation of the first successful colonial archaeological societies and museums in Algeria (1852–1860), in chapter 4 I trace their struggles to maintain funding and the integrity of their collections. Finally, in chapter 5 I suggest the synchronicity of metropolitan and colonial archaeological, cartographic, and epigraphical projects (1860–1870) under Napoleon III. In the brief epilogue, I offer a survey of the archaeological developments that transpired during the first decade and a half of the Third Republic, which, although outside the chronological scope of this book, were built on the foundations of archaeological explorations laid before 1870. They pointed the way forward for archaeological excavations, research, and collections for the first two-thirds of the twentieth century.

Chapter 1

KNOWING AND CONTROLLING

Early Archaeological Exploration in the Algerian Colony

When French warships landed with thirty-seven thousand men at Sidi Ferruch, a port 30 kilometers west of Algiers in July 1830, they found the forces of the reigning Ottoman Dey Hussein ill prepared for their arrival.[1] By this time, Algiers had grown from a modest town of roughly twenty thousand to a capital city of approximately a hundred thousand residents. In addition to a lucrative port, the city boasted a population that included as many as ten thousand janissaries.[2]

Following the debilitating three-year naval blockade of the city, local notables in the Regency of al-Jazā'er were dismayed by the inaction of local Ottoman leaders, who were divided by intrigue and too poorly equipped to wage an effective defense of the territory against the French landing. During the crisis, which followed fierce fighting, they counseled Dey Hussein to pursue a peaceful surrender of the city to French forces under the command of General Louis-Auguste-Victor Bourmont. Local elites such as Hamdan Khodja—a Kouloughli landowner (an ethnic group of mixed Turkish-Arabic heritage), law professor, and counselor to the Ottoman

Figure 6. The bombardment and seizure of Algiers in July 1830. Reproduced by permission of the Bibliothèque nationale de France, Département des estampes et de la photographie.

governor—argued that the city's residents would fare better under such circumstances than if they waged armed resistance to the French forces.[3] Hamdan, who read and spoke French and English in addition to Arabic and Ottoman Turkish, had high expectations of the French and their professed Enlightenment principles. As he recalled in *Le Miroir* (1833), although he and his contemporaries had no particular complaint against their Ottoman overlords, the severity of naval bombardment of Algiers made conditions desperate enough for them to submit to the French overlords without a fight. In accepting the terms of the surrender of the territory, Bourmont granted the Ottoman dey assurances that inhabitants' freedom of religion and property rights would be respected. According to Hamdan, the residents of Algiers had little reason to doubt that the French would honor the terms of the peace treaty.[4]

Despite Bourmont's pledge to protect the civilian population and respect basic property rights, the armée d'Afrique began almost immediately to violate the provisions of the treaty. French soldiers sacked the Kasbah (citadel), confiscated land, destroyed homes, and plundered the civilian residences now occupied by officers and troops.[5] The destruction of the city center in 1831 and 1832 was directed at creating an open space that could accommodate the armée d'Afrique and convey the imposition of French control.[6] France believed that it had title to all of the former dey's wealth, including public buildings and forts, palaces, the regency treasury, and the million or so hectares of agricultural land that comprised the Ottoman territory under his authority. French military officials also seized *habous* lands (A. *waqf*; Ottoman Turkish [T.]: *vakif*) in Algiers, namely the enormous wealth accumulated in the form of inalienable tax-exempt property that supported religious, charitable, and pedagogical foundations in the region as well as the poor in Mecca and Medina.[7] Unabated land grabs by the French throughout the early decades of the occupation exacted a devastating toll on local residents.[8]

With the fall of the Bourbon king Charles X from power just three weeks after the invasion, there was initial hope in some quarters of Algiers that Louis-Philippe's policies would be more moderate than those of his predecessor. But despite the use of the semaphore telegraph to speed communications between Toulon and the invading force, the new king had difficulty establishing direct control of military operations in Algiers. Bourmont was dismissed for refusing to recognize Louis-Philippe. In the general absence of guidance from officials in metropolitan France, many of whom were opposed to military intervention in North Africa, senior commanders of the armée d'Afrique began implementing policies of their own formulation.[9] Some allowed serious matters to devolve to even their most junior subordinate officers. In the first years of the conquest, most French military officers had little sense of the strategic goals of the campaign beyond the poorly defined objective of liberating the Ottoman territory from alleged Oriental despotism.[10] Once in the territory of al-Jazā'er, military commanders pressed strategies that would allow them to expand the territory under their control.

Although Algiers and its surrounding territories were not as unknown to the French as some writers later proclaimed, French officers faced many obstacles to establishing mastery over France's newest possession.[11] Because the French army evicted and exiled the Ottoman administration before learning anything about the existing systems of taxation, landholding, or justice, the arrival of French forces brought

Figure 7. The traverse of the Atlas pass of Téniah (F. Col de Téniah) by the armée d'Afrique, commanded by General Bertrand Clauzel in November 1830, following its defeat of the Bey of Tittery's force of eight thousand troops. Claude-Antoine Rozet, *Voyage dans la Régence d'Alger ou Description du pays occupé par l'armée française en Afrique* (Paris: Arthus Bertrand, Libraire-Éditeur, 1833), Atlas.

about the almost immediate cessation of all governmental institutions and activities. Unable to communicate in Arabic, not to mention in Berber, most French officers had great difficulty conducting even basic interactions with the Indigenous inhabitants. The consequences of this approach were especially severe given the elimination of the Hanafite Islamic tribunal (established by the Ottomans to hear *sharia* cases) on October 22, 1830, at the command of Bourmont's successor, General Bertrand Clauzel.[12] This deficiency caused frequent misunderstandings of local custom and religion. Officers in the cabinet of the duc de Rovigo, commander in chief of French troops in the former Regency of al-Jazā'er from 1831, had neither the resources for nor any apparent interest in a nuanced reading of the situation on the ground in Arab and Kabyle communities. In 1832, the duc de Rovigo was responsible for the seizure and conversion of Algiers's primary house of worship, the Ketchaoua Mosque, which by 1845 had been transformed into the

Cathedral of Saint-Philippe.[13] In this institutional vacuum, the few Arabic translators available gained significant latitude in decision making on the ground.

Symptomatic of Europeans' fuzzy understanding of the Barbary Coast was the conflation of the history of the corsairs with the entire population of the region, despite the fact that the successful capture of booty had declined in the region for as much as a century.[14] As observed by Perceval Barton Lord, a surgeon in the East India Company: "Tyranny and oppression are the features of a piratical government; it encourages those who follow a wild and reckless course, hazarding their lives in the cause of murder and rapine on the ocean; but for the arts of peace, the simple pursuits of the shepherd or the husbandman, it has no sympathy."[15]

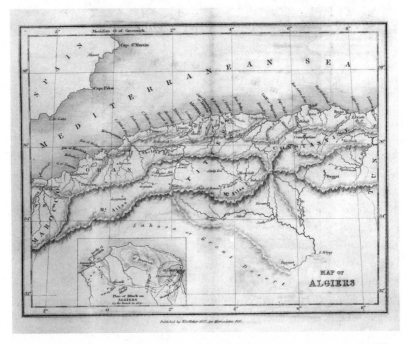

Figure 8. English map of the territory of Algiers and the surrounding region in 1835, much of which was not yet controlled by the armée d'Afrique. Perceval Barton Lord, *Algiers, with Notices of the Neighbouring States of Barbary*, vol. 1 (London: Whittaker, 1835).

Such scathing stereotypes of the population of Algiers and French memoirs of captivity in North Africa written at the turn of the nineteenth century helped render an already toxic situation even worse. Many troops feared for their lives should they fall into the hands of enemy combatants and overreacted to provocation with deadly consequences.[16] In these early years, French forces were involved in several retributive massacres against the Arab population. These included most notoriously the indiscriminate killing of men, women, and children in the city of Blida, 35 kilometers southwest of Algiers, in November 1830, and nearly all of the El-Ouffia tribe in April 1832.[17] Deficiencies in French leadership and the injustice of their actions quickly turned any initial good will or indifference among the Indigenous residents toward the invaders into rising resentment against their prolonged presence in the former Ottoman regency.

In the months and years after the conquest, the French recorded their impressions of the landscape of their new colony.[18] At the same time, they rapidly transformed cosmopolitan centers such as the city of Algiers to meet European expectations of life in the occupied North African territory.[19] These years saw the flight of large numbers of urban-dwelling Indigenous residents, whom the French typically identified by the centuries-old nomenclature of "Maures," descended from a mix of Arabs and more ancient populations. Consequently, the demographics of coastal enclaves changed quickly and dramatically to include French troops and European civilians.[20] The French presence in Algiers during the early years of the war brought an influx of not just soldiers and administrators but also civilian immigrants from Sicily, Sardinia, Corsica, Malta, Spain, and the Balearic and Greek Islands, who sought livelihoods in the new colony.[21] Seizing public and private buildings at will, the French also radically transformed the topography of Algiers in the 1830s and subsequent decades to accommodate French troops, European urban conventions, and larger numbers of wheeled vehicles.[22] Beyond converting the Ketchaoua Mosque of Algiers into the Cathedral of Saint-Philippe and appropriating additional mosques for hospitals and structures meant to serve the army, the French embarked on building campaigns, both official and ad hoc.[23]

Although some blamed the chaos of this period on civilian settlers determined to thwart French military authority,[24] both the army and European colonists were to blame for the violence against Muslim inhabitants and the irreversible damage to existing homes, religious establishments, and former government structures.[25] As residents fled the violence, there was rampant speculation in property as French and European buyers sought to acquire urban and rural land. Some local landholders were threatened with expropriation of their possessions if they did not sell.[26] Early among the victims of indiscriminate destruction by the French were several bazaars in which artisans produced and dyed silk fabrics, manufactured bracelets of African buffalo horn, and worked iron. Their elimination, along with land transfers in and outside the city that threatened the food supply, leveled a severe economic blow against the residents of Algiers, whose livelihoods derived from these local industries.[27] The activities, many of which predated Baron Haussmann's transformation of Paris under Napoleon III, rent the fabric of the city to accommodate European-style structures and open spaces for the future colonial capital.[28]

Similar to the manner in which they had viewed Egyptian Arabs, but with more devastating consequences because their stay in the Maghreb was more permanent, the French regarded the Indigenous residents primarily as an impediment to French ambitions.[29] This blind spot, which has been described as a "space of noncivilization" by Abdelmajid Hannoum, exempted the French from seriously including Arab and Kabyle inhabitants in any colonial undertakings.[30] These silences imposed on contemporary events allowed them to be recast in a manner consistent with the French mission of conquest.[31] In the process of solidifying the colony, French administrators first busied themselves with identifying and appropriating the territory's urban resources. Then, once they had established relatively secure bases, they began to study the territory with an eye to taking advantage of its agricultural resources. Discussion continued throughout the decade as to how the occupation of the territory of Algeria should proceed. Despite the enormous military cost of the venture, Louis-Philippe never seriously considered withdrawal due to the mark it would leave on France's honor. In the early 1830s, policy discussions such as that held by the Commission d'Afrique on March 7, 1834, centered largely on whether the French presence should be restricted to a few coastal cities for defensive and commercial purposes or whether the conquered territory represented the seed for a larger civilian colony.[32] The fact that thousands of French troops were already stationed in North Africa meant that the model of limited French presence and peaceful coexistence with Indigenous inhabitants never had a real opportunity to take root, despite some authorities' acknowledgment of the practicality of this less costly and less violent option.

French control of inland, rural districts, in regions of the former Regency of al-Jazā'er that possessed little infrastructure and were occupied by individuals openly hostile to European incursion, was significantly more difficult for the armée d'Afrique to establish.[33] The challenges of logistics and supply were daunting.[34] In 1835, in the plain of Mitidja, Clauzel ordered troops to clear and drain the marshy, malarial area south of Algiers to make the land suitable for farming. The following year, soldiers founded the first experimental farm at Boufarik, not far from the military Camp d'Erlon, a development that depended on the confiscation of lands from Indigenous residents. In the Tell, the fertile coastal valley in the territory of Algiers most suited to agricultural pursuits, the army displaced much of the existing population, "liberated" preferred farmland, and made these resources available to newly arrived European civilians.[35] From the early 1830s, this kind of settlement pointed to more intensive occupation of the region by the French than had been the practice under Ottoman rule. With a decree in September 1836, French authorities granted sizable concessions to European landholders who promised to build homes, cultivate arable land, and plant trees, with the promise of title to this land if they fulfilled these basic requirements within several years. Developed as an attempt to curb speculation, the measure expropriated lands and dispossessed large numbers of Indigenous inhabitants of their homes, properties, and food security. From the French perspective, the measure was also unsuccessful because the new French and European proprietors often failed to follow through on their commitments by leaving their land fallow.[36]

As it became clear that French presence would be prolonged in the territory of Algiers, army commanders took steps to find alternative sources of military power to reduce dependence on regular units drawn from France for service in North Africa. From 1830, these measures included the creation of battalions of Zouaves and, in 1831, the transfer of the Foreign Legion to Algiers and the establishment of the light cavalry regiments of the Chasseurs d'Afrique. Despite the suggestion by Indigenous observers, who counseled that just and moderate governance by the French would yield positive results, physical force became by default the main language of communication in a land populated by peoples whom Christian Europeans associated primarily with the lucrative occupations of piracy and white slavery.[37] This anachronistic vision prevailed, despite the fact that a total of only eighty prisoners from European shipwrecks were found after the French penetration of Hussein Dey's compound on July 5, 1830.[38]

Over the next several years, the French army expanded its military activities and economic demands to a number of coastal cities in the region, including the ports of Bougie (A. Béjaïa; L. Saldae) and Bône (A. Annaba; L. Hippo Regius) to the east of Algiers, and Oran (A. Wahran) to the west.[39] The army found urban centers easier to secure than rural spaces because they offered physical infrastructure in which to house troops, fortify preexisting defenses, and appropriate precut stone and other building materials from both ancient Roman and more recent structures.[40] With little standing between the troops and the immovable and movable property of Indigenous populations in cosmopolitan areas of the territory of Algiers, French abuse of the Muslim inhabitants became a matter of course.[41] By 1834, the number of troops serving in the French armée d'Afrique, including a growing number of Indigenous recruits among the Zouaves and Spahis, rose another eight thousand men from the initial invasion force of thirty-seven thousand.[42] The army policy of underprovisioning its columns, especially while on campaign, created great pressure on local resources and escalated the already deadly tensions between French soldiers and native Arabs and Kabyles. By 1840, the number of French-led forces serving in Algeria had increased to sixty-five thousand.[43]

Although policymaking was still somewhat receptive and elastic at this early phase, few questioned the validity of the French presence in the region after 1835. By this point, the French presence in North Africa was a fait accompli, and in the eyes of many metropolitan French officials, it was too late to turn back after the sacrifices of the conquest. Debate thus centered mainly on whether the French should engage in restrained occupation or full-blown colonization.[44] Many policymakers favored the latter.

Despite the dramatic and violent measures taken by the military to secure land, however, the anticipated influx of enthusiastic French settlers prepared to take up the plow did not materialize in the first decade of the occupation. In a letter dated December 31, 1835, Captain Nicolas-Anne-Théodule Changarnier, acting battalion commander in the 2nd Light Infantry Regiment, wrote to General Boniface de Castellane: "After five and a half years of occupation, I see *in this colony* a multitude of owners of cabarets and cafes, secondhand dealers of all sorts, but I have not yet seen a man arrive with a plow and with the intention of using it. At the gates of Algiers, the gardens are not cultivated, or they are worse than before the conquest. I do not understand how a colony exists without colonists."[45] Others, like General Pierre Berthézène, whose views made him unpopular with the leadership of the armée d'Afrique and the minister of war, did not see the Algerian colony as a particularly attractive location for settlement. He acknowledged the shortcomings of the current situation and observed with respect to the Algerian venture: "The strange contradictions of the human spirit! We spoke of *humanity* and all of our acts were marked by violence, iniquity, fraud, and cruelty."[46]

Nonetheless, many French military authorities, especially those trained as Arabists, continued to entertain visions of an idyllic future for the Algerian colony. The historian Osama Abi-Mershed has characterized officers' contributions as working "in tandem with and in mutual relation to the making of the post-1830 bourgeois regime in France." They believed that intervention by the armée d'Afrique would bring the benefits of civilization to the inhabitants of Algeria and that this colonial laboratory would become an important resource for revitalizing the French.[47] Indeed, many French officers arrived on the shores of North Africa armed with the stereotype of the Indigenous Muslim population as fanatical, which they attributed directly to its religious orientation, lack of access to formal education, and oppression during centuries of despotic rule by the Ottomans (whom French sources broadly referred to as the "Turks").[48] This perspective, shaped for many authorities by Saint-Simonian philosophy, suggested that exposure to Christian civilization was the best means by which to prime Arab and Kabyle residents for future adaptation to French cultural mores.[49] For this reason, once established in the Algerian territory, the colonial regime proceeded with a variety of projects that its administrators believed would contradict the status quo, including allowing the long-delayed appointment of a bishop in Algiers. In August 1838, Pope Gregory XVI named Antoine-Adolphe Dupuch, a priest of Bordeaux, as bishop of the see of Julia Caesarea (F. Cherchel) and Hippo Regius. But Dupuch's relationship with the French military regime remained rocky throughout his brief tenure as bishop, and he stepped down in 1846.[50] Other innovations of the colonial regime included plans to create new schools, enact health reforms, and institute more benevolent governance, few of which ever came to pass.[51]

French Officers and the Classical Past

Because of the lack of agreement among military commanders and civilian officials over the role of the armée d'Afrique in French-occupied al-Jazā'er, significant tensions arose over the purpose of the French mission. Some military officers based in Algiers and neighboring settlements taken early in the conquest were inspired by the remnants of Roman structures still visible in the Arab cities and towns in which they found themselves. In 1832, the Algiers water supply still depended on ancient aqueducts, and commanding officers were under order to fine and imprison anyone who damaged them or diverted the water they carried.[52] As the newest conquerors of the region, French officers often assimilated the imposing fragments of the ancient past into their historical imaginary. They viewed the Roman legacy as uniquely theirs and understood them as an invitation to leave their distinctive mark on the city. As they modernized the city and made it their own, they erased signs of Arab and Ottoman rule while claiming the more familiar Roman remains as evidence of their tangible heritage.[53] In doing so, they claimed that their defeat of the Ottoman dey and their wholesale appropriation of the resources of Algiers mirrored the actions of the ancient Roman conquerors of North Africa nearly two millennia earlier.[54]

Once the looting stopped, the new overlords of Algiers justified their actions through reference to Roman history, which, along with classical literature, had been such an important part of their schooling. The activities of the Roman army in North Africa provided a compelling narrative by which to explain the ongoing military campaign.[55] Over the following decades, ancient Rome increasingly became an essential link in the story that tied the French to Algerian territory.[56] Officers welcomed the opportunity to make the Mediterranean *mare nostrum* again for the first time since the ancient Romans.[57] The classical past offered a wealth of examples on which they could model the conquest, both positive and negative.[58] As they expanded the territory under French control, these inspirational models buoyed morale and helped enforce discipline among troops facing the challenges of malaria, typhus, cholera, the bubonic plague, and the weather extremes of the Maghreb. Several decades into the conquest, officers still carried modern anthologies of ancient authors created for this purpose with their gear.[59]

Classical history thus made an essential contribution to the French conquest of al-Jazā'er: its annals served as a quarry from which the French could assemble the building blocks of a new colonial edifice, just as they used stones from Roman ruins to construct their fortifications, barracks, hospitals, and roads.[60] The prevailing historical narrative in these early years relied on a parallel understood to exist between the French and preceding conquerors of the region, particularly the Carthaginians and the Romans. The Vandals, Arabs, and Turks occupied distinctly lower positions in such ranked comparisons. Because few Punic monuments survived in Algeria, having been subsumed during the Roman occupation of the region, however, French thinking focused almost exclusively on the ancient Romans.[61] The memoirs of General Pierre Berthézène, who played a central role in the first two years of the French conquest, help explain the tradition of seeing such a distant epoch as ancient Rome as an object lesson for contemporary conquest. In his writings, as in those of his fellow officers, Berthézène maintained that the Indigenous occupants of the Regency of Algiers were little different from their ancient forebears: "Their [Arab] traditions, their customs and the forms of their language have traversed the century and the revolutions, without undergoing almost any alteration. When one reads an Arabic letter, he believes that he has a chapter of the Bible before his eyes. In my opinion, the perfect and entire understanding of this holy book is impossible when one has not lived a long time among them."[62] This orientalist claim about the unchanging nature of the local population, the "permanence berbère," and fixity of Arabic itself allowed the author to erase the millennium and a half that stood between himself and the ancient Romans.[63] Berthézène was thereby able to abolish time and claim that it was as if his men were actually continuing to fight the wars of the classical period.[64] Although he suggested that ancient accounts such as those of Sallust also offered convincing examples of why it was not beneficial to imitate blindly the violence and avarice of the conquering Romans, most French authorities absorbed rather different lessons about how to advance the conquest of the Algerian territory.[65]

From the 1830s, documents produced by a series of governmental commissions and private civilian enterprises that collected relevant information about the territory of Algeria asserted the existence of numerous similarities between the empires despite the millennium and a half that separated them. In 1834, members of the Commission d'Afrique, when considering the expansion of colonial objectives in Bône, framed their work in terms of Roman precedents:[66]

> In no part of the Regency [other than Bône], would French strength gain as many resources with which to expand and develop. One can go as far as the gates of Constantine and even beyond without finding natural obstacles; resources are almost always found on a plain or easily accessible by paths, even for artillery. The Romans have showed us the way: one only has to follow the traces of their military stations and the vestiges of their camps. These mark their progressive steps in the interior and offer skilled evidence of their system of occupation. That which the Romans did, why do we not do with greater means and intelligence?[67]

Deeply familiar with the famous battles fought by ancient military commanders, the members of the Académie des inscriptions et belles-lettres and French military officers who populated such commissions liberally employed references to ancient monuments and inscriptions in their reports. Using Roman structural remains as a blueprint for future French activities, they found that this historical model, if used wisely, not only enabled them to outline a strategy for their presence in North Africa but also provided a practical baseline against which they could measure their accomplishments.

Marshalling ancient sources, military and civilian authorities argued with confidence, for instance, that profits could be derived from the colonized region even if they did not yet seem imminent to contemporary observers.[68] Men such as Claude-Antoine Rozet, a captain in the army general staff who had been trained as a geographer and engineer and collected information about the ancient Roman colony, thus praised without hesitation the potential of the region and the riches that colonization would yield once the Algerian territory was firmly under French control.[69] Even in 1931, during the centenary celebrations of the French conquest of Algeria, Eugène Albertini, director of Algerian Antiquities, still praised uncritically the longtime benefits of this historical approach:

> In the domain of historical sciences, the French conquest had the same consequences as in the economic domain. It allowed Algeria to return into harmony with civilized countries, in the system of general activity. Henceforth, one could travel freely in Algeria, copy the inscriptions, study and excavate the ruins.

If the very early years of the conquest, occupied by more urgent tasks, were sterile from this point of view, ancient history had a place from 1835 among the thoughts of the French who little by little took possession of Algeria.[70]

Placing the colonial undertaking in this teleological trajectory gave it greater weight and reinforced French confidence in the appropriateness of their North African venture.

The classical past was also deeply ingrained into prejudices about the Arab and Kabyle residents of the colony. In 1841, Saint-Marc Girardin, a professor of poetry at the Sorbonne and member of the French Chambre des députés, concluded that classical authors characterized the Indigenous inhabitants of North Africa as passive historical subjects who had little control over their own destiny: "For a long time, Africa has been like the East, and no longer has a nationality. She only changes masters, and these masters are always foreign; the coasts of Africa on the Mediterranean are like Asia Minor, like Syria, like Egypt: all belong to the conquerors."[71] Girardin proposed that the strength of the Romans, who allegedly succeeded in North Africa because of the superiority of their discipline over the impulsiveness and warlike behavior of the Numidians and Carthaginians, stemmed from their indefatigable perseverance and the superior imprint of their civilization.[72] Girardin thus intermingled past and present in his discussion of the French conquest of those whom he described as noble savages. He elided Emir 'Abd el-Qader, the contemporary religious and military leader (*sharif*) of the Indigenous forces resisting French colonization in Algeria, with ancient military leaders such as Syphax and Jugurtha, the latter described by Sallust as noble of appearance, vigorous of body, and brave.[73] Girardin thereby sanctioned and glorified French military activities, and implied that Arab and Kabyle leaders were worthy yet inferior adversaries who existed within an established and respected classical tradition.

Archaeological Practice in Metropolitan France and Colonial Algeria in the 1830s

During the first decade of the colony, the trope of discovery was deeply linked to the possession of ancient Roman sites and the attendant dispossession of the Indigenous peoples of these locales.[74] Indeed, the collection

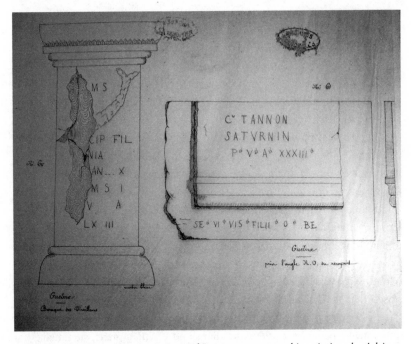

Figure 9. Sketches and transcriptions of Roman monumental inscriptions by Adrien Berbrugger in the region of Guelma (L. Calama). ANOM 80 F 1733. Reproduced by permission of the Archives nationales d'Outre-Mer (ANOM, France).

and application of historical, archaeological, and scientific knowledge, whether by French officers or metropolitan savants, was more than casual yet anything but objective.[75] Integration of the Roman past into French interactions with the Algerian territory thus occurred in myriad and sometimes contradictory ways. John Zarobell has shown that even landscape painters offered ideologically charged imagery of the occupation of the foreign territory.[76]

A close reading of extant sources from the 1830s reveals the uneven and protracted process by which individual French authorities, both military and civilian, collected, interpreted, and employed scientific knowledge. They thereby developed an outlook that effectively gave them license to control the inhabitants, history, and landscape of the Algerian territory. In the relative vacuum of formal policy, military officers' and later civilian scholars' observations enabled the French army to harness both natural

and human-made resources to the perceived benefit of French soldiers and
the small but growing European settler population. Although neither well
organized nor monolithic in their intentions in the first decade of the occupation of Algerian territory, French officers' activities worked to the
disadvantage of Indigenous residents by severely circumscribing or erasing
their contributions to the emerging historical narrative. When convenient
and feasible, they nimbly deployed ancient Roman precedents and ruins
to the advantage of the French colony.

However, because of the lack of encouragement from the Ministry of
War, French military officers' efforts to interpret and reuse Roman remains
to reify French identification with the ancient conquerors of the region were
inconsistent and remained limited in their scope and effectiveness. Most
importantly, Nadia Bayle has observed that the titles of those officers
who published their observations on archaeological topics while serving
in the Algerian territories during the following decades suggest that
they were typically second lieutenants, lieutenants, and captains: officer-
archaeologists tended not to be commanders at the top of the military
hierarchy. Bayle explains that these more junior officers had more direct
contact with archaeological remains because they were often charged with
reconnaissance operations outside the camps. Moreover, the nature of their
duties and the frequency with which they found themselves under fire, meant
that they were more intimately aware of the landscape and the possibilities
for cover than their superiors. No doubt, they also benefited from more
time to write about these topics than their commanders.[77] Although bold
in their aspirations, the efforts of these individual officers in the nineteenth
century necessarily remained quite modest in their enactment, in part due to
the often limited period for which they were stationed in any one location.[78]
According to Bayle's calculations, the vast majority of officer-archaeologists
published fewer than four archaeological site reports.[79]

It is important to remember that the armée d'Afrique's obliteration of a
large percentage of the once-plentiful monuments in Algeria occurred on a
scale with few parallels in this era.[80] Substantial tensions existed between
the military mandate to expedite the maintenance of the strategic goal of
"security" in the new colony, which often required the reuse or recycling of
components of ancient monuments. These constraints limited the potential effectiveness of the minor French officers and the few French civilians
in North Africa who advocated conserving physical remains of the Roman

past. Even if there were military commanders with more historical inclinations who considered ancient monuments to be central to their vision of the colony's future, neither the minister of war nor the governor-general of Algeria was willing to change military strategy or commit substantial funds or legislation to the systematic study, excavation, or preservation of antiquities encountered in the course of military campaigns.

In the 1830s, the discipline of archaeology, including that of the ancient world, was still in its infancy in metropolitan France. Provincial amateurs engaged in archaeology were too diverse a constituency to have earned significant legitimacy with governmental officials or to have attracted substantial funding in either metropolitan France or the Algerian colony. Moreover, because primary schooling was not free or mandated in metropolitan France until the early 1880s, few French soldiers serving in Algeria had sufficient education to cultivate an interest in the ancient past similar to that of their officers.[81] Consequently, in this early period, the emerging discipline remained heavily dependent on historical texts and the *cabinet*, and little had been developed in the way of practical field training.

Nonetheless, a series of landmark events in classical archaeology shifted this imbalance; for French archaeology, these events transpired mainly on distant shores of the Mediterranean, where French scholars such as Jean-François Champollion made his first trip to Egypt in the company of Ippolito Rosselini in 1828.[82] In 1828–1829, following the Treaty of London (1827), French authorities also organized an influential military-scientific venture to the Peloponnese known as the Expédition de Morée, which included an archaeological section based in Olympia. Charles Lenormant, who had accompanied Champollion to Egypt, led this team, which was composed of the epigrapher Edgar Quintet, the architects Abel Blouet and Amable Ravoisié, and the archaeologist Léon-Jean Dubois. The mission focused on recording and acquiring ancient monuments; its success stoked French interest in Greece and led ultimately to the foundation of the École française d'Athènes (1846). This institution became, in time, the base for French archaeological exploration of the Mediterranean and, from 1850, was placed under the direct oversight of the Académie des inscriptions et belles-lettres in Paris.[83]

In contrast to the centrally funded French scholarly expeditions to Egypt and Olympia that engaged classical monuments, however, most provincial amateurs in metropolitan France and officers in the Maghreb who practiced archaeological research were self-directed and self-funded.[84] In France, they had to provide their own financial support and devote their time to a wide variety of archaeological and architectural remains in the regions in which they resided. By contrast, in Algeria, officers occupied themselves almost exclusively with Roman sites in the vicinity where they were stationed. Both disseminated their finds via lectures and published articles in antiquarian journals, which were the main organs of the learned societies that were established from the 1830s in metropolitan France and from the 1850s in Algeria.

Briefly, in metropolitan France from 1810, Parisian authorities helped channel archaeological activities toward the creation of surveys of local antiquities and monuments.[85] Following his appointment as the minister of the interior at the start of the July Monarchy, the liberal historian François Guizot relaunched earlier initiatives to catalogue monuments by calling on departmental prefects to fulfill these requests. Lacking such expertise, however, provincial authorities encouraged the creation of learned societies in their districts to carry out these responsibilities. Although they received little external support from the state for these undertakings, which were supported instead by private wealth or by membership dues of the local learned societies, French amateur antiquarians and archaeologists enthusiastically engaged in the study and documentation of a wide variety of monuments in their respective regions.[86]

To manage the conservation of historically significant structures in metropolitan France, Guizot appointed Ludovic Vitet as the first inspector general of historical monuments in 1833.[87] It quickly became apparent to Vitet that a single inspector could not effectively coordinate this massive undertaking with so few resources.[88] He thus resigned in 1834 so that he might devote himself to becoming a deputy and intervening whenever possible in debates on the French budget that underlay this problem.[89] His immediate successor, Prosper Merimée, was charged with synthesizing and interpreting the results of the completed surveys in metropolitan France.[90] He faced the challenge of dealing with monuments and antiquities threatened as the result of agricultural activities, industrialization, quarrying, the construction of roads, and the dredging of silted rivers. He and his successors also had to address the consequences of the archaeological finds that were disturbed as iron and later steel track was laid for the expanding network of French railways; these artifacts, if not destroyed in the process, were left undocumented and subsequently either dispersed or discarded. In Algeria, by contrast, the minister of war appointed the first inspector general of civil structures over a decade later in 1845, following complaints about the scale on which ancient monuments were being destroyed by the armée d'Afrique.[91] Even more so than Merimée's situation, the appointee Charles Texier was unable to slow the destruction of Roman sites, which served as an important source of precut stone for the French armed forces during the protracted conflict.[92]

In both metropolitan France and the French colony of Algeria, the attention of the inspector general was largely focused on the conservation of aboveground structures of historical value rather than on excavations, which required nothing more stringent than the relevant property owner's permission to proceed.[93] This was the case throughout the century. Even after the promulgation in 1887 of definitive legislation for the protection of ancient monuments—of which article 16 applied to Algeria and the Protectorates—these measures failed to halt the pillage of ancient cemeteries and other subterranean sites located on private land.[94] Although it is impossible to venture an accurate guess as to how many antiquities were thereby destroyed, poorly excavated, or collected and left unpublished, the number must have been enormous given the seriousness of the accusations leveled against unscrupulous amateurs in metropolitan France during the final decades of the century.[95] By contrast, the damage caused to ancient monuments in the Algerian territory by the armée d'Afrique, and later civilian colonists, was devastating.

Because the circumstances under which archaeologists operated in a military zone were exceptional, unmandated archaeological activities in Algeria had few protections in place when they conflicted with the destructive might of the armée d'Afrique.[96] In metropolitan France, as the first minister of public instruction, Guizot sought to build a centralized governmental infrastructure to manage antiquities that would function independently of but in cooperation with the Académie des inscriptions et belles-lettres and existing antiquarian societies.[97] In 1834, Guizot founded the Comité des arts et des monuments (which was later reincarnated as the Comité des travaux historiques) to assist the inspector general in his work.[98] Its projected responsibilities included completion of the aforementioned survey of French historic monuments, formulation of guidelines for archaeological methodology, and preservation of ancient monuments. However, Guizot's modest steps to establish and centralize governmental oversight of antiquities in metropolitan France did not apply to the military-ruled colony in al-Jazā'er, and there was no parallel to Arcisse de Caumont's Société pour la conservation des monuments (later renamed the Société française d'archéologie) to empower regional archaeologists across colonial Algeria.[99] Thus, the frustrations faced by aspiring archaeologists and those interested in the conservation of ancient monuments in metropolitan France and North Africa were on two entirely different scales. While none of these institutions had the budget, will, or expertise to save large numbers of antiquities, officer-archaeologists, unlike their counterparts, the provincial advocates of antiquities in metropolitan France, were frequently a part of the forces that were responsible for their destruction.

In metropolitan France, many of the responsibilities for monument conservation after the 1830s devolved to the better-funded Commission des monuments historiques, created in 1837 by the count de Montalivet, minister of the interior, and run by architects.[100] It rapidly became clear that the commission preferred restoring structures to undertaking excavations, with its budget of 400,000 francs in 1840 dedicated largely to medieval churches (68 percent) and castles and fortifications (9.5 percent), as opposed to Gallo-Roman monuments (8.5 percent).[101] Its objectives also included coordinating research among antiquarian societies and creating a common forum for their discussions through meetings that rotated annually among French cities.[102] Some provincial advocates complained that this new and better-funded arm of French bureaucracy under the Ministry of the Interior represented a threat to not only provincial autonomy but also the future of archaeology, since it employed architects rather than antiquarians and archaeologists to assess the value of ancient and medieval structures.[103] By contrast, in al-Jazā'er, as we see below with the Commission d'exploration scientifique d'Algérie (1839–1842), where architects played a similarly privileged role in the restoration of ancient monuments, sometimes to the disadvantage of would-be archaeologists, they had limited ability to protect monuments.

In metropolitan France, crucial to the advocacy of conservation was the shared notion of the underlying importance of monuments to local and national culture; in Algeria, where only a minority of officers acknowledged the significance of Roman remains, such understanding could not take root. In Caen, for instance, Arcisse de Caumont, a young but highly influential antiquary, rallied provincial contemporaries against those who wished to tame local antiquarians and turn their energies exclusively to fulfilling the needs of Parisian scholars and administrators.[104] By inviting local antiquaries to the public archaeological lectures that he offered in 1831, Caumont expressed his commitment to the idea that all French citizens, not just men of the capital, needed to take responsibility for the historic monuments of their regions and defend them from would-be vandals.[105]

For our purposes here, it bears noting that outside of Caumont's spontaneous course, one of the few places in metropolitan France in which practical archaeological training could be acquired in the 1830s was the École polytechnique in Paris, founded in 1794.[106] The German philologist Karl Benedikt (Charles-Benoît) Hase—a member of the Académie des inscriptions et belles-lettres, a participant in the Expédition de Morée, and an instructor of the young Louis-Napoleon—taught well-subscribed courses on ancient history and numismatics at the École polytechnique from 1830 to 1832. Although ostensibly hired to teach German language and literature, Hase, who was also an epigrapher, offered officer-candidates instruction on how to copy Latin inscriptions. He later contributed to the report of the Académie des inscriptions et belle-lettres for the Commission d'Afrique (1833–1837) that helped lay the groundwork for the Commission d'exploration scientifique d'Algérie.[107] Hase himself traveled to Algeria in September 1839 to document the state of preservation of antiquities and inscriptions, which he characterized as poor. To this end, he visited Bougie, Bône, Philippeville (A. Skikda; L. Rusicade), Blida, and the Atlas Mountains.[108]

As recognized by Caumont, Hase, and other antiquaries, archaeological activities undertaken close to home encouraged residents to take pride in local historical achievements and landmarks.[109] Explaining this tradition, Lynn Meskell has argued, "Archaeology is not free from hegemonic flows, rather it has been indelibly entwined with their politics."[110] Neither at home nor in colonial contexts was the practice of archaeology value free. But whereas artifacts and monuments helped French administrators encourage identification with a local region or metropolitan France, they served less innocuous objectives when used by the French abroad. When archaeologists were able to convince authorities of the usefulness of their contributions and the necessity of institutionalizing their discipline, they had the ability to define what constituted knowledge.[111] The French scientific missions to both Egypt and Algeria were shaped by the predatory circumstances in which participants operated. As antiquities were documented and collected, they were used exclusively to the benefit of those who led the missions and capitalized on the opportunities created by the interpretation and publication of finds. By their very nature, these expeditions excluded Indigenous residents, who were portrayed as ahistorical and thus having no stake in the parameters of these projects or their outcomes.[112] From a very early date, colonial archaeologists' privileged position vis-à-vis antiquities laid the foundation for French historical claims to descent from the ancient peoples that had inhabited these regions and justified contemporary intervention in these territories.[113] Both military officers and civilians saw a connection to their own past in the ancient ruins they encountered.

Despite the shortcomings of the archaeological infrastructure in metropolitan France and former Ottoman al-Jazā'er, what most distinguished archaeological activities in the latter was the violence of the French conquest and the unnumbered civilian victims claimed by the military and archaeological campaigns that supported the establishment of the French colony. The scale of the destruction of ancient monuments and artifacts effected by colonial endeavors far exceeded the damage to antiquities that transpired in metropolitan France during either the French Revolution or the Industrial Revolution in the early decades of the nineteenth century. As noted by Nabila Oulebsir, both elite and lower-level French officers, and later civilians, in the course of these events approached ancient ruins selectively and attempted to conserve only those archaeological remains that had symbolic relevance for them.[114] Even if some French officers passionately interceded by recording, if not preserving, evidence of the Roman rulers of the region, their involvement frequently stemmed from their personal stake in these same ancient remains. Their interactions with Roman ruins often reflected their understanding of the military operations they led or in which they participated. The French fascination with the ancient past, coupled with the extraordinary efforts made by at least some army officers to record, excavate, and preserve fragments of the ancient past, underscored the priorities, ideologies, and preoccupations of the colonial occupation. These activities were anything but an innocent pastime; they were not, as some have suggested, solely a means by which officers filled their free hours when they were not on campaign.[115]

The Challenges of Preserving Roman Monuments in the 1830s

Whereas in the eighteenth century, the French had visited the region's antiquities with significantly more distance and had expressed interest in the ancient ruins they encountered without making personal claims, after the conquest far more was at stake.[116] Once the French controlled Algiers and its surroundings, officers of the armée d'Afrique exhibited what might best be described as an ambivalent relationship to Roman antiquities. Their professed admiration for ancient monuments all too frequently fell victim to more practical concerns. Although they often remarked on being moved by the Roman ruins they encountered during the course of their campaigns, these monuments did not benefit from French protection. From early on in the military invasion, French soldiers' looting of ancient architectural remains plagued the city of Algiers. Marble stones, window casings, and columns all became desirable objects of theft, resale, and export to local settlers and collectors in metropolitan France.[117]

Recognizing the commercial value of such transactions, military authorities in France and the territory of Algiers attempted to control who was permitted to excavate antiquities on state-controlled sites and, in several instances, provided authorization to do so. Yet these instructions were often vague and inconsistent, and the interpretation and application of suggested measures by French officers and other colonial agents were often much messier on the ground than metropolitan authorities anticipated.[118] In August 1831, for instance, the minister of war granted a businessman, M. Espès, permission to dig for antiquities in houses and gardens in Algiers that belonged to the army, provided that he abided by a series of conditions. Beyond giving notice at the office of Governor-General Berthézène of his intentions and informing local inhabitants in advance of his activities, Espès was instructed to disturb residents as little as possible and make necessary repairs following his excavations. In exchange for granting this allowance and offering military support for the undertaking, authorities mandated that half the finds be deposited in the public treasury.[119] No record of the fate of the items excavated by Espès appears to have survived. The lack of evidence suggests that the ancient materials he collected were sold, reused for construction purposes, or destroyed rather than being conserved for future generations.

Under similar circumstances, on December 16, 1831, the minister of war granted excavation permission to another antiquary, M. Sciavi, who likewise petitioned to explore homes and gardens in Algiers for antiquities. In this case, however, the authorities did not restrict his exploration to state properties but stipulated that he had to obtain permission for his activities from private homeowners. Sciavi received instructions to distribute one-third of the finds he made to the state and one-third to the property owners; he was permitted to retain the final third, which he could dispose of as he wished.[120] In both cases, the minister of war matter-of-factly issued instructions that were intended to maintain equilibrium in the affected communities at the time that he sanctioned the basic appropriation and redistribution of antiquities in private hands. In neither instance did the minister of war express concern for conserving the remains because of their historical or aesthetic value, a stance that should not be seen as unusual given the lack of patrimonial legislation and the continuing military engagements in the territory of al-Jazā'er. Not surprisingly, no extant documents chronicle the finds of Sciavi's excavations or their display in later colonial or metropolitan institutions.

Indeed, we know very little about the personal collections of antiquities created by French civilians in the Algerian territory at this time because these proved ephemeral unless they were donated or sold to more permanent institutions. Exceptional evidence survives of a *cabinet* created by a Ligurian-born civilian named Lazare Costa in Constantine (L. Cirta) sometime after October 1837, when the city was conquered by the French.[121] In 1855, the Conseil municipal of Constantine approved the purchase of Costa's collection for the city's new archaeological museum.[122] French military officers likewise appear to have been involved in collecting antiquities, as revealed in a letter from the director of the interior in Algiers, dated June 1839 and addressed to the governor-general:

> Monuments of Roman art found on the soil of Algeria have not been numerous up till now, however, if all of these had been gathered at the time of their discovery and placed in a designated location, they would have formed

a curious collection and the interesting subject of research. However, by an unfortunate fate they were for the most part destroyed as soon as they were found and the few that were treated with respect remain buried with amateurs without any utility for science. Such is the case, for example, with the antiquities collection that Captain Hacker (Backer?) assembled at Guelma following orders from M. Colonel Duvivier and which a health officer of the army seized after the death of the captain.[123]

As in this instance, most privately held collections no doubt proved short-lived, since the artifacts assembled in such a provisory manner faced exportation, dispersion, or destruction when their officer owners departed for service elsewhere or died.

In Algiers, the first sustainable effort to collect and display ancient artifacts occurred after French forces had established sufficient security in the city for resources to be dedicated to this purpose. Adrien Berbrugger, a graduate of the École des chartes, was one of the key figures responsible for creating the first European-led cultural institutions following the French conquest. The Arabist arrived in the Algerian capital in 1835 as secretary to Governor-General Bernard Clauzel and founded what would become the Bibliothèque et Musée d'Alger at the order of his commanding officer that year.[124]

From Berbrugger's perspective, a central part of the French colonial mission was to restore "civilization" to the region, an objective that seems to have been focused exclusively on French beneficiaries, both military and civil.[125] As one of the few advocates of conservation of ancient sites, Berbrugger mourned the loss of ancient monuments during the French military campaigns and colonization of the territory of Algiers, but he recognized their potential to enrich his institution:

> If thus, when an expedition is undertaken for some destination not yet explored in which there is an opportunity to collect manuscripts or antiquities, a representative of science should be there, even helping in the peaceful razzias that might occur. There would be before long a large increase in the collections of the library and the museum. During the taking of the *smala* (treasure) of 'Abd el-Qader, thousands of Arabic manuscripts were taken. More than twenty were procured for us; the rest served to feed the fires of the bivouac and were abandoned unconcernedly along the march for booty that was more attractive in the eyes of soldiers.[126]

Figure 10. Adrien Berbrugger, founder of the Bibliothèque et Musée d'Alger and the Société historique algérienne. Reproduced by permission of the Société de géographie and the Bibliothèque nationale de France.

From its start, the Bibliothèque et Musée d'Alger served French officers and colonists in Algiers; despite his marriage to a Muslim woman, Berbrugger conducted little in the way of positive outreach to other Indigenous residents of Algiers, whom he claimed were indifferent to the pre-Islamic past. The main point of contact between Berbrugger's foundation and the non-European population occurred with the confiscation of Arabic manuscripts, including Qur'ans taken from mosques in Mascara, Tlemcen (L. Pomaria), Médéah, and Constantine.[127] Asserting the practical necessity of such actions in wartime, Berbrugger likewise justified the destruction of some ancient structures as essential to the successful conquest of the territory.[128]

With his creation of the Bibliothèque et Musée d'Alger, which remained the preeminent museum of the territory throughout the period of French rule, Berbrugger effectively laid the groundwork for the colonial government's later conservation efforts and displays of antiquities. However, far from all early initiatives to this effect enjoyed a similar outcome. In 1839, noting the threat posed by the military occupation for the conservation of antiquities, the director of the interior in Algiers asked that the minister of war consider taking steps to preserve ancient artifacts. He suggested that if a monetary reward were given in exchange for saving inscribed stones, bas-reliefs, and medals, the benefits for archaeological science would be significant. These, like the marble statue recently discovered at Stora, the port of Philippeville, could be transported without undue expense and displayed at the Bibliothèque et Musée d'Alger.[129] They might then avoid the brand of shortsighted and selfishly motivated souvenir collecting by authorities such as Ferdinand-Philippe, duc d'Orléans, at Djémila (L. Cuiculum) who recounted in October 1839:

> This place has remained a sort of unexploited Herculaneum that would offer an inexhaustible mine for science. There is an immense space covered with column shafts of stone or European granite, capitals, sculptures, mosaics, etc., that one can hardly gather. I chose two capitals, two medals that a soldier had just uncovered, and a column of which only the end would come out, so that they could be sent to Paris for me. I indicated the place where I wanted someone to dig to find some more objects and, with the heel of my boot, I discovered a mosaic that had not yet been noticed.[130]

On the whole, military authorities expressed little interest in collecting and ranked these requests fairly low among their budgetary priorities in the Algerian colony. Amid the deadly campaigns of the first decade of the French occupation of the former Ottoman regency, no further steps to safeguard antiquities were taken. As is clear from complaints contained in a November 1843 letter from the minister of war to Governor-General Thomas-Robert Bugeaud, little effective progress had been made to protect and document antiquities in the Algerian colony.[131]

Over the course of the 1830s, as the armée d'Afrique expanded the territory under French control and continued its brutal campaign against the Indigenous population, both combatants and civilians, archaeological remains in the Algerian territory continued to attract the attention of some military officers, who envisioned the creation of collections and archaeological societies that would manage and study the artifacts as in metropolitan France. The challenges of doing so in the context of the war, however, were significant due to insufficient financial resources, effective laws protecting antiquities, and stability of personnel, since officers were not often stationed for long periods in any one location. Consequently, other than the Bibliothèque et Musée d'Alger, there were few venues in which valuable ancient remains could be protected from damage by the army. One exception was a small museum in the episcopal palace of Algiers created by Monseigneur Dupuch, the first bishop appointed in Algiers (initially called the see of Julia Caesarea and Hippo Regius), an avid advocate of Christian archaeology during his tenure from 1838 to 1846.[132] In addition, in 1844, a public archaeological collection was established in Cherchel (L. Julia Caesarea); it displayed artifacts gathered by the architect Amable Ravoisié during the Commission d'exploration scientifique d'Algérie (1839–1842). Accommodated initially in a confiscated mosque and covered gallery in the court of a building that housed the Office of Civilian Structures, the Musée de Cherchel was modest in size but designed by its military and civilian founders to highlight the wealth of antiquities found in the urban center. Destroyed by an earthquake in 1846, its collection was temporarily transferred to a nearby military barracks where the already fragmented remains suffered theft and defacement. The artifacts that survived these circumstances constituted the core collection of the Musée de Cherchel after its revival in 1855.[133]

Indeed, even though some officers found ancient Roman remains—especially the stone inscriptions, statuary, and triumphal arches—appealing, they quickly discovered that it was not easy to keep the items safe from military confiscation or more casual vandalism or pillage by French soldiers and civilians in the Algerian territory. At the same time, transporting these war prizes back to France was a costly and difficult undertaking. Even those who wielded significant power in the French military, such as the duc d'Orléans, Louis-Philippe's oldest son, who recognized the symbolic capital of the Roman monuments found in the Algerian territory, were not always able to fulfill their wishes to bring home souvenirs of French ventures overseas. In 1839, the duc d'Orléans launched an ambitious effort to transport the third-century triumphal arch of Djémila to Paris, where he planned to have it installed to honor the armée d'Afrique.[134] However, the logistics of moving such a massive monument overland to the closest port in the absence of reliable roads, waterways, or a railway were complex and required significant monetary investment. Although the minister of war—who pursued the project with enthusiasm after the premature death of the duc d'Orléans—backed the undertaking, the transportation of the heavy stone blocks required a greater investment of technological expertise and funds than anyone was willing or able to commit. The duc d'Orléans's wish was never achieved.[135] Although subsequent decades brought more effective methods for the transport of antiquities to metropolitan France, they focused on smaller items such as sculptures, mosaics, and inscribed stones, which could be appreciated on an entirely different scale and were to be displayed in the galleries of the projected Musée algérien at the Louvre.[136]

Politics and Fact-Finding Missions in the 1830s

In November 1833, three years after the French conquest of Algiers and following the fall of the town of Bougie, the minister of war, Maréchal Jean de Dieu Soult, duc de Dalmatie, debated how best to establish long-term French dominance over the new French colony. He considered the ways in which scientific enterprise might shed light on issues important to the successful European settlement of the territory of Algiers, including the collection of information on topics as diverse as soil fertility, the composition of the Indigenous population, and the practicalities of moving people and goods.[137] Soult prepared a report for Louis-Philippe proposing the creation of the Commission d'Afrique, which was approved by the king in a decree dated December 12, 1833. With the duc Decazes as its president, the commission's eighteen participants were an elite mix of military men and civilians.[138] In January 1834, they began discussions in earnest on the future of the North African colony and how the French might best profit from this new territory.[139] Although some members were disturbed by reports of the French army massacre of Arab civilians of the El-Ouffia tribe and urged moderation in the handling of the Indigenous inhabitants, most members nonetheless advocated pushing on so that the sacrifices already made by French soldiers would not be in vain.[140]

Albeit far from central to the commission's preoccupations, the example of ancient Rome was certainly not absent from its members' thinking. On February 5, one member remarked, "The Romans have shown us the way: one only has to follow the ruins of their military stations, the vestiges of their camps. They mark their progressive march in the interior and favorably bear witness to their system of occupation. That which the Romans did, why would we not do, with more means and intelligence?"[141] Another member noted that following the Roman example demanded that they allow the Indigenous peoples to assimilate rather than exterminating them as the Spanish did in the Americas, a policy that he condemned as contrary to the laws of humanity.[142] This ferment led military authorities, who up until this point had focused almost exclusively on consolidating control over the occupied territories, to gather more information. They started by requesting that the Académie des inscriptions et belles-lettres collaborate in the drafting of a geographical study about Roman Mauretania (a region of the Maghreb north of the Atlas that stretched from modern Morocco to central Algeria).[143]

Led by Charles Walckenaër, the new six-man commission that resulted from this mandate included Karl Benedikt Hase, Adolphe Dureau de la Malle, Amédée Jaubert, Edme François Jomard, and Désiré Raoul-Rochette. In assessing how best to govern the region, the members, all of whom had been selected for their considerable antiquarian expertise, sought to convince the minister of war of the necessity of an expanded academic mission in the Maghreb. They argued for the benefits to be gained by collecting information about ancient North Africa and the

Mediterranean and the relevance of this knowledge to the French campaign in Algeria.[144] By 1834, they had completed both a map of the region as well as the *Programme des instructions pour la commission spéciale à envoyer en Afrique*.[145] Presumably, they intended the guide to be read by French officers and engineers in the armée d'Afrique.

Based in metropolitan France, this committee of the Académie des inscriptions et belles-lettres worked from information gathered by the topographical brigades of the armée d'Afrique and French officers' reconnaissance reports, which often included detailed reference to ancient ruins.[146] Dureau de la Malle requested, in particular, that officers gather data about Roman inscriptions and ruins as an integral facet of their reports. He also asked the army to create squeezes (in this period, three-dimensional imprints of stone inscriptions made with moist paper) to shed light on Roman activities in the territory.[147] The Académie furthermore offered medals to those who voluntarily occupied themselves with archaeological pursuits, such as Paul Prieur, the paymaster and director of the post office in Bougie.[148] Conceding that the situation was not entirely compatible with what ancient conquerors of the region had faced (because they believed that the Romans encountered considerably less resistance from pagans than Arab Muslims now offered), the Académie advocated for the advantages of creating an expanded exploratory mission that imitated the scope of that of Napoleon I in Egypt in 1798.[149]

Shortly after the return of Bertrand Clauzel to Algiers as governor-general in August 1835, he gave orders to Berbrugger to create a library in the capital, a decision that was regularized by a decree of the minister of war. As noted above, because Berbrugger did not have a budget for the acquisition of books, he recruited donations for the collection from European consuls in North Africa and residents of the city as well as through more violent forms of appropriation. With the blessing of French administrators, he accompanied the armée d'Afrique as it engaged in military operations in Mascara, Tlemcen, Médéah, and Constantine between 1835 and 1837. During these expeditions, Berbrugger, who was himself an Arabist, confiscated Arabic manuscripts along with Roman antiquities, which consisted, in this instance, of coins or fragments of stone inscriptions.[150] Rather than being decried as pillage, Berbrugger's efficacious plundering of even Qu'rans during military campaigns earned him official praise for his resourcefulness and put him in good stead with authorities interested in studies that would support military objectives.

By the mid-1830s, with the French army deeply entrenched in former Ottoman al-Jazā'er, it became increasingly imperative to the French to gather accurate data to improve their knowledge of the territory under their control. Scholarly research on myriad facets of the new colony included plans to study the remains of the region's ancient Roman monuments, roads, inscriptions, and coins.[151] Antiquarian studies went hand in hand with the colonial regime's appropriation of the territory's natural resources, including experimentation with agricultural lands for potential new crops, the harvesting of timber and coral, and the reuse of ancient structures and cut stone.[152] As noted by Raoul-Rochette, a historian and antiquarian at the Académie des inscriptions et belles-lettres who had previously participated in the French scholarly commission in the Peloponnese, knowledge of Roman activities in North Africa had distinct benefits for the French: "Were they to prove unfruitful with regard to ancient times, these explorations will nonetheless make better known the localities that we just designated, and will shed new light on the present state of the territory. Extending the sphere of geographical knowledge in these new French possessions is not only for the purpose of multiplying the chances of national prosperity, but it clears the path of civilization and prepares, even outside the western limits of Algeria, the universal triumph of humanity."[153] Members of the Académie advocated on behalf of research carried out on the ground not just by military officers but also skilled civilian scholars.[154]

As late as 1836, however, the scholars of the Académie still lacked direct access to archaeological sites, which was denied to them by military authorities who pointed to the exigencies of the ongoing war in the region.[155] Not only did *academiciens* justify their request for admittance to Algeria on the basis of the scholarly implications of such studies, but they also underlined the ideological potential of the ancient remains encountered on a daily basis by officers. They attempted to win over reluctant military authorities by pointing to direct parallels between the activities of the armée d'Afrique and the Roman army's conquest of North Africa.[156] Despite their argument that the study of antiquities offered military leaders historical tools by which to legitimize French claims to the region, the minister of war nonetheless decided against prioritizing archaeological studies.[157]

Once armed with a somewhat improved knowledge of the geography, climate, ethnography, and history of coastal North Africa from the first six years in the province of Algiers, French military goals became more ambitious. The armée d'Afrique moved from its initial aim of controlling coastal cities near the capital of Algiers and extended its objectives to more distant inland settlements. In November 1836, French commanders set their sights on the province to the east of Algiers, which was nominally governed by the bey of Constantine.

Constantine, a modest-sized urban space of 37 hectares with a population of roughly twenty-five thousand was located 320 kilometers to the east of Algiers and 80 kilometers from the Mediterranean coast.[158] The first poorly executed French campaign against the heavily fortified city, in November 1836, resulted in a disastrous retreat for the attackers, far more of whom died from hypothermia in the snow than from combat-inflicted wounds during the campaign.[159] This devastating defeat was the impetus for a request by authorities in Algeria to the Ministry of War for a more detailed survey

Figure 11. Denis-Marie-Auguste Raffet's portrayal of the first French attempt to take Constantine in November 1836, which was an ill-timed, poorly prepared, and costly failure. Reproduced by permission of the Bibliothèque nationale de France, Département des estampes et de la photographie.

of the region's terrain. The response to this proposal was slow in coming. Only in August 1837 did the minister of war give way to the creation of a commission charged with scientific research, one in which geographical data played a much larger role than antiquities.[160]

Even with this authorization in hand, delays in moving forward with the fact-finding expedition had much to do with subsequent French successes in penetrating the fortifications of Constantine. Emboldened by the favorable provisions of the Treaty of Tafna signed in May 1837, by which Emir ʿAbd el-Qader, leader of the forces resisting French military occupation, recognized the lands conquered in the territory as belonging to the French, military officers turned their attention once more to the territory of Ahmed Bey based in Constantine.[161] In October 1837, driven by the desire to restore the honor of the badly defeated armée d'Afrique, the French launched a second assault against the cliff-top city.

Following a brief siege, French soldiers successfully penetrated Constantine's massive stone walls and plundered the urban center for several days. The violent takeover caused the deaths of many civilian residents, some at the hands of the attackers, but hundreds of others plunged to their deaths in a desperate attempt to flee the cliff-top city after its defeat by the French. Following this bloody victory, the army's profit from the city's wealth whetted the appetite of soldiers and officers in the armée d'Afrique and the French public for deeper penetration of the province.[162]

News of the fall of the antiquities-rich region of Constantine, a city much closer to the heartland of Roman North Africa and one in which Ottoman influence was much less pronounced than in Algiers, generated great excitement among scholars of the Académie, who insistently pressed the minister of war for their long-awaited mission to the Algerian colony.[163] Despite this urging, they received little in the way of a concrete commitment from the colonial authorities. The long delay in authorization for an archaeological survey pushed leading scholars to abandon official channels in frustration, and they created an alternative organization to explore the territory of Algiers. By this means, they believed that they could organize and sponsor excavations in the new French colony and in the Ottoman Regency of Tunis. Various European consuls to Tunis had established the precedent for this brand of privately sponsored society, which enabled them to undertake excavations of the monuments of Carthage.[164]

Figure 12. In October 1837, the armée d'Afrique launched a second attack on the cliff-top city of Constantine, in which they lost their commander, General Damrémont; the French assault resulted in the death of a significant number of the civilian inhabitants, some of whom jumped or fell to their deaths from the plateau. Horace Vernet, "Attaque de Constantine de Octobre 1837" (detail). Châteaux de Versailles et de Trianon, Versailles, France. Photo: Gérard Blot, © RMN-Grand Palais/Art Resource, NY.

Founding the Société pour l'exploration et les fouilles de l'ancienne Carthage in August 1837,[165] Dureau de la Malle worked with Isaac Silvestre de Sacy, the orientalist responsible for training a generation of Arabists in Paris, to fund this program by subscription.[166] Before the organization could advance its objectives, however, Silvestre de Sacy died. Having lost its well-known leader in its first year, the society attracted only nineteen members to its ranks. Although these less than ideal conditions precluded members' ability to finance extended private excavations, the organization nonetheless managed to publish its first volume in 1838. This preliminary survey of antiquities was based on the self-sponsored travels of the Englishman Sir Grenville Temple and the Danish consul Christian Tuxen Falbe, who received permission from the French minister of war to journey to the region of Constantine just after its fall to the French.[167] Falbe had already worked in Carthage five years earlier collecting archaeological and cartographic data.[168] The volume that Temple and Falbe composed together appears to have been the only product of this innovative venture, which lacked sufficient financial backing to meet the high cost of overseas excavations. Although the Société pour l'exploration et les fouilles de l'ancienne Carthage predated archaeological societies in Algeria by more than a decade and a half, its objectives were soon superseded by two belated French governmental initiatives.

The first expedition sponsored by the French state was sparked by the need for better maps of the territory under the control of the armée d'Afrique. In January 1838, General Simon Bernard, the minister of war, gave instructions to Governor-General Sylvain-Charles Valée to constitute a five-man topographic section headed by Squadron Commander Saint-Hypolite and whose workforce included captains Puillon de Boblaye, Desaint, Martimprey, and Guérin de Tourville.[169] The second expedition took the form of much delayed financial backing for a broader scholarly mission to the Algerian colony starting in late 1839, which fell under the aegis of the Commission d'exploration scientifique d'Algérie. Putting together a list of participants for the latter required great sensitivity to the demands of the army. To satisfy the minister of war, the Académie mediated between scholarly candidates with deep knowledge of their subjects based in metropolitan France and French military officers in Algeria who had far less academic preparation but more experience on the ground, some proven immunity to the diseases prevalent in the region, and knowledge of the challenges of working in a war zone.[170]

Jean-Baptiste Bory de Saint-Vincent—a naturalist, veteran participant of the expedition to the Peloponnese, and colonel of the army general staff—was granted the leadership of the scientific mission.[171] Although he was perhaps not the most suitable director of the enterprise, having never been to the colony, he was a pragmatist and made a strong case for the necessity of the survey.[172] By August 1839, the commission comprised twenty-one paid members, a number that rose with the addition of eighteen associated members, most of whom were already resident in the territory. The component of the group residing in metropolitan France, which departed for Algiers in December 1839 despite worsening violence in the colony, consisted of ten scholars drawn from the army and eleven civilians. Ten were members of the Académie des sciences and five were members of the Académie des inscriptions et belles-lettres.[173]

With many regions of the territory off limits to the scholars, the commission was a mixed success. Governor-General Valée and his subordinates offered significant resistance to their interventions.[174] Moreover, Bory de Saint-Vincent found himself unable to rein in the individual trajectories of some of the group's members, especially the Saint-Simonian advocate Prosper Enfantin, who had a rather different project in mind from the one envisioned by the minister of war. Still others fell sick once they arrived in the Algerian colony, and one member and one adjunct member contracted fevers and died during the course of their duties in North Africa. With violence worsening and budgetary issues becoming more pressing, the minister of war, at the urging of Governor-General Bugeaud, abruptly recalled the commission participants from the Algerian territory in September 1841.[175] Although a few members negotiated more time to complete studies still underway, most returned to France by late 1841. The commission also received at least one offer of additional drawings of antiquities from a nonmember, who hoped to find a place for the sketches he had made during two visits to the French colony.[176]

The original commission plans had called for the creation of a Musée algérien in the Louvre, which would be composed of a variety of collections gathered in the Maghreban territory along with a library to support further research on the colony. But lack of funding and the shortened time frame shifted emphasis exclusively to publications by its constituent members, many of whom did so without sufficient leave or remuneration to allow them to accomplish this task efficiently.[177] The editorial board, directed by Baron Charles Walckenaër, the perpetual secretary of the Académie des inscriptions et belles lettres, spent a fraught summer and fall in 1841 determining the subject matter of the proposed volumes.[178] In the end, the cost of the expedition and its associated publications amounted to over a million francs.[179] The series, which was titled *Exploration scientifique de l'Algérie pendant les années 1840, 1841, 1842, publiée par ordre du Gouvernement* (1844–1867), comprised thirty-nine volumes, not all of which achieved the same level of scholarly erudition and some of which took several decades to appear. Those that were approved for publication (and, indeed, some were not) were relatively homogenous.[180]

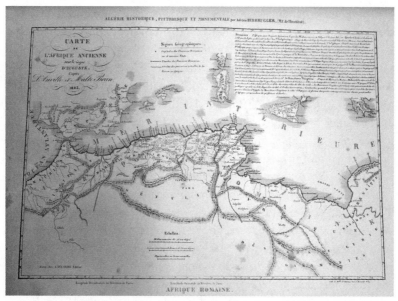

Figure 13. Map of Roman North Africa published by Adrien Berbrugger in 1843. Adrien Berbrugger, *Algérie historique, pittoresque et monumentale ou Recueil de vues, costumes, et portraits faits d'après nature dans les provinces d'Alger, Bône, Constantine et Oran*, vol. 1 (Paris: Chez J. Delehaye, 1843).

Their objective was to define regional differences in the Algerian territory, whether caused by history, geography, archaeology, the arts, or the natural sciences.[181] Additional works by members of the commission such as Berbrugger were published outside the series. In 1884, the successor of this abbreviated mission was the Commission de l'Afrique du Nord, which was constituted following the establishment of the French Protectorate of Tunisia in May 1881.[182]

Despite the input of the Académie des inscriptions et belles-lettres from the start of the commission, just three volumes in the series directly addressed the subjects of archaeology, architecture, and the arts, which had the most bearing on the legacy of ancient Rome. The size of this contribution was no doubt the consequence of the skepticism of Ministry of War and French military officials in the North African colony as to the value of such an undertaking.[183] Captain Adolphe-Hedwige-Alphonse Delamare wrote about archaeological remains in the Algerian territory, and the architect Amable Ravoisié, a veteran of the Peloponnese mission,

contributed two volumes on larger North African monuments of architectural significance.[184] The latter's charge covered similar materials to
those addressed by Delamare, with the addition of a small number of
more recent structures that dated to the Arab period; as previously noted,
some of the objects collected by Ravoisié resulted in the establishment of
a museum in Cherchel.[185] Closely related to these works and containing
at least some archaeological content were Ernest Carette's surveys of the
geography and ethnography of the Algerian territory, the first of which
documented the roads in the colony and the second of which focused on
Kabylia.[186] The publications of Berbrugger and Dureau de la Malle appeared outside the series, much to the consternation of the commission.[187]
These volumes offered historical, archaeological, and ethnographic studies of the newly conquered territory.[188] By contrast, Pellissier de Reynaud,
who had already published the three-volume *Annales algériennes* (1836)
prior to the creation of the commission, composed a historical study for
the series focused on the region to the east of French possessions in the
Algerian colony in his *Description de la Régence de Tunis* (1853).[189]

Delamare, who was a graduate of the École polytechnique and the École
d'artillerie de Douai, as well as a veteran of Napoleon I's Grande Armée,
was among those already familiar with the colony of Algeria prior to being
chosen to serve as an adjunct and then full member of the Commission
d'exploration scientifique d'Algérie. Although his selection for the project
depended more on his drawing skills and perseverance than on any previous archaeological experience, he developed a real passion for ancient
monuments and inscriptions during his tenure. Indeed, he found it very
difficult to conduct archaeology while serving in the armée d'Afrique.[190]
Delamare faced significant challenges in fulfilling his duties because of the
basic incompatibility between the activities of the commission and the demands made on him by his military duties. Although his service on the
commission was supposed to end in 1841 and he was not paid for months
at a time, he managed to prolong his stay in Algeria. By 1845, when he departed for France with a shipment of antiquities, Delamare had completed
an archaeological volume replete with 193 plates and 32 pages of text.[191]

In the fall of 1850, the minister of war authorized Commander Delamare to return for a final time to Algeria, where he remained until the
spring of 1851. His main responsibility was to assist the epigrapher Léon
Renier, who had received sponsorship from the minister of the interior

to transcribe thousands of inscriptions discovered at Lambaesis (F. Lambèse; A. Tazzoult) and nearby sites in the Aurès Mountains. The real fruit
of Delamare's contribution were the thousands of drawings he produced
during these years, some of which were published and others of which
survive only in manuscript form.[192] This documentation, which focused
on not just magnificent but also more modest remains, was as invaluable
to scholars then as they remain today. Many of the antiquities he captured
in his drawings between the late 1830s and early 1850s were damaged
irreparably or destroyed by the subsequent activities of French military
officers and civilians in the Algerian colony.[193]

The Power of Colonial Maps and Images

In assessing the legacy of the Expédition scientifique, Michael Heffernan
has argued that the authoritative appearance of the ponderous tomes its
members produced disguised the very speculative nature of the texts, drawings, and maps they contained. The works were not just optimistic and as-
pirational but also constituted a "complex rhetorical smokescreen behind
which the more brutal realities of European imperial conquest continued
uninterrupted."[194] Such mapmaking activities helped Europeans take possession of land.[195] At the same time, they erased what was long known to
the Indigenous peoples of the region.[196] Indeed, the French claimed that
cartographic knowledge of North Africa was almost a blank slate when
French warships landed at Sidi Ferruch in July 1830, armed with little more
than classical descriptions of the region.[197] Instead of consulting local residents, officers relied heavily on the works of ancient geographers. These authors were useful primarily for their help in reconstructing the itineraries of
the ancient Roman roads in the region, evidence that underlined the close
connection between the French invaders and their Roman predecessors.[198]
French emphasis on cartography had a long tradition: royal and academic
authorities had long recognized mapmaking as an invaluable political resource and had applied it during Napoleon's invasion of Egypt in 1798.[199]

When on campaign, officers made new maps by hand on the fly and
under fire; only some of these would eventually be put into more permanent
form in metropolitan France. The preferable method for printing maps was
to engrave them on copper plates, even though less costly, more durable

(but inferior) printing options existed, including lithography from 1816 (in France) and steel-facing (*aciérage*) from the 1860s.[200] Collecting sufficient data to create an accurate picture of Algiers and its surroundings took cartographers nearly three years to complete.[201] The wartime conditions under which these scholars worked, and the fact that large parts of the territory under consideration were not accessible to their exploration, did not seem to dampen their enthusiasm for drawing sweeping conclusions about the bright future of the French colony after the allegedly dark period of the Arab conquest.

Such research, however, was not limited to maps but included nostalgic descriptions of the former Roman territory in narrative form. Jean-André-Napoléon Périer, the physician whose study was the first volume in the commission series dedicated to medical science, remarked:

> Well! Similarly in the distant past, [the site of] our conquest [i.e., Algeria] was the seat of flourishing colonies. The magnificent ruins that one finds at each step in certain provinces and that our arms will recover one day, attest to its prosperity in a different era. This land, then the object of powerful exploitation, was neither deforested nor depopulated as we see it today; along with Sicily and Africa proper, it was the abundant granary of Rome and of Italy, "Romam magnâ ex parte sustentabat Africae fertilitas."[202] It was ignorance [and] human degeneration that created agricultural decadence and endemic invasions.[203]

In the section of the series dedicated to art, archaeology, and architecture, moreover, participants in the commission saw their research as not just glorifying and reconstructing the ancient past but also conserving remains that might no longer exist in physical form. The artist and architect Amable Ravoisié, in recounting his experience in the Algerian territory and the level of destruction he observed as a consequence of the actions of the armée d'Afrique, noted that:

> The study of Roman monuments from a historical and architectural perspective was thus a new undertaking; let us say more precisely that it was a necessary and pressing project in a land destined to undergo continual transformation as a consequence of the evolution and exigencies of the conquest. It was thus important for the history of art to follow, step by step, the progress of our weapons, to study and describe in great detail the Roman ruins

so numerous in this land, to the extent that chance or circumstances brought about their discovery, with the goal of saving at least from oblivion those that imperious necessities, no doubt but regrettably, forced to be destroyed to the great disadvantage of history and fine arts.[204]

Even if they could not bring an end to the current devastation of ancient sites, the historians and antiquarians who contributed volumes to the *Expédition scientifique* evidently found some solace in the fact that they were able to offer a substitute, a simulacrum of Roman finds. In some cases, those that were not scrupulously true to reality offered something better than the original. Ravoisié, for instance, often included not just the architectural remains as he saw them but rather also as they might ideally be restored.[205] Even if less authentic than the original Roman ruins that stood in the path of the armée d'Afrique, his published drawings enjoyed far greater permanence than the majority of pieces that were dismantled or appropriated in the course of construction projects in the new colony.[206] Such idealized imagery probably suggested to the French readers of the commission volumes how the colonial regime might perfect the contributions of the ancient Romans.

Despite the lack of an official policy for Roman antiquities, from the time of their arrival in North Africa, French scholars in the commission worked hand in hand with the armée d'Afrique. Those recording ancient Roman artifacts emphasized that they were the legacy of European, as opposed to a Muslim or Arab presence, in the region. Consequently, in a further effort to sanction their rightful possession of ancient remains, the French typically accused Arab and Kabyle residents of being irresponsible caretakers of ancient sites. This idea was based on their claim that Indigenous engagement with the ruins had been motivated by profit rather than the acquisition of knowledge about the past. From the perspective of European travelers, antiquaries, and proto-archaeologists in North Africa and the Ottoman Empire, many of whom were already uncomfortable in their interactions with the local populations, the existing residents were ignorant and an obstacle to research. Not only did they inconveniently own or live on the land on which archaeological finds were situated but in some cases they strenuously objected to European interventions of this kind.[207]

On encountering the desert conditions of the Algerian territory, the French blamed the Arab "invaders" for destroying the once fertile landscape described in ancient Roman sources and substantiated by the expansive aqueducts, habitations, and public buildings found in now-abandoned settlements.[208] French officers and civilians did not make these deceptive comments lightly or innocently: at stake were historical and territorial claims to these ancient remains and the ancestors with whom they were associated. Scholarly attention to ancient remains also starkly downplayed the historical contributions of the Indigenous peoples to the destiny of the Algerian territory.[209] Across North Africa and the Middle East, claims to a personal connection to and scholarly appreciation of classical antiquities supported Europeans' efforts to proclaim themselves more "modern" than the current inhabitants of Ottoman-controlled and former Ottoman lands.[210] Nevertheless, as noted by Aimé Césaire, European intervention did not often bring progress.[211] French interest in modernizing North Africa raised the destruction of antiquities in the nineteenth century to a level never heretofore experienced.[212] The obliteration of the very symbols used to legitimize the French conquest of North Africa offers tangible evidence of the fundamental incoherence of the colonial venture.

The potential ideological value of archaeological artifacts to the colonial project in the Algerian territory suggests that we must be critical of European contempt for and censure of the handling of antiquities by Indigenous peoples. A prime example, building on a decade of such contempt, was occasioned by Berbrugger's visit to the territory of the tribes of the Beni-Mzab in the late 1840s. According to Léon Renier, the director of the Bibliothèque et Musée d'Alger asked his hosts if he might visit reputed Roman ruins in the area. The local chiefs tried to discourage him from going by claiming that the ruins were Arab and not Roman. Berbrugger saw this behavior as dishonest; he compared his local contacts to debtors who acted in poor faith because they refused to show proof or allow him to verify this on his own.[213] Failing to view their reaction more sympathetically, or as an act of self-preservation, Berbrugger interpreted their reticence as intransigence whereas it likely stemmed from their recognition that acknowledging Roman ruins in the region might weaken their claims to the land and ancient monuments (which offered shelter, landmarks, and water) vis-à-vis the French military authorities. Such alleged encounters, or at least the French interpretation of them, make evident how fraught the interpretation of antiquities was for contemporary advocates of military and settlement efforts in the Algerian territory.

Similarly, many military maps of the period included archaeological features because they were important to the army's activities, providing refuge, a reliable water supply, and landmarks to rapidly moving but vulnerable columns.[214] With the growth in popularity of thematic cartography from the 1820s, officers and engineers possessed a powerful visual tool by which they could communicate a wealth of statistical information from the Algerian colony, including demographic, agricultural, and meteorological data. Although the teaching time allotted to cartographic studies at the École polytechnique was reduced from what it had been under the Napoleonic Empire, graduates of the École polytechnique, just as the École des ponts et chaussées, made important contributions to metropolitan understanding of the natural resources potentially available in the Algerian colony.[215] We may view drawings and cartographic representations of the Algerian colony as methods by which the French inscribed their authority on the landscape by submitting it to familiar language, imagery, structures, and symbols.[216]

Not only did these maps convey topographical data and the locations of roads, man-made waterways, and ancient ruins, but they also connoted possession. In integrating ancient ruins into their maps, the topographical brigades of the armée d'Afrique, just like Delamare and Ravoisié did much more than just make it possible for columns of soldiers to penetrate Algerian territory effectively during their expeditions. French drawings and maps, whether created by graduates of the École polytechnique or the École des ponts et chaussées, left a powerful imprint on the way that Europeans imagined contemporary Algeria. As forms of classification, they shaped the ways in which the new colony was occupied and controlled, and they reflected the new colonial hierarchy and its inherent inequalities more than the scientific rules they espoused or the objectivity they claimed.[217] In the French vision of Algeria, contemporary campaigns blended seamlessly with those of the ancient Roman army more than a millennium and a half earlier.[218] Indeed, the ancient landmarks that earned pride of place on such topographical maps alluded to the future aspirations of the French colony.

It thus is now time to turn to the 1840s, when the armée d'Afrique asserted itself ever more aggressively against the Indigenous population and when ancient texts and Roman monuments provided a road map for the military officers who doggedly sought to open the Algerian colony to civilian settlers.

Chapter 2

ENVISIONING THE FUTURE

French Generals' Use of Ancient Rome in the 1840s

By the time France formalized its occupation of Algeria in 1841 and divided the territory into the provinces of Algiers, Oran, and Constantine in 1842, the activities and goals of the armée d'Afrique had far exceeded the limited military presence originally envisioned by civilian administrators in the metropole.[1] French officers justified their expanded control of the North African territory as part of a long-term endeavor crucial to the well-being of metropolitan France, one that necessitated appropriate infrastructural support. In June 1844, the minister of war issued a decree to establish a communications network of semaphore telegraphy to unite strategic centers in the colony, a project that was finished a decade later.[2]

Many French political leaders embraced the hope that the conquest and settlement of the colony of Algeria might offer moral renewal and provide a solution to urban poverty in the metropole, which had worsened with industrial development.[3] Following a visit to Algeria in 1846, the French traveler and author Xavier Marmier recognized the sacrifices that had been made to acquire the territory and the consequent importance to metropolitan France of the mission to North Africa: "It [Algeria] is tied to the very heart of France by the blood that France has spilled there, by the glory that she has earned there, and by the works that she undertook there."[4] Although public figures remained deeply divided as to the purpose of the conquest and especially the value of investing so deeply in an ambitious project that competed with financial interests in the south of France, the tide of opinion even among those of a liberal bent shifted steadily in favor of expanding France's presence in its newest colony.[5]

However, some nineteenth-century French authors focused on the culturally alien nature of Arab society, simplifying the complex dynamics of Muslim life in Algeria.[6] Novelist Gautier, for instance, professed his admiration of Islam but recounted that the destabilizing effect of his visit made him feel like an outsider.[7] He nonetheless reveled in the exoticism of the people and beauty of Algeria following a visit in the summer of 1845, and he returned to Paris having acquired Arab apparel (the *burnous*), a cultivated hashish habit, and a pet lion.[8] Rarely were humanitarian concerns voiced with respect to the plight of the Indigenous people who lived in the territory.

At the start of the second decade of the conquest, public intellectuals and statesmen such as Alexis de Tocqueville, who had been sharply critical of the military enterprise as late as 1837, altered the negative tone of their characterizations of French military operations in North Africa.[9] In 1841, following a visit to Algeria with his brother Hippolyte, Tocqueville composed an essay that not only justified the existence of the colony but sanctioned military authorities' violence against Arab and Kabyle civilians in the name of public security. Although this document was never intended for circulation and remained unpublished until 1962, Tocqueville used the essay not only to make sense of the characteristics of the city of Algiers but also to distill his thoughts on how the successful settlement of the Algerian colony benefited metropolitan France and provided new opportunities for its burgeoning population.[10] In the early 1840s, Victor Hugo, who publicly remained fairly quiet on the topic of Algeria but expressed his views in unpublished notes, embraced colonization as part of the natural course of French history. He grew critical of the enterprise's impact only at the end of the 1840s, when the French army turned a heavy hand against French citizens in metropolitan France and Algeria. In the early 1850s, Hugo spoke out against the decision to exile French political prisoners to North Africa.[11]

Another traveler to the region, Jean-Joseph-François Poujoulat, a legitimist historian who was elected deputy of the Bouches-du-Rhône in 1848, concurred with the colonization of Algeria on rather different grounds. In 1844, he visited Algeria to make pilgrimage to Hippo Regius (F. Bône; A. Annaba). His journey took place just two years after Monseigneur Antoine-Adolphe Dupuch, installed in 1838 as the first modern bishop of Algiers, successfully petitioned the archbishop of Pavia, Aloysius Tosi, for the relics of the forearm of Saint Augustine of Hippo. He planned to install the holy remains in Bône, where he had erected a monument in honor of the ancient bishop's see.[12] Drawn to ancient sites of Christian significance in the North African colony, Poujoulat, like a minority of others in this period, were part of a religious undercurrent that bucked the anticlerical tendencies of the military leaders and a growing number of civilian colonists in Algeria.[13] Instead of pointing to the Roman imperial conquest of the region for a model, he viewed the modern French undertaking as the fulfillment of Louis IX's crusading ambitions in North Africa (downplaying the fact that the king, who was later canonized, died from dysentery soon after landing in Tunis in 1270 during the eighth crusade).[14] Borrowing from medieval theology, a subject in which he was well versed, Poujoulat argued that the fight against barbarians justified barbaric acts in the name of good.[15]

Although the activities of Dupuch, who saw his mission as the revival of Christian North Africa as it had existed in the time of Cyprian of Carthage and Augustine of Hippo, were favored by many in Catholic circles, he was disliked by French military officials, who considered his proselytizing among the Muslim population as a potential source of unrest.[16] After he managed to incur a significant debt for the diocese, authorities were finally able to force him to leave his office in 1846.[17] Under his successor, the French-appointed Louis-Antoine-Augustin Pavy, who served from 1846 to 1866, the number of parishes in Algeria increased from 29 to 187, and the number of priests grew from 48 to 273. Because they were officially forbidden to proselytize among the Muslim population, however, the main role of the clergy and a number of monastic congregations that settled in Algeria was to minister to and teach the children of European civilian settlers, especially those who were not from France. Their decisive role in Catholic education continued in the colony well after the start of the Third Republic, ceasing only with passage of the Lois Jules Ferry in 1881–1882, which made all public education secular.[18]

What also distinguished Bishop Dupuch from the military authorities was his deep-seated faith in the connections between ancient Christian history in coastal Algeria and the responsibilities of modern France in the region. In 1847, a year after leaving Algeria, Dupuch published his *Essai sur l'Algérie chrétienne, romaine et française*, which was intended to translate selections from Stephano Antonio Morcelli's *Africa christiana* (1816–1817) and update them with information gathered since the start of the French conquest about Christian North Africa.[19] Similarly, Abbé Bourgade, who served in Algiers briefly after 1838 before he moved to Tunis, where he worked from 1841 to 1858, recorded the lasting imprint of the ancient Christian past on the North African landscape.[20] This brand of Catholic advocacy for the colonial project in Algeria nonetheless was unappreciated by the French colonial administration during this era. Most French officers who ventured westward from Algiers to pay homage to Hippo trained their attention on more practical matters such as the historic vulnerability of this outpost, which had not weathered the fifth-century Vandal onslaught without incident.[21]

Although there were vocal critics in the Chambre des députés in metropolitan France in the 1840s, opposition to the ongoing war in the former Ottoman territory had softened considerably from what it had been in the 1830s.[22] The second decade of French military operations in the region saw erection of a modest number of memorials in Algiers, Constantine, and elsewhere in the colony commemorating French military victories and generals.[23] One of the few remaining deputies to speak out decisively against the occupation of Algeria was Jacques-François-Claire-Henri Joly, a lawyer from Limoux (Aude), who courageously denounced the imperial undertaking in June 1844: "The war, always the war, expenses without result, a conquest without a future, and above all, colonization that is both ruinous and impractical."[24] According to Amédée Desjobert, a deputy who had already represented Seine-Maritime for a decade, the French occupation of Algeria continued unabated only because of widespread ignorance of what was actually happening on the ground. His argument took into account the high mortality rate of French servicemen in Algeria from cholera and dysentery: in Desjobert's reckoning, roughly eleven thousand troops had succumbed to disease in 1840 alone (compared to 227 who died in battle). Based on these demographics and the typical seven-year term of enlistment for French soldiers, he calculated that the armée d'Afrique would require more than twenty thousand new recruits annually to maintain the fighting force of one hundred thousand men that was deployed in North Africa by 1846. Of the projected cohorts of twenty thousand young men conscripted to fight in France's name in Algeria, he estimated that an average of only fourteen thousand would return.[25] In his view, the deficit of young French lives, financial cost of the military operation, and senseless violence committed overseas compromised the well-being of metropolitan France.[26] Others, such as Jean-André-Napoléon Périer, a participant in the Commission d'exploration scientifique d'Algérie, nonetheless argued that French troops and colonists would adapt to the environment of the region despite these challenges.[27]

Within the Ministry of War and the armée d'Afrique, where few opposed colonial expansion, significant differences of opinion divided authorities on essential topics such as effective military tactics and the most appropriate candidates for colonial settlement. Meanwhile, pressure mounted on those in a position to make policy decisions as the military and civilian presence in Algeria continued to grow. As in the first decade of the French occupation, the memory of imperial Rome occupied an increasingly dominant place in French discussions of the Algerian colony's future during the 1840s.[28] For French officers, the Roman past offered both inspiration and guidance in carrying out their missions.[29] Broadly speaking, those involved in military operations, as well as the scholars they consulted, gleaned what they could from the relatively spare ancient texts that described the North African coast and its peoples. Supplementing this information, as we have already seen, were the brief missions sanctioned or accommodated by the minister of war in the early 1840s; they offered additional evidence from inscriptions and key ruins in Algeria. Reference to the classical period by policymakers and officers shaped their interactions with Arabs and Kabyles, offered important models for military strategy, and laid an important narrative foundation for colonial ideology.

Azéma de Montgravier, a graduate of the École polytechnique (1828) and an artillery captain attached to the Bureaux arabes in the Division of Oran, was one officer among many who remarked on Roman achievements in the region. Having served in Algeria several times during the 1830s and 1840s, and later elected a member of the Société historique algérienne in Algiers (founded in 1856), Montgravier wrote passionately about the parallels between the Roman experience in North Africa and that of the French in his own time. By his estimation, ancient remains served not just historians but also modern-day conquerors and colonists: "In every epoch, the establishment of colonies was the most useful and fruitful act of humanity; this expansive force was destined by its incessant action against the barbarian world to enlarge the domain of civilization and prepare the way for Roman unity. For nations foreign to the great city, it became the superior limit of political and social progress that they could attain."[30] Montgravier thus exhorted his contemporaries to embrace the past by engaging in thoughtful yet critical study of their Roman predecessors in the region: "Let us therefore do research on the remains of Roman domination, not to propose a servile imitation of it that would reject the bold allures of our own century and the adventurous spirit of the nation but rather to inspire us with the wisdom of the ancients, and leave, if we can, to our descendants, some examples of our own wisdom."[31] In Montgravier's eyes, the possibilities were limitless: "War has enabled us to get to know the largest part of their [the Romans'] military establishments; peace and the study of the lands pertaining to colonization allow us to discover each day their civil and agricultural establishments."[32] He thereby suggested that successive phases of colonial development might profit from what could be learned from critical consideration of Roman antecedents.

For an individual who had authorization from the Ministry of War to visit Algeria for any length of time in the 1840s, however, there could be little doubt as to the violence of the French occupation. Claiming that the behavior of French soldiers in North Africa was civilized required turning a blind eye to the day-to-day conflicts of an increasingly bloody military endeavor. By 1840, troop levels reached a new height of sixty-one thousand men, and the European civilian population numbered nearly twenty-nine thousand souls; both figures came close to doubling within a space of just five years as the French occupation wreaked devastation on Muslim residents.[33] The era was shaped in particular by Thomas-Robert Bugeaud's deadly term as governor-general from 1841 to 1847, during which extreme violence against Arab and Kabyle peoples became normative in the French quest to pacify the region under their authority.[34] Beyond the immediate hardships provoked by the massacres and dislocation that supported Bugeaud's ambitions for an expanded French territory in the region, historians concur that the events of this decade contributed to the severe humanitarian crisis that transpired during the drought and famine of 1867–1868. The confiscation and reallocation of the scarce resources of Algeria to European colonists worked to the severe disadvantage of Muslim inhabitants. From the start of the French occupation, human-made conditions created enormous vulnerability to drought, typhus, malaria, and cholera, debilitating challenges that disproportionately affected local residents. The demographic catastrophe was brought on by a fatal combination of colonial policies that dated to the earliest years of the conquest.[35]

Dawson Borrer, a British traveler in the unusual position of being embedded with French columns during their campaigns in the mountainous region of Kabylia in 1847, commented on the savage violence used by French troops against the Indigenous population. He drew attention, in particular, to the all-too-frequent application of the *razzia*,[36] a retributive tactic that the French borrowed from the Arabic and Ottoman word *ghaza* but that originally denoted a limited raid at a much lower level of violence than the kind of punitive activity conducted by the French.[37]

The French attributed the custom of the razzia to ancient Indigenous leaders such as Tacfarinas.[38] Despite French claims that they were engaged in a "native" custom of war, they transformed what had been a regular custom of tribal raiding into the punitive destruction of the livelihood of tribes that opposed colonial rule. When they burned Arab and Kabyle crops, homes, and food storage facilities; confiscated their flocks; chopped down their fruit, nut, and olive trees; and took hostage or massacred women, children, and the elderly, they took this practice to a new extreme.[39] Borrer recognized that the French employed the brutality of the razzia explicitly to terrorize Muslim civilians while blaming them for their alleged savagery.

Borrer's counsel that the French would benefit from heeding Cicero's exhortation on the importance of piety, religion, and wisdom to any governing nation went unheeded by military authorities.[40] In the meantime, French commanders relied on ancient historians to very different ends: namely, justifying their treatment of Muslim residents by alleging that the Arab population had squandered the abundant resources of the land described in antiquity.[41] Officers and metropolitan administrators alike selectively read Roman sources on the prosperity of the region more than

Figure 14. Denis-Auguste-Marie Raffet portrayal of "Une razzia," an illustration in Charles Nodier's *Journal de l'expédition des Portes de Fer* (1844). Photograph: Emilie Cambier. Musée de l'armée, Paris. © Musée de l'Armée/RMN-Grand Palais/Art Resource, NY.

fifteen centuries earlier to absolve themselves of responsibility for the desolation they themselves were helping create. Roman imagery filled the negative spaces from which the Indigenous population had been expunged or reduced to invisibility.[42] This narrative distracted attention from the brutal nature of French campaigns by blaming the victims for their woes. It also allowed French officers and administrators to delude themselves that they were returning the land to its full potential.[43]

In this same period in metropolitan France, there were remarkably few critics of the extreme violence and massacres of what amounted to thousands of civilians; this silence resulted, at least in part, from careful censorship by the Ministry of War of reports addressing French activities in the Algerian territory. One important exception to this news blackout was the unauthorized circulation of reports of the murder by asphyxiation of at least eight hundred civilians from the Oued Riah tribe in the caverns of Dahra, west of Algiers, in June 1845. That French forces had built bonfires at the entrances of the caves where men, women, and children sought

Figure 15. Tony Johannot's portrayal of "Les grottes du Dahra, 18 Juin 1845" and the asphyxiation of members of the Oued Riah tribe who had taken refuge there. Photograph: Emilie Cambier. Musée de l'armée, Paris. © Musée de l'Armée/RMN-Grand Palais/Art Resource, NY.

refuge caused considerable consternation in metropolitan France, but this did not lead to the prosecution of the perpetrators, some of whom went on to positions of enormous influence in the French military.[44]

Another frank historical account of Algeria was composed by Pierre Christian, the pseudonym of Jean-Baptiste Pitois, a journalist and bibliographer in the Ministry of Public Instruction who from 1843 to 1844 served as Governor-General Thomas-Robert Bugeaud's personal secretary.[45] Criticizing the French colonial mission as having little to do with pacification, Pitois provocatively compared French tactics in Algeria to those of the ancient Huns and Vandals.[46]

The classical past constituted a key element in French colonial ideology throughout the 1840s. A pointedly nostalgic vision of Algeria justified and sustained central policy considerations by French administrators and officers during a period when the main players in the venture had still not reached a mutual consensus as to the nature and parameters of either the conquest or the shape of the future colony. Indeed, the classical past represented a multivalent symbol that allowed French military and civilian officials to highlight selected aspects of history that best suited their objectives and ignore the ones that did not. Yet the consequences of envisioning French actions within a much longer historical trajectory of the foreign occupation of North Africa were severe. Although a few officers in the 1840s such as Franciade-Fleurus Duvivier echoed criticisms raised in the late 1830s, pointing to the counterproductive nature of policies that diverged from the contemporary understanding of ancient Rome and made enemies of the inhabitants of the territory, their voices were increasingly in the minority. In this era, the lens of the classical past enabled many French officers to avoid reckoning with officially sanctioned terror and its implications for the future of Algeria and metropolitan France. Nor were French authorities exceptional in their use of the ancient past to fulfill both national and imperial ambitions. Yannis Hamilakis has observed that the study of the ancient remains largely lacked objectivity and critical judgment, regardless of where it was practiced: "Therein lies one of the central paradoxes of national archaeology: it often invokes objectivity, neutrality, accuracy, and precision, it privileges empirical observation over explanation and interpretation, yet at the same time it overtly or covertly creates a national past and a national archaeological record, by deliberate selection, de-contextualization, sanitization, and often imaginative re-creation of the past."[47] In the context of Algeria, reference to imperial Rome allowed French officers to justify the extraordinarily cruel measures taken by the armée d'Afrique as necessary for the "restoration" of civilization to the Maghreb.

Eternal and Unchanging Peoples: Encountering Arabs and Kabyles

As we have seen from the example of General Pierre Berthézène, who played a central role in the first two years of the French conquest, the Roman Empire offered a model for the French domination of the Algerian territory. He, like many of his contemporaries, believed that the Arabs and Kabyles he encountered in Algiers were almost entirely unchanged from their ancient ancestors.[48] His civilian contemporary, the artist Eugène Delacroix, had a similar reaction during a visit to Morocco in 1832; he imagined that Cato, Brutus, and Cicero could have easily encountered the peoples he saw all around him.[49] Such tropes became increasingly common in the next decade and continued throughout the occupation.[50] Berthézène's successors, such as Armand-Jacques Leroy de Saint-Arnaud, perceived Arabs and Kabyles as untouched by the advances of modern civilization. In a letter sent from Algiers on June 7, 1838, to his younger brother, he wrote: "Among no other people, I believe, are there as many contrasts as among the Arabs, and there is no people that is less advanced, less changed than that group. Every day I see the days of Abraham, of Isaac, and of Jacob. I see the Numidians of Juba and of Massinissa. I saw, near Constantine, the war bands of Jugurtha. The men are the same, the horses are the same, the dress is entirely the same. What have time and civilization brought them?"[51]

Saint-Arnaud characterized the territory of Algiers as a place in which essentially no time had elapsed between the ancient Roman and modern French invasions. However, unlike Polybius, who praised Massinissa as having successfully reigned in Numidia for more than sixty years, Saint-Arnaud's view of the native people of Algeria was far less charitable.[52] He focused mainly on their unpredictable and warlike behavior, including Livy's description of Massinissa's impulsive nature when he married the beautiful Carthaginian Sophonisba, the wife of Syphax and daughter of Hasdrubal, to save her from being taken prisoner by the Romans.[53] This predilection for eliding past and contemporary conquests meant that nineteenth-century French officers envisaged classical Roman activities as highly relevant to contemporary military campaigns and colonization efforts in Algeria.[54]

Framing the region's residents in terms of the ancient past also empowered French officers to draw sharp contrasts between themselves and the non-Arab Indigenous peoples, especially the Berbers, to whom they typically referred as Kabyles or mountain people. This reference point allowed them to suggest that their interlocutors were primitive and veritable noble savages "ripe" for the civilizing influence of the French colony.[55] In November 1841, Captain Jean-Joseph-Gustave Cler, a graduate of the military academy of Saint-Cyr, was commissioned in the 2nd Light

Saint-Arnaud.

Figure 16. Armand-Jacques Leroy de Saint-Arnaud. Ferdinand-Désiré Quesnoy, *L'armée d'Afrique depuis la conquête d'Alger* (Paris: Furne Jouvet et Cie, 1888).

Infantry, a battalion of soldiers who had been convicted of various crimes and had already served their prison sentences.[56] (Although these former inmates still owed military service, they were not considered fit to serve with ordinary enlisted men.) Writing in 1842, Cler viewed contemporary North Africa through the lens of ancient history. He observed that, just as in the period of the Roman conquest of the coastal areas of North Africa, the Kabyles remained loyal to their mountain enclaves.[57] Arrested in time and clinging to the safety of their rocky promontories, they now resisted mixing blood with conquerors just as their ancestors had done with the ancient Carthaginians and Romans:

> There is, I assure you, in the primitive nature of the Kabyle more good than bad. The first inhabitants of North Africa, they were conquered but not subjugated by the Numidians, the Carthaginians, the Romans, the Vandals, and the Arabs. In the midst of all the revolutions that must have accompanied these conquests, they always remained the same and did not borrow from the last masters but a few religious dogmas that accommodated their customs and passions. France will never subjugate them because . . . they have their poverty and impracticable mountains to defend them. If we act with firmness, frankness, and wisdom with them, we will make from these people an ally that prefers our domination to that of the Arabs, who were always their avid despoilers.[58]

The Kabyle myth, which encouraged the French to think that Berber peoples had more potential as allies than Arabs,[59] rested in large part on works of ethnology such as Eugène Bodichon's *Considérations sur l'Algérie* (1845).[60] In addition, the French understanding of classical Roman colonization of North Africa and their alleged isolation from Indigenous inhabitants contributed to this construct.[61] Even later authors who believed that the Kabyles had mixed with conquering nations still held to the idea that they had not changed much over the centuries and would need to be enticed rather than forced to recognize French dominion.[62]

Like their belief in the allegedly unchanging nature of the Kabyle, many French officers felt a direct connection to the Romans, whose legacy they remembered whenever they contemplated the ancient stones all around them. In August 1845, Aléxis Robardey, a second lieutenant in the 6th Light Infantry Battalion, conveyed some of the excitement still conjured by seeing the ruins of the ancient Roman city of Castellum Tingitanum, from which Governor-General Thomas-Robert Bugeaud ordered the construction of the city of Orléansville (A. Chlef). Robardey noted: "The excavations that were done furnished incontestable proof of its ancient opulence. In addition to medals with effigies of the emperor, cameos, capitals, marbles, [and] a bust, a beautiful mosaic was discovered that was the square of a chapel where St. Reparatus, bishop, had been buried in 436, as was indicated by an inscription on the mosaic."[63]

For some, the proximity of the ancient past went beyond excitement because it offered a model for their own domination of Algeria. Although Colonel Saint-Arnaud never fulfilled his intention to re-erect Reparatus's church in Orléansville, and the ruins still lay covered by the city's market in the twentieth century, it was not because he did not feel the weight of the ancient Roman legacy.[64] In 1844, when Saint-Arnaud oversaw the construction and defense of the city, he sensed the intimate reverberations of its predecessor's ruins: "We live on top of a Roman city, and our cheap tunics float with the same wind that rustled ample tunics and very noble Roman togas. I ordered that my great street be leveled, and in excavating the land we found some superb stones, marble columns, well-preserved tombs and their complete bones, and a classical urn filled with copper coins, *as* or *deniers*. The ancient city sleeps under our feet."[65] Inserting themselves in the grandeur of an ancient historical narrative, French officers claimed a personal connection to the Roman past. Their self-identification with its rulers allowed them to characterize their actions as waking the region from a deep sleep.

In the 1840s, as French officers increasingly embraced their mission of drawing Algeria back into the sphere of European dominance, references to ancient Rome became more common. In 1842, Captain Nicolas-Gilles-Toussaint Desvaux, a cavalry officer visiting Tébessa (L. Theveste) in the province of Constantine, alleged that only the French, not the Arabs, had the right to step into the shoes of the ancient Romans:

> on this land covered by colossal ruins left by the genius and strength of a people without equal, of a conquering people [the Romans], this religion of Islam just recognized the domination of the *Roumi* [Europeans] who are for them the direct descendants of the founders of the city. This Christian religion, so beautiful, so charitable when it is not tested, will live at the side of the religion of Muhammad [*mohamètisme*], in the places where it flourished in the past. The glorious flag will shine on these ruins to say that if any people could walk in the traces of the Romans, it is the French people![66]

Desvaux did not hesitate to parallel the dominance of the armée d'Afrique with its Roman predecessor despite the long interlude that separated the two invasions.

Léon Blondel, a French civilian administrator and director of finance in Algiers from 1834 to 1845, noted that he, like many French, instinctively identified with and was buoyed by the ghosts of the ancient Roman conquerors of the Maghreb.[67] Not only did his arrival in North Africa awake in him a sense of historical homecoming, but the Algerian territory also impressed on him the possibility of France's renewal: "In treading upon this old land, in seeing this part of the Roman Empire, dead since the fifth century, shake off its shroud, leave its tomb and be revived solely through contact with France, I felt in this solitude . . . invincibly protected by the moral strength that victory gave us; I thought of myself as greater and was very proud of my country."[68] In the shadow of the humiliation experienced by the French with the final defeat of Napoleon in 1815, French officers and civilians in Algeria welcomed the North African conquest because they surmised that this military action, like its ancient Roman precedents, would provide ample opportunity for the pursuit of honor essential to French healing and regeneration.

Franciade-Fleurus Duvivier's Quest to Restore Ancient Rome in North Africa

The career of a little-remembered French commander who made a name for himself in the Algerian conflict illuminates how the echoes of ancient Rome shaped the campaigns of the armée d'Afrique and served as a model for the newly established colony. Born in Rouen in 1794, Franciade-Fleurus Duvivier entered the École impériale polytechnique in 1812 at the height of the Napoleonic Empire.[69] In 1814, he undertook training as a military engineer at the École d'application de l'artillerie et du génie de Metz. Before he had finished his studies, however, the fortunes of Napoleon I and the French Empire changed dramatically: Duvivier found himself fighting in defense of the city of Paris against Coalition forces in July 1815 following the emperor's loss at Waterloo. In the years after Napoleon's fall from power, Duvivier served successfully (if not happily) in Corsica, the Îles d'Hyères (in the Mediterranean, near the coast of the French department of Var), and Saint-Pierre in Martinique. He was steadily promoted through the ranks of the French army. By the time he obtained permission from the Bourbon monarchy to return to France, he had

Duvivier.

Figure 17. Franciade-Fleurus Duvivier. Ferdinand-Désiré Quesnoy, *L'armée d'Afrique depuis la conquête d'Alger* (Paris: Furne Jouvet et Cie, 1888).

attained the grade of captain. While working in the engineering unit at Verdun in 1830, Duvivier learned of Charles X's ambitions in North Africa and made a formal request to join the armée d'Afrique in its imminent bid to conquer Algiers. Among his qualifications, he listed his experience in warm climates and his introductory acquaintance with the Arabic language.[70]

Duvivier's petition was granted and, months before the actual invasion, he received orders to report to Toulon, the main port of departure for the North African campaign.[71]

As commander of the 67th Line Infantry, one of two battalions of Zouaves composed of an uncomfortable blend of Indigenous infantrymen and Parisian volunteers arriving from the barricades, Duvivier was an enthusiastic leader. His accomplishments earned him coveted citations as a knight and then officer of the Legion of Honor in 1831 and 1832, respectively.[72] Although poor health enabled him to request leave to convalesce for months at a time in metropolitan France, such complaints were not uncommon for French officers stationed in the Algerian territory. In the former Ottoman regency, it was less frequently battle wounds than cholera, malaria, typhus, and the bubonic plague that severely weakened French troops. Illness was frequent among enlisted men, and to a lesser extent among better-fed officers.[73] Whatever the nature of his unnamed ailments, Duvivier recovered sufficiently each time from his maladies to return to North Africa and take on new and challenging responsibilities in the rapidly expanding French colony.[74]

Duvivier's military superiors valued him for his courage in battle: he and the men under his command covered the evacuation of Bône and the retreat of French troops from a failed expedition to Médéah in 1831.[75] However, they also considered him one of the most promising officers serving under arms in Africa due to his rapid mastery of vernacular Arabic. Following the creation of a Bureau arabe in 1833 at the initiative of Captain Christophe Louis Léon Juchault de Lamoricière, commander of a battalion of Zouaves, a superior officer recommended Duvivier as an ideal candidate to contribute expertise to the undertaking.[76] Although his familiarity with the Berber language of the Kabyles was still incomplete and represented a liability in certain circumstances, Duvivier was considered sufficiently proficient in Arabic to merit a temporary appointment in 1835 and 1836 as the "agha des Arabes."[77] In this position, which would be eliminated in 1837 and replaced by the Directorate of Arab Affairs (later the Bureaux arabes or Office of Arab Affairs), he served as the primary spokesman of the armée d'Afrique.[78] As agha, his responsibilities included mediating between tribal leaders and their Arab or Kabyle dependents on behalf of the French government. Taking part in both the failed expedition of Constantine in late 1836 and the cliff-top city's subsequent defeat in the autumn of the following year, Duvivier served in rapid succession as lieutenant colonel, colonel, and brigadier general in Algeria. His accomplishments included creating a military base with four hundred men in Guelma (L. Calama) (1837), fortifying the military camp of Blida (1838–1839), commanding men in a fraught battle in the pass of Téniah in the Atlas Mountains (1840), and successfully occupying the city of Médéah (1840).[79]

As a loyal supporter of then Governor-General Sylvain-Charles Valée, Duvivier was deeply dismayed by his superior's recall to metropolitan France in late 1840 and his replacement by Thomas-Robert Bugeaud in early 1841.[80] Consequently, in February 1841, after more than a decade of illustrious service in Algeria, Duvivier petitioned Jean de Dieu Soult, duc de Dalmatie, then minister of war, that he be allowed to return to France. Diplomatically, he cited his desire to finish out the last years of his career on the European continent.[81] Although the time was not as restful as anticipated, he published prolifically on historical and political topics related to the past and future of the Algerian colony. On April 17, 1843, Duvivier requested and soon afterward received permission from the minister of war to go into retirement so as to devote himself more fully to his writing.[82] However, the 1848 Revolution rudely interrupted the relative peace of Duvivier's scholarly pursuits. On February 26, 1848, the provisional government in Paris called him back into service and appointed him superior commander of twenty-four battalions of the Mobile National Guard in Paris and the Department of the Seine.[83] Although he relinquished these functions after becoming a representative in the Assemblée nationale, Duvivier died later that year during the turmoil occasioned by the June Days.[84]

Throughout his successful career in the armed services, Duvivier's commanders praised him for his scholarly enthusiasm. The author of the 1838 General Inspection saw this attribute as a positive complement to his extensive military accomplishments and loyal service: "Colonel Duvivier is a commander who already has much experience and even more of a future. He has extensive knowledge and is well versed in sciences and literature. He is no stranger to any specialty of war, having worked in different branches of the armed services."[85] By 1837, when he was stationed in Guelma, Duvivier had developed an interest in the Roman archaeological monuments uncovered during the course of engineering works at the site; his superiors commended his activities, including uncovering traces of the ancient city with the help of his troops.[86] Documents from his military career, today preserved at the Service historique de la défense in Vincennes, France, include, for instance, line drawings and transcriptions of Roman inscriptions, which he made while stationed in Guelma.[87] A detailed understanding of the site's ancient remains had practical advantages for Duvivier, since the hard-pressed soldiers under his command were eager to repurpose the monumental fortifications built by the Romans on their own behalf. In the course of his service of the armée d'Afrique, Duvivier oversaw the repair and reuse of the ancient Byzantine fort's walls, which were doubled in height, and the construction of barracks from Roman cut stone found nearby.[88]

Duvivier's fascination with antiquities seems to have extended beyond practical concerns and included considerations as to their prospects for short- and long-term conservation. As the superior commander of the military outpost of Guelma, he complained of his soldiers' lack of scruples in destroying the inscriptions of ancient Calama in the course of building projects.[89] Given the high toll on ancient monuments of the activities of the armée d'Afrique, French military officers had to make an extraordinary effort to protect Roman historical remains from their men.[90] Duvivier also ordered civilian inhabitants to leave ancient inscriptions, decorative details, and sculptures undisturbed. Although it is unclear how and to what degree these provisions were enforced, Duvivier directed residents to offer any movable antiquities found in the course of daily activities to local military authorities. He intended that these artifacts be transmitted to the Académie des inscriptions et belles-lettres or placed in a future museum.[91] Yet, Duvivier achieved only some of his short-term objectives for antiquities at Guelma; he lacked the institutional infrastructure to extend these protections beyond the time of his service in the armée d'Afrique. However, although Duvivier did not control the resources necessary to move the sculptures and bas-reliefs from Guelma to Paris while he remained in Algeria, his objectives were not entirely abandoned. In the mid-1840s, Captain Adolphe-Hedwige-Alphonse Delamare successfully petitioned the minister of war for funds and clearance to move some of the antiquities of Guelma to the Louvre as part of a larger shipment of antiquities for which he was responsible.[92]

Duvivier's career, which included a decade of campaigning in the Algerian territory, contrasts with that of Governor-General Sylvain-Charles

Valée, though the two shared a deep awareness of and respect for Roman precedents. Born on December 17, 1773, Valée attended the École d'artillerie de Châlons from September 1, 1792. During the 1820s and 1830s, he helped update French uses of artillery and served first as the general inspector of artillery (from 1828) and then as the director of the service of gunpowder and saltpetre (from 1835). In 1836, Valée set foot on Algerian soil when he was called to assist the armée d'Afrique in its first, ill-timed attempt to take the cliff-top city of Constantine in November 1836. The defenders of Ahmed Bey, the last resident Ottoman representative in the region, brought about the untimely demise of Governor-General Charles-Marie-Denys Damrémont, who was wounded by a cannonball during the siege of Constantine and died immediately afterward. Following this incident, Valée took command in the field as the leading military official in the colony and occupied this role until the end of 1840.[93]

Within just a few months of his arrival in Algeria, Valée had begun to share Duvivier's appreciation for Roman achievements in the region. As an officer whose career was dedicated to ordnance and fortifications, Valée recognized the signal importance of Roman remains in determining where the French should establish encampments, identify and secure reliable water supplies, and build roads. Unlike his immediate successor, Thomas-Robert Bugeaud, who opted for a more aggressive, mobile approach to Indigenous combatants, Valée's strategy relied heavily on fortified defenses that were constructed on former Roman citadels like Cherchel (G. Iol; L. Julia Caesarea), Médéah, and Miliana.[94] He thus valued ancient remains as essential to the French military effort. In October 1838, Valée documented how he had used Roman remains to fortify his headquarters in the Kasbah, formerly the Roman citadel of Constantine.[95] On January 5, 1841, just after his return to France, he reported his operational successes to the minister of war and underlined how his knowledge of the Roman army allowed him to advance the French cause: "All the establishments that I founded in the province of Constantine were dictated by the thought of recreating the Roman occupation. This is the same system that I am applying in the West. This explanation is to help you understand, Mr. Maréchal, the importance that I ascribed to the discovery of the route that the [Roman] army followed to return to Miliana and the desire that I had to put this city in communication with Cherchel."[96] Identification of the remains of Roman occupation, and especially roads, allowed Valée to achieve his strategic goals. Although the governor-general did not produce any detailed publications on the subject, his approach to ruins suggests that Colonel Duvivier's interest in ancient Roman sites was far from unique among commanding officers in the armée d'Afrique in the early 1840s.

While not many of Duvivier's personal papers appear to have survived, his publications on Roman North Africa and more contemporary issues composed both during his service in Algeria and subsequent retirement in France offer insight into the significance of the Roman era for French military officers in the late 1830s and 1840s. In 1841, Duvivier published *Recherches et notes sur la portion de l'Algérie au sud de Guelma*, the most significant of his archaeological contributions. This work, which comprised a geographical survey of Roman ruins and modern-day tribes, was based in large part on interviews he conducted with local Muslim witnesses when he was based in Guelma. He used their responses to confirm and supplement information he had extracted from a variety of ancient and more recent sources on North Africa, including the late Roman map (which survived only in a medieval copy) known as the Peutinger Table, travel writings of the eighteenth-century cleric Thomas Shaw, and studies of the provinces of Algiers and Constantine by Adolphe Dureau de la Malle (published in 1838 and 1837, respectively).[97]

Intensive fieldwork on this project, which lasted five months in total toward the end of 1837, helped distract Duvivier from the privations faced by his men during their two successive assaults on Constantine: "study was the only thing that could bring contentment and that could make all the crossings and campaigns slip away unnoticed; it is the best companion given to us . . . during the short passage of an instant on earth. . . . I resolved to carry this [my research] out through the materials that were at my disposition."[98] Archaeological studies, in addition to the time spent interviewing residents about Roman antiquities found in their native regions, offered welcome relief from arduous military campaigning. Following his return to France, Duvivier finalized the volume and spent more than 600 francs of his own funds to print and bind five hundred copies along with a map of ancient Roman roads, aqueducts, and other remains.[99]

Duvivier's archaeological ambitions were not limited to this important work. Five years later, in a somewhat stranger publication, he revisited his study of ancient monuments. In this self-published volume, he made the improbable claim that he had recently mastered the reading of Phoenician, Punic, and Numidian inscriptions. With this allegedly new method of translation, which he hoped to popularize in France, Duvivier fancied that he was able to improve the work of several well-known scholars of his day with dramatic readings of what he characterized as their dry (and inaccurate) interpretations of these texts.[100] Despite praise from the minister of war, the work had all the hallmarks of great originality but few scholarly merits. Its complete absence from contemporary discussions suggests that Duvivier's work did not garner the warm reception that he anticipated from its publication.[101] We might nonetheless interpret Duvivier's excessive confidence in his linguistic ability as a sign of the relatively laissez-faire attitude with which French officers approached vestiges of the ancient past. Not only did they not view the study of inscriptions as the exclusive purview of epigraphers, but they were also convinced that their personal contact with ancient remains in Algeria afforded them remarkable facility in interpreting these materials in new, meaningful, and exciting ways.

Closely connected to Duvivier's writings based on archaeological research were his publications on contemporary developments in French Algeria, including the most important, his *Solution de la question de l'Algérie* (1841). With more than a decade of experience in North Africa to his name, the general offered his thoughts on the potential contributions to be made by the army in shaping the French colony of Algeria. At the heart of his vision was the fusion of the French and Indigenous populations; he believed that this approach required French investment in the education of Arab and Kabyle inhabitants, since only in this fashion would they be able to foster intellectual, material, and productive unity between their peoples.[102] To accomplish these objectives, Duvivier argued that the French needed to establish good relations with the Indigenous peoples to gain the cooperation necessary for the colony's stability and security. Taking an object lesson from the ancient Romans, who made a critical strategic error by isolating rebellious tribes, Duvivier cautioned against massacres as a solution to the French colony's dilemmas.[103] The Romans had learned through experience that they could not count on the loyalty of hostile peoples forced into submission because their obedience lasted only as long as they were compelled to cooperate.[104]

From his desk in metropolitan France, Duvivier advocated that the armée d'Afrique adopt a more moderate strategy in Algeria, one that he suggested should be a civilizing role and not driven just by military objectives. He entreated his contemporaries to find a middle ground between colonial conquest and their Christian upbringing:

> The first principle of Christian civilization is to remember that all people descend from the same father, to regard every man as one's own brother, to be charitable to him, indulgent toward his faults, and forgetful of his offenses. Calm the spirits [of those involved in the conflict], multiply all the material obstacles that will diminish the causes for shedding blood and pillaging, tolerate the indigenous people too old to fight, win over as much as possible the youth through Christian instruction.[105]

However, by the time he wrote these words, a year into the radical strategic military shift initiated in the colony by Governor-General Bugeaud, Duvivier's advocacy of relative restraint effectively had lost its audience. A more aggressive approach to the Algerian conflict, one that largely went unquestioned, now dominated the wartime experience of French officers of the armée d'Afrique. And, more intensive efforts by Catholic missionaries to engage in a "mission civilisatrice" still lay several decades in the future.

Thomas-Robert Bugeaud's Total War and the Inspiration of Rome

Born to a wealthy family in Limoges in October 1784, Thomas-Robert Bugeaud suffered significant hardship during the French Revolution. At the age of twenty, Bugeaud reluctantly joined the foot grenadiers of the French Imperial Guard because he had few other career options. Serving in Central Europe and then Spain, he witnessed firsthand what he described as widespread brigandage, which he thought a common feature of military activity of the time. These formative experiences were lessons he never forgot. Rather than receiving his education in a French military academy, Bugeaud owed his rank in the army to his courageous conduct in combat. By the age of twenty-nine, he received promotion to lieutenant

Figure 18. Charles-Philippe Larivière, "Thomas-Robert Bugeaud de la Piconnerie, maréchal de France en 1843." Chateaux de Versailles et de Trianon, Versailles, France. Photograph: Gérard Blot, © RMN-Grand Palais/Art Resource, NY.

colonel of the 14th Line Regiment (1813), serving under both Napoleon and his Bourbon successor.[106] Initially an ambivalent supporter of the war in the former Ottoman regency, Bugeaud was concerned about the large number of troops being sent to North Africa instead of being stationed on the Continent to defend France's European interests. Although he recognized the practicality of having an overseas training ground for the French army and thought it a convenient outlet for disruptive individuals who might otherwise destabilize metropolitan France, he criticized French statesmen for having no real idea of the quagmire into which they were descending with their pursuit of renewed colonial ambitions in North Africa.[107]

After he received a commission in Algeria in 1836, Bugeaud served in Oran as a temporary regional commander. Despite his reputation for being headstrong, he quickly earned the loyalty of his troops and senior officials owing to his skills as an effective leader in a war that seemed otherwise to be making slow progress. As resistance to French presence grew in the region under the direction of the militant Sufi Emir 'Abd el-Qader, who commanded Indigenous forces against the French occupation, Bugeaud became a vocal critic of current military strategy in North Africa. In advocating for the necessity of satisfying practical economic needs of the emerging colony, he found himself particularly at odds with Governor-General Damrémont during the negotiations that led to the Treaty of Tafna, which Bugeaud signed with 'Abd el-Qader in May 1837.[108] Unable to embrace partial occupation, which he thought impractical and difficult to achieve, Bugeaud launched a strategy of total conquest and colonization of Algeria: "Limited occupation, and, by extension, the concentration of troops, is the abandonment of the whole country, the destruction of our governance of the Arabs, the restoration of the power of 'Abd el-Qader. The system is contrary to that which maintained and will maintain our conquest and the honor of our flag."[109] Bugeaud thus sharply opposed the policies of newcomers to Algeria such as Damrémont's immediate successor Valée, who brought continental sensibilities to the office of the Government-General in late 1837. Bugeaud's position also made him unpopular with moderate officers like Duvivier, who had a long record of service in North Africa but expressed a commitment to the future integration of French and Muslim populations.[110]

As French strategic goals expanded to the complete subjugation of the Arabs and Kabyles, Bugeaud opposed any drawdown in troops, and in fact argued for the very opposite to support French successes in the region.[111] He and the officers under his command frequently compared the situation in which they found themselves to conditions faced by the ancient Romans in North Africa. Just as Bugeaud viewed Emir 'Abd el-Qader as an archetypal foe, Bugeaud's contemporary Azéma de Montgravier compared 'Abd el-Qader to Jugurtha, king of Numidia, whose wars against the Romans in the late second century BCE were chronicled by Sallust.[112] Bugeaud, too, thought that the seven years of bitter struggle against Rome waged by Jugurtha paralleled the Algerian conflict of his own time. From his perspective, classical sources describing the spirit of independence of the Indigenous peoples of North Africa were relevant to understanding the Kabyles of Algeria.[113] The historical conflict justified nineteenth-century advocacy for seeing the complete submission of the Indigenous peoples as a necessity.

Despite his lack of the formal training in one of France's military academies enjoyed by most of his contemporaries, Bugeaud recognized the practical and ideological importance of capitalizing on the presence of Roman remains in the new French colony. Regarding the former, in describing progress on building Orléansville in the Chellif Valley (A. Chlef) in 1843, Bugeaud noted that the troops were working to restore the Roman aqueduct from Tighaout to the city and thus ensure a reliable water supply.[114] Elsewhere, he noted the importance of Roman cisterns that were still intact from ancient Rusicade. These required cleaning to make them serviceable for the city of Philippeville, which was then being constructed by the French from the large quantity of ancient cut stone available on site.[115]

Consequently, in two successive circulars of January 20 and March 25, 1844, Bugeaud instructed generals and colonels under his command to protect antiquities reported to them by civilians.[116] Although not motivated mainly by conservationist concerns, he also sought to maintain the oriental character of the city of Constantine after its conquest.[117] However, such policies were largely ineffective in saving ancient monuments. Operational considerations took priority over other objectives. Moreover, many officers profited personally from their access to antiquities. As recalled by the currency commissioner Charles Marcotte de Quivières during a visit to Cherchel in the early 1840s, their homes were known to display lavish antiquities:

> The port was littered with the ruins of an immense temple that crowned a promontory, at the entrance of the city. There only remained some vestiges that nonetheless sufficed to give an idea of these grandiose constructions. Some mosaics were still fairly well preserved, and I think that the superior commander had them collected like other specimens that I was able to admire at his home. I noticed, among other antiquities, at the home of Colonel Admirault, which is the name of the commander of Cherchel, a small charming statue of white marble, which was missing a part of its head and one arm. It was called the *Puller of Thorns.* It was a work of the most correct style and ancient purity.[118]

In an attempt to quell criticism of the destruction of so many Roman sites, more lasting measures were put into place the following year. As will be discussed below, shortly after the establishment of the first civil territories within Algeria in 1845, the minister of war insisted on the appointment of an inspector of civil structures, a post filled by Charles Texier.[119]

During his time in North Africa, and especially after he became governor-general in February 1841, Bugeaud made considerable changes to the way in which the armée d'Afrique waged war. For the purposes of morale, he advocated closer contact of officers with their men, and thereby earned the support and loyalty of many soldiers serving in the French army.[120] Borrowing from his experience in Spain, he also created rotating military patrols to collect intelligence and employed highly mobile strike columns to surprise his opponents. Some contemporaries claimed that Bugeaud imitated the tactic of favoring the use of foot soldiers over cavalry from ancient Rome.[121] Although that characterization is not entirely accurate, there is no doubt that in response to the challenges of guerilla warfare, Bugeaud lessened dependence on heavy artillery units to diminish the vulnerability of his troops. Yet in contrast to ancient Roman practice, soldiers now carried little but their weapons and ammunition, leaving the rest of their supplies and potable water to be transported by a mule corps.[122]

With these innovations, the model of Rome figured large in Bugeaud's commanding officers' strategic vision of the future of Algeria as a colony and the basis of more permanent French presence in the region. Expedition journals of commanders in this period included casual and more formal observations of the antiquities they encountered. In June 1841, for instance, General Louis-Achille Baraguey d'Hilliers recorded the location, dimensions, and state of conservation of ancient cisterns on the route from Blida that might later be of importance to the armée d'Afrique.[123] In July 1847, L. H. Bartel, a lieutenant carabineer in the 13th Light Infantry regiment, completed a detailed manuscript recording monuments and inscriptions he had encountered in the city of Bougie.[124] In November 1841, the head of the engineering battalion in Blida, Polytechnicien Martial Bouteilloux, observed:

> The question of Africa is not a question of expeditions, it is an affair of occupation. It is, in a word, a question of rubble. The Romans envisaged it in this manner, and their domination is written on the landscape, which is dotted Roman roads and structures of all sorts. We will not master this country except by following their traces, that is to say by beginning to establish ourselves solidly there where we are and in building roads to communicate with our establishments in the interior and to make them real (and not at all illusory) bases of operation for the far-flung war, if it is necessary.[125]

The landscape of Roman monuments and roads laid out a possible map as to how the French might best settle the territory; it taught this particular military engineer the absolute necessity of a durable communication network.

Most important, at least in terms of its impact on the civilian inhabitants of the areas through which the French army passed, Bugeaud secured the rapid expansion of the number of soldiers serving in Algeria from sixty-three thousand to more than one hundred thousand men in less than six years. Many of the officers and troops that made this large deployment possible arrived from theaters of war like Spain and Guadeloupe, where resistance to French conquest was punished with violence against civilian populations. In Algeria, too, few superior officers were willing to relieve commanders of duty if they slaughtered civilians.[126] At the same time, Bugeaud reduced the amount of food and fodder provided to troops while on campaign, forcing them to seize livestock, cattle, and grain to supplement their meager rations and those of their service animals during protracted marches.[127] As recalled by Pierre de Castellane in his memoirs published in the *Revue des deux mondes*, military life in North Africa was not just difficult but also tedious:

> Little do they know or realise in France the tortures of the life we lead here [in the armée d'Afrique]. To see perpetually the same faces, though they be those of men one may esteem and even love, but whom one knows to weariness down to their least joke! To be a prisoner [of the armed services], so to speak, and buried alive; passing days and weeks without the smallest mental aliment; completely cut off from all intercourse with the outer world, although not far off in point of actual distance. Believe me, it is a hard life—an existence rather—before which the strongest spirits will sometimes quail.[128]

With hunger and fatigue as unrelenting motivators, French soldiers achieved reckless military successes in the 1840s as Bugeaud's adjustments of the tactics of the armée d'Afrique made life more difficult for the men under his command.

Whatever the hardships of French soldiers, however, conditions on the ground were far worse for Arabs and Kabyles; they were perhaps as intolerable for the Indigenous inhabitants then as they had been in Roman times. In their wake, French columns left a swath of flattened villages, charred fields and orchards, and empty pastures, all essential elements of the fragile agricultural economy that sustained life in the interior and desert regions of Algeria. In a letter dated April 7, 1842, Saint-Arnaud wrote to his brother from a bivouac near Cherchel and described the devastating actions that his men had taken against the Kabyle tribe of the Beni Menasser:

> The rest of the land of the Beni-Menasser is superb and one of the richest that I have seen in Africa. The villages and habitations are very close together. We burned everything, destroyed everything. Oh! War, war! Women and children, having taken refuge in the snow of the Atlas, died there of cold and misery. Our rearguard did not have to fight more than two hundred Kabyles. There were only five killed and forty wounded in [our] army, but the field hospital is full of feverish men and sick whom we will leave in Cherchel.[129]

Since the production of wheat and barley were incredibly labor-intensive and the timing of their reaping was critical, French interruption of the harvest or their confiscation of grain proved disastrous to the food supply of affected communities. There is terrible irony, given the French affinity for ancient Roman models, that the destructive role of French soldiers in this sense differed from Roman precedent in North Africa: soldiers of the Third Augustan Legion were known to have assisted in harvests when extra manpower was required, but only after these regions had been violently subdued.[130]

With an increasing number of tactical successes under Bugeaud's direction, the French went on the offensive as they expanded their reach from the coast into the Sahara and Kabylia.[131] Seldom able to force Arab and Kabyle forces into definitive engagements on the battlefield, French generals identified the most vulnerable targets in their effort to "punish" and subdue the elusive enemy. Their tactics were both ancient, focused on pillage and destruction, and modern, taking pitiless lessons from recent French military involvement in conflicts in Spain and Saint-Domingue, where many officers and soldiers in the armée d'Afrique had previously served.[132] On October 18, 1841, Nicolas-Anne-Théodule Changarnier, at this time a brigadier general all too familiar with the use of razzia against Muslim communities, wrote to General Castellane from Algiers to complain of Bugeaud's misrepresentation of the reality of Algerian campaigns: "colonial politics have not achieved up till now any of the proclaimed successes that were boasted of in advance. To compensate for them, General Bugeaud has sought, in an account that owes greater honor to his imagination than to the truth, to elevate a miserable razzia to the height of combat. In it, the indigenous cavalry (Spahis) cut the throats of several dozen women and elderly people who could not defend themselves."[133] Bugeaud continued to justify the violence of his troops' tactics as the only way to achieve "security" for current and future European colonists among what he described as Muslim fanatics. He insisted that they understood nothing other than the language of force.[134]

French dehumanization of the Arabs and Kabyles as enemies and the consequent desensitization of soldiers to carnage justified the use of any and all tactics to bring defiant opponents to heel.[135] Under such circumstances, officers and soldiers followed orders from their commanders, who pushed their men to the limit; on October 13, 1841, the minister of war chastised Comte Achilles Baraguey d'Hilliers, commander of operations in the province of Tittery, for driving his men excessively hard in the heat without adequate water, with the result that some of his soldiers died during forced marches.[136] These same troops' gruesome acts of violence were heightened by their hunger, thirst, greed, fear, frustration, and desire for revenge; they took vengeance on the Indigenous people in a way they could not do against their commanding officers, who spurred them on both with threats and the deprivation of sustenance and water. French soldiers plundered the homes of civilians, stole their horses, and confiscated flocks of sheep and goats to feed the persistently undersupplied army. Even more extreme forms of the razzia, such as the Dahra massacre in 1845, also came to pass.[137] Rather than condemning the actions of commanding officers like Colonel Aimable Pélissier, who sanctioned the asphyxiation of Muslim civilians, French commanding officers viewed these tactics as indispensable to forcing the population to submit.[138]

Officers' reward for their service in Algeria was the possibility of earning promotions twice as quickly as on the Continent.[139] Bravery in combat situations might also win them a knighthood in the Legion of Honor. However, the cost of this brand of warfare was high for the French army, since officers and soldiers who served in the Algerian theater had difficulty moderating their violence when they returned to campaigns in continental Europe. Commentators described those who had served in Algeria as poorly disciplined and prone to excessive force;[140] these men became a liability to the army because the laxness of their training and lack of respect for civilian lives made their behavior intolerable in other circumstances.[141] Bugeaud himself was a case in point. In February 1848, a year after his resignation as governor-general and the surrender and exile of 'Abd el-Qader to metropolitan France, the maréchal ordered men under his command in Paris to deploy similar tactics to those used in Algeria. These included French soldiers allowing French civilians in the uprising no quarter and aiming their weapons point-blank at the crowds.[142] Forced to desist from these tactics by the civil administration, which ultimately led to his departure for his estates in the Dordogne, Bugeaud unrepentantly viewed their hesitance as a sign of Louis-Philippe's cowardice. Despite this controversy, when Bugeaud died the following year during an outbreak of cholera, the former governor-general was remembered foremost for his accomplishments in Algeria and not his unremitting violence against all whom he viewed as enemies of France. In 1849, he received a state funeral at the Hôtel des Invalides.[143]

Bugeaud's Dream of Rome: A Colony of Military Veterans

In promoting the need for a campaign of total war in Algeria, Bugeaud, like his contemporaries, made ample use of examples from the Roman past. The history of Algeria, which he set out in a variety of writings, including a two-volume monograph published a year after his death in 1849, constituted the underlying framework of Bugeaud's vision of the future of the French colony.[144] In the opening of this work, Bugeaud characterized North Africa not just as the breadbasket of the ancient world but as a verdant Eden in which "the grains, the fodder, the flour, the aromatic plants (*umbelliferae*) acquired there a prodigious development. The trees, the vegetables of other parts of the world became naturalized and propagated themselves almost without cultivation."[145] Although the Romans themselves were surely to blame for the overcultivation of North Africa with agricultural techniques that produced about four million bushels of grain for export to Rome, nineteenth-century French colonial authorities like Bugeaud typically praised the yield of ancient production. By contrast, the French exclusively blamed the Arabs' nomadic system of land use for soil degradation and the lack of abundant agricultural production in the modern era.[146] This approach was less fraught than pointing out, as did Amédée Desjobert in 1844 based on his reading of book 5.1–5 of Pliny the Elder's *Natural History*, that the Roman breadbasket had been based around Tunis (Africa Proconsularis, which included late ancient Byzacena) and Tripoli (Cyrenaica) rather than in modern Algeria (Mauretania Caesariensis and Numidia).[147] Although Pliny testified that the Numidians were nomadic, he did not suggest that this practice was the cause of the region's lower fertility.[148] And as late as at least the seventeenth century, European observers had noted the great desirability of the fields and gardens near Algiers.[149]

An important historical model to which Bugeaud pointed to justify a scorched earth strategy in Algeria was the Numidian revolt led by Tacfarinas, a former Roman soldier thought to have been of Berber origin. During the French conquest, this rebellion was thought by military authorities to have had significant parallels to the contemporary resistance of Emir 'Abd el-Qader to the French. According to Tacitus's *Annals* 4.23–25, Tacfarinas led local transhumant tribes against the Romans between 15 and 24 CE, the year in which he willingly met his death in battle to avoid captivity.[150] Bugeaud appreciated the lessons taught by this North African rebellion in part because the Romans' ultimate defeat of the Numidian pastoralists allowed them to convert vast tracts of pastureland into the fields they required to produce grain for their capital. More important, however, Bugeaud derived from this account a lesson about the future possibilities of mixing between conquerors and conquered peoples. Although the more than forty-year reign of Juba II (d. 23 CE), a Numidian king restored to his throne in Julia Caesarea (A. Cherchel) by Augustus, had afforded significant integration between Romans and the Indigenous population, Bugeaud understood that this brief period of accommodation was insufficient for long-term blending. In Bugeaud's eyes, the revolt of Tacfarinas had its roots in the incomplete forging of a bond between peoples. Since the nomads had not yet mastered the trappings of Roman civilization, they had developed no deep-seated loyalty to Rome.[151]

The example of Rome, however, could be read in a variety of ways. In 1841, the professor and statesman Saint-Marc Girardin, writing in the *Revue des deux mondes*, counseled that Roman victories resulted from the imperial army's patience in implementing a measured campaign: they initially left the Indigenous people in place and avoided appropriating land until after they had consolidated their authority.[152] By contrast, Bugeaud's reading of ancient Roman history led him to believe that a warrior instinct and "vague sense of nationality" "smoldered like a poorly extinguished fire" among the conquered inhabitants of North Africa and represented a potent source of insurrection.[153] Ancient historical examples helped Bugeaud make the case for the application of unforgiving military force, though he distinguished his own time from that era in specific ways. In looking to the ancient past more generally, he argued that the French faced far greater challenges than the Romans because their predecessors had not had to contend with Islam and its followers' eagerness to engage in holy war against foreign overlords.[154]

These concepts were not abstractions: they translated directly into French military policy. Prevailing conditions justified French reliance on extreme applications of violence as propagated through tactics like the razzia, which were used against Arab and Kabyle tribes that failed to submit to the French. French officers characterized the Indigenous people as cowardly due to their reliance on guerilla attacks, yet sought retribution in unforgiving forms that would not have been deemed acceptable in a continental context. Bugeaud justified these methods, noting:

> Without a doubt, these terrible operations that one calls the razzias are sad and unpleasant necessities, but each of them saves more French blood than it would cost in Arab blood, and [those that express] this singular sentimentalism, which so often in France moves one to pity the vanquished, should have saved a bit of this praiseworthy and humane pity for the large number of French whose throats were cut with such revolting inhumanity, or who were clubbed to death in their midst, by an enemy who left no trace of himself.[155]

So convinced was Bugeaud of the historical imperative driving the French conquest of the region that he was unable to comprehend why the Indigenous people might have resisted the arrival of the French.[156] Even tribes that allied with France fared poorly since they faced high penalties if they failed to achieve full compliance with French demands. The mercilous nature of these policies had a drastic effect on tribal cohesion and well-being. The Arabs and Kabyles in Algeria resisted because they had nothing to lose, which boded poorly for the erstwhile hope of integrating European and Indigenous populations.[157] As argued by Frantz Fanon in 1961, French behavior taught the Muslim population of Algeria that their colonizers understood only the language of force.[158]

Despite Bugeaud's personal enthusiasm for these cruel tactics, at least some officers serving under his command expressed qualms about an approach to fighting that made little distinction between fighting men and civilians. They recognized this brand of warfare as causing severe demoralization of the officer corps and troops. In a letter to his brother of January 31, 1840, Saint-Arnaud, one of Bugeaud's captains, referred to it succinctly as "holy baptism by fire" (*le saint baptême de feu*). He offered more detail: "Many superior officers of all ranks in the regiments recently arrived in Africa, disgusted, frightened by the sight of such a war in which heads fly like June bugs, ask to retire. The maréchal sends them back without pity."[159] On February 11, 1841, Major de Lioux, a battalion commander in the 53rd Infantry Regiment, then stationed at the Camp of Tixeraïm (A. Birkhadem) several miles south of Algiers, wrote to General Boniface de Castellane, a veteran of Algeria then serving in the Pyrénées-Orientales.[160] Giving his senior colleague and mentor recent news of developments affecting the French armée d'Afrique, de Lioux mentioned that he was discouraged by the slow progress of the conquest and the brutal tactics of the recently appointed governor-general. He candidly described the negative effect of this existence on the soldiers under his command: "I do not believe that in Algeria, one learns the art of war; it is a hunting party on a large scale, in which the regiments are worn out and disappear in a short time; three months after their arrival, they no longer know how to fall into line; all that they were taught soon disappears; the hospitals devour half of them: and the state of things is truly deplorable, and a kind of demoralization, one must say . . . is the result."[161] Especially for older officers who had served under Napoleon I, few engagements during the Algerian campaign resembled anything they had experienced under the emperor. For the more junior officers, the forced marches, insufficient provisions, bitter cold, and attacks on the rearguards of their columns that characterized the life of the armée d'Afrique threw cold water on dreams of glorious campaigns.[162]

Similarly disillusioned with the armée d'Afrique was Captain Cler, who on July 1, 1842, wrote to General de Castellane from the coastal city of Cherchel. Cler had been stationed just five months in Algeria, but after nearly four straight months on campaign, he observed bitterly: "During this time, I have searched in vain for an opportunity to fight without finding it. We have only made war on herds [of livestock], habitations, crops, and the lowliest part of the population that is unarmed and driven by hunger and misery, that prefers to surrender rather than to fight."[163] This war thus little resembled the conflicts that officers like Cler and Castellane studied in preparation for their service as officers at the École polytechnique, the École spéciale militaire de Saint-Cyr, and the École d'application de l'artillerie et du génie de Metz.[164] The tactics were also condemned abroad, especially in Britain, where the historian John Morell imagined the long-term effect of the Algerian conflict on the comportment of French soldiers:

> Not withstanding that war is ever a scourge, and desolation has too often marked the track of its columns, the French army has ever upheld its high reputation for prowess in the valleys of Atlas; though it has not always united the humanising spirit of civilised warfare with the innate gallantry of its race. We are fully aware of the fact, that long service in Africa, as elsewhere, has hardened the men into soldiers of fortune, whose regiment is

their country, and who do not scruple to trample on liberty at home or elsewhere, in mechanical obedience to their commanding officer.[165]

Knowing that the consequences of disobedience were high and hoping for
rapid promotion to more desirable positions, most officers nonetheless
complied with the orders they received and declined to spare the vulnerable civilian populations in the path of the armée d'Afrique.[166]

According to their commanding officers, soldiers serving in Africa
complained of prolonged maneuvers that demoralized the troops because
they lacked defining engagements on the battlefield. Although French
campaigns in the territory of Algeria were intended to achieve an end
goal euphemistically termed "pacification" by contemporary administrators, the men who fought engaged in a war of extreme violence, including
deadly force directed against civilians. Some contemporaries such as Poujoulat even suggested that a special military academy be created in Algeria
specifically to address these unique requirements:

> One observation that struck me during my Algerian studies was the igno-
> rance of every newly arrived officer on the subject matter of the African war.
> The officer who arrives begins his education, and it is always at the expense
> of the army. Why should there not be a school in Algiers where young offi-
> cers destined for the war in Africa could be trained? They would learn the
> art of fighting the Arabs, which has nothing in common with European mil-
> itary art; they would get acquainted with the practices, questions, and af-
> fairs of the country; they would finally learn how one could gain an empire
> in the spirit of the Muslim races.[167]

Recent scholars have variously characterized the strategy of the armée
d'Afrique, especially as formulated by Bugeaud, as occupation by brute
force, total war, or genocide.[168] It is not too far distant from the strategy
that scholars now believe the Roman army under Julius Caesar applied in
Gaul, despite some of his claims to the contrary.[169]

Between 1840 and 1846, the number of European civilian settlers in
Algeria rose from a little over twenty-eight thousand to over one hundred
nine thousand, about 43 percent of whom were French and of whom
only 10 percent occupied agricultural villages established by authorities.[170] This rapid rise in numbers came in response to a measure passed

in April 1841 that granted free passage, land, and accommodation to Europeans ready to settle in Algeria, provided they remained long enough to make a good-faith attempt at cultivating the land.[171] However, the cost of the war continued to mount and an insufficient number of settlers arrived prepared to farm, both issues crucial to the survival of the future colony.[172] In 1844, Director of Finance Léon Blondel reminded his readers that settlement required organization and patience. He observed that Bugeaud's focus on physical force had made it difficult to shift emphasis to the herculean effort and financial investment that successful immigration and agricultural innovation required.[173] Although by that time, colonial administrators had distributed nearly 7,500 parcels of land as a part of an official settlement policy, very little of it, about 3,400 hectares, was under cultivation because so few of the arrivals were ready to engage in farming.[174] In 1847, when 'Abd el-Qader surrendered, the French colony was still heavily dependent on imports, which amounted to more than ten times the goods being exported from Algeria in the same period.[175]

Seeking long-term resolution to these challenges, Bugeaud looked to military colonization, an idea he developed in a work titled *De la colonisation de l'Algérie* (1847). In this treatise, Bugeaud distilled the central elements of his long advocacy for such policies, one in which army veterans would play a central role in settling the province. He borrowed this idea in general terms but not in detail from the Roman example during the reign of Claudius and afterward. He argued that settlement of the territory by military men was the only way to assure the security and cost effectiveness of the French colony.[176] Not only could former soldiers defend their lands against a hostile population, but they would build the roads and bridges integral to the infrastructure and successful operation of the new French colony.[177] He thus envisioned a system in which veterans, after a six-month leave to return home to France and marry, would receive land, a home built at the cost of the state and outfitted with necessities, basic implements, and some animals. He believed that this offer was sufficiently attractive to convince former soldiers, who theoretically had gained immunity to local endemic diseases during their military service, to return to Algeria with their families for a required period of at least three years. The roughly 3,000 francs per soldier Bugeaud estimated it would cost to settle such colonists, was, in his estimation, money well spent. He believed the trial period sufficiently long to ensure that they would give up their military lifestyle and settle more permanently as part of a civilian community.[178]

However, just as Bugeaud had great praise for the Romans' approach to colonization, he also emphasized that conditions had changed significantly and that French occupation of Algeria needed to vary from this precedent in significant ways. As conquerors, the Romans were content to allow the Indigenous peoples to be ruled by their own kings; they did not feel it necessary to establish their presence in the colonies until they had sufficiently absorbed the mores of Roman civilization. By contrast, the French had in mind more substantive settlement and cultivation of the conquered territory.[179] Although Duvivier strongly criticized Bugeaud for confusing colonization with extermination or replacement of the Indigenous population, it appears that Bugeaud's vision of the new colony was more nuanced than Duvivier allowed.[180] The governor-general planned to accommodate the Arabs and Kabyles under French rule but wanted to restrict their residence and activities to discrete locations. His regulations for the future development of Constantine, for instance, designated a distinct urban quarter for Muslim inhabitants: this policy helped retain a greater Arab presence in the city than many of the coastal centers occupied by the French from the earliest years of the invasion.[181]

Bugeaud also aspired to direct rule of Arab and Kabyle residents as opposed to their indirect oversight through tribal intermediaries, which was current French just as ancient Roman practice. Yet even he recognized that such developments lay a long distance in the future despite the creation of the Bureaux arabes on February 1, 1844.[182] To this end, Bugeaud's ordinance officer Captain Rivet reported that the governor-general acknowledged that the French military was not yet prepared to administer to Indigenous civilians on this scale: "The great difficulty was to create between the indigenous populations and the superior authority of the French charged with governing them, some intermediaries, living delegations of this authority, speaking the language of those administered, familiar with their customs, knowing their needs of every kind, sufficiently assimilated to speak to these populations from a political and administrative perspective. The corps of army interpreters, even if they counted some distinguished representatives in this period, was insufficient to fulfill this task well."[183] As late as 1846, Bugeaud noted that fewer than thirty French officers could speak Arabic in addition to having at least some basic knowledge of local laws, history, religious custom, and cultural norms. The French civil administration was even less well equipped to govern Indigenous residents. Given these shortcomings, Bugeaud concluded that French success in the near future necessitated winning over the local population through beneficent paternalism.[184]

Judging from the devastation regularly visited on Arab and Kabyle villages by French troops, however, such policies were largely absent from the practical application of military rule. At least some officers serving under Bugeaud expressed significant skepticism that their liberal application of razzias was likely to yield a positive transformation. In 1843, Élie-Frédéric Forey, commander of the 6th Light Infantry Battalion and a graduate of Saint-Cyr, wrote:

> All of us were stupefied by so much natural beauty [of the mountain habitations of the Kabyles], but our orders were imperative, and I believed I was conscientiously fulfilling my mission in not leaving a village standing, not a tree, not a field. The harm that my column did as it passed through is incalculable. Is it harm? Is it good? Or better is it harm for good? It is something that the future will decide. In my estimation, I think that it is the only way to bring about the submission or the emigration of these inhabitants, whom one feels sorry for, definitively, because they are between two sides, and cannot choose one without incurring the vengeance of the other.[185]

While such tactics brought about temporary submission, they put great stress on Indigenous communities and yielded few permanent results other than earning their hatred of the French.[186]

Moreover, French challenges in settling Algeria did not end through conflict with the Muslim population. One and a half decades after the initial invasion, the French still faced significant obstacles to recruiting farmers to Algeria to cultivate the land. The historian Poujoulat described his 1844 visit to civilian settlements in the Sahel as heartbreaking: "When leaving each of the new villages on the Massif inhabited by the French, I was saddened as if I had parted from exiles, because the poor families who had settled in the Sahel of the territory of Algiers have not yet found the sweetness in life that could compensate for their separation from France."[187] He advocated that the addition of local churches and priests might make their life more bearable. Similarly, Adrien Berbrugger, founder of the Bibliothèque et Musée d'Algers, advocated on behalf of cultural institutions and the preservation of Roman antiquities as key to attracting settlers to Algeria.[188] To preclude demoralization of the French army in what he described as "primitive" conditions, Berbrugger argued that the colony needed to imitate the conventions of metropolitan society if it was to push inhabitants toward civilization. Libraries and museums were essential institutions for this purpose.[189]

Although such developments did come to pass, some officers did not agree that civilian measures could resolve the issue so easily. In Major de Lioux's letter of 1841 to General Castellane, the battalion commander wrote:

> With regard to the word "colony," do not believe it, I suggest; it is a lie. There are no settlers of any value, at least if one takes into account a thousand wine and *eau-de-vie* sellers who poison our soldiers, and they are in any case for the most part Maltese, Italians, Spanish, and Germans, and thus the people for whom France ruins itself and spends its most vigorous children! No, there is not yet a French colony in Africa; we only have up till now a glorious flag around which a hundred thousand men in the last ten years have come to die.[190]

Given the current policy of the burning down entire villages and cutting down thousands of fruit and olive trees standing in nearby orchards, it was difficult for officers like de Lioux to imagine that this land would be suitable for future colonists. Two years later, in 1843, de Lioux observed: "I cannot explain this last sort of devastation [referring to a recent razzia he and his men had recently conducted against the Beni-Abbas and other tribes], whether one really wants to occupy the country or solely demand tribute. Besides, we have hardly experienced any resistance from the enemy."[191] Indeed, the long-term hostilities created by the depravities of the razzia were but one of many problems in attracting suitable colonists who had the will and experience to farm the land.[192] The French administration, however, also faced an increasingly powerful lobby of civilian colonists who strongly opposed Bugeaud's veteran settlement policy, which limited nonmilitary settlers to a band of land in more stable coastal areas. In reaction to their criticisms, Bugeaud complained that French officials did not appreciate his concerns for the number of troops necessary to protect civilian families and lands. In 1847, in large part

because of the criticism and rejection of his vision for the future, Bugeaud resigned from his responsibilities as governor-general in Algeria and
returned for the last time to metropolitan France, where he led troops
against the February 1848 uprising before dying in an epidemic the following year.[193] By 1848, the number of soldiers serving in the armée
d'Afrique were drawn down to seventy-eight thousand. However, the war
by this point had cost France an estimated 1.5 billion francs and the loss
of life of roughly seventy-five thousand French soldiers and possibly as
many as a million Algerian inhabitants, most of them civilians.[194]

Dismantling Roman North Africa to Build a French Colony

We can now turn to the fate of the physical remains of the ancient Romans to
help complete our understanding of the impact of French imperial ideology
on Roman antiquities in the early 1840s. Visible in many parts of the
country but most numerous in the province of Constantine, Roman ruins
offered a potential blueprint for as of yet ill-defined colonial strategies in a
land that the French were only beginning to understand more intimately.[195]
Some, like Edmond Pellissier de Reynaud, a member of the Commission
d'exploration scientifique d'Algérie that began its work in 1839, advocated
the necessity of deeper study of remains. He noted: "Already in the current
state of things, archaeology, everywhere we can penetrate, comes to the aid
of geography, In effect, the Arabs having let things perish more rather than
destroying them, the ruins of ancient monuments have remained in place,
and it is always fruitful when one excavates them."[196] Ruins thus gave clues
into how intensively settled this now sparsely inhabited landscape was in
ancient times. Yet this objective ran counter to the reuse of ancient remains
as building materiel: as noted above, French officers regularly sanctioned
the repurposing of Roman monuments for pressing practical ends, including
the construction of much needed roads, aqueducts, bridges, and cisterns
crucial to French military and settlement efforts in Algeria. As observed by
Michael Greenhalgh, this human-made landscape was absolutely essential
to the success of early French military campaigns.[197] Thus, despite frequent
deference to classical antiquity in their writings, French officers' actions
contributed directly to the demise of the still-extant Roman infrastructure
that the armée d'Afrique encountered in the Algerian territory.

Only a few contemporary visitors dared to characterize military engineers' redeployment of Roman stone as acts of plunder; they claimed that these tactical decisions stemmed from a lack of respect for ancient sites, whether pagan or Christian.[198] The situation, however, was more nuanced: officers' knowledge of the disposition and function of classical monuments had significant value to French endeavors. Learning from disastrous failures such as the October 1836 assault on Constantine, in which almost complete ignorance of the topography and climate of the cliff-top city proved to be an act of gross negligence on the part of the French command, many military officers came to recognize how essential practical knowledge of ancient sites actually was.[199] Roman remains frequently oriented the objectives of their campaigns and suggested to officers possible strategies by which to control the territory.[200] They thus sought to capitalize on the ruins of Roman infrastructure like aqueducts, fortifications, and roads to meet successfully the unique challenges of waging war in the climate of extremes and subduing the Arabs and Kabyles of the Maghreb.

This dependence helps explain why, despite French rhetoric that liberally deployed references to the Roman past for a variety of objectives, classical remains from the period of their domination did not fare well during the first two decades of the occupation by the armée d'Afrique. Even in metropolitan France, the discipline of archaeology and institutions founded to identify and safeguard ancient structures were still in their infancy in the 1830s and 1840s.[201] It would be anachronistic to anticipate that the armée d'Afrique would treat antiquities in North Africa differently than civilians did at home in the midst of an industrial revolution.[202] However, the case of Algeria was extreme. Many structures faced demolition simply because they offered a valuable supply of cut stone, to which the French would continue to help themselves throughout the 132 years of their occupation of Algeria.[203] In light of French readiness to capitalize on all the available resources of the object of their conquest, there were few reasons to spare ancient structures any more than the other resources of the colony.

One contemporary witness well informed about the level of redeployment of monumental structures was Captain Delamare, a member of the Commission d'exploration scientifique. He first visited the city of Philippeville (A. Skikda) in 1840, just two years after it was founded on the ruins of the

Figure 19. Ancient Roman sculptural remains from Philippeville. Amable Ravoisié, *Exploration scientifique de l'Algérie pendant les années 1840, 1841, 1842*. Beaux-arts, architecture et sculpture 2 (Paris: Chez Firmin Didot Frères, 1846–50), pl. 60. Reproduced by permission of the Bibliothèque de l'Arsenal, Bibliothèque nationale de France.

Roman city of Russicada under the direction of General Valée.[204] At this time, Delamare reported that the French had incorporated remains of the ancient Roman city's bridges into the new ones being constructed; he also observed that the French were busy repairing and modernizing Roman water fountains, aqueducts, and cisterns for their current needs.[205] Continuing such practices during the six years he served as governor-general, Bugeaud's aggressive extension of French dominion to a broader footprint that included the Sahara thus had long-term implications for the survival of ancient structures. From early in his command of the colony, Bugeaud ordered the systematic scavenging of spolia for the construction of fortifications in the new colony.[206]

More problematic from the perspective of those with antiquarian leanings, however, was the wholesale destruction of ancient structures at Philippeville as early as 1838 to build structures required by the armée d'Afrique. Over the course of the next decade, in their relentless search for cut stone, the French ordered the demolition of the city's ancient Roman amphitheater, theater, forum, basilica, temple, and water tower.[207] Just a few years later, the historian Poujoulat lamented that classical ruins in Algeria constituted primarily a stockpile of supplies for engineers: "There remained some beautiful remains of ancient Russicada which has been replaced by Philippeville; one could still admire the theater and the circus; but the engineering corps is more terrible than the weather and sees only some stones in the monuments imprinted with the majesty of centuries."[208] Poujoulat mourned that rather than being preserved for posterity, an end he judged fitting for such august monuments, the structures were disappearing before they could even be recorded.

Due to the partial or complete destruction of many ancient sites, metropolitan authorities, spurred by the members of the Commission d'exploration scientifique d'Algérie, acknowledged the importance of protecting ancient monuments rather than seeing them primarily as a resource to help meet the needs of the armée d'Afrique.[209] Correspondence between Bugeaud and Maréchal Soult, the minister of war, suggests that antiquities were often on the latter's mind. In November 1843, Soult complained about the ongoing destruction of Roman antiquities in the Algerian colony and reprimanded Bugeaud:

A suite of laws and administrative dispositions let us ensure, in France, the conservation of ancient monuments as the property of the State. Up till now, no measure has been taken in Algeria to preserve the precious remains of antiquities, which one finds at every step, from destruction; they were also not always respected. In many locations, their materials supported public constructions as well as private ones, without authorities being consulted in advance about the possibility of preserving intact ruins, or [asked] to consecrate them to specific usages.[210]

Soult admonished Bugeaud to command all officers, engineers, forest agents, and civilians under his command in Algeria to create inventories of finds, so that Bugeaud, in turn, might redact these and send them to Paris. The minister of war required these data so that he could make further assessments as to what kind of policy was necessary for their conservation. Bugeaud thereafter issued a directive dated January 20, 1844, to this effect.[211] However, in a letter of February 6, 1844, with new reports of destruction in hand, Soult again reminded Bugeaud of the protocol that was to be followed with ancient monuments, and advised that smaller antiquities or pieces of art be delivered to the Bibliothèque et Musée d'Alger.[212]

On March 23, Bugeaud issued additional instructions worded similarly to the recommendations of the minister of war. In a lengthy circular on the ancient monuments and artifacts, the governor-general indicated that all ancient finds were to be considered the property of the state and as such were to be respected rather than destroyed. The only allowable exceptions to these conservation measures might be made under urgent circumstances. In all other instances, the disturbance of ancient remains now required documentation, the recommendation of an administrative commission, and the permission of the governor-general, before it could be undertaken.[213] When these measures did not yield immediate results, the minister of war could no longer contain his frustration. In April 1844, Soult wrote from Paris: "You understand, Monsieur le Maréchal, how important it is for the history of this land, from the Roman epoch until that of the invasion of the Arabs, that the inscriptions, which alone can fill in the vast lacunae that these two periods present, be preserved."[214] To this end, the minister of war demanded that Bugeaud issue a circular to all serving under his authority to preserve intact the architectural remains, bas-reliefs, statues, and inscriptions that came into their hands.

One immediate result of this impasse was the appointment in 1845 of Charles Texier as the first inspector general of civil structures in the final years of Bugeaud's command of the colony as governor-general.[215] As noted in the last chapter, the minister of war charged Texier, an architect and specialist in Phoenician antiquities, with the task of creating a system in some ways parallel to the post of inspector general of historical monuments that had existed in metropolitan France since 1830.[216] Texier's functions as inspector in Algeria were intended to appease government critics and academics who complained of the French army's unnecessary violence toward ancient monuments and inscriptions in the colony.[217] With responsibility for all civil structures found in the newly conquered territory, Texier reported regularly to the French minister of war and met with scholars at the Académie des inscriptions et belles-lettres in Paris. In characterizing his approach to Algerian antiquities, Texier underlined the connection between the present and the past: "French domination, in bringing civilization to Africa, is thus connected above all to the great monuments of Roman domination, [that is,] everywhere they can be re-established."[218] In his interactions with French authorities, he emphasized the importance of Roman ruins and the necessity of combating the wanton pillage of monuments that had already occurred during the first decade and a half of French military activities in North Africa.

Despite his stated responsibilities for the conservation of ancient structures, however, Texier had few effective means of altering the policies of the French army and the growing number of European settlers in the Algerian territory, whom he accused of having little regard for antiquities. When he overstepped his authority in late 1847 by taking an excursion into the Sahara to see the state of Roman remains in the region, the minister of war took him to task for this relatively minor affront.[219] Although his overture to the Ministry of the Interior for a more extensive mission within Algeria was rejected, Texier continued his conservation work.[220] However, before 1854 and the appointment of Adrien Berbrugger as the inspector general of historical monuments and archaeological museums in Algeria, very little progress was made in saving historic structures in the French colony.[221] Monuments in the ancient cities, military camps, and settlements around the territory thus continued to suffer after his appointment, due in no small part to the army's rush to create fortifications and ready the land for French colonization.

Despite their professed admiration for these reminders of the ingenuity of classical Roman engineering, French military authorities viewed ancient structures primarily as a source of conveniently accessible construction materials.[222] Additional well-documented examples of monuments dismantled or severely damaged in this period included Cherchel, where the theater served as a quarry to build military barracks; Tipasa, where ancient stone was employed to construct a hospital; and Guelma, where the Roman amphitheater and other structures fell victim to French military needs.[223] As painstakingly documented by Michael Greenhalgh, these were far from the only sites affected by the French military effort amid the enormous devastation caused by the armée d'Afrique in just two decades.[224] For this reason, the next chapter turns to a detailed assessment of French intervention in the camps of the Third Augustan Legion located at Lambaesis (F. Lambèse; A. Tazzoult), where the collision between imperial ideology and military appropriation of ancient sites created ever greater tensions in the late 1840s and early 1850s.

Chapter 3

The View from Ancient Lambaesis

On September 27, 1844, Karl Benedikt (Charles-Benoît) Hase, a Greek
and Latin epigrapher and member of the Académie des inscriptions et
belles-lettres as well as the three-man commission responsible for overseeing the publications of the Commission d'exploration scientifique
d'Algérie, produced a report on the two volumes prepared by Captain Alphonse Delamare on the Roman monuments of Algeria.[1] Praising Delamare for his zeal and service to the commission, Hase drew attention to
the officer's contributions to French understanding of the functioning of
aqueducts and cisterns near Constantine and his skilled drawings documenting the region's antiquities. However, he also took this opportunity to
implore authorities to safeguard the antiquities of Algeria. Because of the
mandated departure of the commission's members from Algeria two years
earlier in 1842, still more work was necessary. He noted, moreover, that:

> we believe it is our obligation at the same time to call to the attention of the
> minister of war the carelessness, one could say, a kind of silent persecution,

that endeavors to make all that remains of ancient monuments disappear in French Africa. Each year, each day adds to their destruction. To cite just one example: before his departure for Biskra [L. Vescara] last February, Captain Delamare saw the mosaic of Mansoura still fairly well preserved. Today, it is three-quarters destroyed; in a little more time, nothing will remain; the walls themselves will collapse amid new construction. Would it not be possible to take some conservation measures before and during works that are required by the remediation of the cities, the establishment of caserns, the imperial needs of colonization?[2]

Hase argued that any number of museums, including Paris or Marseilles, would be pleased to house the Roman remains found at such sites. In his view, active intervention by the Ministry of War was the only means by which to stop the armée d'Afrique's wanton destruction of ancient monuments that the Arabs had spared from harm for so many centuries.[3]

To give a sense of the rapid and devastating degradation of archaeological sites in the early decades of the conquest, we turn now to an exploration of the history of an exemplary site that faced significant challenges to its integrity as a result of the activities of the armée d'Afrique. Roman Lambaesis (F. Lambèse or Lambessa; A. Tazzoult), located roughly 140 kilometers south of Constantine, was an ancient military encampment known to nineteenth-century scholars and officers mainly from works of classical geography like Ptolemy's *Geographia* and the *Antonine Itinerary* and from travel accounts by hardy European adventurers of the late eighteenth and early nineteenth centuries.[4] However, the site was not as well documented as might be expected given the attention it had received since the 1840s: in 1892, René Cagnat was the first to undertake a holistic study of Lambaesis in his account of the Roman army in Africa.[5] Although he referred to just one camp, it is now thought that Lambaesis consisted of three camps linked to the Third Augustan Legion. Dated by inscriptions in situ, this premier military installation grew steadily to encompass the Eastern Camp or the Camp of Titus founded in 81 CE (and rediscovered in 1954), the Grand Camp dated to about 129 (on the basis of the earliest inscription but possibly older), and a third camp to the southwest constructed in honor of a visit of Emperor Hadrian in 128.[6] Much research remains to be done at the site today, though in recent years access has been impeded by political insecurity in the region.[7]

Besides the military encampments, an ancient Roman city by the same name was also established at the site. It contained substantial civic structures and essential infrastructure such as aqueducts and cisterns for a civilian population that served the encampments.[8] Already important under the Severan dynasty in the late second century, Lambaesis briefly became the governmental seat of the Roman province of Numidia Militiana in the late third century, although this ended when it was abolished by Constantine some time before 320.[9] By the early fourth century, the territory of the Aurès Mountains had been extensively Christianized.[10] Following the departure of the legion in the 390s, however, Lambaesis declined rapidly. The status of the Christian community of Lambaesis waned at roughly the same time, with its numbers dropping to such an extent that it no longer merited the appointment of a bishop.[11] The date of its ultimate abandonment as a settlement remains unclear.

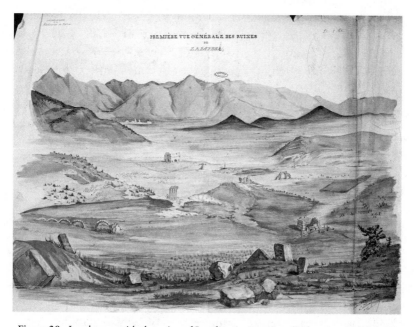

Figure 20. Landscape with the ruins of Lambaesis. Jean-Luc Carbuccia, *Archéologie de la subdivision de Batna: Première campagne du 1er novembre 1848 à juillet 1849*. Bibliothèque de l'Institut de France, Ms. 1369 A, pl. 1ter. Photograph: René-Gabriel Ojéda. Reproduced by permission of the Institut de France. © RMN-Grand Palais/Art Resource, NY.

From the eighteenth century onward, Lambaesis's abundance of monumental remains captured the imagination of a series of European visitors. Until the last quarter of the nineteenth century, Lambaesis constituted the premier archaeological site in French colonial Algeria and was far better known than the more lavish monuments of ancient Thamugadis (F. Timgad; A. Tubna), which, though not distant, later overshadowed it as a tourist destination. Whereas some turned their attention to studying prominent structures on the site like the so-called *praetorium* and a temple dedicated to Asclepius, god of medicine and healing, these activities were dwarfed by efforts to transcribe and analyze the site's wealth of epigraphy. One of the earliest civilian epigraphers to visit was the historian Léon Renier, then the deputy-librarian at the Sorbonne, who traveled there from Paris twice in the early 1850s. He was lured to Lambaesis by the remains of thousands of Latin inscriptions found scattered over the site. In 1856, the publication that resulted from Renier's sojourn earned him membership in the Académie des inscriptions et belles-lettres and the newly created chair of epigraphy and Roman antiquity at the Collège de France (1861).[12] By contrast, although the inscriptions of Thamugadis received attention from Renier in the early 1850s, the latter site was not formally excavated until 1875, when Émile Mascqueray, a teacher at the Lycée d'Alger, received funding for this project from the Ministry of Public Instruction and Beaux-Arts. This late date and Thamugadis's greater distance from the army columns heading to the Sahara probably spared it much of the damage suffered by Lambaesis at the hands of the armée d'Afrique during and after its transformation into a penitentiary in the 1850s.[13]

The intention here in revisiting the ruins of Lambaesis is somewhat different from that of reconstructing the original location and appearance of its component pieces. Because the site was utilized in a large variety of ways, it presents a microcosm, albeit an extraordinary one, of the impact of colonial efforts on Roman remains and the Arab and Kabyle inhabitants associated with them. Close scrutiny of the documents reporting on the discovery, excavation, and interpretation of Lambaesis's monumental remains, especially in the 1840s and early 1850s, exposes how the tenor of discussions of the site changed with French conquest of the region and its integration into metropolitan France. The site also provides a glimpse into the disconnect between mid-nineteenth-century visitors' imagination of the glorious past of Roman Lambaesis and their negative view of the living inhabitants of the Aurès Mountains. The backdrop of these investigations were the military events that gravely threatened both the archaeological site and the communities living in its vicinity.

Nineteenth-century interactions with Lambaesis allow us to see that French understanding of the ancient past was not static but evolved over time. On a practical level, the site intersected with key military operations of the 1840s: the ruins of the Third Augustan Legion provided a staging ground and spiritual base for aggressive and devastating French military campaigns against Kabyle communities in the Aurès Mountains and the Algerian Sahara. At various times, the ancient Roman encampments also served as a laboratory in which officers and civilian scholars experimented with reform of the mercenaries who joined the Foreign Legion and unruly French citizens who had been deported from metropolitan France in the 1840s and 1850s. The ruins became the backdrop for the reeducation of individuals whom authorities had labeled as unsuitable residents of metropolitan France, either because they had questioned the inequities of the French political system or because, as foreigners, they had chosen careers as soldiers of fortune. Their time at Lambaesis thus offered the promise of renewal as French citizens or soldiers. Finally, Lambaesis offered military officers of the armée d'Afrique a flattering mirror in which to reimagine their own historical contribution: in this setting, they could contrast themselves favorably not only with the ancient Romans but with the modest but warlike Kabyles who inhabited the region.[14]

Lambaesis's Monuments and Residents in the Eighteenth Century

As early as the first third of the eighteenth century, Lambaesis left a strong impression on European visitors who secured the permission of Ottoman authorities to journey to the Aurès Mountains.[15] Among those who visited the site were the French geographer Jean-André Peyssonnel, writing in the mid-1720s (in a work that remained unpublished until 1838), who traveled there with an escort of fifty horsemen provided courtesy of the bey of Constantine.

Peyssonnel enjoyed his day trip to the ruins of what he referred to as Lamba, which he recognized from the magnificent ruins and inscriptions

TEMPLE D'ESCULAPE A LAMBA.

Figure 21. Idealized rendering of the temple of Asclepius at Lambaesis by
Jean-André Peysonnel in the 1720s. Adolphe Dureau de la Malle, *Peyssonnel et
Desfontaines: Voyages dans les régences de Tunis et d'Alger* 1 (Paris: Gide, 1838), 351.
Reproduced by permission of the Bibliothèque nationale de France.

as being the site of ancient Lambaesis. Moved above all by what he described as its forty gates, he wrote—perhaps with some longing for the
comforts of France—that these structures reminded him of Paris. He also
reported firsthand on the ruins of a temple of Asclepius, imposing funerary monuments, an amphitheater, an aqueduct, and a sizable number of
inscriptions located at the site.[16] Peyssonnel offered his readers a figural
or imaginative rendering of the temple: his depiction projected the appearance of the structure back to the period of its construction. Rather than
portraying the ruins as they then stood, he presented them in an idealized manner typical of the work of anatomists, geographers, and botanists
prior to the mid-nineteenth century. He thus offered to his readers an
improved example of ancient ingenuity rather than providing accurate
images that reflected the present condition (and faults) of the structure in
question.[17]

As a geographer, Peyssonnel did not limit his attention to the ruins or the rivers that flowed through the Aurès. Offering an ethnographic description of the rural Kabyles who populated the region, Peyssonnel noted that the inhabitants of this area of the Aurès Mountains, whom he identified as the Ouled-bel-Cassem, should be recognized as descendants of the ancient *Chauvies*.[18] He possibly came to this conclusion on the basis of a false etymology of the name of the local Kabyles, whom Arab historians called the Chaouïa or *Chawi*, a term in Arabic that referred generically to shepherds rather than a specific transhumant group south of Constantine and in the Aurès.[19] Not only did Peysonnel describe the mountain people living in the Aurès as a hardy and independent group who maintained their distance from their Ottoman overlords, but he also alleged that their lighter skin color, separate language, and lack of affinity for Islam distinguished them from Arab inhabitants of the region.[20]

Visiting a little more than a decade later, the British cleric Thomas Shaw exhibited a deeper mastery of classical references to the site than his French predecessor. Trained at the University of Oxford, he was the first to interpret and highlight the discovery on site of definitive inscriptional evidence of the Third Augustan Legion.[21] Following his thirteen-year appointment as the British consular chaplain in Algiers and travels in the region in the 1720s and early 1730s, he returned to Queens College, where he was elected a fellow.[22] Perhaps envisioning himself following in the footsteps of ancient geographers, Shaw also took an ethnographic interest in the peoples he encountered. Beyond copying some of the inscriptions for his readers, he commented that the physiognomy of the population of this mountainous region bore the signs of earlier occupations:

> the Inhabitants have a quite different Mien and Aspect from their Neighbours. For Their Complections are so far from being swarthy, that They are fair and ruddy; and Their Hair, which, among the other *Kabyles*, is of a dark Colour, is, with Them, of a deep Yellow. These Circumstances, (notwithstanding They are *Mahometans*, and speak the common Language only of the *Kabyles*) may induce us to take Them, if not for the Tribe mentioned by Procopius, yet at least for some Remnant or other of the *Vandals*, who, notwithstanding they were dispossessed, in His Time, of these strong Holds, and dispersed among the *African* Families; might have had several Opportunities afterwards of collecting Themselves into Bodies, and reinstating Themselves.[23]

Not only had the Romans made their imprint on the landscape, but it also appeared to this British observer that European colonization of the region left an indelible mark on its people. Even if no memory of these origins remained among the Kabyle inhabitants, Shaw believed that he could discern the continuing legacy of the ancient past in the light skin, eye color, and reddish hair of the Chaouïa who resided near Lambaesis.

Shaw's choice of Vandals as the forebears of the Kabyles, however, may not have been entirely innocent in its inflection. Although Procopius indeed described the Vandal invasion, he nowhere mentioned its impact on Lambaesis, which had been in decline a generation before their arrival. While Shaw seemed to praise the Kabyles' untamed savagery and love of independence, linking their origins to Germanic peoples, and particularly the fearsome Vandals, he thereby also identified the Indigenous people as one and the same as the alleged destroyers of Roman North Africa.[24] When a third traveler, James Bruce, a Scot who served briefly as the British consul of Algiers before heading eastward to find the source of the Nile, passed through the site in 1763 with the permission of the dey of Algiers, he echoed Shaw's observations about the legacy of European presence on the appearance of local inhabitants.[25] The alleged link between the Vandals and Lambaesis proved enduring.[26] Charles Diehl's *L'Afrique byzantine* (1896) breathed new life into allegations of the Vandal heritage of the Chaouïa late in the nineteenth century, and these forebears long remained part of the unsubstantiated lore associated with Lambaesis.[27]

Bruce, who traveled with a camera obscura for the purpose of drawing accurate, large format images of the antiquities he encountered, had as his sources both classical geographers and more recent visitors such as Shaw. In anticipation of his sojourn in Africa, Bruce had spent time at Herculaneum, Pompeii, and Paestum in southern Italy learning about classical antiquities. Aided by geographical, astronomical, and meteorological instruments, he also aimed to create a map and a fuller study of the natural attributes of the regions he encountered. During the course of his journey through the region, which was just one phase of a more ambitious expedition to the Nile, he gathered antiquities, including medals, vases, and bronze statues.[28] At Lambaesis, he was most impressed with the ruined structure that would eighty years later come to be known as the praetorium. Bruce posited improbably that the large building had served the Third Augustan Legion as an elephant stable or quarters for storing military machines.[29]

Dated to well before the advent of formal archaeological methodology, the travels of Peyssonnel and Shaw preceded the most famous archaeological excavations of the period: those of Herculaneum and Pompeii in the Kingdom of Naples, which began in the 1740s and 1750s, respectively.[30] Like Constantin Volney's *Travels through Syria and Egypt, in the Years 1783, 1784, and 1785* (1787), eighteenth-century travel narratives typically drew a contrast between the ills of so-called barbarous lands and the benefits of European progress. Although impressed by the ruins they saw, authors of such exotic accounts claimed that local antiquities pertained to European heritage rather than having relevance for the Indigenous people of the lands through which they passed.[31]

We should not be surprised that none of the eighteenth-century visitors to Lambaesis who recorded their impressions of the ruins and the appearance of local residents attempted to do any digging at the site or carry off substantial numbers of souvenirs. Each spent less than a day at the ancient encampments and mainly sketched ruins and inscriptions. Consequently, they added little that was substantive to what was already known from ancient sources about the site; deeper understanding of Lambaesis awaited the transcription of its inscriptions in the mid nineteenth-century. These narratives simply made Lambaesis one of a few recognizable locations in the Maghreb, a region with which Europeans were otherwise almost entirely unfamiliar. In the following decades, however, fewer visitors made their way to Lambaesis and the site largely receded from European consciousness. Only in the late 1830s, following French conquest of the Ottoman Beylik of Constantine, did new accounts of visits to Lambaesis surface again.

Wartime Visits to Lambaesis in the Mid-1840s

In contrast to the ease with which tourists could travel by train and carriage to Lambaesis by the 1890s, the eastern, mountainous region of the province of Constantine in which Lambaesis was situated remained largely inaccessible to Europeans following the invasion of Algiers in July 1830.[32] In anticipation of their 1836 and 1837 campaigns against the beylik of Constantine, the armée d'Afrique established military bases in the eastern part of the Algerian territories to provision troops en route to the heavily fortified city. Located between Bône and Constantine, Guelma was the site of one early encampment that also exhibited a wealth of ancient ruins. While stationed there in the late 1830s, Colonel Franciade Fleurus Duvivier took the opportunity to conduct exploratory research in the antiquities-rich region. He depended to a large extent on the writings of earlier explorers for specific information, including the observations of Shaw (which had been translated into French), the *Antonine Itinerary*, and the Peutinger Table, which he supplemented with information from Indigenous eyewitnesses.[33] His inability to travel to Lambaesis from Guelma suggests that in the late 1830s, the ruins remained inaccessible even to French officers interested in Roman antiquities.[34]

In 1838, however, Adolphe Dureau de la Malle's publication of Peyssonnel's eighteenth-century travel account increased scholarly awareness of Lambaesis. The editor used his preface to this influential work to issue a scathing indictment of the French military occupation. Not only did Dureau de la Malle complain that the conquest had not improved knowledge of North Africa, but he also blamed the invasion for engendering great hostility among the native peoples toward Europeans. In his estimation, this situation made it more difficult to study antiquities in the territory than had been the case more than a century earlier.[35]

With the appointment in December 1840 of Thomas-Robert Bugeaud as governor-general of Algeria, relations with Arabs and Kabyles continued to deteriorate. Under his command, the size of the armée d'Afrique grew exponentially, expanding from sixty thousand to more than ninety thousand troops in just five years.[36] With the increasing regularity of military patrols and application of punitive razzias against Arab and Kabyle habitations, crops, and civilians, French forces normalized violence against the Indigenous population and increased the mobility of their troops so that they would be prepared to engage in guerilla warfare. Their aggressive tactics began to yield decisive victories against the tribes led by the Sufi Emir 'Abd el-Qader at the same time that the civilian death toll mounted rapidly.[37] In 1843, under the direction of Bugeaud, the French began to involve themselves in the Aurès Mountains. As leader of these campaigns, Louis-Achille Baraguey d'Hilliers, the new commander of Constantine who had just one year earlier been reprimanded by the minister of war and the governor-general for his boundless ambition, allied the French forces with certain chiefs of the Ouled Abiad tribes. He then conducted destructive razzias against any groups that resisted French domination.[38] These assaults had a devastating effect on the subsistence economy of the mountainous region bordering on the Sahara desert.[39] They also disrupted the ties that bound together Berber tribal groups, whose composition was very fluid in the 1840s and 1850s.[40]

An uptick in military activity in the Aurès Mountains occurred next when Bugeaud turned his ambitions to the conquest of the Sahara. Among his various subterfuges to expand French control to the south without the full permission of the minister of war was the duc d'Aumale's expedition in 1844 to the Saharan oasis town of Biskra, the only urban center in the Aurès region at the time.[41] Anticipation of this campaign led to the establishment in February of the strategically placed military encampment of Batna. This French outpost in the Aurès Mountains guarded the route between the Tell and the Sahara and could be used to monitor if not control the movements of desert nomads.[42] Although the response of local tribes to this provocation and the demand that they turn over large quantities of their grain to the French was swift, they were unable to dislodge the French or prevent them from attacking the oasis of Biskra.[43]

Just 11 kilometers to the southeast of Batna, along the partially surviving Roman road, lay the Indigenous settlement of Tazzoult and the ruins of Roman Lambaesis. The Roman army had constructed their camp in this important mountain pass to the desert more than a millennium and a half earlier. The close proximity of the ancient Roman and French camps meant that from the mid-1840s, Lambaesis attracted a steady stream of French visitors. These were mainly officers and civilian administrators, who passed its abundant ruins as they made their way to or from what had become the French garrison of Biskra and points beyond. Civilians who wished to conduct studies of antiquities in the vicinity, including scholars sent by the Ministry of Public Instruction and the Académie des inscriptions et belles-lettres, required authorization from the minister of war to travel in this region.[44]

From early in the duc d'Aumale's expedition, French military exercises included Lambaesis. He gave orders to an engineering captain in his column named M. Lagrenée to create a detailed overview of the ruins, knowledge of which was seen as having practical utility for the French army. In 1844, Captain Alphonse Delamare, the artillery officer and polytechnicien who had been appointed to the Commission d'exploration scientifique d'Algérie between 1839 and 1842 to provide drawings of ancient monuments, also accompanied the column led by the duc d'Aumale.[45] During this visit and his return to the site with the epigrapher Renier from the fall of 1850 to the spring of 1851, Delamare recorded detailed images of Roman structures at Lambaesis. Many were the same ruins that had been sketched by Peyssonnel and Shaw a century before, although Delamare executed them with greater accuracy than his predecessors' idealized renderings.[46] Despite his complaints of living in a poorly insulated tent in the Aurès during winter snows, Delamare produced the most complete artistic drawings of Lambaesis made by the French to date. His images captured the site both before and during the intensive archaeological excavations of the mid-1840s and the early 1850s.[47] As noted by Monique Dondin-Payre, who has studied the polytechnicien's career and oeuvre in great detail, Delamare was motivated to conduct this work regardless of the challenges it created for his military career because he believed in the signal importance of Roman precedents in shaping French strategy in the region. He was confident that the armée d'Afrique was following in the glorious tradition established by the Third Augustan Legion nearly seventeen centuries earlier.[48]

In 1844, Jean Guyon, a physician charged with the medical inspection of the province of Constantine, traveled to the southern part of the Ziban, a Saharan term for the "region of the oases," with two other doctors.[49] Accompanied by a military escort, the men traveled through the Aurès Mountains and included Lambaesis on their itinerary. In several evocative passages describing the ruins, Guyon recalled the lasting impression Lambaesis made on him:

> I never saw such a vast field of ruins, I never saw ruins that were both so considerable and so imposing! . . . I think that those of Baalbeck [Heliopolis] or Nineveh would not be able to impress more. And, in the midst of so many witnesses of destroyed generations, regarding so much past splendor, no human voice is raised today! One hears nothing more than the cries of birds of prey mixed with the howling of wild beasts![50]

We can attribute Guyon's hyperbolic comparison of Lambaesis vis-à-vis these other ancient sites to news of archaeological exploration of ancient sites in both Lebanon and Assyria in roughly the same period.[51] However, Guyon's romantic embrace of the brief temporality of human existence

seems ominous (and knowingly disingenuous) given contemporary violence and the intensification of the military administration of Arab and
Kabyle populations during a highly volatile period of the French "pacification" of the region.[52]

Indeed, further along in his narrative, Guyon related how he and his
companions received a warm reception from the Chaouïa, who did not
delay in presenting the weary travelers with carpets on which to rest and a
first meal of dates, couscous, eggs, dairy, and water, which the women carried on their heads to the ruins.[53] Thus, the site was not empty as claimed
by Guyon. His misrepresentation of events suggests that he disqualified
the resident Kabyle population as being historically relevant to the ancient
ruins. He took this stance at the same time that he observed, as had Shaw,
that light skin, hair, and eye color (as well as, allegedly, syphilis and breast
cancer) distinguished the local population from most Muslim residents
of Algeria. On the basis of his brief visit to the region, Guyon, like Shaw
and Bruce before him, entertained the possibility that the local inhabitants
were descended from the Vandals.[54]

Guyon's views had many affinities with the writing of Édouard Lapène,
a lieutenant colonel in the artillery, who observed that Kabyle ancestry
was shaped by a series of foreign invasions of the Philistines, Vandals,
Goths, and Arabs. Going against Procopius's affirmation of the lack of
intimate contact between Maures and Vandals, Lapène read the light com-
plexions of at least some Kabyles as evidence of Germanic biological contributions to the population of North Africa.[55] This ascription furthered
both European myths of the Kabyle and their negative reception of any
possible connection between these pastoral communities and the ancient
Roman builders of monumental Lambaesis.[56]

Another of those who left a record of his visit to the ruins was Dawson Borrer, an Englishman embedded with a French column traveling
from Constantine to Biskra; in the autumn of 1846, he was escorted from
Batna to Lambaesis by General Émile Herbillon, several staff officers, and
a cavalry detachment of fifty dragoons. Beyond offering typical praise of
the forty gates of the city, the temple of Asclepius, the amphitheater, and
numerous inscriptions half-buried on site, Borrer observed that there was
enough raw material to keep an antiquarian busy for a half-century.[57] His
call to recognize the value of Lambaesis's abundant monuments was all
the more poignant because the armée d'Afrique had already begun to take

advantage of the encampment's supply of ancient cut stone for the construction of the French camp at Batna. Borrer's ruminations on Lambaesis also diverged from the eagerness of French officers to link the site to the contemporary conquest. Borrer focused more on Lambaesis as a lens by which to understand the persecution of Christians under Roman rule during the third and fourth centuries than on the ruins' potential to glorify the subjugation of the Indigenous peoples.[58] Perhaps as an English civilian, one whose future and reason for witnessing Lambaesis was less intimately identified with the deeds of the ancient Roman army, Borrer's thinking was not bound by the themes typically addressed by contemporary French officers visiting the extraordinary ruins.

During his time at Lambaesis in 1846, Borrer noted that the residents of the Aurès Mountains, who spoke the Chaouïan ("Showiah" in Borrer's text) dialect of Berber, looked more German than Arab. Borrer posited:

> As one regards these fair-faced gentry, he can but accept the supposition of their being descendants of sons of the North, living tokens of that Vandal horde, which, in the early part of the fifth century, "urged onward by the hand of God," left devastated Spain in their rear, to carry fire and sword into the heart of the three Mauritanias, to found an empire within the fairest dominions of Rome, and to place kings upon the throne of Carthage.[59]

Although he concurred with General Émile Herbillon's reports that the Chaouïa were more civilized than the Arabs, living settled rather than nomadic lives and paying their tribute regularly, Borrer acknowledged the challenges engendered by their warlike nature. He suggested that the mountain-dwelling Kabyles' love of independence made it likely that they would rise up again and risk forfeiting all if the right opportunity to fight the French presented itself.[60]

In 1847, Lieutenant Champion de Nansouty and Sub-Lieutenant Duzun of the 2nd Line Infantry Regiment of the armée d'Afrique received orders to study the region of Batna and its inhabitants. In their report, the two minor officers described the ruins of Lambaesis, which they noted was called "El Arba," by natives. They characterized the site as an immense city of the dead. Compared to the large number of people who had once occupied the thriving site in the Roman period, they estimated that roughly 7,752 Indigenous inhabitants from three separate tribes resided within five leagues of Batna and Lambaesis. By contrast, at this early date, there were just 166 Europeans in Batna, of whom 40 were women and 18 children. Champion de Nansouty and Duzun concluded that the best way to win over the much larger and "fanatical" Indigenous contingent was to extend to them the economic benefits of French presence in the area.[61]

In early 1848, Charles Texier, a civilian architect and the inaugural inspector general of civil structures in Algeria appointed in 1845, visited Lambaesis following an excursion with the armée d'Afrique into the Sahara.[62] Besides drawing the attention of scholars in metropolitan France to the still extant riches of Roman North Africa, Texier's main contribution on Lambaesis was a report on the large structure at the entrance of the city, variously referred to in previous archaeological accounts as a triumphal arch, a place to lodge elephants, or a temple. Identifying it as a praetorium, Texier imagined the ceremonies that must have once transpired in the imperial center. He posited that ancient Romans used the structure for public assemblies that could not be held in open air for much of the year owing to the mountainous terrain and severe weather conditions of the locale.[63] Such thinking reinforced nineteenth-century integration of the site into the Roman military apparatus and its ceremonies in North Africa.

Resurrecting the Third Augustan Legion and Taming the Residents of Kabylia

Despite the multitude of visits to Lambaesis that followed the French conquest of Constantine, the first sustained attempt to excavate the ruins at the legionary camp occurred shortly after Colonel Jean-Luc Carbuccia's arrival in Batna in 1848. A French officer born in Corsica, Carbuccia had attended the École spéciale militaire de Saint-Cyr. Graduating in 1830 at the age of twenty-two, Carbuccia was awarded a commission as a second lieutenant during the invasion of Algiers. He remained in Algeria until 1836, when he returned to metropolitan France for a period of four years. Serving again in French North Africa from 1840, he continued to move upward through the ranks of the army despite receiving mixed reviews from his superiors for his display of an impetuous temper and a tendency toward excessive displays of military force.[64] Although some alleged that he was too familiar with his subordinates, others cited his devotion to the French army.[65] Returning to Algeria for a third tour in September 1848, Carbuccia took command of the 2nd Regiment of the Foreign Legion. In October, he was additionally assigned military authority over the administrative subdivision of Batna, just six months after Algeria was declared an integral part of French territories and a month before the 1848 Constitution allowed French settlers in Algeria to elect representatives to the Assemblée nationale.[66]

Although it appears that he had no prior archaeological experience, Carbuccia expressed interest in ancient Roman monuments throughout his stay in Batna. He steadily began to divert resources at his disposal— including officers, soldiers, horses, mules, wagons, surveying equipment, shovels, and picks—to the archaeological exploration of the territory under his command.[67] One of the most important members of his team was Lieutenant Viénot of the 2nd Regiment of the Foreign Legion, a graduate of the École polytechnique and a skilled draftsman, whom he sent to make a watercolor drawing of a mosaic he had sketched at Henchir Guessaria in the valley of Chemorra in March 1849. Carbuccia recognized the mosaic as belonging to a church and planned to undertake an excavation at the site, trusting Viénot to render an accurate facsimile of the monument.[68]

Although he directed the works done at Lambaesis and other sites in the region, Carbuccia did not conduct most of the excavations personally due to his heavy responsibilities that necessitated frequent travel through the subdivision under his direction. In late 1848, he charged Viénot with the task of surveying archaeological sites at Lambaesis; Viénot had an additional seven soldiers supporting him in these duties. After a month, Carbuccia charged Sergeant Steffen, a former lieutenant in the Prussian artillery and mathematics instructor at the military academy in Berlin, with oversight of the soldiers whose task was the excavation of the temple of Asclepius. They worked together through the first six months of 1849. In March, he ordered these same officers to travel briefly to Thamugadis, but the mission was recalled after just forty-eight hours due to security threats.[69] Carbuccia sent other officers elsewhere in the region of Batna to make measurements and drawings of monuments that might help fill in gaps in the map of Roman Africa. Among the capable officers, noncommissioned officers, and soldiers under his command whom he credited with helping enormously in this project, were Sergeant Major Tuilliez and Sub-Lieutenant Rousseau.[70]

Between November 1848 and July 1849, Lambaesis thus figured large in the imagination and rituals of Carbuccia and his motley crew of soldiers based in Batna. During the same period that he engaged in extreme displays of military force without any real strategic value, including the destruction of three villages in Narah to the southeast of the region in April 1849 and January 1850, Carbuccia's sponsorship of research made it possible for him to draw important strategic distinctions between the Roman occupation of the region and that of the French:[71]

> These considerations did not escape the French government, when it wanted to occupy this region, and it chose Batna as the center of its authority. Indeed, differences exist between our domination and that of the Romans. The Romans had built Lambaesis and Thamugadis at the foot of the Aurès on the basis of political considerations and command of this region. The general of the dominion, Duc d'Aumale, built Batna with an eye to ensuring that France would have a monopoly over the business of import and export [of goods] from central Africa. For that, he placed his men in the principal valley through which those engaged in commerce were obliged to pass.[72]

Carbuccia's excavation notes from August 31, 1849, suggest that he recognized the archaeological ruins and inscriptions of Lambaesis as having great potential for clarifying the objectives of the French mission against the backdrop of their Roman predecessors. With some digging, he also thought that French scholars could extract from the site information relevant to topics beyond that of warfare, on issues as diverse as the success of Roman farming ventures and mortality rates among Roman children.

Among the events that highlight the symbolic significance of Carbuccia's sponsorship of excavations at the Roman camp of Lambaesis was the discovery of a statue of Asclepius in the temple dedicated to the Roman god. Its extraction from the site occasioned a large triumphal procession. Pulled by eight horses, a wagon carrying the statue was accompanied to Batna by an honor guard of cavalry, Carbuccia described how it was thereafter displayed at the military base: "Until the chief work could decorate the first place that would be created in our nascent city, Asclepius was

Figure 22. The ruins of the temple of Asclepius at Lambaesis in 1848. Jean-Luc Carbuccia, *Archéologie de la subdivision de Batna. Première campagne du 1er novembre 1848 à juillet 1849.* Bibliothèque de l'Institut de France, Ms. 1369B, pl. 22. Photograph: Thierry Le Mage. Reproduced by permission of the Institut de France. © RMN-Grand Palais/Art Resource, NY.

shown in the garden of the *hôtel* of the subdivision, where it did not cease to be the object of admiration among all the Arabs of the province. A large number came to Batna just to see this statue."[73] This statue joined an ancient marble pedestal of a column that had also been taken from Lambaesis and placed at the center of the military camp. It had recently been embellished with an inscription honoring the duc d'Aumale's campaigns in the province of Constantine.[74]

Edme-François Jomard, a polytechnicien and geographer who had participated in Napoleon I's expedition to Egypt in 1798, reported to the Académie des inscriptions et belles-lettres that active study of ancient Rome had a positive, transformative effect on the soldiers of the Foreign Legion.[75] In his view, the troops' archaeological activities under Carbuccia's

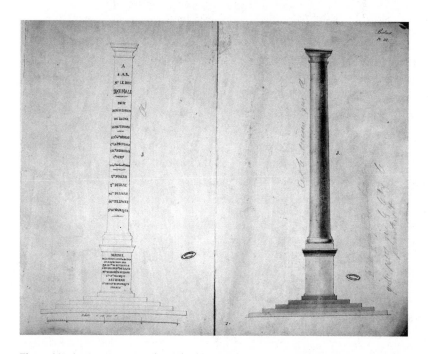

Figure 23. Ancient Roman column freshly inscribed and erected at Batna by the armée d'Afrique and dedicated to the duc d'Aumale. Jean-Luc Carbuccia, *Archéologie de la subdivision de Batna: Première campagne du 1er novembre 1848 à juillet 1849.* Bibliothèque de l'Institut de France, Ms. 1369A, pl. 3. Photograph: Thierry Le Mage. Reproduced by permission of the Institut de France. © RMN-Grand Palais/Art Resource, NY.

command allowed them to take from the site a better understanding of their own responsibilities in North Africa:

> Each soldier, transformed, one could say, into an improvised antiquary and obedient to the directions that were imparted to him, executed with eagerness, even with joy, the orders of the commander. This is not all: following in the steps of the first, some new explorers verified the measures, directions, distances, and others proofread the copies of the inscriptions; many were busy evaluating the relative heights of the sites, and took note of how to estimate the terrain in relief. . . . Finally, many topographic maps were put on the drawing board; they also, at some bridges, effected trigonometric calculations.[76]

According to Jomard, the soldiers assigned to the 2nd Regiment of the Foreign Legion, a unit composed of men often condemned as rough and poorly disciplined, were thereby inspired by their archaeological work to serve France more faithfully.[77]

However much we might be tempted to interpret this rhetoric as superficial or clumsy, it was deadly serious. The readiness of Carbuccia to see the destruction of archaeological sites as a "political crime" was demonstrated by his "severe punishment" of a tribe in the valley of Chemorra. They had wisely failed to deliver to him the children whom he claimed had thrown stones at and broken a Christian inscription that formed part of the mosaic he had recently seen at the church of Henchir Guessaria.[78]

Moreover, there is no doubt that Roman sites, and especially Lambaesis, were employed as motivational tools for shaping the behavior of the ragtag men then serving in the Foreign Legion. Contemporary reports make clear that Carbuccia consciously encouraged devotion to the ancient past as a model for his soldiers' comportment. As reported in the *Revue archéologique*, in March 1849, for instance, Carbuccia gathered the garrison of Batna before the funerary monument of Titus Flavius Maximus, prefect of the Third Augustan Legion at the camp of Lambaesis, who served under Severus Alexander.[79] A group of soldiers under M. Lambert, commander of a detachment of men at Batna from the 11th Artillery Regiment, had recently discovered this funerary monument after it had been damaged by earthquakes and restored it with local stone.[80] During the ceremony, which included a military gun salute, they reburied the ancient Roman officer's ashes and bones in a zinc container intended to replace the original lead one, which had broken into pieces after being

TOMBEAU DE FLAVIUS

à mètres du Prœtorium de Lambèse.

Figure 24. Funerary monument erected in early 1849 by Carbuccia and the soldiers of the Foreign Legion to house the ashes of Titus Flavius Maximus at Lambaesis. The structure was destroyed in 1983. Jean-Luc Carbuccia, *Archéologie de la subdivision de Batna: Première campagne du 1er novembre 1848 à juillet 1849*. Bibliothèque de l'Institut de France, Ms. 1369B, pl. 44. Photograph: Thierry Le Mage. Reproduced by permission of the Institut de France. © RMN-Grand Palais/Art Resource, NY.

exposed to the air. They embellished the monument's ancient epitaph with a second inscription commemorating the contributions of the soldiers in the Foreign Legion under the direction of Carbuccia.[81] These rites, which neatly elided more than a millennium and a half of history, linked the soldiers intimately to their Roman predecessors, whose leader they now laid to rest with a time-honored ceremony.[82]

While Carbuccia's idealized vision of the Roman past was inextricably intertwined with the comportment of French-led troops, an equally important link existed between his archaeological explorations and contemporary maneuvers in which soldiers under his command participated. Stationed in Batna with his troops to assist in campaigns in the Sahara and the Aurès Mountains (and not primarily to excavate ancient Roman sites, as one might surmise from his excavation journal), Carbuccia contributed to French efforts to quell regional unrest that followed news of the events of 1848 in metropolitan France. Just three months after the ceremony to honor Titus Flavius Maximus, Carbuccia led soldiers under his command in a predawn retributive razzia against the Ouled Sahnoun tribe in the pre-Saharan desert in July 1849. The surprise attack, which was meant to punish the population for an earlier uprising at the fortified oasis town of Zaatcha that had caused French casualties, exacted a high toll among civilians, including women and children. Three days later, Carbuccia's men assaulted Zaatcha but were forced to withdraw after encountering stiff resistance.[83] In October 1849, a thousand of Carbuccia's men took part in the final French assault on Zaatcha, which resulted in a bloody siege in which hundreds died on both sides. Following their breach of the city's fortifications and the felling of more than ten thousand date palms that represented the inhabitants' main source of income, the French leveled the settlement and massacred the defenders and most of the civilian population that had not fled the oasis.[84]

Nonetheless, the precise nature of the legacy of Carbuccia's activities at Lambaesis is disputed. There is no doubt that Carbuccia's archaeological activity in the region of Batna led to the creation of valuable drawings and maps of Lambaesis and nearby archaeological sites, in addition to providing detailed descriptions of the remains of the military camp of the Third Augustan Legion.[85] Moreover, at Carbuccia's order, Rousseau, now a lieutenant, created a detailed map at a scale of 1/100,000, on which he recorded not just geological features, place names, and tribes

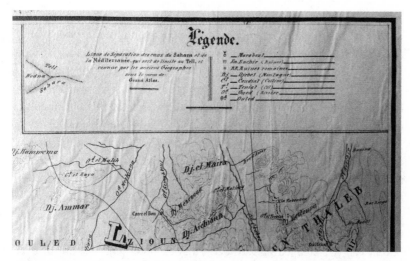

Figure 25. Key of one version of the topographical map created by Rousseau for the
military administrative district of Batna with particular attention to Roman ruins.
Carte de la Subdivision de Batna par le Lieutenant Rousseau du 2e régiment de la
Légion etrangère sur les levés qu'il a fait lui même, et sur des renseignements
pris au bureau topographique de Constantine, October 7, 1851. © Service historique
de la Défense, CHA, Vincennes, 1M 1314.

but also Roman ruins, roads, and other signs of imperial occupation of
the Aurès.[86] These cartographic efforts earned Carbuccia the acclaim of
the Académie des inscriptions et belles-lettres, which awarded him a gold
medal in the competition on antiquities and encouraged him to continue
in these endeavors. He also received tribute through his selection as an
officer of the Legion of Honor.[87] In 1858, the epigrapher Renier praised
Carbuccia's extremely detailed map and told Napoleon III that he had
benefited greatly from it. He suggested that this example could serve as a
praiseworthy cartographic model for other parts of Algeria.[88]

The minister of war, however, seemed determined to stymie Carbuccia's
efforts by demanding that he not have direct contact with the Académie
des inscriptions et belles-lettres despite its members' recognition of his
work. In May 1851, the minister of war also declined to publish the fruit
of Carbuccia's research, citing the lack of funds for such purposes. The
historian Monique Dondin-Payre posits that this reluctance stemmed from
accusations that Carbuccia had taken advantage of military resources by
requisitioning soldiers in the Foreign Legion to contribute a considerable

number of man-hours to this archaeological project, the total of which was estimated by one contemporary to be fourteen thousand days.[89] For their labors, the soldiers received no compensation beyond funds provided personally by Carbuccia.[90] Yet the army must have seen some utility in Carbuccia's project since it took steps to recognize several of the leading officers and lower-ranked officers in these archaeological undertakings and rewarded them with transfer from the Foreign Legion to more prestigious brigades of the armée d'Afrique.[91] While the minister of war declined to print Carbuccia's book because it was of insufficient interest to the army (and perhaps, although this went unsaid, because the rough quality of the draft required substantial reworking), he did offer to publish Carbuccia's archaeological map.[92] This plan did not, however, come to fruition. In the end, disagreement stemming from accusations that Carbuccia had overstepped his authority, among other tensions, boiled over and led to Carbuccia's abrupt departure from North Africa in 1851. The well-liked officer returned to France, receiving a promotion to the rank of general soon afterward. Carbuccia was subsequently sent to the Crimea to lead a brigade of the Foreign Legion but died of cholera on the Gallipoli Peninsula in July 1854.[93]

In her assessment of Carbuccia, Dondin-Payre has remarked on the relative incompetence that characterized his archaeological efforts. Undated comments in pencil in the margins of the manuscript of his archaeological report likewise suggest that someone at the Académie des inscriptions et belles-lettres was less than overwhelmed by Carbuccia's historical analysis and eclectic observations.[94] Nonetheless, Dondin-Payre acknowledges that the officer's detailed documentation of Lambaesis and other sites in the region were indispensable to his successors. Fanny Colonna has elaborated on this point by observing the powerful impact of not just Carbuccia's archaeological work, but also his stereotypical descriptions of the impenetrable nature of the Aurès, on Émile Masqueray and the École d'Alger twenty-five years later.[95] The texts, surveys, drawings, and maps produced by Carbuccia in concert with officers under his command, captured and preserved for posterity the main features of Roman authority over the Aurès Mountains, which were soon threatened by renewed French military activity.

With respect to archaeological conservation, Nacéra Benseddik lays blame squarely on Carbuccia and not the minister of war for the decision to construct a French penitentiary at Lambaesis to house political prisoners from June 1848.[96] This project received authorization from the minister of war in January 1850, and actual construction began in March 1851.[97] Carbuccia also requested the construction of a colonial village on the ancient site, a project that was not realized for another decade. Indeed, the authorities appear to have chosen the site largely on account of the ready availability of cut stone.[98] Despite the protests of contemporary scholars aware of Lambaesis's importance and Carbuccia's own apparent appreciation of archaeology, Roman remains and houses of the village soon became the quarry from which soldiers and later prisoners built the penitentiary.[99] Word quickly got out of Algeria regarding how rapidly the site was being degraded from its pristine condition in the early 1840s. According to a surgeon in the infantry regiment of Zouaves (composed predominantly of Indigenous troops) stationed at Batna who visited Lambaesis several times, the temple of Asclepius's marble columns were no longer standing by April 1850.[100]

Because of Lambaesis's location, French infantry columns in the late 1840s continued to witness its most famous monuments on their way to campaigns in the Aurès Mountains and the Sahara. Just two months after the destruction of Zaatcha, in late December 1849, Colonel François-Certain de Canrobert's column of four thousand men passed within sight of the ruins, known by this time from Carbuccia's excavations, as they headed to put down a rebellion in the mountain town of Narah.[101] Having massacred most of the inhabitants and burned standing structures in the town, the French returned to Batna three weeks later, convinced that they had forced the Indigenous population into submission.[102] On May 1, 1850, General Armand Jacques Leroy de Saint-Arnaud arrived at Lambaesis from Constantine with a column of soldiers intent on showing French dominance in the Aurès and Nementchas Mountains. In letters to his wife and brother, he recounted the eight hours he spent at Lambaesis visiting the ruins, admiring the statue of Asclepius recently found on site, and contemplating how the Romans left such a lasting mark on the land. Before his men headed south, he spent over an hour meditating in the temple of Asclepius while troops of the Foreign Legion played Strauss waltzes in honor of his visit.[103] Thereafter, concerned by plans for the construction of the penitentiary so close to the ruins, Saint-Arnaud ordered local authorities to move its location further toward the perimeter of the ancient camp so as to preserve better the impressive remains of the Third Augustan Legion.[104]

It is thus imperative to consider how contemporary military conflicts shaped engagement with extant Roman remains at Lambaesis by officers like Carbuccia and Saint-Arnaud. Although Carbuccia's journal, which he kept during the campaign to document antiquities the column encountered on the way, is single-minded in its perceived purpose, it makes little reference to any of the skirmishes, deaths, or hardships in the course of his military engagements.[105] By contrast, Carbuccia reported on the numerous tribes that camped in the area, acted peacefully, followed orders, and in no way interrupted the ongoing excavations of the temple of Asclepius. From his perspective, the real threat to digging was from the lions that occasionally made their way into the camp.[106] Yet here, too, Carbuccia seized the opportunity for self-reference in the ongoing war: he related that French soldiers paralleled their taming of a captured lion they kept as a pet in the camp of Batna in 1850 to their role in civilizing the inhabitants of the Aurès Mountains.[107]

Nonetheless, we should not allow the distinction that Carbuccia drew between archaeological and military activities to lead us to dismiss the morale boost gained through excavations and the colorful ceremonies that encouraged identification with the Roman past. French troops drew from Lambaesis's ruins an understanding of the historic weight of their role in North Africa; they often literally marched on the roads built by the ancient Romans and sheltered in their fortresses. Perhaps thoughts of these deeds of old helped allay any qualms (which seem to have been few) about the moral shortcomings of the shocking violence they brought to the region. Driven by their self-perception as saviors of Algeria, a sentiment accompanied by a deadly thirst for vengeance for their own losses, French officers gave scarce acknowledgment to the slaughter of innocents at the oasis of Zaatcha, the mountain town of Narah, or on the road to Khenchela, east of Lambaesis.[108] Their recollections of the campaign focused almost exclusively on the privations faced by their own soldiers. As a new generation of conquerors, they saw their purpose as returning the region to European rule, settlement, and civilization. All were necessary components in the development of what was known by about 1840 as the "mission civilisatrice," a concept that first became official policy during the Third Republic.[109]

Imprisonment at Lambaesis: Roman Ruins as Penitentiary

Attracted by the store of ready stone and the relative isolation of the site, French authorities chose Lambaesis in early 1850 as the location of a penitentiary to house those whom they determined to be the most intransigent political prisoners of the June 1848 uprising against the Second Republic.[110] Following the abolition of the death penalty for political prisoners in metropolitan France, the expulsion of these detainees was aimed at creating as great a separation possible between them and potentially unruly sectors of the French population in a time of significant unrest.[111] Although government officials had originally excluded Algeria as a possible destination for political prisoners, so as not to discourage recruitment of civilian colonists, their outlook changed considerably when the latter did not arrive in sufficient numbers to meet agricultural targets. The end of slavery in France's Caribbean possessions also destabilized other potential venues for the deportees.[112] Consequently, authorities concluded that expulsion to Algeria offered prisoners the possibility of rehabilitation through agricultural work and other forms of hard labor, even if the practical application of these ideas did not come to fruition in North Africa. The subsequent experience of the exiled prisoners demonstrated how embedded the colony was in metropolitan affairs.[113]

Interned without trial first at Belle-Île, an island located 14 kilometers south of the Quiberon Peninsula in Brittany, 462 French male prisoners were identified by French judges as the most dangerous and selected for transport to Algeria in January 1850.[114] The next month, the men, many of whom were in their twenties and thirties but some as young as twelve, embarked on their journey across the Mediterranean and into exile in Algeria, where French authorities believed that they posed less threat to the security of metropolitan France.[115] Saint-Arnaud, who met the prisoners temporarily housed in the Kasbah of Bône, had only harsh words for the newly arrived exiles:

> A heterogeneous mass of all that could reunite the debris of a defeated revolution; a mix of artisans and instruments of disorder: journalists, poets, Masons, teachers, painters, then some prison escapees . . . , all socialists, all red, but above all, all enraged madmen, posing as a martyr to that which no one thought of inflicting on them; howling, shouting, demanding judges, crying

loudly everything, except that which is honest; sworn enemies of a society that they wanted to overturn and which repelled them. They are dangerous men, but I do not fear them.[116]

After the prisoners experienced more than two years of incarceration in the port city of Bône with little opportunity to undertake the labor originally intended to rehabilitate them, French authorities decided to transfer the exiles of 1848. A new group of prisoners, political adversaries to Napoleon III's coup d'état of 1851, were expected to arrive soon, and officials wanted to keep the two groups apart. However, although the minister of war had authorized construction of the prison at Lambaesis in late January 1850, work at the site did not actually begin until March 1851.[117] Consequently, when, in May 1852, the exiles of 1848 arrived in Lambaesis after marching 200 kilometers in a southwesterly direction to their new base of confinement, the prison facilities were not yet finished. Accompanied by an army escort during the roughly twelve-day journey, the prisoners were expected to help complete the construction of the prison in which they were to be detained.[118] Those who refused, roughly eighty men in total, were sent to exile in French Guiana.[119]

One of the older men among the detainees of 1848 deported from France without the benefit of a trial was Jean Terson, a defrocked priest and a former Saint-Simonian mystic. He stood accused of spreading revolutionary ideas through public speeches in June 1848 that excoriated the condition of the working class. Imprisoned at first in Perpignan, he was transferred to caserns outside Paris, then Cherbourg, and finally the citadel of Belle-Île. From there, he was transported across the Mediterranean by ship to the Kasbah of Bône.[120] Although contemporary government sources documenting the alleged crimes of the exiles described him as a "dangerous liar, provocateur, and an evil spirit," Terson recalled the violence to which the men were subjected by their guards, who killed some of the inmates who refused to cooperate.[121] By contrast, he highlighted what he viewed as the generous spirit of the prisoners, who volunteered to aid the soldiers escorting them by offering to carry their heavy bags and rifles as they set out by foot in May 1852 to the partially constructed prison at Lambaesis. He recalled that these selfless acts and others like them made the French soldiers somewhat more sympathetic to the plight of the political prisoners.[122]

Another inmate who marched from Bône to Lambaesis in the spring of 1852 was Jacques-Eugène Leiris (or Leyris), whom authorities vilified as "very fanatical, a propagandist, and a man of action."[123] In fact, Leiris's older brother Jean-François died on November 12, 1849, when—incarcerated and unarmed—he was attacked by guards at Belle-Île.[124] Not only did the younger Leiris correspond regularly with his sister and brother-in-law, but he expressed great longing to see his family once again. After passing through snow and cold on his way southward, Leiris's first impression was that he had reached the promised land; he felt great eagerness to explore the ancient ruins after his long imprisonment in the Kasbah of Bône.[125] In this same group was the journalist Émile Thuillier of Sedan, with whom Leiris became close friends.[126] Although contemporary French documents described him as "dangerous, fanatical and a man of intelligence, silent intrigues; a propagandist, [and] bad in every respect,"[127] Thuillier was described much more sympathetically by Leiris, who praised his fellow inmate's good sense of humor.[128]

As Terson made his way overland with other prisoners in the convoy of May 1852, they passed through the military garrison of Batna before arriving in Lambaesis. On his arrival at the former Roman camp, Terson observed the absence of walls at the hastily assembled and still incomplete French penitentiary; he remarked that the Sahara made additional security unnecessary. The exiles' sense of isolation was reinforced by knowledge that their overseers had offered Kabyle inhabitants of the mountainous region a bounty of 10 francs per head (a sum that apparently rose to 25 francs by the mid-1850s) for capturing and returning fleeing prisoners, with no differential in the price whether the returned escapees were dead or alive. Beyond contributing to continuing construction on the prison, some of the six hundred detainees created a kitchen garden while others engaged in intellectual activities. As part of their duties, all the men, aside from those who were ill, were required daily to help gather sticks and water used for heat and cooking.[129]

Terson, who desperately searched for a way to fight off the isolation of his incarceration at Lambaesis following the construction of the penitentiary, was among the first to request permission to excavate the ruins he saw about them. Although participation in archaeological excavations was entirely voluntary, it was one of the rare outlets for the prisoners with scholarly inclinations. Captain Toussaint, who led the engineering unit from Batna that built the prison and oversaw the detainees in Lambaesis, offered his enthusiastic support for the enterprise and granted Terson authorization to oversee the dozen or so men interested in conducting archaeological research. With Toussaint's encouragement, Terson walked 11 kilometers to Batna with an armed escort to speak with Colonel Nicolas-Gilles-Toussaint Desvaux, the cavalry officer who had taken over command of the administrative subdivision of Batna in late January 1851, following the hasty departure of Carbuccia. Among his various responsibilities was supervision of all operations at Lambaesis, including oversight of its political prisoners.[130]

Desvaux, who had taught himself some spoken Arabic and was sympathetic to the Saint-Simonian cause, was also deeply interested in the Roman past. In the 1840s, he made a practice of copying inscriptions at Constantine, Tébessa, and some of the other ancient cities through which

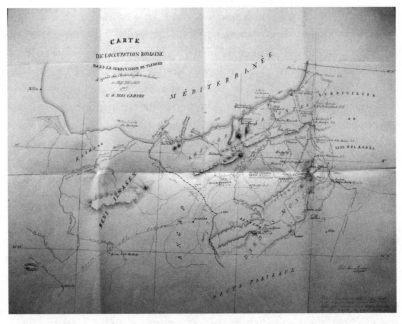

Figure 26. Report by Oscar MacCarthy titled "De l'occupation romaine dans la subdivisions de Tlemsen" dated September 5, 1851. The map's key notes that it displays only information related to the Roman period, namely ruins and inscriptions. Scale is 1/400,000. ANOM 80 F 1587. Reproduced by permission of the Archives nationales d'Outre-Mer (ANOM, France).

he passed in the course of his military duties as captain of the 3rd Regiment of the Chasseurs d'Afrique (light mounted cavalry) and from 1845 the squadron chief of the 3rd Regiment of the Spahis (Indigenous cavalry).[131] Although he was now frequently underway and had little time to pursue his archaeological interests, the colonel generously put at the disposal of the prisoners in Lambaesis his personal library with many of the relevant works of classical history and more recent archaeological publications. Terson noted that Desvaux's collection was well stocked with ancient works such as the writings of Procopius, Cassius Dio, Sallust, and Ptolemy, and modern works, including among others Peyssonnel, Shaw, Dureau de la Malle, and Delamare.[132] By the mid-1840s, larger posts like Batna also had a small library of several hundred volumes provided by the minister of war to prevent the officers from falling into "nostalgia."[133] It is certainly possible that Terson and the other prisoners had access to these books as well. Besides working with the authorization of Desvaux, the detainees labored on behalf of specific soldiers who expressed interest in the site. Terson remarked, for instance, that M. Benvenuti, a Roman painter and soldier in the Foreign Legion, received the help of the prisoners when he turned his attention to excavations.[134] Terson also received assistance from local inhabitants such as the father of a local man referred to as Muhammed ben-Abdellah.

Dismayed by what he described as the criminal pleasure that many soldiers took in the destruction of both remains and human life, Terson quickly observed that the study of Latin inscriptions offered a haven in which he could give life and movement to the ancient past.[135] Rescuing a statue from the temple of Asclepius, which had languished since the Vandal period, also provided Terson some hope of future relief, which he captured in a poem:

> The deportees had gathered in this place,
> Some precious debris snatched from the ruins,
> Here, some pedestals ornamented with figures,
> There, some busts without their heads and torsos without arms.
> Rejoice, you Roman. O you who consecrate
> To divine Asclepius a noble statue
> But which a Vandal had thrown in the sand;
> Our arms have remounted it on its former pedestal.

May it protect against evil strokes
Our colonists menaced by the venom of fevers,
Which ice the heart and burn the lips![136]

The deportee Leiris likewise reminisced that the exploration of Roman ruins offered him a brief respite from the travails of his present reality: although he felt unqualified as an excavator, the broken fragments he handled allowed him to imagine Roman life in all its glory.[137] In late November 1852, enthused by the success of the excavations to date, Desvaux approved a request for thirty-five political exiles, who were to be accompanied by three officers and two Spahis, to travel to nearby Thamugadis for an exploration of its monuments.[138] To the great disappointment of the men, however, an unseasonal snowstorm aborted the two-week mission shortly after it began.[139] After nearly being attacked by a lion, the prisoners returned to Lambaesis empty-handed.[140]

Between 1852 and 1853, anywhere from twelve to thirty prisoners at Lambaesis dug at a time, depending on how much the site was affected by rain and snow, and how many men fell ill from the fevers that likewise decimated French troops. Working on occasion in concert with soldiers who helped them move large quantities of soil from the structures and inscriptions in which they were primarily interested, their activities focused on several key sites including the temple of Asclepius, the baths, and the triumphal arch.[141] Within the first year of the excavations, the camp of Lambaesis boasted one of the earliest open-air museums in Algeria. Located in the so-called praetorium, which the prisoners covered provisionally with cloth, the museum displayed a couple hundred finds. Among them were statues and inscriptions that Carbuccia had originally transported from Lambaesis to decorate his lodgings in Batna but which Desvaux had returned to the site of their discovery.[142]

Soon after the failed visit to Thamugadis in November 1852, Terson's stay ended at Lambaesis and his confinement was transferred to Constantine, where, armed with a very positive recommendation from Desvaux, he found work as an agent in a military task force and gave lessons in French and Latin. Following Terson's departure for Constantine, archaeological work at Lambaesis nonetheless continued, and an architect named Beury was put in charge of inscriptions and mosaics.[143] The activity was fueled by a regular stream of exiles, since the detainees of 1848 were soon augmented by imprisoned adversaries to Napoleon III's imperial ambitions. Terson, by contrast, remained in Constantine until at least 1859, when a general amnesty was extended to all the exiles of 1848 and 1851. Like the majority of deportees who had survived their stay in Algeria, he returned to metropolitan France.[144] Despite the wealth of Roman remains in Constantine, during his nine years there, Terson appears never to have returned to the study of antiquities, the bittersweet activity of his incarceration. In early 1883, more than twenty years after his return to metropolitan France, Terson ended his life by suicide.[145]

Although earlier military authorities had expressed displeasure with Carbuccia's diversion of military resources to archaeology, the new minister of war, Maréchal Saint-Arnaud (December 1851–March 1854), a firm supporter of Lambaesis, encouraged archaeological undertakings at the site. He acknowledged that the exiles were not only contributing to French science but also making good use of this opportunity to rehabilitate themselves.[146] Similar to their view of soldiers in the Foreign Legion, French authorities thought that the prisoners might cultivate greater loyalty to France through extensive contact with the ruins of the ancient Roman military, seen as the forebears of the French. Although Saint-Arnaud suggested that some of the most accomplished participants in the archaeological activities at Lambaesis might be rewarded with an improvement in their situation, just as Desvaux had assisted Terson find a more suitable situation in Constantine, it was too late for the unfortunate political detainees who had died from cholera or typhus soon after their arrival in the Aurès Mountains.[147]

Unfortunately, the freedoms afforded to the political prisoners did not last long after Terson's departure. Following an escape attempt in 1853 by a number of men held at Lambaesis, the detainees lost many of their freedoms and the escapees who were caught were sent to French Guiana.[148] The boredom and hopelessness brought on by unending incarceration in the Aurès Mountains weighed heavily on the French exiles.[149] And with the departure of some of the deported prisoners of 1848 for other sites in Algeria in 1854, archaeological work at Lambaesis for the most part ceased. Even so, Gaspard Rouffet, one of the earliest among the exiles of 1851 to arrive in Lambaesis on May 16, 1854, noted that the prisoners were still allowed to take walks among the abundant ruins. This small privilege was withdrawn, however, once the prison became more crowded.[150] One of the few officers to conduct excavations in the second half of the decade was Captain A. Moll, who published several short notices about the site in 1856 and 1857 in the journal of Constantine's archaeological society. In the course of his work on the prison's water supply, Moll made several discoveries of previously undocumented inscriptions in and near Lambaesis.[151]

It is striking to note that in his memoirs, Terson recalled only positive experiences in his excavation of Roman remains. Despite his status as a political detainee and the lack of any incentive to promote an idyllic picture of the French in Algeria, Terson did not question the existence of the French colony or its ideological claims to the ancient Roman past. As neither a representative of the French army nor a professional scholar employed by the state, but instead a political prisoner condemned for his outspoken protest against French policies, his outlook toward Lambaesis suggests how deeply identification with ancient Roman rule of North Africa had already penetrated the consciousness of French residents of Algeria. While the internment of the political exiles of 1848 and 1851 at Lambaesis was one of the more unusual aspects of the reuse of the Roman past, the housing and voluntary excavations of French deportees at Lambaesis from May 1852 onward offered one of the few documented instances of civilian interaction with archaeological remains in North Africa prior to 1870.

Victor Hugo, who voted in the French National Assembly against the creation of the penitentiary at Lambaesis, highlighted the suffering of the prisoners exiled to Algeria. In his poetry collection *Châtiments* (1853), which he published during his self-imposed exile from France, Hugo criticized both the exportation of political prisoners to Algeria and the barbarizing effect that such brutality was having on the French army and the inmates.[152] Hugo specifically evoked the foreboding prison of Lambaesis in a poem dedicated to the memory of the Catholic activist Pauline Roland, who was imprisoned first for her involvement in the uprisings of 1848.[153] After her exile to Algeria for her opposition to Louis Bonaparte's coup of 1851, she died of fever in December 1852 before she could be reunited in France with her three children. Roland, however, made no mention in her letters of spending time in Lambaesis, having been transferred during her detention through a series of locations in Algeria, including Mers-el-Kébir, Saint-Grégoire near Oran, El Biar, Bougie, Sétif, Constantine, Philippeville, and Bône.[154] Although Hugo did not directly condemn the colonization of Algeria, he harshly criticized the use of force against French citizens like Roland. For Hugo, Lambaesis represented the epitome of such practices.[155]

After the departure of the political exiles, the excavation of Lambaesis continued in fits and starts in the 1860s, receiving new impetus from Napoleon III's second state visit to Algeria. The imperial journey included a stop at the so-called praetorium of Lambaesis on June 2, 1865, during which the emperor claimed for the Louvre a statue of Jupiter displayed in the site's open-air museum created by the prisoners. The large sculpture departed overland and then by steamship for metropolitan France, reaching Paris by October of the same year.[156] The emperor's interest in this important Roman archaeological site, as well as his request that more information be gathered about the Roman roads that led to Lambaesis,[157] no doubt encouraged M. Barnéond, director of the penitentiary, to renew the armée d'Afrique's commitment to conducting research on the Roman site.[158] During the revolts of 1871, however, the praetorium, the site of the museum of Lambaesis, was pillaged by French units from Bouches-du-Rhône housed there. They scrawled graffiti on the statues and broke many of the remains that were still relatively intact.[159]

French, Arab, and Kabyle Perspectives of the Ancient Past

At Lambaesis as elsewhere in Algeria, French officers and civilians alike privileged the Roman past over the more recent history of the region to promote the legacy of the conquerors with whom they most closely identified over all possible contenders. Not only did French emphasis on classical archaeology telescope time, eliminating twelve hundred years of Arab presence in the region, but it "cleaned" ancient sites of both late antique Christians and more modern inhabitants.[160] Scholarly attention to the monumental remnants of the ancient Romans overshadowed and masked the realities of the current French assault on Algerian civilians.[161] Nicholas Dirks's observations regarding British-occupied India are helpful in examining European colonial politics and the artificial tensions they created with Indigenous peoples over ancient monuments. He suggests that the willful consignment of a population to oblivion aided nineteenth-century British imperial ventures. As he has noted: "colonial governmentality produced a different kind of relationship to the past, and to its collection, preservation, and destruction, than had been the case in the imperial metropole. In many ways, the archive was the literal document that expressed the rupture between nation and state engendered by the colonial form."[162] Having constructed a narrative emphasizing the alleged barbarism and primitivism of the Arab and Kabyle population, the French could similarly dismiss as irrelevant their past contributions; they could allege that these populations had advanced little over millennia.[163]

From the time of the French conquest in 1830, at least some officers had observed that Arabs and Kabyles had an ongoing relationship with the Roman ruins found throughout the territory. In the early 1830s, Captain Rozet, who was part of the topographical section of the armée d'Afrique, made observations about the ancient monuments located between Algiers and Oran.[164] To the members of the Académie des inscriptions et belles-lettres, Rozet reported that some of the ancient sites he encountered were not in pristine condition.[165] They had been disturbed by recent digging and apparent plundering that he attributed to the Indigenous inhabitants:

> We saw in the interior of Rustonium [a ruined Roman settlement on the prom-ontory of Matifou, east of the bay of Algiers], many excavations of which some were still very recent: they were the result of excavations undertaken by the Arabs, either to extract the stones to build since they found them already cut, or to look for coins and other art objects, regarding which I was told that in different periods of time one had found a large quantity [of such items].[166]

Indeed, across the Maghreb, Arabs and Kabyles had long been familiar with Roman structures, because either they maintained and still used them (as in the case of aqueducts, cisterns, roads, and bridges), or they viewed these locations as a source of worked stone for building projects. In both the medieval and the early modern period, ancient marble columns were particularly desirable for high profile structures such as mosques and pal-aces.[167] As Rozet suggested, some excavators may have also sought coins, small statues, and other treasures that they might sell for a profit. Despite the evident similarity between their activities and those of the French, mil-itary officers like Rozet were eager to distinguish themselves from Muslim inhabitants, whom they condemned as uncivilized. They complained that the latter were motivated to seek out antiquities mainly by the desire to profit personally from attractive building stone and valuable coins.

By the early 1850s, however, French archaeologists, a significant number of whom were by this point metropolitan scholars or civilian settlers rather than military officers, were content to claim that Arabs and Kabyles were entirely uninterested in Roman antiquities.[168] Members of the Société archéologique de la province de Constantine, founded in 1852, alleged that Muslim ignorance of and disdain for the classical past made them poor stewards of ancient remains.[169] Oscar MacCarthy, Berbrugger's successor as director of the Bibliothèque et Musée d'Alger from 1869, attributed Arab and Berber motives for engagement with classical monuments to greed. He criticized the Indigenous inhabitants for being sufficiently naïve as to believe that they would find hidden gold and silver if they dug at ancient sites.[170] Metropolitan scholars, too, took a hard position against the value of Muslim interaction with antiquities. Renier, in the midst of his scholarly mission to Lambaesis in the early 1850s to record its ancient Latin inscriptions, suggested that the Indigenous population had no historical claim to Algeria. He argued that the French, heirs of the ancient Romans, possessed exclusive moral title to the territory.[171] This rhetoric seems to have been widely accepted, even if, as some later acknowledged, the armée d'Afrique had destroyed far more ancient monuments in its short time in North Africa than had been disturbed by the Arabs and Berbers over more than a millennium.[172]

In sharp contradistinction to French claims of the dissimilarities between the meaning of ancient monuments to Europeans and conquered peoples, respectively, we must consider the possibility that local inhabitants had long-standing and complex relationships with remains of the ancient past. Antiquities played an integral part in their daily lives, belief systems, and customs, as has been demonstrated in contemporary cases in other parts of the Mediterranean such as newly independent Greece.[173] This observation is relevant not solely to predominantly Christian regions of the former Ottoman Empire but also to Muslim Egypt and Lebanon. There, identification with the ancient past in the nineteenth and early twentieth centuries served a variety of causes, including the building of modern nation-states, the development of historical narratives for those entities, and the passage of legislation identifying and protecting national patrimony.[174] For this reason, it is important to interrogate standard generalizations about distaste for the pre-Islamic past in Muslim countries, including the Maghreb, ideas that were initially propagated in colonial publications but have been reiterated in more recent studies.[175]

It is clear that in colonial Algeria, archaeological projects led by French officers and civilians, who were part and parcel of the French regime, effectively silenced the voices of Muslim inhabitants, both Arab and Kabyle. By excluding these actors and rendering their perspectives irrelevant, colonial archaeologists effectively robbed members of the Indigenous population of agency over their own past.[176] Reading against the grain of colonial reporters, however, we can discover in French sources a small number of brief but tantalizing descriptions of Arab and Kabyle interactions with Roman remains that survived in nineteenth-century Algeria, including at Lambaesis. These accounts suggest that traditional generalizations about Indigenous disinterest in antiquities do not accurately reflect the subtle intricacies of the relationships of non-Europeans with ancient ruins. Although their interactions with Roman sites in Algeria may not have been "archaeological" and their understanding of ancient times might be interpreted as "unorthodox" by modern standards, Arab and Kabyle knowledge of these sites nonetheless had practical, historical, and spiritual significance.

Although our limited source base prevents us from understanding precisely what the largely illiterate Kabyle inhabitants of the Aurès Mountains thought about Roman sites, we can posit that they were quite familiar with the ancient landscape that survived in their own day. French officers and archaeologists with some knowledge of Arabic or Berber, or those who had access to interpreters, seem to have regularly taken the opportunity to interrogate native inhabitants as potential informants. Until the French successfully mapped the territory for themselves, they depended heavily on local knowledge about topography and travel routes through the region they were taking by conquest.[177] They also relied on Arabs and Kabyles for firsthand information about ancient monuments.

In the late 1830s, for instance, Colonel Duvivier acknowledged his dependence on Indigenous contributions to his project of compiling an atlas of Roman finds in the region of Guelma (L. Calama) east of Constantine. While he recognized the importance of knowledge of ancient and medieval sources to this project, he could not personally confirm the current state of many of the ancient sites of interest, including Lambaesis, since they were located in areas still unsafe for exploration. For this

Figure 27. Home near Lambaesis with ancient Roman spolia embedded in the walls. Médéric Meusement, "Lambèse: Fragments romains sur une maison" (1893). Fol NS 1201. Reproduced by permission of the Bibliothèque nationale de France, Département des estampes et de la photographie.

reason, when "a large number of indigenous people from all the tribes came to Guelma [where I was stationed], I questioned them, and took note of all their responses. Soon I saw that I could arrive at creating a map of many of the lands that we probably would not visit for a long time. This is the result that I now publish. It took me five months, working at least eighteen hours per day."[178] He described Arab and Kabyle knowledge of Roman monuments in the Aurès Mountains as intimate and reliable, since some of the tribesmen then passing through Guelma had lived in this area during childhood but had later been expelled by the French.[179] Judging from Duvivier's brief descriptions of ancient sites in and near Lambaesis, the local population's familiarity with this material appears to have gone beyond practical use of these sites as stone depots. He judged native oral accounts as sufficiently reliable to be excerpted in his works on antiquities.

In the case of Jean Guyon, whose visit to Lambaesis was described above, the physician was considerably more hostile to Indigenous informants. He denied the possibility that the resident Kabyle population had any meaningful connection, either historical or contemporary, to the ruins of Lambaesis. Nonetheless, his description of the hospitality he received from local residents during his visit to Lambaesis in 1844 belies his claim that the site was empty of inhabitants. His exceptionally detailed account of spontaneous interaction suggests that residents were indeed very familiar with the ruins of Lambaesis.[180] Guyon's was just one of several extant first-person accounts by French officers and archaeologists who recalled interactions with Indigenous peoples on the ancient site. As was the case elsewhere in Algeria, European visitors to Lambaesis benefited from information about local antiquities offered at regular intervals by the Chaouïa.

By the mid-1840s, however, the possibility of this sort of exchange was becoming increasingly rare. A combination of growing French distrust of the Arabs and Kabyles, the continuing effects of the deadly razzia, and the progressive *cantonnement* of the Muslim population that resulted in their segregation from French military and civilian colonists stifled many potential opportunities for exchange. One of the exceptions to this dearth of communication was the political exile Terson, who recounted positive interactions with local inhabitants during his imprisonment and excavations at Lambaesis. Although he could not speak Arabic or Berber fluently, during his exile in Algeria, Terson recorded in his diary that he had picked up some polite phrases with which he liked to converse with residents. Among the individuals with whom he spoke, he related that one man, whom he identified only as the son of Muhammed-ben-Abdellah, told him that his father had once been very engaged in studying the ruins of Lambaesis.[181] Terson's interlocutor suggested, moreover, that if Terson were interested, his father would be delighted to share his knowledge of the site. After explaining that his father knew some Latin and Greek, the visitor asked for a copy of Terson's transcriptions, which his father, who was now blind, would understand if they were read to him.[182]

Whether anything came of this extraordinary exchange is unknown, since Terson did not record it in his diary. The conversation, however, suggests that greater local knowledge of ancient Roman culture existed than has traditionally been attributed to the Kabyle tribes that traveled hundreds of kilometers regularly between the Aurès Mountains and the city of Constantine to sell their sheep, wool, goats, and services.[183] It seems entirely possible that some members of the Berber-speaking tribes received some degree of education, like those descended from saintly lineages who traveled to northern Algeria and the Ziban oases for more advanced school-ing. There, they learned law, grammar, astronomy, arithmetic, metaphys-ics, and logic.[184] And while it is unlikely, we cannot dismiss the additional possibility that the Kabyles of the Aurès Mountains may have included among their members individuals of European descent who had entered Constantine prior to 1830 as either maritime captives or traders.[185]

Not all the political exiles who excavated at the site of Lambaesis and helped create an open-air museum at the so-called praetorium, however, had positive opinions of the Indigenous peoples in the Aurès Mountains. In the early 1850s, Thuillier Pellotier, one of the prisoners of 1848, com-plained of the unpredictable nature of Indigenous interactions with an-cient remains: "The praetorium, open to all coming, haunted by the Arabs and their flocks, exposed to the brutality of ignorance or to the profana-tion of fanaticism offered but uncertain asylum to the objects which were entrusted to it."[186] His sentiments were shared, no doubt, by many other French arrivals in Algeria who distrusted the continuing presence of Arabs and Kabyles in the Aurès Mountains and sought to discredit their engage-ment with ancient ruins and thus any legitimate or long-standing claim to a heritage based in this region.

As we have seen in this survey of French (and, through them, Indig-enous) interactions with Lambaesis from the mid-1840s to the early 1850s and beyond, French officers and civilians actively involved in the conquest of Algeria relied heavily on the touchstone of Rome for a variety of practi-cal and ideological purposes. This convention, which implicated archaeo-logical research in the mechanisms of the French conquest, superficially concealed deep ills in both the French metropolitan and colonial appara-tus. The finds made at Lambaesis helped the French construct an alterna-tive history of the conquest, one written for fellow Frenchmen more than anyone else. Through their interactions with the ruins of the camps of the Third Augustan Legion, French witnesses proclaimed themselves the heirs of the Romans, and as such they followed a path they believed to have been ordained for them as the Romans' worthy successors.

Shortly after visiting Lambaesis in May 1850, Saint-Arnaud wrote to his brother of his encounters with Roman antiquities: "I have already seen ruins in Greece, Italy, Asia, but they impressed me less. Perhaps my admiration for Antiquity was less developed, because I reflected on them little; perhaps too I find the ruins more worthy of attention as I bring myself closer to them? These enormous secular stones that have remained standing in the midst of storms and the destruction of worlds express a very poetic and deep language."[187] In the hands of French officers like Saint-Arnaud, sites like Lambaesis conveyed the timelessness of the activity of conquest. In the midst of a savage war, the "destruction of worlds" to which Saint-Arnaud referred, perhaps such remains gave French military officers license for their brutality, and relieved any possible misgivings they had about their involvement in them.

Others had a different perspective of Lambaesis shaped by personal travail. Terson hoped that the ancient Roman past might also offer a source of redemption for French colonists:

> If the echo of the desert could carry my voice
> To the temple of laws,
> I would pray that the Solons of our dear France,
> Transform this place of penitence
> Into a hall of rest for our valiant settlers,
> Whitened in the furrows
> And the rough labors which Triptolemus teaches;[188]
> And there, under the gaze of Asclepius himself,
> These noble laborers
> Would lift both their arms and their hearts to the heavens
> To bless their country
> And the last breath of their spirit moved
> Like the last sound of a harmonious lute,
> Would rise into the celestial regions.[189]

Fully engaged in the patriotism of the French mission in Algeria, and the role it played in the future of metropolitan France, Terson imagined an idealized and blessed Lambaesis that belied the harsh conditions of the penitentiary in which he was unjustly held during his exile. It was there that France would inherit the true legacy of ancient Rome.

As a whole, French interactions with the Roman past at Lambaesis—whether performed by copying inscriptions, excavating ancient temples, or honoring Roman war dead—made it easier to envision the colonial mission as triumphant. This glory, however, could be grasped only through an embrace of an alternative reality, one that required not just the physical but the historical removal of the Indigenous people from the landscape of Lambaesis. By suggesting or accepting that the Chaouïa of the Aurès were the descendants of the Vandals, the alleged destroyers of Roman civilization in North Africa, French officers and scholars erased living links to the Roman ruins. In this colonial context, classical archaeology telescoped time and robbed the Indigenous population familiar with these sites of agency in their past and present. While most French officers' archaeological interventions at Lambaesis may have been incidental, they were far from innocent: Carbuccia, Saint-Arnaud, and Desvaux, among others, gained a distinct advantage through carefully orchestrated encounters with monuments of the Third Augustan Legion. The same site gave Terson hope for the future improvement of not just the colony but metropolitan France. As recounted in the next chapter on the military and civilian colonists of Algeria during the 1850s, the entanglement of French activities with ancient Roman monuments suggested that Lambaesis and many other classical sites constituted far more than footnotes in the French "pacification" and settlement of Algeria.

Chapter 4

Institutionalizing Algerian Archaeology

With the calamitous events of the 1848 Revolution, some of the predicted aftereffects of the Algerian conquest and colonization came home to roost in metropolitan France.[1] During the uprising in Paris, Maréchal Thomas-Robert Bugeaud, General Franciade Fleurus Duvivier, and other veterans of the Algerian conquest had now returned to France and were charged with commanding the National Guard. Armed in the streets of Paris, they unleashed the brutal tactics they had used against Arabs and Kabyles in Algeria and turned them against French citizens.[2] Despite public outcry against violent policing in a metropolitan context, however, French confidence wavered little as to their right to settle Algeria and the benefit of their mission to share "human progress" with its Indigenous inhabitants.[3] Moreover, following the June insurrection in Paris, authorities decided to transport and resettle nearly fourteen thousand French citizens fleeing unrest in the metropolitan capital to the Algerian colony, which in December 1848 was incorporated into France as the departments of Oran, Algiers, and Constantine. As recounted by Michael Heffernan, these erstwhile colonists were, for the most part, urban poor from Paris and the arrondissement of Saint-Denis to its north. The ill-prepared families that journeyed to North Africa late that year had little choice as to where they might reside or what kind of livelihood they might undertake: the newly appointed Governor-General Viala Charon selected forty-two sites recently emptied of their residents for French settlements scattered across Algeria's three provinces. Many of these lands were neither suitable for agricultural pursuits nor legally in the possession of the French state. Not only did the impoverished French arrivals encounter inadequate housing and a cholera outbreak in 1849, but they faced brutal French military oversight and the stark realities of agricultural life in Algeria. Most of the volunteers who survived this disastrous social experiment returned either to France or fled to one of Algeria's urban centers.[4]

Although few of these unlucky migrants remained in the agricultural settlements beyond 1852, other European colonists quickly took their place and accounted for an overall increase of close to ten thousand European civilians in the Algerian colony.[5] Improved ease of travel to the region helped support the growing number of civilian immigrants. Writing of his travels to North Africa in the mid-1850s, Joseph Bard, an archaeologist and inspector of historical monuments from eastern France who traveled to the region, described transport between Marseilles and the ports of Stora (near Philippeville), Algiers, and Mers-el-Kébir (near Oran) as safe, dependable, and fast. Civilians could purchase tickets for the same liners as military personnel and functionaries, who journeyed to and from their duties in the colony free of charge.[6] Late in the 1860s, French authorities laid the first steel track in Algeria and established a railroad network that significantly facilitated travel in the region within the coming generation.[7] However, in the years before the establishment of the Third Republic, the port of Algiers was not freely accessible to private companies, and contemporaries noted that much potential business was lost to the Ottoman-controlled ports of Tunis, Tangiers, and Tripoli. In the 1850s and 1860s, the service offered by commercial vessels sailing between Toulon and Tunis; Alexandria, Malta, and Tunis; and Palermo and Tunis represented accessible and dependable alternatives for civilian transport and trade.[8]

Most settlers bound for Algeria headed not for rural areas but cities. In the 1850s, the composition of the city of Algiers' population of just over one hundred thousand included over 67 percent European nationals. As documented by Julia Clancy-Smith, fewer than half of these immigrants were French citizens (including those from Corsica), with others arriving in the Algerian capital from Sicily, Sardinia, Malta, the Balearic and Greek islands, and Spain.[9] The remaining third of Algiers's residents were indigenous Muslims, Jews, and "Nègres" (circa 25 percent), and "undocumented" individuals (10 percent), the last an ill-defined category that included refugees, sailors who had abandoned ship, the indigent, and criminals.[10]

Although many regions of the French colony of Algeria were no longer in an active state of war following the final departure of Governor-General Bugeaud for metropolitan France in July 1846, his wartime policies and land confiscations widened the gulf considerably between Arab and Kabyle residents and French and European immigrants in Algeria.[11] Stereotypes of non-Europeans in the military-governed colony hardened, and European residents and visitors, as in previous decades, continued to compare Muslim inhabitants unfavorably with those of European stock.[12] Bard, who journeyed across North Africa in 1854, alleged matter-of-factly that Indigenous Algerians remained unchanged from their ancient, primitive state:

> In arriving in Africa, the French will find there indigenous people such as those the Romans themselves had found, [and] such as those that these latter conquerors had found in ancient Gaul, where they encountered dispersed tribes, fortresses, markets, and few centers. The peoples all resembled a certain phase and given epoch of history, and the large veil (*haïck*) or the heavy robes (*burnous*) of the Arabs are not different, nearly the same color, as the Gallic mantle (*sagum gallicum*) of our rough ancestors. . . . Between [the Roman] epoch and the conquest by French arms, the Arabs did not take any steps toward civilization.[13]

His attribution of developments in the region to the Roman period rather than any technological or intellectual achievements on the part of the Arab and Kabyle populations in the intervening centuries, was symptomatic of attitudes shaped by imperial and orientalist bias. This teleological approach supported the economic prerogatives of the colonial regime.[14]

Nonetheless, after decades of conflict in the colony, many military and civilian administrators questioned the efficacy of current approaches to pacifying the Indigenous population. Keeping close tabs on the shifting demographics of the colony, Parisian authorities concluded that the number of residents of European origin in some urban zones was substantial enough to merit altering their status from *zones mixtes* to *zones civiles*. In September 1847, the governor-general created municipal councils in six population centers with substantial enough proportions of European settlers to warrant the application of civil law: these included the districts of Algiers, Blida, Oran, Mostaganem, Bône, and Philippeville. At the same time, the officers of the Bureaux arabes, the still modest but powerful administrative structure that managed the Muslim populations outside the *zones civiles*, shed light on the consequences of the colonial regime's decimation of the leadership in Indigenous communities.[15] Consequently, in the late 1840s, French administrators ended the so-called assimilationist policies that had left the Muslim population extremely vulnerable to land confiscations by French settlers. On the whole, however, administrative policies of the 1850s following the integration of the three French departments of Oran, Algiers, and Constantine, enforced more formal separation between European arrivals and Muslim and Jewish populations of Algeria. They further entrenched the segregation of the Indigenous population from settlers by expanding French control over Muslim institutions and residents in the fields of law, education, economic activities, and religious affairs.[16]

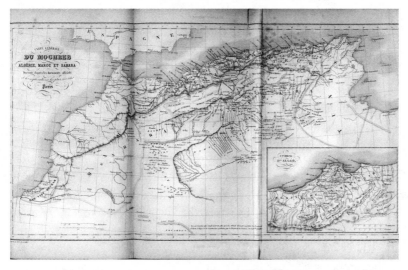

Figure 28. Map of Algeria showing increasingly dense occupation by the French; it was drawn by Pierre Christian in 1846. Pierre Christian, *L'Afrique française, l'empire de Maroc et les déserts de Sahara* (Paris: A. Barbier, 1846).

By contrast, although detailed demographic statistics are lacking for this period, it is thought that rural areas of Algeria, which had been sustained for centuries by subsistence agriculture, were inhabited mainly by Arabs and Kabyles. About a third of these residents were sedentary, village-dwelling Kabyles who lived from farming. The rest of the nonurban population consisted mainly of nomadic and pastoral Arab tribes. French arrivals thus encountered a land that, at least in their eyes, was not systematically exploited. Moreover, much of the land was held communally rather than individually.[17] Historians have estimated that during the 1840s, the number of French and European colonists in Algeria grew from roughly twenty-seven thousand to one-hundred-twenty-six thousand, and these immigrants created pressure and encroached on tribal lands.[18] Under the leadership of Governor-General Maréchal Jacques-Louis Randon from 1851 to 1857, French authorities therefore increased protections of Arab- and Berber-held lands to prevent their wholesale acquisition by European colonists and sought to strengthen tribal institutions. Yet, although the conclusion of military operations in the region of Kabylia in July 1857 reduced the overall extent of the activity of the armée d'Afrique in the colony, the expansion of the authority of civil administrators and the legal measures instituted by the colonial regime did little to improve the conditions in which Algeria's Indigenous residents lived and died.[19]

Indeed, these measures may have been too late to help restore the damage already done in the two previous decades. John Ruedy has calculated that by 1852, French and European settlers controlled over 158,721 hectares of beylik land—property previously controlled directly by the Ottoman beys—in the three Algerian provinces. Colonists' heightened demands for agricultural land and pasturage, which they could not procure easily on their own, pushed French administrators to resort to harsh policies like *refoulement*, the displacement of Muslim residents, *resserrement sur place*, the forced concentration of Indigenous habitants, and *cantonnement* or containment, by which the French dispossessed the Muslim population of their "surplus" lands. The fact that those who seized land illegally could be prosecuted only with great difficulty emboldened the perpetrators of such activities: the colony's punitive legal apparatus made it nearly impossible for Indigenous residents to appeal the appropriation of their lands by European offenders.[20]

With the intensification of the French policy of cantonnement in the 1850s, the armée d'Afrique and civilian colonists undermined the nomadic and pastoral economy of local tribes by restricting their movement and confiscating their most fertile lands.[21] Despite these advantages, European settlers were nonetheless impatient with the colonial administration. They demanded still greater access to agricultural land, liberty to govern the colony as they wished, and freedom to dominate the Arab and Kabyle inhabitants with little governmental oversight.[22] By 1856, the number of colonists of European origin was roughly one-hundred-seventy thousand as compared to 2.3 million resident Algerian Arabs, Kabyles, and Jews. Most colonists of European descent were concentrated in urban centers like Algiers, Oran, and Bône, and only about 5 percent lived under military rule.[23] However, European landholding continued to increase. Between 1850 and 1870, the amount of land under their control expanded from 115,000 to 765,000 hectares. Very little of this land, perhaps less than one-third, was actively cultivated.[24]

Protecting Algeria's Monuments from Civilian Settlers

Making note of the rapid increase in the number of civilian arrivals in Algeria by 1847, nine-tenths of whom lived in urban zones, the French consul of Sousse (Regency of Tunis), Edmond Pellissier de Reynaud, who had previously served as director of Indigenous affairs in Algeria and as a member of the Commission d'exploration scientifique d'Algérie (1839–1842), characterized the Algerian colony as being affected negatively by land speculation. Metropolitan French interests were rapidly acquiring land in Algeria despite the fact that the colony, up until that time, had proved itself a net importer and consumer rather than an exporter. Pellissier de Reynaud also complained that urban development was being undertaken with little forethought or planning. In particular, he drew attention to many Europeans' preference to reside in the province of Constantine rather than distributing themselves more evenly across the colony.[25] This trend also indicated that a disproportionate number of new arrivals were heading to the most monuments-rich region of the territory. Consequently, as the engines of construction shifted to meet settlement needs, the armée d'Afrique perhaps no longer constituted the greatest threat to ancient sites: it was now civilian colonists.[26] Pellissier de Reynaud and his contemporaries wrote with greater concern about the impact of their growing numbers on Roman antiquities than on the Indigenous population.

Noting the danger of the influx of settlers for ancient monuments, Bard likewise observed during his journey in the mid-1850s that many Algerian locations had substantial Roman ruins; he described Philippeville as a land "tattooed with Roman debris" and remarked that the site had significant interest for Roman history.[27] He similarly noted the visible imprint of Roman architectural mores on French military engineers, who modeled their own structures after the solidity of classical architecture. Because these ancient monuments linked modern arrivals in a physical way to the soil of their newly acquired land in Algeria, Bard concluded that it was of utmost importance that they be preserved. New cultural institutions were necessary to support the colonial enterprise.[28]

In 1849, an anonymous author, no doubt one of the editors, published a notice in the last pages of the *Revue archéologique*, metropolitan France's premier journal for archaeology founded in 1844. He alleged that the articles recently published on the monuments of Algeria, and particularly those located in the province of Constantine, were attracting colonists to sites built by the ancient Romans. Rather than learning important lessons from these remains about how to govern the region, colonists in Algeria, he insisted, were driven foremost by the desire to advance themselves personally. They established their homes in locations the Romans had demonstrated suitable for projecting their power over the region. The author cautioned:

> Let us hope that the numerous and majestic ruins that cover this beautiful land and prove its ancient splendor, will be respected as much as possible by the new inhabitants of these regions, and that, when necessary, authorities will come with the help of the quarries that one finds in this territory. By making available to colonists the materials that are necessary, they will not be obliged, in the course of building their homes, to destroy the Roman ruins, which [if left intact] will attract more and more travelers and will be one of the sources of wealth for the colony.[29]

Although it is unlikely that many European colonists were avid readers of the *Revue archéologique*, this scholar's concerns reveal that at least some French thinkers recognized the threat posed to Roman antiquities by steady streams of civilians ambitious to profit from their new surroundings. Lured by the promise of fertile land, European settlers were, like the armée d'Afrique, in search of accessible building materials, especially cut stone, to facilitate the construction of their homes. In comparison to the destruction occasioned by military officials in the early years of the conquest, which were justified by the desperate conditions of the war, most contemporaries thought that the damage that civilian colonists exacted on ancient monuments was far less defensible.[30]

In 1858, the journalist Charles Nozeran observed the relevance of ancient remains to the modern colony of Algeria. While in Cherchel, he noted that the ruins of Roman Julia Caesarea lay less than half a meter under the modern city. He was struck, however, by the blunt indifference with which businessmen and industrialists conducted their daily affairs despite their proximity to the past. They had little appreciation of the remains they encountered whenever they sunk a well, laid the foundation of a new building, or cleared their fields.[31] As Nozeran reminded his readers, all these monuments were signs of the ancient glory of a city that possibly rivaled Rome and Carthage. Although these abandoned remains called out for excavation and conservation measures, he complained of the muted and ineffective reaction of officials to their continuing destruction. In 1856, such frustrations led Adrien Berbrugger to urge his readers to recognize that "on the path that France finds itself engaged, knowledge of Roman organization in North Africa is no longer an archaeological curiosity for the exclusive use of scholars: it is a useful, retrospective lesson in which the past can furnish practical indications for the present time."[32]

The settlement schemes envisioned by Bugeaud in the 1840s valued the classical past uncritically for the examples of colonization it offered French administrators. However, by the 1850s and 1860s, some archaeologists were willing to critique classical models more readily than they had in earlier decades. They observed, for instance, that ancient examples were not always suited to French objectives, particularly if it was evident that certain Roman strategies had not worked to the benefit of the empire. This approach might thus be understood as a greater commitment to the success of the colonial enterprise, especially now that the three Algerian regions were officially integrated into metropolitan France as administrative departments. For instance, in September 1851, in his geographical study of Tlemcen (A. Tlemsen) in the province of Oran, Oscar MacCarthy suggested that a comparison between the French and Roman regimes showed that a central weakness of Roman rule had been its policy of absorbing the Indigenous population.[33] French scholars and administrators thus recognized the Roman model as fallible and encouraged colonial administrators to avoid "servile imitation" of the Roman example; the colonial regime could not afford to follow its ancient model blindly as it pursued mastery of the land now under occupation.[34] There is no question that greater flexibility in the interpretation of the ancient past helped justify the appropriation of not just ancient ruins and agricultural lands but now also forests, including cork concessions.[35] Despite the increasing number of archaeological and epigraphical studies of the Roman past, some military and civilian administrators consciously turned their back on ancient structures and practices and forged a new path forward.

Closely related to this more aggressive approach to land tenure was the claim of French administrators and settlers that the Arab and Kabyle populations had historically treated the natural resources of Algeria with little respect. Namely, as European settlers challenged policies protecting the property of the Indigenous population in the 1850s, they looked to ancient texts and monuments to allege that the desert landscape of their own time contrasted with the fertility of the land in classical antiquity as described by Roman authors.[36] Although French authorities and colonists did not actively deploy this ideological narrative until the 1870s, it cast a long shadow on activities in the territory.[37] Only recently have scholars like Brent Shaw and Jean-Louis Ballais challenged such long-held views and demonstrated that the impact of intensive agricultural exploitation of the Maghreb was far greater during the Roman period. In fact, the deforestation of Algeria was more severe during the 130 years of French colonial occupation than it had been during all of the intervening centuries of Arab pastoralism.[38]

As we have seen, however, any deference that French military and civilian authorities displayed toward the historical legacy of ancient Rome did not necessarily translate into respectful treatment of its physical remains. When French authorities began to question the relevance of ancient narratives to the present and suggested that they did not offer the right path forward, classical Roman monuments fared no better, and perhaps even worse, than before. We thus turn now to a discussion of the way in which individual advocates of the conservation of Algeria's ancient past persevered and took on the project of creating archaeological infrastructure in the absence of active governmental intervention. Expertise gained during these undertakings allowed French military and civilian settlers in Algeria to take the first steps toward professionalizing archaeological practice in the colony.

Metropolitan Expertise and the International Race for Antiquities

In 1842, the minister of public instruction created the Service des voyages et missions scientifiques et littéraires, which, from 1843, possessed a budget of 112,000 francs to be used for scientific exploration abroad.[39] Although these funds were not often granted to archaeologists working in the Maghreb, support for archaeological endeavors expanded under the presidency of Louis-Napoleon Bonaparte and, following his coup in December 1851, Napoleon III's Second Empire. Indeed, structural developments in metropolitan France steadily allowed new resources and attention to flow to archaeological endeavors, still often based on the initiative of individuals, both on the continent and overseas. Although the École française d'Athènes was founded in 1846, Ève and Jean Gran-Aymerich have pointed to the significance of the year 1850, when Louis-Napoleon turned over the institution's intellectual leadership to the Académie des inscriptions et belles-lettres. This adjustment allowed for the establishment of a scientific program in archaeology, philology, and history that bore fruit for classical archaeology in subsequent decades.[40] Members of the École française like Jules Girard, Alexandre Bertrand, Charles-Ernest Beulé, Alfred Mézières, and Léon Heuzey all participated in missions to various parts of Greece at the start of their influential careers.[41]

The mid-nineteenth century was an exciting time for French archaeology abroad, with news reaching the metropole of Paul-Émile Botta's exploration of the palace complex of the Assyrian king Sargon II in the northern Mesopotamian village of Khorsabad during the waning years of Louis-Philippe (1843–1846), and Auguste Mariette's more successfully disseminated excavations at the Serapeum of Saqqara, Egypt (1851).[42] Despite these exciting developments, the French faced significant uncertainty due to fierce rivalry with Britain in imperial and archaeological endeavors. As European competition to collect classical antiquities for display in imperial galleries gathered steam in the 1850s, European elites not only physically controlled antiquities but also possessed the intellectual authority to integrate them into new systems of meaning and power in which they were entangled.[43] French involvement in the Crimean War, for instance, offered officers the opportunity to claim that their activities connected them to the ancient Greeks. It was British military transport vessels, however, that moved antiquities from the region. The little that was left in situ rather than being shipped to the British Museum was destroyed by participants in the conflict.[44]

Closer to their colonial possessions, the French also encountered fraught competition over antiquities. French academicians expressed concern over the threat posed by German philologists like Heinrich Barth, who traversed North Africa from Morocco to Egypt between 1845 and 1847. He participated in an English expedition to the interior of Africa (1850–1855) that included documentation of Roman sites in the Ottoman Regency of Tripoli. These pressures from rivals spurred the first French attempts to explore the region. In 1847, the dragoman-chancellor of the French Consulate General of Tripoli, Joseph Vattier de Bourville, was sponsored to undertake a two-year mission to Benghazi and Cyrenaica, where he engaged in the study of ancient inscriptions, numismatics, and marbles.[45] These activities were followed by the arrival of two British naval lieutenants, Robert Murdoch Smith and Edward Augustus Porcher, who spent nearly eleven months excavating and collecting antiquities of Cyrenaica in 1861. Their stay was productive and resulted in the yield of two shipments of antiquities, which were transported to the British Museum in June and October by HMS *Assurance* and HMS *Melpomene*, respectively.[46] Similarly, in Carthage in the 1850s, the British Foreign Office funded Nathan Davis's excavations (1856–1859) so as to enrich the British Museum with anticipated finds.[47] In 1859, Charles-Ernest Beulé's arrival in the Regency of Tunis and his allegedly self-financed excavations helped the French counter the work of this perceived interloper, whom the French archaeologist accused of lacking necessary appreciation for the architectural context of his finds to be effective.[48]

The epigraphical career of Léon Renier, who was then serving as the deputy librarian at the Sorbonne, also reveals how Algeria fit into the increasingly competitive international antiquities race in the 1850s. Due to infighting between the Ministry of Public Instruction, the Académie des

Figure 29. Portrait of Léon Renier (1809–1885), member of the Institut de France, by Eugène Pirou (1884–1886). Photograph: Gerard Blot. Reproduced by permission of the Institut de France. © RMN-Grand Palais/Art Resource, NY.

inscriptions et belles-lettres, and the Ministry of War, the French were relatively late to involve themselves in large-scale, collaborative projects to catalogue inscriptions.[49] In 1849, however, members of the Académie des inscriptions et belles-lettres received reports from Alphonse Delamare and Jean-Luc Carbuccia about the multitude of antiquities accessible at Lambaesis and in its vicinity. With the threats posed by military activities and planned construction of a penitentiary on the archaeological site, and no doubt the rapid inroads being made by contemporary German philologists and epigraphers, there was plenty of incentive for Renier to develop an epigraphical project in Algeria. In July 1850, Renier thus appealed successfully to the minister of public instruction to allow him to go on an individual mission to Lambaesis to document the important inscriptions in the region. As he reminded the minister, it was France's moral obligation to allow scholars to study the documents that might shed light on Algeria. Because the members of the academic mission of 1839 had been forced to return to France with greater haste than anticipated in 1842, they had not been able to visit the most important parts of the former Ottoman Beylik of Constantine from the perspective of archaeology and epigraphy.[50]

According to Renier, despite the danger posed by ongoing military activities in Algeria to civilian-scholars, the time was ripe to proceed, particularly because Lambaesis was menaced by destruction.[51] Although Armand Leroy de Saint-Arnaud, following a visit to Lambaesis in May 1850, had succeeded in shifting the location of the planned penitentiary from the center to the periphery of the site, Renier informed the minister of war that he feared greatly for the well-being of the thousands of inscriptions known to be present there. He insisted that an expert in the newest methods of epigraphy was needed to examine this rich archive of the Roman army in North Africa, and he volunteered to take responsibility in person for the critical project.[52] His mission to Algeria became a turning point in his rising career. It also contributed to reviving France's reputation in the field of epigraphy, although German scholarship ultimately came to the fore in the 1860s under the leadership of Theodor Mommsen.[53]

In September 1850, Renier received a favorable response from the minister of war, who granted authorization for a mission sponsored by the minister of public instruction. The minister of war's approval of Renier's request stemmed at least in part from the desire to quell criticism of the still largely incomplete publications of the Commission de l'exploration scientifique d'Algérie.[54] The minister not only gave him permission to travel into the military zone and transcribe inscriptions at Lambaesis and nearby locations but also provided him with the guidance and artistic services of Major Alphonse Delamare, who already knew the site well. The latter had considerable skills in drawing ancient monuments which once again proved useful.[55] Delamare's familiarity with Lambaesis also allowed Renier to comprehend the extent of the French army's devastation of its monuments in the course of just a few years. His presence, and that of some of the officers stationed at the site, gave urgency to the task of measuring, transcribing, and drawing thousands of inscriptions: "I had hardly arrived at the camp, but before I settled into my lodging, I went to find my friend M. Toussaint, captain of the corps of engineers responsible for constructing the prison. I did not want to delay informing him about my discoveries, in which I knew that he had great interest. . . . He received this request with his ordinary benevolence, a thing for which I was then, and still remain today, extremely grateful."[56] Although their mission was initially intended to last just three months from the time of their arrival in November 1850, Renier and Delamare asked for and received an extension until April 1851, owing to the large quantity of unique material they were uncovering and documenting in advance of the penitentiary's construction.[57]

Renier's expertise in identifying errors in earlier transcriptions of inscriptions made it possible to create more accurate records of these threatened sources. Since traditional historical sources were relatively limited on this topic, the inscriptions constituted the main source of new evidence about the Third Augustan Legion and its labors in North Africa.[58] Although deep snow and lack of sufficient housing forced Renier to stop his work at Lambaesis during part of the winter, this interlude gave him an excuse to explore the nearby Sahara for evidence of the extent of Roman military presence in the region.[59] Despite delays caused by the weather, by the end of his first visit to Algeria, Renier had copied more than 1,600 inscriptions from Lambaesis and nearby ancient Roman sites like Verecunda and Thamugadis (F. Timgad). He also assembled information about another 1,500 inscriptions collected by Delamare and a host of French officers of an antiquarian bent stationed in the region.[60] Following a brief second visit to Lambaesis in August 1852, the crowning achievement of Renier's labors was the publication of this raw data, namely 4,417 individual inscriptions or fragments thereof, in *Inscriptions romaines de l'Algérie* (1855).[61] For the most part, the work ignored the other ancient monuments found in the vicinity.[62] The wealth of inscriptions transcribed at Lambaesis, and the personal details they revealed about the workings of the Third Augustan Legion, shaped subsequent classical scholarship on the Roman army not only in North Africa but around the Mediterranean.[63]

The privileging of epigraphy over archaeological remains was not unique to Renier.[64] The very large number of Latin inscriptions from North Africa meant that epigraphy constituted a distinctive feature of Algerian archaeology from its earliest days, and it continues to dominate historical understanding of classical North Africa.[65] However, the significance of these written reminders of the Roman inhabitants of the region offered much more than historical evidence: in the eyes of men like Renier and Adrien Berbrugger, founder of the Bibliothèque et Musée d'Alger, they represented title to the territory. As recounted by Renier, when Berbrugger encountered the tribes of the Beni-Mzab, Berbrugger alleged that local leaders tried to prevent him from seeing what they described as Arab ruins. Berbrugger, who believed them to be Roman in origin, understood this attempt to deny him access to the remains as a conscious effort to stymie French hegemony in the territory.[66] At least in the eyes of French scholars, Latin inscriptions constituted essential evidence of French claims to be the heirs of the ancient Roman conquerors of North Africa.

Renier's success in transcribing the written evidence found at Lambaesis and other nearby ancient locations was praised enthusiastically by his contemporaries in France and buoyed the impressive trajectory of his professional career in Paris. In Berlin, Mommsen, too, considered Renier's work meritworthy. In 1866, he sought to enlist Renier's cooperation in the Berlin-based project known as the *Corpus inscriptionum latinarum (CIL)* by reporting on the epigraphy of Algeria and Gaul once an agreement between the academies of Berlin and Paris made collaboration possible.[67] Renier's participation in the project was interrupted irrevocably, however, by the Franco-Prussian War of 1870–1871, after which he ceased working with the Akademie der Wissenschaften in Berlin on patriotic grounds. Renier formally resigned in February 1872.[68] His career-long accomplishments nonetheless helped expand the popularity of Roman epigraphy in metropolitan France, which up till then had largely been focused on Italy and southern Gaul to the exclusion of other parts of the Roman world.[69]

The long-term legacy of Renier's work in Algeria, however, was uneven. With unfettered access to the Latin inscriptions of the military colony of Algeria, the French had enjoyed an overwhelming scholarly advantage. The minister of war's control of which civilians and foreign nationals might enter the military colony and where they could travel meant that French academics had little to fear from German or British competition.

However, military rule exacted a high cost on the antiquities; as discussed above, French military engineers and soldiers did not share Renier's and Berbrugger's reverence or respect for ancient inscriptions. Within twenty years, many of the epigraphical remains Renier had transcribed no longer existed outside of the facsimiles in his publication. The productive relations that had existed between French and German philologists in past decades reached an all-time low in the 1870s.[70]

Following Renier's withdrawal from work on the *CIL*, Mommsen sent his former student and then professor at the University of Strasbourg, the German epigrapher Gustav Wilmanns, to Algeria and Tunisia in March 1873. His mission was to catalogue North African inscriptions for the eighth volume of the *CIL*.[71] Consequently, his presence in the French colony also allowed him to see firsthand the devastation that had been wrought by military and colonial activity. As reported by Wilmanns, who died prematurely in 1878 before the publication of the North African *CIL* volume, the level of vandalism at Lambaesis was deplorable. Of the thousands of inscriptions published by Renier in 1855, only half were still extant, the others being plundered for construction projects of the armée d'Afrique.[72] Wilmanns also publicly complained of the dearth of French epigraphical competence, deficiencies in their protection of antiquities, and the lack of scholarly courtesies displayed in the colony, the last of which, as Renier pointed out, was no doubt caused in part by Wilmanns's university appointment in annexed French territory.[73]

The fate suffered by these inscriptions suggests that ancient remains were of lesser import to French philologists once they had been accurately transcribed and published. However, Renier's sojourn in the Aurès mountains caused him to think differently. He argued that stone inscriptions were essential physical proof of the rightful establishment of a French colony in Algeria. As mentioned above, Renier suggested that France's best claim to the region could be made through the language of epigraphy, and in an oft-cited passage he argued:

Roman monuments, especially the inscriptions, are in the eyes of the Arabs our most legitimate title to the possession of Algeria. During my stay in Zana, the sheik of the country and a venerated marabout Si Mohammed Bokarana, came one day and found me among the ruins. I copied an inscription: "You understand this writing?" he asked. I responded, "Not only do

I understand, but I can write it; look: these are our letters, this is our language." He responded by addressing the Arabs who accompanied him, "It is true; the *Roumis* are the sons of the *Roumâns*;[74] when they took this land, they were simply taking back the property of their fathers."[75]

Although the account was probably apocryphal, Renier used it to allege a direct connection between the French and the Romans, one claimed by the French and—more improbably—recognized by the Indigenous peoples.[76] In this view, ancient Latin inscriptions found in abundance at Lambaesis pointedly excluded Arabs and Kabyles from sharing any connection to a Roman heritage.[77] Moreover, Renier proposed that they were unimpeachable evidence of the transmission of the conqueror's mantle from the Romans to the French, a notion that he unabashedly claimed was widely accepted by the Indigenous inhabitants of Algeria.[78]

From his experience at Lambaesis, Renier learned firsthand of the ephemeral nature of archaeological remains unearthed during military maneuvers and colonial settlement. Given that neither the French civil nor military authorities were willing to invest heavily in the study or conservation of the antiquities of Algeria, he recognized that encouraging involvement by volunteers was crucial to the success of documenting what would otherwise be lost. In 1859, this sentiment no doubt led to Renier's publication of a short instructional manual. In it, he observed the multiple benefits of preserving Roman antiquities, which offered a starting point for settlers to identify with the territory in addition to representing a future source of economic growth:

There is no doubt that one wants to reproduce the same phenomenon [of conservation] there [in all Algerian cities], by which archaeological studies will not be the only things to profit, it is permitted to remark, but also matters of political importance. Indeed, it [the preservation of monuments] is an index of the development of municipal mores, [and] of the birth of love of the local country, the lack of which is one of the principal maladies of the new colonies. These cities will thereby be endowed, in a few years and almost without cost, with institutions of which they can be proud, and which, in attracting travelers to them, as do the cities of the south of France with ancient monuments and collections of the same type that one has created there, will contribute to some degree to the development of their prosperity.[79]

For military officers and civilian settlers interested in recording or excavating the antiquity-rich territory of Algeria, Renier offered guidance on how to identify potentially fruitful locations, transcribe inscriptions, and preserve and publish antiquities.

Although the work is considerably less well known today than his publication of the inscriptions from Lambaesis and surrounding sites, Renier's manual specifically encouraged amateur enthusiasts with the advice that they did not need significant resources to undertake valuable archaeological projects. Different from the more collaborative, professionalized approach to epigraphy that would be engineered by Mommsen later in the century (a feature of *Großwissenschaft*), Renier maintained that archaeology could be practiced successfully with the support of just five or six workers armed with iron levers and spades or shovels.[80] Although he reserved interpretive work for those with advanced skills, readers of his manual learned how to preserve the inscriptions they found by creating molded paper squeezes and marble rubbings. Once collected, these materials would allow more accomplished epigraphers to read them firsthand, free of the errors introduced during inexpert transcriptions.[81]

A final aspect of Renier's brief sojourn in Algeria in the early 1850s was his effort to move valuable artifacts from Lambaesis to metropolitan France. The seizure of ancient monuments in Algeria (and in Tunisia, following the creation of the French Protectorate in 1881) has been studied less well than those of Egypt and the Middle East.[82] However, French colonial officials in Algeria had a relatively easy time laying claim to artifacts in a context in which property law was not yet well established.[83] The main impediments to taking these objects back to France were the expense and logistics of transporting heavy pieces of stone in a region where roads were poor, waterways distant, and railways still nonexistent.[84] For this reason, the number of items slated for overseas removal remained comparatively small and consisted largely of sculpture. However, as the constituency of civilian colonists grew, so did calls for keeping archaeological remains in Algerian museums such as those of Algiers and Constantine.[85]

In 1851, before returning to France, Renier ambitiously recommended that a number of marble busts, epigraphical monuments, and a mosaic he had studied in the region of Batna be transported to the Louvre.[86] As a critic of the destruction of ancient monuments, he expressed in this stance his belief that moving the pieces to metropolitan France was necessary for their protection and conservation. Renier likewise thought that this arrangement would better support their study by formally trained scholars, who would thereby have ease of access to the most important pieces.[87] He also

Figure 30. Inscription of the Third Augustan Legion paying hommage to the Severan emperors, dated August 22, 202. Musée du Louvre, Paris. Photograph: Thierry. © Musée du Louvre, Dist. RMN-Grand Palais/Art Resource, NY.

attempted to arrange the shipment of several key inscriptions related to the Third Augustan Legion to the Bibliothèque nationale, where he intended them to "display to citizens and strangers this inestimable trophy of French arms."[88] Although he received a one-time credit of 1,000 francs for the conservation of antiquities at Lambaesis,[89] neither the minister of war nor the minister of the interior was willing to pay for the cost of the transport of ponderous stone monuments to Paris, especially if they lacked the aesthetic attractions of more finely sculpted marble.[90] Indeed, only one inscription from Renier's trip to Algeria appears to have successfully made its way to the Louvre in the 1850s: a key piece dedicated to the Tribune of the Imperial Officer's Guard of the Third Augustan Legion.[91]

After ministerial authorities declined to provide additional funding for the preservation of the inscriptions of Lambaesis, Renier turned for help to the aforementioned Captain Toussaint, who commanded the engineering detachment from Batna responsible for directing the construction of the penitentiary. In a desperate measure to spare the most important inscriptions from destruction as the work began in the spring of 1851, Toussaint came up with the ingenious and inexpensive solution of embedding them facing outward in the wall of the prison.[92] He mounted another 109 in the walls of the structure housing the engineering office.[93] In 1874, more than thirty years after Renier's work at Lambaesis, Antoine Héron de Villefosse, at the urging of his mentor, was at last able to ship fifteen crates of antiquities from Lambaesis to France, including many busts still on display in the Louvre today.[94] By this time, however, it was too late to save many of the inscriptions originally recorded and recommended for export by Renier since they had been destroyed or incorporated into French military construction projects.

Officers and Archaeological Societies

Military and civilian advocates like Karl Benedikt Hase had long cautioned that the conservation of ancient Roman monuments required more substantive actions than improvised and uncoordinated efforts by French military officers who lacked the capacity to be the long-term guardians of such sites.[95] In 1845, in response to complaints about the widespread demolition of Roman structures in the Algerian territory during the expansionary regime of Governor-General Bugeaud, the minister of war appointed Charles Texier as the first inspector general of civil structures.[96] Texier spent the next three years producing a report on extant monuments for the minister of war.[97] His tenure, however, seems to have had little noticeable impact on the pace of destruction of ancient sites by the armée d'Afrique, which confiscated ancient remains as building materiel during the protracted conflict.[98] No effective legislative mandate allowed Texier to safeguard archaeological sites or regulate the excavations undertaken by either French officers or civilian residents.[99]

Archaeological enthusiasts in both metropolitan France and Algeria therefore continued to petition French authorities to grant Roman remains special status due to their unique capacity to document France's relationship with the former conquerors of North Africa. The period following the incorporation of Algeria's three departments into metropolitan France in 1848 finally offered conditions that allowed archaeological societies to thrive in Algeria. Of particular significance in the colony's achievement of a modicum of stability were the defeat, imprisonment, and exile of Emir 'Abd el-Qader to metropolitan France that year, after the long period in which the Sufi ascetic and military leader had united Indigenous tribes against the French.[100] In addition, the fall of the Saharan stronghold of Laghouat to the French in 1852 freed up military resources that had been tied to the defensive and expansionary activities of the previous decade. The appointment of Jacques-Louis Randon as governor-general also furthered such objectives since the military commander had some appreciation for antiquities.[101] Although not all French administrators in the Algerian colony signaled their support for Louis-Napoleon's coup in December 1851, despite the central role in the power grab played by Jacques Leroy de Saint-Arnaud and other officers who had served in the armée d'Afrique, no one could deny the new emperor's commitment to the arts and ancient history. All these factors allowed military officers and civilian residents to muster the necessary resources and enthusiasm for founding sustainable learned associations in Algeria and documenting ancient remains.[102]

These men took their model from metropolitan France, where the institutions that dealt with patrimonial matters on a day-to-day basis were regional academies and antiquarian societies situated in provincial urban centers, both small and large. Most of the latter had been founded after the fall of the Napoleonic Empire, the earliest in the 1820s but the majority during or subsequent to the tenure of François Guizot as minister of the interior and then the minister of public instruction at the start of the July Monarchy.[103] These organizations attracted constituents both from the lower nobility and among bourgeois landowners, professionals, and clerics. Yet most metropolitan learned societies were never more than private associations that, for instance, required prefectural approval before they could hold regular meetings. They typically received a modest annual allocation from their respective cities and prefectures and, if well connected, from the ministry of public instruction. The main source of their income, however, came from the membership dues they collected from constituents.[104] Although their numbers included influential individuals as honorary members, most archaeological societies were distant from the powerful metropolitan capital and had relatively little sway over the legislative bodies that could influence conservation policy.

Learned bodies like the Société archéologique du Midi de la France, established by luminaries in Toulouse in 1831, emphasized the contributions that might be made by adherents who studied and helped preserve local monuments damaged during the French Revolution or those that were now threatened by industrialization.[105] Alexandre du Mège—a co-founder of the association, former military engineer, and advocate of Toulousan culture—also sought to acquire monuments from Algeria.[106] In the year in which he co-founded the archaeological society and its associated museum, he thus proposed that French military officers stationed in Bône send a statues for display in the archaeological society's new museum, observing, "A few blows from pick-axes near the remains of an ancient building would produce a beautiful head made of marble and some other very interesting fragments."[107] The unsuccesful request was symptomatic of the lack of legislative clout of provincial antiquarian societies. By the 1840s, these metropolitan organizations formed an ad hoc provincial network united mainly by the informal exchange of their publications. Some also participated in the annual meetings of the Assises scientifiques and the Congrès archéologiques de France; both organizations were created in the early 1830s by the Norman antiquary Arcisse de Caumont to strengthen ties among antiquaries located in diverse parts of the country.[108]

In the Algerian colony, military officers, civilian residents, and archaeologically minded visitors looked to metropolitan learned societies as a model for their activities despite the latter's relative ineffectiveness in preserving endangered ancient monuments. There were also precedents for such organizations in other North African contexts such as the Egyptian Society, founded in Cairo in 1836, which was directed mainly at European travelers and "literary and scientific men" passing through the *wilāyah* (province) of Egypt, who found themselves in need of a reference library.[109] During the first decade of the French occupation of former Ottoman Regency of al-Jazā'er, at least two such organizations of this nature were established. In 1835, Colonel de Larochette and a group of fellow officers in Bougie (A. Béjaïa; L. Saldae civitas) convened what is thought to have been the earliest such association in the colony, the Société d'essai et des recherches. The Société scientifique de Constantine was formed in the same year as the successful military conquest of the beylik.[110] The existence of both associations, however, proved ephemeral and neither survived past the end of the first decade of the conquest.[111]

In Bône, a literary organization was also established in the colonial city from 1841 to 1845. Called the Société littéraire de Saint-Augustin, the organization's name alluded to the late Roman bishop of renown whose see was based in Hippo Regius (the predecessor of Bône, known in Arabic as Annaba). This society, however, failed to thrive. In 1863, it was replaced by the more successful Académie d'Hippone, which published a bulletin from 1865. This journal addressed a range of topics from discussions of local crops and fauna to history and craniology; in its first two decades of publication, the space allotted to classical archaeology was relatively limited.[112] Other short-lived organizations in the colony included the Société des sciences, lettres et arts (1847) and the Société algérienne des Beaux-Arts (1851), both established in Algiers.[113]

The members of learned societies in Algeria, among them a substantial number of military officers, aimed to educate recent European arrivals to the French colony about the ancient history, geography, and archaeology of their new surroundings.[114] Nozeran heralded this favorable shift toward protection of antiquities in *L'Algérie nouvelle*, a political daily in the colony, in December 1858: "Until now, as we know, the questions of war and colonization have dominated; it is necessary first to master the land before opening the field for scientific research. But today the work of the conquest is finished, the sword is returned to its sheath; a new era of peace and prosperity has just opened for Algeria."[115] The improved documentation of Algeria's monuments was also symptomatic of an increasingly technocratic approach to the administration of the colony by the Bureaux arabes, which was also revealed in the intensification of efforts to collect information about the Indigenous population.[116]

Unsurprisingly, Constantine, built on the site of the ancient Numidian and later Roman city of Cirta and thus one of the richest sites of accessible antiquities, saw the establishment of the first successful archaeological society in Algeria. The city ruled by Hadj Ahmed Bey was conquered by the French following two consecutive sieges in 1836 and 1837. In the latter incident, when the bey fled, the violent French assault decimated the city's original population. Subsequent appropriation of real estate and property speculation by French officers and European settlers prevented many of the survivors from returning to their prewar homes. In the decades that followed, the number of European residents climbed rapidly from around three hundred in 1841 to around twelve thousand five hundred in 1867.[117]

In 1852, the Société archéologique de la province de Constantine was founded with the objective of collecting, preserving, and documenting the wealth of monuments in the region.[118] Leading this endeavor were Auguste Cherbonneau and Colonel Casimir Creuly.[119] Cherbonneau, who was one of the few civilian members of the organization at this early stage, had trained at the École des langues orientales. From 1846, he held the chair of Arabic in Constantine. After its foundation in 1852, he served as the association's secretary until his departure for Algiers in 1863.[120] Despite his training as a scholar of Arabic, however, Cherbonneau expressed little esteem for the Muslim population of Algeria. He noted, "The ignorance of Muslims, too often taken by their imagination, had bestowed upon the triumphal arch the name *Kasr-el-Ghoula* 'the castle of the evil fairy.'"[121] By contrast, he looked much more favorably on ancient imperial accomplishments in the city, including Roman technological achievements such as aqueducts, stone bridges, and triumphal arches.

The society's other leading member, Creuly, had been a student at the École impériale polytechnique (1812) and thereafter at the École d'application de l'artillerie et du génie de Metz (1814). As an engineering specialist, Creuly earned praise from his superiors for his distinguished education and perfect mastery of Latin. After serving in Spain, Senegal, and metropolitan France, Creuly arrived in Algeria in 1850, where he was commissioned first as the director of fortifications in Blida and shortly afterwards in Constantine, where he served as commander of the engineering corps.[122] He believed that an archaeological society was an effective means by which to inform contemporary military officers about the urgency of protecting ancient sites: "It [our purpose] is above all to expand a taste for archaeology among officers under our orders, who are able to offer so many services to science that we took the initiative to found a society embracing, within the scope of its studies, all the antiquities of the province."[123] Creuly was well aware of the Romans' achievements in the region and deplored the acts of vandalism that degraded ancient monuments at places like Lambaesis. In reaction to concerns about the destruction of the city's antiquities, the archaeological society opened a modest museum in 1853.[124] He believed that the institution could be effective in educating officers about the harmful actions perpetrated by French soldiers against the region's ancient monuments.[125] In 1859, however, Creuly's reputation as an accomplished classical archaeologist led to his return to metropolitan France and his appointment by Napoleon III as a member of the Commission de topographie des Gaules.[126]

James Malarkey notes that although the European-born residents who helped found Constantine's archaeological society were neither men of leisure nor particularly erudite, they were united by their commitment to the conquest and colonization of North Africa.[127] They credited Renier with having inspired the creation of the association with his work on Latin inscriptions in Lambaesis and its vicinity.[128] Among the society's earliest members were military officers, colonial bureaucrats, medical doctors, judges, an Arabic teacher, and an architect. Texier, the former first inspector general of civil structures in Algeria, was likewise among the early members of the organization.[129] Even if many who joined did not achieve the level of proficiency of their contemporaries on the European continent, the Byzantinist Charles Diehl noted that their palpable enthusiasm for archaeology in such improvised conditions had an important impact on subsequent research in the region.[130]

As Constantine was rebuilt after the French siege and European immigrants pushed the Indigenous population into more dilapidated quarters of the city, the archaeological society's journal, which was first published in 1853, reflected the sensibilities of Constantine's new occupants rather than those whom they replaced. The publication was intended to cultivate interest in North African antiquities among subscribers in Algeria and metropolitan France and mirrored contemporary confidence in the connections between French achievements and those of the ancient Roman empire in the region. Essays in the early issues of the revue were dedicated for the most part to the subject of Roman archaeology and somewhat less frequently to Libico-Berber and Punic remains. By comparison, only about 20 percent of the journal's articles covered later historical or ethnographic questions, few of which were based on Arab and Ottoman sources.[131]

In Algeria, members of such newly created archaeological societies embraced Roman archaeology and epigraphy as a means of documenting their unique historical ties to the landscape. Such familiar markers of the Roman past helped diffuse the disorientation that many recent immigrants felt on arriving in Algeria.[132] It was hoped that such sites might help foster first- and second-generation French colonists' attachment to their adopted homeland. Populating the landscape with meaningful references was thought more generally to ease immigrants' adaptation to colonial environs.[133] The learned organization thus created a venue in which leading members of the community were encouraged to take pride in local remnants of the ancient past and, by extension, their new lives in North Africa. Archaeological research in particular helped French and European colonists in Algeria forge an intimate connection with their new home, even if this feeling did not come as naturally as in their birthplaces in France or elsewhere in Europe.[134]

With the evident successes enjoyed by Constantine's archaeological society, Governor-General Randon encouraged the foundation of additional scholarly associations in the provinces of Algiers and Oran. While Oran lacked a significant number of Roman antiquities as compared to Algiers and Constantine, Algiers became the home of the influential Société historique algérienne and its journal, the *Revue africaine* (first published by the publisher Jourdan in 1856).[135] The society was headed by the ambitious Arabist Adrien Berbrugger, a graduate of the École des chartes and founder of the Bibliothèque et Musée d'Alger (1835).[136] The organization earned the immediate support of officers like Captain (and Baron) Estève-Laurent Boissonnet, who became the aide-de-camp of Division General Ducos de la Hitte in June 1853 and later commanded the artillery corps in Algiers. A polytechnicien, artillery specialist, and speaker of both Arabic and Berber who had earlier directed the Bureaux arabes in Constantine, Boissonnet was an active participant in both archaeological and ethnographic research.[137] The organization's objectives included the publication of historical research and the conservation of monuments. Just as libraries, museums, and hospitals benefited metropolitan France, Berbrugger, Boissonnet, and their contemporaries believed that archaeological museums, learned societies, and other familiar cultural institutions had an important role to play in France's colonization of Algeria.[138]

Based in the colonial capital, the founding members of Berbrugger's archaeological association ambitiously reached out to their colleagues (and erstwhile competitors) in Constantine and sought to affiliate their activities with classical scholars in the metropolitan capital. To this end, they appointed epigraphers like Renier, Hase, and other members of the Académie des inscriptions et belles-lettres as honorary members of their organization.[139] These measures were probably intended to capitalize on the prestigious connections forged by Berbrugger a decade earlier when he served on the Commission d'exploration scientifique d'Algérie. They also helped vocalize Berbrugger's determination that the organization would be the premier learned society of the colony. Even if it was not the earliest, coming second to Constantine, Berbrugger's association took advantage of the privileged status of the collection and extensive resources available at the Bibliothèque et Musée d'Alger.[140] Within a few years of the foundation of the society, however, perhaps due to a failure to attract sufficient membership, organizers opened the doors of the Société historique algérienne wider than they had at the start. They liberalized the membership policy to welcome any honorable European resident of the colony interested in helping the association meet its goals.[141] Extant sources suggest that the Indigenous population continued to be excluded from such ventures.

Despite the enthusiasm in Algiers and Constantine among advocates for conservation of the Roman legacy, the two archaeological societies had few resources by which to leverage improved treatment of ancient monuments by military and civilian administrators who encountered classical remains on a regular basis.[142] Berbrugger himself understood the region as destined to be the scene of war as it had been in the period of ancient Rome: "Also, it was always its [North Africa's] destiny to be a battlefield in which foreign civilization and indigenous barbarity clashed more than once."[143] The seizure of lands and structures deemed essential to France's military operations, however, narrowed the window for effective progress on archaeological standards and conservation efforts.[144] As noted by Berbrugger, there was much to be learned from the strategy of the ancient Roman army, which was documented in the monuments and inscriptions being found in Algeria:

> The analogue bears exploration since there are the same traces of military organization that exist in the other Roman provinces, and observation demonstrates that they are very easily discovered. As for personnel, we find here the legion with its auxiliary as a principal element in the mobile corps; next to them, the indigenous troops, organized as a sort of local militia and employed permanently in guarding the outposts. We find the camps, the official residences, the towers, and even the simple lookouts where forces were stationed to oversee the security of the country.[145]

This message was little heeded due not only to military exigency but also repeated disagreements between officials in Paris and the military administration in Algiers as to how to prioritize Roman monuments in the midst of the colonial conquest and occupation.[146] French understanding of patrimony in this period was, in any case, narrow. Only those monuments with symbolic and historical value for the French, typically those of ancient Rome, stood a chance of being studied and protected, and many of these also came under threat.[147] Despite the ideological value of archaeological activities, many military officials saw the reverence for antiquities as a distraction from (and potentially an impediment to) the objectives of the French military mission in North Africa. They created restraints on the freedom with which the armée d'Afrique could operate in the field.[148]

Competitive Stakes of Museum Building in Algeria

As we have seen, closely linked with the foundation of archaeological societies and journals in Algeria was the creation of museums to house and protect Roman antiquities. These collections often benefited from the enthusiasm and expertise of historians and archaeologists among their members, who fervently denounced the departure of antiquities for metropolitan France.[149] Case in point, just a year after its start in 1852, the Société archéologique de la province de Constantine established its own collection so that it might retain some of the region's wealth of archaeological materials in situ rather than allowing these objects to be moved to Algiers or Paris.[150] In April 1854, the prefect of Constantine wrote to

voice his support for the activities of the archaeological society and the efforts of its members to preserve monuments and inscriptions: "Composed
of men who as a consequence of their positions are up-to-date in their
knowledge of discoveries that occur each day in construction and excavations, this praiseworthy society, on the basis of its objectives and composition, allows us nonetheless to hope for archaeological science that
no ancient remains of value will go unnoticed or be destroyed."[151] Finding sufficient funding to achieve this goal, however, was a challenge. As
in Egypt following Muhammad ʿAli's decree of August 15, 1835, ban-
ning the export of antiquities and establishing a museum of antiquities in
Cairo, such measures did not necessarily bring about consistent or effective protections for ancient monuments.[152]

Members of Constantine's archaeological society faced the additional
challenge of refuting the contentions of the prefect of Algiers and the
governor-general that secondary museums beyond that of Algiers were
incapable of safeguarding antiquities.[153] Making the case in favor of housing ancient remains locally, Colonel Creuly argued that the newly created
learned society in Constantine was committed to responding effectively to
the history of abuses by the armée d'Afrique:

> The engineering service of the province of Constantine has not been left un-
> touched by the general interest inspired by the archaeological wealth of this
> region. Through its care, some precious objects were saved from destruc-
> tion, but it is necessary to confess that many others perished because their
> importance was not sufficiently understood. Ignorance is not the only enemy
> to fear; there are individuals who refuse to recognize the utility of historical
> studies and even seem to find a certain pleasure in the destruction of monu-
> ments of the past. We have seen in this regard acts of incredible vandalism.[154]

Creuly understood that establishing a local a collection was essential to
the future success of these objectives. With the compelling argument that
the armée d'Afrique had destroyed too many valuable antiquities, authorities in Constantine won the backing of the provincial administration to
undertake the conservation, display, and publication of ancient remains in
the city as opposed to outside the province.

Shortly after its inauguration, the Musée de Constantine achieved
another important victory. In 1856, just three years after opening, the

museum received authorization to spend 10,000 francs for the purchase of a private antiquities collection from the Ligurian colonist and antiquarian Lazare Costa, who also joined the Société archéologique.[155] His collection, which included 1,500 silver and bronze coins and over a thousand artifacts made of marble, stone, ceramic, mosaic, precious metals, ivory, bone, and glass, augmented the young museum's holdings considerably.[156] Like other institutions of this era, the museum was not focused solely on archaeology but also had a rich collection of natural history and mineralogical specimens. Curiously, however, the collection did not include any Libyan inscriptions despite the fact that hundreds were found in the city and region. Moreover, the rapid and unpredictable growth of the museum's collection created significant challenges for the regional museum. The institution had to move several times over the next few years to accommodate its expanding acquisitions. During each of these transitions, the museum lost a considerable number of ancient artifacts to vandalism, breakage, theft, and loss during transport.[157]

Even more egregious than the moves was the mayor of Constantine's unauthorized sale of hundreds of the museum's inscribed stones, which had been exhibited in the open air in the city's Square Valée, as materiel for construction of a road from Constantine to Batna in the 1850s.[158] Although this instance was not isolated, there were few means by which such activities could be halted and little or no way to levy penalties against those who caused harm to the museum's collection.[159] During a visit to Constantine in March 1873, Héron de Villefosse, curator at the Louvre and a former student of Renier, reported that the situation had not improved over time: "As for the museum [of Constantine], it is very badly maintained: only the small objects are placed safely in a room of city hall; the lapidary museum is outside the city in a little-supervised garden and the monuments of small dimension are scattered to the right and left like pebbles: it is said that they are going to remedy all of this by uniting the library and museum in a new venue."[160] Another three years passed before A. Poulle, then president of the archaeological society in Constantine, turned his attention to improving the condition of the museum. In 1882, the appointment of Captain V. Prud'homme as the museum's curator offered impetus for the updated organization and installation of the collection.[161]

Another contemporary example of an archaeological museum was that created by the exiled prisoners of 1848 who were housed at Lambaesis from 1852. Using the interior space of the praetorium, the open-air museum contained sculptures and other carved stone fragments.[162] Although the specific provenance of many of the pieces was not noted, presumably most came from the surrounding archaeological site.[163] After Napoleon III saw the collection in 1865 and departed with a statue of Jupiter, however, the makeshift collection fare poorly. During the revolts of 1871, French military units from Bouches-du-Rhône that camped at Lambaesis left graffiti on the statues and severely damaged the stone remains.[164] Consequently, in 1874, Héron de Villefosse, with the blessing of Renier but over the protest of resident archaeologists in Algeria, received permission to transport the site's most important antiquities to Paris so that they could be displayed in the Louvre.[165]

A more successful example of an archaeological museum's longevity in Algeria was the Bibliothèque et Musée d'Alger. Soon after landing in North Africa in 1835, Berbrugger received the charge from Governor-General Bertrand Clauzel, whom he served as secretary, to edit the colony's official gazette, *Le Moniteur algérien,* and create a library in the city of Algiers.[166] With the benefit of substantial state support, Berbrugger opened the library that year, to which he added the museum in 1838. The institution was operational fully two decades before the establishment of the Société historique algériene and its journal *Revue africaine* began publication in Algiers in 1856, which were created nearly contemporary to those of Constantine. From 1848, the Bibliothèque et Musée d'Alger came under the authority of the Ministry of Public Instruction and constituted the main center for antiquities in Algeria, regardless of their provenance.[167]

While one might be led from extant correspondence to think that Berbrugger's independent path as a librarian and curator owed much to his domineering personality, his training at the École des chartes and some of his early publications refute any suggestion that he did not have the necessary qualifications to do so effectively.[168] Since the institution had limited resources for new acquisitions in its early years, Berbrugger capitalized on the campaigns of the armée d'Afrique to expand the nascent museum's collection of Arabic manuscripts and antiquities through wartime confiscations. By the mid-1840s, the library had almost six thousand books and manuscripts, in addition to its art and antiquities collection.[169] These resources allowed him to compose *L'Algérie historique, pittoresque et monumentale* (1845), a four-volume illustrated journey through Algeria aimed at promoting colonial propaganda and inculcating respect for the region's classical antiquities among an educated French readership in the metropole.[170] From 1848, the institution benefited from an enviable state budget of 10,000 francs per year for staffing—including a curator, guard, and porter—as well as for maintenance of the museum, a generous sum even by metropolitan standards.[171]

The Bibliothèque et Musée d'Alger served a broad range of purposes for colonial inhabitants of the capital. In addition to displaying ancient artifacts and monuments and housing manuscripts and printed works, the institution offered European colonists in Algiers regular Arabic classes

Figure 31. Berbrugger's "Conquête et civilisation (5 Juillet 1830)" depicts the landing of the French on the shores of Sidi Ferruch (A. Sidi Fredj) as the continuation of the civilizing activities first begun by the Romans. Adrien Berbrugger, *Algérie historique, pittoresque et monumentale ou Recueil de vues, costumes, et portraits faits d'après nature dans les provinces d'Alger, Bône, Constantine et Oran* 1 (Paris: Chez J. Delehaye, 1843), frontispiece.

and saw a steady stream of visitors to its library.[172]Additionally, at least until the mid-1850s, the Bibliothèque et Musée d'Alger contained a Galérie zoologique, a feature of the museum for which Berbrugger expressed little enthusiasm. In fact, Berbrugger's willful neglect of the museum's natural history collection led some contemporaries like Eugène Couturier to complain about the institution's paltry offering of local specimens.[173] Just like Abbé Bourgade's Musée Saint-Louis, established in Carthage in the late 1840s, Berbrugger perceived archaeological remains as a key tool in the French colonization of the region.[174] Beyond providing housing and a budgetary allotment for the state-funded Bibliothèque et Musée d'Alger, however, metropolitan authorities did not fully back Berbrugger's attempts to enlarge the space, prestige, and scope of the Algiers collection. Some claimed that his transcriptions of inscriptions in the collection were faulty and the catalogue he produced in 1861 contained many errors.[175]

In the decade subsequent to the foundation of the Bibliothèque et Musée d'Alger, the minister of war dedicated the vast majority of funding for scientific research to the Commission d'exploration scientifique d'Algérie. Comparatively few resources went to local conservation. Rather than enhancing existing or building new museums in the Algerian colony, most of the operation's budget was dedicated to paying for the travel and wages of personnel, publishing the mission reports, and facilitating acquisitions for the Louvre Museum. In June 1845, the minister of war sponsored the shipment to Paris of a mosaic discovered near Koudiat-Ati near Constantine along with ancient Roman statues, busts, and inscriptions from a variety of locations in the Algerian colony.[176] Organized by Captain Alphonse Delamare, the transport of 343 cases of antiquities from Constantine, Philippeville, Djémila, Bône, Médéah, Sétif (L. Sitifis Colonia), and other important archaeological sites proceeded despite a challenge from a military engineer named Laborie in Philippeville, who pushed for at least some of the pieces to remain in his community.[177] In July 1845, these artifacts reached the port of Le Havre and were transported to the Palais du Louvre in August 1845, where they became the principal part of the museum's Algerian collection. They joined a number of mosaics from Carthage shipped by the French consul in Tunis, M. de Lagau. Later that summer, sculptural remains from Cherchel (L. Iulia Caesarea) collected by Delamare's colleague from the commission, the architect Amable Ravoisié, also arrived in Paris.[178]

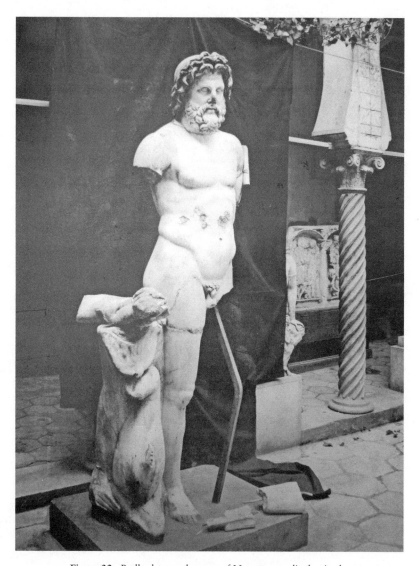

Figure 32. Badly damaged statue of Neptune on display in the
Bibliothèque et Musée d'Alger. Alexandre Leroux, *L'Algérie illustrée*, vol. 2
(Algiers: A. Leroux, 1888–1892).

Although the bulk of the artifacts transported from Algeria to France
were the fruit of the commission's excavations and research, authorities sought to regularize future efforts to gather antiquities for display
in the metropolitan capital. On August 26, 1845, the governor-general

issued a circular to provincial commanders in the colony, enjoining them to inform authorities in Algiers of any items suitable to be transported to Paris. These objects were intended for display in the Louvre's future Musée algérien, a gallery conceived of as celebrating the cultural capital of France's newest colony as had been done with Egyptian antiquities under Napoleon I.[179] However, in Paris, the reception of statues and other monuments culled from the colony was not warm; one might suggest, as has Timothy Mitchell with respect to Egypt, that fragmented artifacts could not compete with the imagined ideal of the orientalized gaze.[180] Although Delamare himself helped install some of the recently arrived artifacts like a mosaic from Koudiat-Ati,[181] the powerful Louvre curator, Adrien de Longpérier, greeted the Roman sculpture sent from Algeria with consternation rather than enthusiasm: "Is it not rendering a disservice to geographical science, for example, to uproot Roman mile markers to send them to Paris? I am, as you know, Monsieur, entirely removed from the organization of the Algerian gallery of the Louvre; it is not under my authority."[182] He complained, moreover, that many of the pieces did not meet the museum's exacting standards. Despite his resistance, additional shipments arrived in the early 1850s from various parties and points of origin including Oran, Cherchel, and Tunis.[183] Although internal opposition was no doubt to blame for the indefinite delay of the opening of the long-planned gallery of the Musée algérien, Longpérier's displeasure with this project suggests deeper obstacles existed to the display of Roman antiquities from Algeria.[184] In contrast to the mid-nineteenth-century fervor for collecting classical antiquities from Italy and Greece, the aesthetic merits of often fragmentary Algerian antiquities failed to attract similar enthusiasm in elite Parisian circles.

From the perspective of metropolitan officials, the Bibliothèque et Musée d'Alger was a repository of secondary importance to the Louvre. It represented a depot in which the state might display monuments too heavy for transport to France or antiquities that were seen as aesthetically unworthy of inclusion in the Louvre. Yet during the 1850s, as the number of exports of antiquities to the metropole grew, colonial archaeologists and enthusiasts protested these removals, arguing that Roman artifacts needed to remain in the colony for the benefit of current and future French and European settlers.[185] They called on authorities to do more to improve the conditions of the colony's antiquities-rich cities like Cherchel, where classical remains deteriorated dramatically during the French

Figure 33. The poor state of preservation of the antiquities, like this statue of Hercules displayed at the Musée de Cherchel, was symptomatic of the circumstances in which they were collected. Paul Gauckler, *Musée de Cherchel* (Paris: Ernest Leroux, 1895).

military occupation and colonial expansion.[186] In Cherchel, the army actively pillaged the ancient amphitheater, used the Roman theater to build caserns, and stored their wine in one of the ancient city's cisterns.[187]

Ironically, some of the city's losses also resulted from the work of the architect Ravoisié for the Commission d'exploration scientifique d'Algérie, since he marked many of the finer yields of his research as appropriate for shipment to Paris. Throughout Algeria, the conservation of existing monuments was also impoverished by the appropriation of artifacts by military engineers and other officers for private collections, which often did not survive the departure of their new owners, who were subsequently deployed elsewhere, died, or retired from military service.[188]

The Musée de Cherchel's origins dated to the final months of the Commission d'exploration scientifique d'Algérie in 1842, when Ravoisié excavated a monument known to Arab residents as the Palais du Sultan and used the site, and a nearby military storage depot, to display ancient Roman artifacts that were not earmarked for shipment to Paris. Some French engineers based in Cherchel were also enterprising, such as M. Giret, who made a small museum in the court of his home to preserve local finds from rapacious army officials.[189] Soon afterward, the collections of the Musée de Cherchel were transferred to a confiscated mosque, complemented by a second venue at the Office of Civilian Structures. In November 1846, however, both collections suffered severe damage in an earthquake that rocked the city. While surviving artifacts were salvaged and moved to another structure in 1852, city authorities chose to demolish the building the following year and did little to curb the vandalism perpetrated against artifacts stored temporarily in nearby military barracks.[190]

To rectify these deplorable conditions and establish clearer policies governing the ownership of ancient remains, Governor-General Randon appointed Berbrugger as inspector general of historical monuments and archaeological museums in Algeria on November 15, 1854.[191] Taking on the Sisyphean responsibilities attempted with little success by Charles Texier nearly a decade earlier, Berbrugger, who was still the curator of the Bibliothèque et Musée d'Alger and the president of the Société historique algérienne, undertook the task of cataloguing the monuments of Algeria. He distinguished between the artifacts that should enter local public collections and those that should go to Algiers, and he prescribed research on particularly important finds.[192] In this period, however, the inspector general did not conduct regular excavations as would be the case by the 1880s.[193] In January 1862, additional responsibility for architectural remains fell to Ernest Feydeau, whom Napoleon III named the corresponding inspector for the Office of Historical Monuments of Algeria, which fell under the jurisdiction of the State Department. During the period in which he was resident in Algeria, the architect began the work of classifying the colony's historical monuments.[194]

With a budget of only 2,000 francs and no additional staff, Berbrugger faced challenges similar to those that had dogged Texier. Among other things, Berbrugger had few means by which to enforce the colonial policy of claiming artifacts such as gold coins from those who had discovered them.[195] Such demands by the colonial state seem to have been restricted at least in part by article 716 of the Napoleonic Civil Code, a measure that guaranteed half of what was discovered to the finders.[196] In this case, even Randon conceded that compensation for those who willing gave up such items might facilitate their acquisition by public collections, whether in Algeria or Paris. Although the governor-general failed to dedicate funds to this purpose, he conceded at least theoretically that locally found antiquities, especially Roman ones, afforded French colonists an important mechanism by which to identify with their new home of Algeria.[197] This admission suggested that Randon and other authorities in the 1850s acknowledged the potential ideological value of the newly created museums in cities like Constantine, Cherchel, and Philippeville.

Admittedly, as the inspector general, Berbrugger was far from objective and rarely supportive of the well-being of rival museums to his foundation in Algiers. In fulfillment of his ongoing duties as curator in Algiers, he worked aggressively to advantage the institution he had created and continued to champion it as the premier antiquities collection of the colony.[198] As we have seen, government funding for archaeological projects was rare, so Berbrugger initially advocated shutting down smaller institutions in provincial centers in Algeria in favor of shifting resources toward the larger collection in the colonial capital. From as early as January 1854, Berbrugger proposed transporting the Musée de Cherchel's collection to Algiers:

> Thus, instead of augmenting the Musée de Cherchel, instead of proposing to create new museums in localities where settlers' plows encounter ruins; rather than proposing to endow each of these secondary museums with a curator or a simple guardian, to whom it would be necessary to give a payment or some sort of salary to obtain good service, I would be in favor of the advice of transporting to the Musée central d'Alger not only all the objects at

Cherchel but also those that excavations in the future might discover. The system of local museums does not have a limit. . . . From this dispersion of accessions is inevitably born the dispersion of collections.[199]

It is clear that Berbrugger was not a disinterested figure at the center of archaeological policy making in Algeria. While Berbrugger's bold actions are likely to have pleased members of the Société historique algérienne and did not offend colonial municipalities with insufficient resources to open their own museums, the inspector general earned the enmity of Cherchel's colonists.[200] Consequently, the minister of war and the governor-general periodically had to intervene to mediate such conflicts among regional museums. The situation was similar to the one that prevailed in metropolitan France, where provincial collections suffered from the Louvre's demands to display the best pieces in Paris.[201]

Yet as circumstances changed, Berbrugger adapted by offering strong support for local institutions. In 1855, one of his first successful acts as inspector general was a report outlining the consequences of the insalubrious

Figure 34. The haphazard appearance of the courtyard of the Musée de Cherchel c. 1895. Paul Gauckler, *Musée de Cherchel* (Paris: Ernest Leroux, 1895).

history of the antiquities of Cherchel, whose fate convinced the governor-general to find more secure housing and staffing for the Musée de Cherchel.[202] Berbrugger's intervention in Cherchel resulted in a suitable building for the museum and the appointment of Pierre de Lhotellerie, a local numismatist, as its first full-time curator in 1855. The new appointee dedicated his time to drafting the Musée de Cherchel's inaugural catalogue, and he was afforded sufficient resources to sponsor local excavations.[203] Despite the very uneven history of the museum, Héron de Villefosse described it as the most beautiful and richly endowed collection of Roman North Africa.[204]

In the end, however, Berbrugger did not relinquish his ambitions for his own museum in Algiers. In 1856, he used the authority of his position to confiscate some of Cherchel's finest antiquities, with an initial target of acquiring the sixty late imperial gold solidi found in the city. These entered the collection of the Bibliothèque et Musée d'Alger later that year.[205] In response to this aggressive tactic, seventy inhabitants of Cherchel, including members of the municipal council, petitioned that the city retain the wealth of monuments of which its citizens were rightly proud. Perhaps the threat to local antiquities led them to identify more closely with the ancient resources of their new community and challenge the ease with which Berbrugger transferred their best finds to the colonial capital. They also regretted the damage to local pride and the loss of business from travelers to the city that Berbrugger's appropriations had caused.[206] Although it was apparently deemed impossible to return the confiscated antiquities that had been transferred to either Algiers or Paris, Prince Jerome-Napoleon, minister of Algeria and the colonies, sought to lessen the tensions that pitted advocates for conserving Roman antiquities in Algeria against one another. On December 31, 1858, the emperor issued a circular that protected antiquities in situ. This measure, theoretically at least, protected the Musée de Cherchel against further spoliation by either metropolitan or colonial authorities.[207]

Without the support of an archaeological society, however, since the Société archéologique de Cherchel (1860) was active only briefly, Lhotellerie ultimately decided to abandon the challenges of his curatorial responsibilities. In 1869, the city of Cherchel suppressed his post and did not appoint a replacement for more than a decade. In effect, the museum stood abandoned during the 1870s, and Héron de Villefosse regretted that more of the collection had not been transported to metropolitan museums.[208]

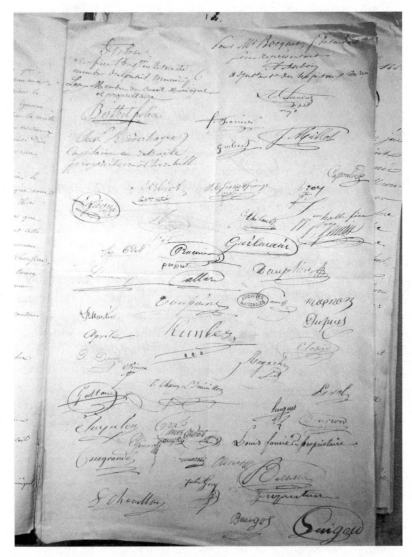

Figure 35. Signatures of colonists of Cherchel attached to a petition to Governor-General Randon dated December 2, 1856, requesting the retention of antiquities in their city. They asked that the collection not be removed to Algiers or elsewhere. ANOM 80 F 1587. Reproduced by permission of the Archives nationales d'Outre-Mer (ANOM, France).

In 1886, intensive excavation of the city began again under the direction of Victor Waille, a teacher at the École supérieure des lettres d'Alger. As late as 1895, Paul Gauckler described the installation of the museum as picturesque but defective. He saw little chance of an effective remedy for the fragmentary collection of antiquities.[209]

Likewise, in the coastal city of Philippeville—even though the colonial city was built in the 1840s on the site of ruins dating back to Phoenician times, which included remains of the Roman city of Russicada—significant obstacles existed for anyone interested in establishing an antiquities museum. During the construction of the new French city, the armée d'Afrique turned up significant numbers of ancient structures and artifacts. They reused some monuments immediately with few modifications, while others they sacrificed to the prerequisites of the colonial occupation.[210] As is well documented from the work of photographers like Félix-Jacques-Antoine Moulin, who worked in the mid-1850s in Constantine, Philippeville, and Stora (the latter's port city which was largely inhabited

Figure 36. Roman statuary and architectural fragments in the open-air Musée de Philippeville in the late 1880s or early 1890s. Alexandre Leroux, *L'Algérie illustrée*, vol. 2 (Algiers: A. Leroux, 1888–1892).

by Indigenous residents), the urban conglomeration suffered substantial losses of archaeological material during this period.[211] Under such challenging circumstances, those desirous of preserving some of this material intact set their hopes on a museum that might house what remained.

In 1859, French colonists established the Musée de Philippeville at the site of a Roman theater that had been serving as army barracks. Over a hundred individuals offered a wide variety of objects found in the region to the nascent institution as the basis for the collection. In 1860, Joseph Roger, an architect residing in the city and an active donor, published a brief catalogue of the Musée de Philippeville at his own expense.[212] In the absence of a local archaeological society, A. Wallet, the mayor, and M. de Toulgoet, the prefect of Constantine, initially took responsibility for overseeing the collections under the scrutiny of Minister Jerome-Napoleon.[213] However, Roger ultimately became the collection's curator. Given the lack of funding from either the municipal or imperial administrations, the challenges in running the institution were immense. Following a request for support in 1867, Roger's efforts to bring the institution to its full potential were once again stymied.[214]

It is striking that despite considerable investment by authorities of the Second Empire in the archaeological endeavors and the creation of museums that glorified the ancient past, the Musée de Philippeville, like other local institutions in the Algerian colony, was never able to achieve its envisioned objectives. Although learned societies and their associated museums fostered some European colonists' identification with ancient Roman artifacts, the shortage of financial resources and the alternative priorities of newly arrived settlers in Algeria effectively prevented the successful growth of local institutions. The next chapter thus turns to a detailed exploration of important archaeological developments that occurred in the late 1850s and the 1860s. With the backing of Napoleon III, these activities included topographic missions related to Roman roads, the advent in metropolitan France of excavations that integrated the expertise of French military men—some of whom had served in colonial Algeria, and the start of archaeological tourism.

Chapter 5

CARTOGRAPHY AND FIELD ARCHAEOLOGY DURING THE SECOND EMPIRE

During the 1860s, the French colony of Algeria faced continuing up-heaval, with the policies that supported the violent subjugation of the Arab and Kabyle population finally reaching a tipping point. The military "pacification" of Kabylia, which ended only in July 1857, provoked both secular and religious resistance to ongoing French intervention among Indigenous inhabitants.[1] Impeding their very survival was an increasingly vocal, independent, and urban constituency of European settlers in Algeria, which called for an end to military rule and an expansion of civilian control of the territory's resources.[2] Their impatience with the colonial government led Napoleon III, who until then had remained aloof from the affairs of Algeria, to implement policies leading to the full incorporation of Algeria into metropolitan France. Thus, in June 1858, when the emperor passed legislation that ended metropolitan subsidies for European colonization, he also lifted restrictions on European access to tribal lands and transferred the power of the governor-general to the newly created Ministry of Algeria and the Colonies.[3] Between August 1859 and February

1860, lands in French civilian jurisdictions ballooned from 748,995 to 1,854,990 hectares. With few remaining constraints on the confiscation or purchase of communally held Indigenous property (*arsh*) by European settlers, their ownership of former tribal lands grew exponentially. In 1859 alone, this figure increased from a total of 175,000 to 295,000 hectares.[4]

The disastrous spoliation of "surplus" tribal lands, a policy known as cantonnement, was just one of several damaging legal maneuvers and met with significant resistance in interior regions of Algeria.[5] These devastating developments and Napoleon III's brief but informative visit to the colony in September 1860, during which he saw some of the grave consequences of French policies on the Muslim population, convinced the emperor to backtrack on his rapid overhaul of the administrative structure of Algeria. That fall, he eliminated the short-lived Ministry of Algeria and reestablished the Algerian Government-General with reduced powers.

Given Napoleon III's intention to slow the rate of land appropriations by European colonists, however, his appointment of Aimable-Jean-Jacques Pélissier as governor-general of Algeria in November 1860 was ill advised. The military career of Pélissier, a veteran officer in the armée d'Afrique, had been forged entirely in Algeria. A graduate of the École spéciale militaire de Saint-Cyr, he earned a notorious reputation for his role in the asphyxiation of many members of the Oued Riah tribe at Dahra in April 1845, when soldiers under his command started fires that suffocated nearly a thousand civilians who had taken refuge in the caves. When word of the massacre reached metropolitan France and caused widespread outcry, Governor-General Thomas-Robert Bugeaud justified the event as a "cruel necessity," and Pélissier escaped censure.[6] Seven years later, in 1852, Pélissier organized the bloody seizure of the Saharan oasis of Laghouat.[7] The choice of Pélissier as governor-general thus suggested both military commanders' considerable influence over the vetting process and opposition to gentler handling of the Indigenous population. In this position, Pélissier took advantage of existing law to confiscate Muslim-held property, a direct affront to the emperor's policy objectives.

Having come under the influence of the Saint-Simonian thinker Ismaÿl Urbain and career officers of the Bureaux arabes, about 60 percent of whom had graduated from the École Saint-Cyr or the École polytechnique, Napoleon III recognized that further measures were necessary if he was to improve the living conditions of Algeria's Arab and Kabyle population.[8] With the desire to initiate reform and reinvigorate France's interactions with Muslim inhabitants, the emperor made plans to jettison his earlier and disastrous assimilationist policy.[9] Laying the groundwork for the so-called *Royaume arabe* or Arab Kingdom that was intended to serve all its inhabitants, Napoleon III issued a *senatus consult* outlining his new policies on April 22, 1863. Although formulated with an eye to improving the deplorable circumstances in which the Arabs and Kabyles lived, these measures remained notoriously difficult to implement. Moreover, Napoleon III's vision was not met enthusiastically by Indigenous authorities, because it further weakened remaining tribal power structures.[10]

Consequently, when the poorly implemented imperial measures of 1863 resolved few of the pressures created by colonial expansion, renewed tribal rebellions broke out in Kabylia in 1864.[11] Following Pélissier's death in May of that year, Napoleon III delayed appointing a successor for four months. In September 1864, Patrice Maurice de Mac-Mahon, who had provided more than twenty years of service in the armée d'Afrique, took command of the colony as governor-general. His selection was motivated no doubt by the anticipation of further unrest in Algeria. Although he had served as an officer of the Bureaux arabes immediately before becoming governor-general, he had participated during his military career in many of the colony's hardest-fought battles, including the conquest of Constantine (1837) and the defeat of Biskra (1853). In 1857, Mac-Mahon gained renown by commanding one of the divisions involved in the submission of Kabylia. Mac-Mahon's regime, which lasted until July 1870, undertook military operations against Indigenous armed resistance in this region.[12] These activities ceased only in 1866 and left the economy of Kabylia in ruins.[13]

Napoleon III's distance from or denial of these military realities is evident from a speech he made to Muslim representatives from Algiers during his second visit to the colony from late April to early June 1865. In an address to leaders of the Arab community, the emperor praised the warriors who had resisted French dominance. Strikingly, he described the experience as not very different from the way in which the Gallic peoples had resisted Roman incursion into their territory: "Like you, twenty centuries ago, our ancestors also courageously resisted a foreign invasion, but nonetheless, their defeat brought about their regeneration. The defeated Gauls assimilated with their Roman conquerors, and from the forced union between the contrary virtues of the two opposing peoples was born, in time, the French nationality which, in its turn, has spread its ideas throughout the world."[14] Napoleon III went on to describe his vision of a similar fusion of the French and Arab races with time; although it had thus far been painful, he sought to reassure Indigenous leaders that French dominance would ultimately bring important civilizational advances to their peoples. Owing to the contradictions between this discourse and the conditions that existed on the ground, it is unlikely that his speech brought much relief to the people most in need of it.[15] The ineffectiveness of Napoleon III's policies in Algeria, and his failure to ameliorate the precarious reality of land appropriations underway in the colony, may be seen in the amount of land that continued to move to European hands during this period.[16] By 1870, European holdings in Algeria had reached the breathtaking figure of 765,000 hectares, a nearly fivefold increase from 1859. This development was all the more ominous given the fact that most of the colonists of European descent inhabited Algeria's urban centers and did not actually occupy most of the lands over which they now exercised control.[17]

While the French occupation was extremely violent from its start, the second decade of Napoleon III's reign ushered in ever more daunting prospects for the survival of the non-European residents. Despite the emperor's benevolent, though admittedly ineffectual, gestures early in the 1860s, the growing population of settlers encroached increasingly on the basic resources of Arabs and Kabyles. Officers of the Bureaux arabes seem to have been unable or unwilling to do much in their defense.[18] Since French naturalization required renouncing the Muslim faith, it was not an option for most native Algerians (by contrast, the Crémieux decree granted most inhabitants of Jewish descent citizenship in 1873).[19] Although the precise number of Indigenous residents who died directly at the hands of the French army is unknown, Kamel Kateb has argued that the number of people who were either killed by the French or who died as a result of the scorched-earth policy during the first forty-five years of the French colony may be estimated at least as high as eight hundred twenty-five thousand, although there is no way to verify this number with any certitude.[20]

Demographic losses were so devastating that some French colonists characterized the demise of the Muslim population as a foregone conclusion, something that needed to be combatted through a change in French

policy if its extinction was to be avoided. As noted by the geologist, paleontologist, and later member and president of the Conseil général in
Oran, Auguste Pomel, French colonization had worsened an already fragile situation: "The miseries of this infantile and barbaric people are, in
large part, due certainly to their atavistic shortcomings and the immobility
of their social condition; however, our domination would have aggravated
these, above all with the mistakes under which it [the French colony] was
constituted."[21] Others, by contrast, saw the complete eradication of Arabs
as desirable or at least unavoidable, the product of natural selection and
comparable to the fate of Native Americans and Aboriginal peoples in
Australia.[22] Continuing tactics of the armée d'Afrique like the razzia, the
scorched-earth policy used by the French from the late 1830s, not only
reaped enormous violence against the non-European civilian population
but destroyed essential infrastructure, such as food supplies, shelter, and
flocks necessary to the survival of Arabs and Kabyles.[23]

   In the 1850s and 1860s, the impact of the confiscation of tribal lands
through cantonnement was magnified by French demands that tribes hand
over the one-tenth tax of their harvests (*achour*) and their livestock (*zek-
kat*, one of the five pillars of Islam). These policies not only restricted
the Arab and Kabyle population's access to arable and grazing lands but
also decimated their food reserves.[24] Although the crop yield was notoriously uneven in this period, the colonial government rapidly escalated the
amount of grain exported from Algeria by roughly 255 percent between
1862 and 1867. Having lost much of their best land and food stores to
European concerns, those of the Indigenous population who were able to
leave emigrated to Tunisia.[25] High levels of undernutrition and malnutri-
tion experienced by the Muslim population in the 1850s and 1860s, a
consequence of drought and famine and exports, appear not to have affected contemporary European settlers in the colony to anywhere near the
same degree.[26]

   Colonial policies aimed at breaking tribal cohesion, often facilitated by
the *Maghzen*, or Indigenous agents in service to the French through the Bureaux arabes, also had the effect of destroying Muslim support networks
and subsistence infrastructure. The colonial administration prioritized the
well-being of French and European settlers over that of Arabs and Kabyles with the establishment of better schools, medical care, food supply,
and sanitation in the civilian neighborhoods where the former lived.[27] By

contrast, in both civilian- and military-controlled districts, the dispersion of thousands of Indigenous residents from their homes led to their exposure to extreme conditions, and multiplied the terrible consequences of drought (1868–1870), invasions of locusts, and two consecutive years of severe winter weather (1867–1868 and 1868–1869). In 1866–1867, epidemics of cholera (brought by the French), typhus (spread through body lice), and the bubonic plague (spread by rats and fleas) swept across Algeria, taking a heavy toll on the already malnourished inhabitants suffering from the punitive measures of the colonial regime. The consequence was demographic collapse, during which Djilali Sari has estimated that the humanitarian catastrophe took the lives of somewhere between one-third to one-half of the native population of Algeria.[28]

As this toxic combination of natural and human-made factors conspired against the well-being of Indigenous peoples, settlers like Pomel still focused on historical evidence rather than contemporary conditions to suggest why the Kabyles might be predisposed to revolt. Instead of expressing concern at the contemporary situation created by colonial policies, Pomel chose to focus on the Kabyles' alleged descent from Tacfarinas, an Indigenous member of a Roman auxiliary unit who deserted and fought successfully in the early first century against the Third Augustan Legion. On the basis of this alleged genealogy, Pomel shifted blame for the crisis onto the Kabyles without acknowledging the impact of French colonial policies.[29]

As the famine and epidemics worsened among the Kabyles and Arabs, Governor-General Mac-Mahon attempted to censor news that might lead to an outcry in metropolitan France. However, Mac-Mahon was unable to muzzle the communications of the recently appointed archbishop of Algiers, Charles Lavigerie. Appointed by Pius IX as the metropolitan of the North African Church, the former bishop of Nancy arrived in Algeria in May 1868 and was not subject to the orders of the governor-general regarding the unfolding humanitarian catastrophe.[30] To deal with the famine and its aftermath in Algeria, Lavigerie founded the Société des missionnaires d'Afrique, also known as the Pères blancs (1868), and the Soeurs missionnaires d'Afrique (1869). Under the direction of Alfred-Louis Delattre, and with the encouragement and direction of Lavigerie, the former order also became known for its archaeological undertakings in Carthage from 1875.[31]

Figure 37. Archbishop Charles Lavigerie in the late 1880s or early 1890s. Alexandre Leroux, *L'Algérie illustrée*, vol. 2 (Algiers: A. Leroux, 1888–1892).

Lavigerie's motives in addressing the crisis were not purely altruistic, and he took a more radical line than had been accepted previously by the military administration in dealing with the Indigenous population. Lavigerie used Catholic intervention in the human tragedy that transpired in the late

1860s to advance efforts to proselytize among the Muslim population of Algeria, and especially the Kabyles, whom many French clerics believed were ripe for conversion.[32] Although his blatant advocacy for making missionary inroads among Arabs and Kabyles was supported by the papacy, it differed sharply from the policies of his predecessors, who included clerical proponents of multiconfessional education like Abbé Bourgade. Bourgade, who supported the study of antiquities with a small museum to this effect in Carthage, had been recalled from North Africa by the papacy in 1858 for his more liberal approach to the Muslim population.[33] Although Lavigerie's activities were generally opposed by the French military authorities, who were concerned about the unrest that Catholic missionary work would provoke among the Indigenous inhabitants, they were not a complete departure from past precedent, since the Jesuits had worked in the region since 1863. In the end, however, initiatives to convert the Kabyles and Arabs of Algeria to Catholicism were largely unsuccessful beyond a modest number of orphans taken in by the Church.[34]

On the whole, there is little indication of the extent to which the calamitous events of the 1860s interrupted the daily lives of European settlers in Algeria. As civilian presence in the region grew in size and influence, the archaeological pursuits of French officers and civilian colonists not only continued but became more diverse. Supported by active learned societies in Constantine and Algiers and their respective publications from the 1850s, archaeology flourished and broached a broader range of topics than previously. Although one officer-archaeologist named Payen, who headed the Bureaux arabes in Batna, complained that unrest led by local marabouts (religious leaders and often holy men) cut into his time for archaeology, such asides were surprisingly rare in contemporary publications.[35] Potential interactions between French officers and settlers, on the one hand, and French officers and the Indigenous population, on the other, seem to have become so circumscribed that the terrible suffering of Arabs and Kabyles during the worsening famine went unacknowledged by French military officers and European civilian colonists.

Cartography in French Algeria

In his introduction to *La cité antique* (1864), thirty-four years after the invasion of Algiers, the French historian Numa-Denis Fustel de Coulanges cautioned that the world of ancient Greece and Rome was very different from that of modern times. Emphasizing significant distinctions between the classical past and the present, he underlined the danger of using poorly understood Greek and Roman history as a model for the future of France:

> The ideas that we derive from Greece and Rome have often troubled our generations. Having poorly observed the institutions of the ancient city, we imagine it possible to revive it among us. We have had the illusion of the liberty of the ancients and by this means have only imperiled liberty among modern peoples. The last eighty years have shown clearly that one of the great difficulties that hinders the progress of modern society is the practice that has arisen of always having Greek and Roman antiquity before our eyes.[36]

Fustel de Coulanges indeed lived to see the consequences of allowing the past to determine present events in metropolitan France. Just six years after the publication of *La cité antique*, following France's devastating losses in the Franco-Prussian War, the historian angrily called out Prussian colleagues for twisting narratives of the Germanic invasions to suit the objectives of the modern military undertaking against France.[37]

During much of the 1860s, however, reservations like those expressed by Fustel de Coulanges were rare in reference to the colony of Algeria. While a few scholars cautioned prudence in reading too much from fragmentary primary sources, French civilian administrators, military commanders, and scholars continued to use the Roman past to support a variety of objectives during the region's "pacification" and settlement.[38] Even if Fustel de Coulanges did not speak specifically to instances of ancient narratives being used for practical and ideological purposes in the conquest and settlement of North Africa, the contrast could scarcely be greater between the historian's suspicion of historical claims being put to the use of present conflicts and French military and civilian authorities' regular emphasis on the ancient past.[39] Classical history remained a popular subject of study and its practical applications to disciplines such as cartography were integral to this embrace.[40]

During the first forty years of colonial expansion in Algeria, the Société de géographie de Paris (1821), which had as its objective the collection of information about far-flung parts of the world from travelers, officers, and statesmen, grew increasingly influential.[41] During the brief tenure of the Commission d'exploration scientifique d'Algérie from 1839 to 1842, geography occupied a central place.[42] Captain Ernest Carette, who studied at the École polytechnique from 1828, was a military engineer who professed strong sympathy for Saint-Simonian ideals. As the chief geographer and cartographer of the expedition, Carette advocated that scientific maps shape the French military approach to the conquest of the Ottoman Regency of al-Jazā'er.[43] He underlined the importance of cartographic advances in introducing European civilization to North Africa.[44] However, a lack of recent data from reconnaissance missions conducted by the armée d'Afrique impeded Carette's ability to make accurate calculations and forced him to depend to a large degree on the reports of early modern Arabic and European historians and geographers. Although some reliable regional maps that accorded with modern realities were completed in subsequent decades, an all-inclusive map of French Algeria had not yet been achieved by the War Depot by 1865.[45]

Despite these shortcomings, from the early 1840s, Carette's ambitious geographic and ethnographic studies of Algeria exercised a profound influence on colonial policy. Although they were far from comprehensive, these undertakings measured a variety of features of the territory, including the future potential of the Tell's agricultural produce in the heartland and Saharan commerce for the rapidly expanding colonial project.[46] During the 1850s, Carette's research produced a well-timed publication surveying the Indigenous population of Kabylia, the region that, following Bugeaud's conquest of the Sahara, became the next strategic object of French military intervention due to its proximity to the colonial capital.[47] Because the work of the army's topographical brigades did not begin to yield fruit in Algeria until 1879, when Constant Mercier took charge, more modest cartographic projects of this era exercised an outsized practical and ideological influence and helped actualize French claims to the territory.[48]

While Carette collected topographical and ethnographic data critical to the future of the colonial enterprise, some of his surveys also documented in detail the physical remains of the classical past. He believed that both contributed to the same objective.[49] Thus, in 1863, he took over an unfinished project begun by Frédéric Lacroix at the command of Maréchal Randon in 1851, which had been cut short by Lacroix's passing.[50] Whereas the original survey had intended to address various facets of Roman colonization from the perspective of ancient written sources,

Carette's publications also turned to the abundant data offered by the material remains of classical Rome.[51] Among the physical monuments that figured in Carette's calculations of distances and locations were extant Roman mile markers, roads, inscriptions, and churches.[52] In the late 1860s, detailed statistical surveys and maps of individual districts, such as those undertaken by Captain Charles de Vigneral in Guelma and Djurdjura, followed up on the foundations laid by Carette.[53]

Napoleon III stood personally behind some of the topographic initiatives undertaken in North Africa. These included the mission of Adolphe Daux, a civil engineer and former student of the École des Mines, who had been employed previously by the bey of Tunis to restore function to the ancient Roman hydraulic system in the territory. In 1868, the emperor appointed Daux to direct an official cartographic mission of the North African coast as it was in the Roman period, a task that he coupled with excavations of ancient water systems and visits to more than three hundred ancient sites, many of which were Roman.[54] Occupied in large part with the coast of Tunisia, Daux's activity was more strategic than archaeological in nature since the Ottoman Regency was the next French territorial objective. Both facets of his work, however, had significance for the future territorial ambitions of France.[55]

Both Carette's and Daux's careers underline the intimate connection between officers' scientific inquiries into the ancient past and practical concerns for the effective French appropriation of North African agricultural, human, and strategic resources.[56] Because there was not yet consistent support for this genre of exploration, however, cartographic projects documenting ancient Roman sites in Algeria—and, shortly afterward, Tunisia—only gained more substantial impetus and infrastructure after 1881, this time in the capable hands of the French topographical brigades.[57]

Napoleon III and the Commission de topographie des Gaules

However, even if they had not yet gained the institutional support they would acquire in subsequent decades, cartographic projects, including those related to antiquity, represented an integral part of the historical and ideological framing of the Second Empire. Those on the classical period undertaken by the French in North Africa were intimately related to similar initiatives undertaken in the metropole. As is well known, during the late 1850s and the 1860s, Napoleon III became an enthusiastic proponent and generous supporter of studies of Gallo-Roman geography and history. His interest centered above all on the military exploits of Julius Caesar, whose biography offered a suitable precedent for his own regime. Excavations that pushed the origins of France to the Gallic past, and thus a date well before the rise of the Franks, therefore occupied a special place among the emperor's preoccupations to this end. Among other objectives, they served to bolster the legitimacy of his reign.[58] Disposable funds from the civil list, which annually provided Napoleon III with roughly 25 million francs (30 to 38 million, if one includes income generated by his properties), allowed the emperor to support more extensive archaeological undertakings than had previously transpired in metropolitan France.[59] Unsurprisingly, just as in the case of his recent coup, military men who had served in Algeria played a prominent role in these undertakings.

The earliest of the large-scale ancient excavations in metropolitan France sponsored by Napoleon III transpired at the Camp de Châlons in Champagne, at a date well before the emperor had professed openly his plan to write about Caesar, a theme that had also occupied Charlemagne and Napoleon I.[60] Namely, in the course of establishing a French military installation at the site in 1856–1857, authorities uncovered remains that some attributed to the famed Battle of the Catalaunian Plains (451) between the Roman general Flavius Aetius, allied with Theoderic I, and Attila the Hun and his followers.[61] Although not as well-known as the ancient excavations that followed shortly afterward, Napoleon III's archaeological undertakings in Champagne enticed him to sponsor further activities of this genre. His intervention—and no doubt his generous investment in archaeological exploration—encouraged antiquaries in the region to emulate Napoleon III's intervention in ancient sites.[62]

Following this archaeological venture, Napoleon III issued a decree on July 17, 1858, that established the Commission de topographie des Gaules. He placed it under the direction of Captain Félicien de Saulcy, who was a polytechnicien, numismatist, and curator of the Musée d'artillerie, today the Musee de l'Armée in the Hôtel national des Invalides. The commission, which consisted of ten members, five of whom were based at the Institut de France, was given the task of drawing a map related to Caesar's activities in Gaul, a map of Roman Gaul more generally, and a map of Merovingian Gaul, in addition to creating dictionaries of Celtic and Gallo-Roman archaeology.[63] In addition to using traditional historical sources, members of the commission employed ancient cartographic and archaeological sources like the Peutinger Table, the *Antonine Itinerary*, and the engraved goblets of Aquae Apollinares (Vicarello), which had been discovered in 1852. They also conducted topographic surveys and documented mile markers found in various parts of France and Belgium like Tongeren (F. Tongres) (Limburg), Autun (Saône-et-Loire), and Allichamp (Haute-Marne).[64]

Despite its focus on Gaul, the commission's activities were by no means limited to metropolitan France. Its expert members included, among others, Georges Perrot, who embarked on a mission to Asia Minor; Léon Heuzey, who conducted archaeological research in Macedonia; and Saulcy himself, who undertook excavations in Jerusalem in 1863 and is considered the founder of modern biblical archaeology.[65] Besides their cartographic responsibilities, the commission's members were supposed to assemble a broad variety of documents and materials to assist in the emperor's historical research on Caesar.[66] Napoleon III's evident interest in the classical past may have also emboldened officers based in Algeria to request imperial funding for the repair of the ancient Roman transportation infrastructure. Petitions included a proposal in October 1861 by the duc de Malakoff, then governor-general, for resources to restore the famous Roman bridge at El-Kantara, north of Biskra.[67]

For the most part, however, Napoleon's interest in Gallo-Roman and imperial history was physically disconnected from Algeria. During the Second Empire, metropolitan-sponsored archaeological intervention in the colony, in the years following the conclusion of the expedition of the Commission d'exploration scientifique d'Algérie (1842) and Léon Renier's missions to Lambaesis (1850–1852), was mainly limited to the costly project of acquiring artifacts for the Louvre and publishing the data collected by members of the commission. Nonetheless, as we will see below, there were some important exceptions such as at Tombeau de la Chrétienne. More importantly, those who had served in the French colony and had knowledge of ancient history and monuments represented an important resource from which Napoleon III drew in the late 1850s and 1860s to fulfill his archaeological and imperial ambitions.

Casimir Creuly: Military Expertise in Metropolitan Archaeology

While the actual work of the Commission de topographie des Gaules centered on metropolitan France, it benefited, almost from the time of its creation, from the military cartographic expertise of officer-archaeologists. At least one of its most active participants had served in Algeria: Colonel Casimir Creuly, who arrived in Constantine in 1850 to oversee the cliff-top city's fortifications. During his North African assignment, Creuly played an influential role in the foundation of the Société archéologique de la province de Constantine. In 1852, he also conducted excavations in support of Léon Renier's epigraphical project, mainly with the objective of discovering additional inscriptions to those that the epigrapher had recorded on his first visit to the region.[68] By the end of the decade, Creuly had earned the rank of general on the basis of his laudable reputation among his superior officers as a fortifications engineer and the accolades he had earned as a knowledgeable classicist with perfect command of Latin.[69] As a result, no doubt, of the respect the officer had earned and metropolitan connections established while serving overseas, Napoleon III appointed Creuly as the vice-president of the Commission de topographie des Gaules in 1859.[70] Not only did this invitation bring Creuly to Paris, where he again had the opportunity to work with Renier, but the position facilitated his entry into the immediate circle of scholars such as Alexandre Bertrand, the newly appointed editor of the *Revue archéologique*. The group of scholars supported Napoleon III in his historical and archaeological undertakings inside and outside the metropole.

Once appointed a member of the commission, Creuly found himself in the unique position of integrating his military cartographic skills and war-time experience honed in Algeria with the mission of formulating maps of ancient Gaul and copying more than 1,300 pages of Latin inscriptions.[71] In a rare published personal aside during his work for the commission, for instance, Creuly acknowledged that his North African experience served him well in recognizing the practical realities as opposed to theoretical approximations of Roman calculations of distance: "In Algeria, where I engaged in studies of this type, I recognized that the coefficient of 4/5 applied to mountainous territories, but for land that was not very hilly, as is here the case, one could not evaluate the curves of the routes at more than 1/6, and likewise I do not propose reducing the itinerary distances so much because Caesar describes the landscape as covered by trees and poorly penetrated, *incertis itineribus per silvas* (chap. 37)."[72] In another instance, Creuly approximated the possible pace of an Alpine crossing of the Roman army on the basis of his detailed knowledge of contemporary marches undertaken by French columns across the mountainous landscape of Algeria. To quell doubts of those who questioned the speed at which he thought that the Roman army could move, he cited the rapid traverse of 105 kilometers in the Atlas Mountains by a column of eight thousand to ten thousand men under the command of General Armand Jacques Leroy de Saint-Arnaud during a five-day period in May 1851.[73] A combination of his knowledge of classical history, his proficiency in reading the relevant Latin texts, and his military experience allowed Creuly, like other officers in the direct employment of the emperor, to visualize the capabilities of the ancient Roman army.[74] He was thus able to contribute effectively and influentially to some of the most important components of Napoleon III's favored ancient history projects.

In the early 1860s, Napoleon III directed the activities of the Commission de topographie des Gaules toward the identification and exploration of the battle sites of the famed Gallic leader Vercingetorix. Most important among these undertakings were excavations at the summit of Mont-Auxois at Alise-Sainte-Reine (Côte-d'Or) (1861–1865) and Gergovie (Puy-de-Dôme) (1861–1862).[75] Although the location of the former had been disputed in the late 1850s by the architect Alphonse Delacroix and the art historian and archaeologist Jules Quicherat, most prominently, who pointed instead to Alaise (Doubs) as the site of the battle of Alésia, neither the emperor nor military officers who had served in Algeria like the duc d'Aumale were swayed to this perspective.[76] Quicherat's arguments not only hinged on the details of ancient sources but also included criticism of the merit of the scholarly contributions of those military officers who had so effectively promoted Alise-Sainte-Reine as the location of Alésia.[77] While there were military men on both sides of this controversy, Quicherat's line of attack ultimately proved ineffective against officers who coupled close readings of ancient sources with detailed topographical studies and field experience.[78] However, the animosity of Quicherat's critique exposed the discomfiture felt by at least some civilian scholars at Napoleon III's readiness in his Gallo-Roman projects to place as much if not greater confidence in officer-archaeologists than more traditionally trained scholars of classical history.[79]

From April 20, 1861, Captain Saulcy, the head of the Commission de topographie des Gaules, directed excavations at Alise-Sainte-Reine. Since its constituent members were unable to spend large amounts of time at the site, the expedition was left largely under the technical supervision of Paul Millet, the borough surveyor (*agent-voyer*) for Flavigny-sur-Ozerain. The day-to-day direction of operations fell to a young but enthusiastic local amateur named Victor Pernet.[80] With funds drawn from the emperor's civil list, as many as fifty laborers at a time earned 2.5 francs per day, a figure that was raised to 3 francs per day in March 1862.[81] In addition to Saulcy and Creuly, others involved in this phase of the undertaking included Major Raymond de Coynard, a graduate of Saint-Cyr, and Bertrand.[82]

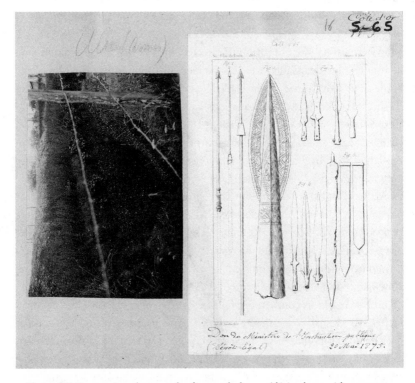

Figure 38. Excavation photograph of a trench dug at Alésia along with weaponry found at the same site. Musée d'archéologie nationale, Saint-Germain-en-Laye, France. Photograph: Tony Querrec. © RMN-Grand Palais/Art Resource, NY.

The initial weeks of the project at Alise-Sainte-Reine and neighboring sites turned up few promising traces of fortifications, in part because the commission was not in a position to question the misguided approximations of Napoleon III. Nonetheless, the time-consuming approach of digging parallel trenches for the purpose of finding walls or other archaeological vestiges like disturbed soil and artifacts eventually yielded important results.[83] Millet documented these undertakings in topographical and site maps and produced detailed drawings of the profiles of the trenches they dug.[84] Due to the care with which the laborers (*terrassiers*) employed in the excavation monitored the stratigraphic layers of the soil, they were able to identify ancient fortifications thought to be associated with the battle as described in Julius Caesar's *Commentaries*.[85] Indeed, Creuly claimed that pickaxes used in excavations by the commission and military engineers at Alise-Sainte-Reine and elsewhere, had effectively resolved the protracted conflict over the location of Alésia. With optimism that was not shared in all quarters, Creuly suggested that the discovery of extensive fortifications, the fruit of applied survey archaeology, had definitively put to rest the remaining text-based questions.[86] To house the finds from Mont-Auxois, plans moved forward for the establishment of an onsite archaeological museum, originally called the Musée impérial d'antiquités (Côte-d'Or), which was placed under the authority of the Commission de topographie des Gaules.[87]

The commission's composition suggests that although Creuly was not the only officer involved in the emperor's Gallo-Roman projects, he was the least controversial and the only one to have served in Algeria. Others involved in Napoleon III's research on Roman Gaul included Commander Eugène Stoffel, a graduate of the École polytechnique and the École d'application de Metz, and an artillery officer who fought in the French armée d'Italie in 1859 under the command of Maréchal Randon.[88] In 1860, on his return to France from Italy, Stoffel was stationed at Auxonne-sur-la-Saône (Côte-d'Or) and took it on himself to visit the sites of both Alaise and Alise-Saint-Reine. After comparing their topography with descriptions of Caesar's famed conflict with Vercingetorix at Alésia, he published an essay in the *Moniteur* on August 6 and 7, 1860, that defended the identification of the battle site described in the *Commentaries of Caesar* with Alise-Sainte-Reine on Mont-Auxois. This piece, which played publicly to the emperor's position, made a strong impression on Napoleon III, who thereafter called Stoffel to his summer residence in Biarritz for a personal audience. Following the commission's discovery at Alise-Sainte-Reine of ditches related to Caesar's military activities, Napoleon III invited Stoffel again to Biarritz in the summer of 1861, so that the two might collaborate on the emperor's project.[89]

On March 23, 1862, just eleven days after Major Stoffel was promoted to the rank of squadron chief of artillery, Napoleon III named him to a special appointment as an imperial ordnance officer. He served in this irregular post, which gave him privileged access to the emperor, for four years.[90] His favored status led to significant antagonism from established scholars working on the Gallo-Roman project, especially after he was given the charge of surveying sites related to the movements of Caesar. In July and August 1862, Stoffel took over excavations at Gergovie. Immediately thereafter, Napoleon III commanded that Stoffel effectively replace the commission at the site of Alise-Sainte-Reine, with the excuse that the latter was preoccupied with a variety of other tasks. Under Stoffel's close oversight and with the benefit of the emperor's expanded funding, excavations continued for an additional three years. Although documentation under his direction was thinner than it had been previously, Stoffel identified the camps that the commission had missed during its more limited engagement.[91]

However, among the circle of scholars working for the emperor, the unpopular decision by the emperor to promote Stoffel to this favored position created the impression that what had previously been an scholarly excavation had now become a more personal affair. Contemporary classicists, and indeed successors, perceived the continued operation as less professional than it had been earlier. Perhaps unjustly, they discounted Stoffel's valuable contributions, including his correction of some of the commission's errors.[92] However, to be fair, Stoffel never published a report of the excavation. His findings were subsumed instead in Napoleon III's three-volume *Histoire de Jules César*, the last of which was an atlas. Stoffel later produced his own three-volume work (likewise containing an atlas) titled *Histoire de Jules César: Guerre civile* (1887). Because of the small size of the print run, this publication never circulated widely.[93] Consequently, Stoffel's academic reputation suffered due to detractors like Salomon Reinach, who worked under Bertrand and succeeded him as director of the Musée des antiquités nationales in Saint-Germain-en-Laye in 1902.[94]

Despite the haste and scale of archaeological undertakings at Alésia, the relative inexperience of those overseeing the operation, and their heavy reliance on ancient historical descriptions of the battle site, late twentieth-century reexploration of the site determined that the unpublished records and observations of the commission and Stoffel were of a high standard for the era.[95] Although the Franco-Prussian War and the fall of Napoleon III ended any thought of returning to Alise-Sainte-Reine for renewed excavations for more than a generation, the battle site continued to attract French officer-archaeologists. In the early twentieth century, another officer, Commandant Émile Espérandieu, a veteran of Algeria, reopened excavations on the remains of Alésia on Mont-Auxois.[96]

On the whole, what distinguished the excavations at Gergovie and Alésia from those that came before and after in France was the scale of the open-air survey excavations: at any one time, the operations under the direction of Stoffel employed as many as three hundred laborers.[97] With the aid of unpublished notes, drawings, letters, and maps produced by those involved in these missions, in addition to renewed exploration at Mont-Auxois in the 1990s, recent scholars have documented how workers at Alise-Sainte-Reine uncovered almost 40 kilometers of Roman fortifications in the course of two years.[98] Prior to this time, there was no precedent for an archaeological undertaking of this size in metropolitan France, Germany, or Britain. Centrally coordinated, large-scale German archaeological projects, foremost those of the Reichs-Limes-Kommission (1892), were still several decades off.[99] The excavations that Germans conducted abroad, most infamously Heinrich Schliemann's at Hissarlik (1870) and Ernst Curtius's in Olympia (1875), likewise lay in the future. Stoffel's innovative approaches owed in no small part to his military experience. Napoleon III had confidence in the abilities of this young but ambitious military officer and was willing to invest enough in the archaeological undertaking to yield rapid and comprehensive results.

Indeed, before the mid-1860s, no comparable examples of large-scale archaeological projects were undertaken in Algeria. Creuly, as a fortifications specialist, was familiar only with the use of smaller groups of soldiers or prisoners for the efficacious excavation of military and archaeological installations in the administrative circle of Batna, and Lambaesis in particular. In part, this had to do with other priorities of the armée d'Afrique as well as safety concerns that still discouraged even the most enthusiastic officers from wandering too far afield without an escort in search of ruins and inscriptions. Moreover, what passed for excavation in Algeria in this period might mean activities as modest as removing debris from stones, turning them over so that their inscriptions might be read, or rebuilding fallen monuments.[100] No undertakings similar to the scope of Alésia were yet envisioned in the Maghreb. Although occasionally visited in the 1840s, and reported upon by Émile Masqueray at the request of the governor-general in 1876, the spectacular town of Thamugadis, located 35 kilometers east of Batna, was not comprehensively excavated until decades later.[101]

One of the few contemporary examples of a French archaeologist organizing excavations on this scale in the 1860s and 1870s was Auguste Mariette Pasha. With a concession over all of Egyptian archaeology, Mariette received access to, among other things, the archaeological corvée—more specifically the men, women, and children subject to forced labor on Egyptian archaeological sites. The corvée had previously been used by Muhammed 'Ali on behalf of French and British consuls to move the amount of soil, sand, and stone necessary to uncover Egyptian antiquities.[102] This example, however, contrasts markedly with Napoleon III's engagement with Alésia, which was largely made possible by his own generous funding. In metropolitan France, the civil list, and not forced labor, provided the manpower that underlay the excavation of sizable sites at remarkable speed.[103]

Creuly, Napoleon III, and Julius Caesar

In addition to his service on the Commission de topographie des Gaules, Casimir Creuly benefited in other ways from Napoleon III's deepening commitment to large-scale projects on the Gallo-Roman period. Many of these undertakings followed the emperor's partial reconciliation in 1860 with his childhood friend, Madame Hortense Cornu. Cornu had conducted research on behalf of Louis-Napoleon on Charlemagne (a project he later abandoned) and assisted him in his publication on the history of artillery while he was imprisoned in the fortress of Ham in the 1840s. Much like the emperor himself, she spoke and wrote multiple languages. Moreover, she regularly attended the meetings of the Académie des inscriptions et belles-lettres and conducted a well renowned scholarly salon at her home.[104] Although Cornu has not often received the credit she merits for her involvement in these imperial endeavors, her renewed friendship with the emperor, despite her unequivocal liberal allegiances, placed her in a powerful position from which to influence court politics and advise the emperor on how to expend funds from the civil list for research.[105] Among other contributions, she suggested which scholars might help him fulfill his historical and archaeological objectives.[106] Cornu, for instance, was behind Ernest Renan's successful bid for an exploratory research trip in search of Phoenician antiquities in the eastern Mediterranean.[107] It was no coincidence, moreover, that Napoleon III chose her husband, the painter Sebastien Cornu, to work with Renier to negotiate the acquisition of the controversial Campana Collection, meant to fill the short-lived Musée Napoléon III at the Palais d'industrie in 1861.[108]

Creuly, as a member of the commission, became one of a stable of experts in classical history and archaeology gathered at Napoleon III's court to support his project on Julius Caesar, which we have seen was closely connected to ongoing archaeological activities at Alise-Saint-Reine and Gergovie.[109] One aspect of this involvement was Bertrand and Creuly's translation of Caesar's *Commentaries on the War of the Gauls* (1865).[110] With the backing of Renier and Cornu, the emperor also appointed Alfred Maury as the librarian of the Tuileries (1860) and Victor Duruy as the minister of public instruction (1863), both of whom participated in the project on Caesar, albeit the latter more peripherally.[111] Among the other contributors to the undertaking were Wilhelm (Guillaume) Froehner, then employed at the Louvre but whom the emperor had hired to read German works for him;[112] Paul Foucart, a specialist in Greek epigraphy; and Prosper Mérimée, former inspector of historical monuments in metropolitan France.[113] The end result was Napoleon III's three-volume *Histoire de Jules César* (1865–1866), a project whose merits few dared to challenge until after the fall of the Second Empire.[114]

Another project in which Creuly participated was a consultative commission established in April 1865 to oversee planning for a long-awaited archaeological museum on the Gallo-Roman period that Napoleon III had decreed in 1862 be established in his château at Saint-Germain-en-Laye. Headed by Comte Émilien de Nieuwerkerke, the powerful superintendent of beaux-arts during the Second Empire, the consultative commission took charge of organizing the future scope and content of the institution. The task had previously been overseen by Claude Rossignol, who had come to the emperor's attention during the excavations of Alise-Sainte-Reine but had made insufficient progress in the museum's planning over more than three years.[115] Civilian members of the commission that replaced him included Maury, Bertrand, Saulcy, the physical anthropologist Paul Broca, and the architects Viollet-le-Duc and Damour. In addition, there were at least three officers beside Creuly, including Commander Auguste Verchère de Reffye and Colonel Octave Penguilly-L'Haridon, both archaeological specialists, and Colonel Oppermann, a specialist in mythology.[116]

Of these men, Verchère de Reffye—a polytechnicien, artillery specialist, and inventor whose interests and inventions spanned from modern artillery to ancient siege engines—had one of the closest relationships to Napoleon III. His work had strong appeal for the emperor, who had a long-standing interest in historical artillery and, as mentioned above, published the two-volume *Études sur le passé et l'avenir d'artillerie* (1846 and 1851) with the research support of Cornu.[117] Verchère de Reffye seems to have come to the notice of Napoleon III around 1860 as a result of his construction of model war machines, which were built to the specifications of ancient Roman and Greek classical texts (and were especially important since, prior to World War I, there were no known surviving archaeological examples). Like Stoffel, Verchère de Reffye received a special appointment as an imperial ordnance officer, a title that allowed him to work directly in the service of the emperor from 1862.[118] Although he neither excavated nor published extensively, his duties for Napoleon III included studying and conserving the material remains found at Alise-Sainte-Reine by Stoffel, including some number of ancient weapons.[119] With the emperor's financial backing for the endeavor, Verchère de Reffye also built models of artillery at an imperial workshop in Meudon (now Hauts-de-Seine) dedicated to both ancient and modern weaponry, about which little documentation survives today.[120] As a consequence of what Hélène Chew has described as Verchère de Reffye's successful engagement in experimental archaeology and his regular interaction with the emperor, the consultative commission chose Verchère de Reffye, along with Bertrand and Rossignol, to draw up the report documenting the group's recommendations for the future museum at Saint-Germain-en-Laye.[121]

Following their consultations, the commission agreed to broaden considerably the mission and scope of Napoleon III's future museum. Although the emperor had originally envisioned the institution as exclusively housing Gallo-Roman antiquities, the commission enlarged the scope of the collection to include all finds related to national history dated to before the reign of Charlemagne. However, this charge excluded the recently created departments of Algeria based in Oran, Algiers, and Constantine (1848). After long years of planning, the inauguration of the Musée de Saint-Germain, later known as the Musée des antiquités nationales, was timed in conjunction with the Exposition universelle de Paris in 1867. By this point, the emperor had appointed Bertrand as the museum's director, a post he occupied until his death in 1902.[122] Long after the museum opened its doors, however, Verchère de Reffye remained active at Saint-Germain-en-Laye, where he continued to design models of ancient machines of war. Some of these are still extant in the collection of the Musée d'archéologie nationale.

Army Translator Laurent-Charles Féraud and the Celtic Remains of Algeria

Although French officer-archaeologists focused nearly exclusively on Roman military remains in the first two decades of the conquest of Algeria, a few tentative efforts to expand the range of archaeological inquiry in the region occurred during the 1850s and 1860s. Captain Moll of the engineering corps at Tébessa (F. Theveste), for instance, initiated study of Christian monuments in the vicinity of the ruins of Tébessa.[123] His survey included attention to the ancient basilica and its mosaic, which were excavated first by Commander Sériziat of the circle of Batna in 1867.[124] His successor, Commander Émile-Jean-Baptiste Clarinval, continued the work in 1870.[125] The officers' understanding of these sites after their brief encounters was simplistic, however, and they failed to use such examples to nuance discussions of the divisiveness of late Roman Christianity in North Africa. Study of the heterodox Donatist movement began only in the 1890s.[126]

Officers with an interest in archaeology more rarely turned their attention to non-Roman remains, including the exploration of prehistoric sites like the standing stones that intrigued Claude-Antoine Rozet in the early 1830s when he first landed in the French colony.[127] Although sustained

French attention to prehistoric remains occurred first in the 1860s, this very distinctive example demonstrates that the Roman sites were not the only monumental possibilities that might be exploited to justify French military intervention in North Africa. However, for a number of reasons that will be outlined below, prehistoric remains proved not to have the same ideological potential as Roman ones in legitimizing the French conquest and colonization of Algeria. The touchstone of ancient Rome proved more successful in its application than reference to an earlier, lesser-known period that was the subject of international, rather than exclusively French, investigation.

Following the publication of Charles Darwin's *Origin of Species* in 1859, which was translated to French in a controversial edition by the anthropologist Clémence Royer in 1862, prehistoric archaeology attracted attention not only in metropolitan France and colonial Algeria but across Europe.[128] The development of this discipline opened up the possibility of new subjects of scholarly inquiry for those interested in the distant past.[129] Conducted in large part by officers and translators of the Bureaux arabes, the exploration of prehistoric monuments also benefited from its practitioners' mastery of Arabic and sometime acquisition of Berber linguistic skills, which allowed them direct access to Indigenous inhabitants, whom they interviewed for lore about prehistoric sites.[130] They also profited from access to the archives and libraries of the Bureaux arabes, which, from the early 1850s, typically contained not just statistics on local populations but also works of ancient and modern North African history.[131] Yet the fact that the men of the Bureaux arabes wielded absolute authority over the livelihoods of local tribes, what Abdelhamid Zouzou has termed the "politics of the baton,"[132] meant that their archaeological and ethnographic research was a product of the severely unequal hierarchy of this relationship.[133] They incorporated prehistoric monuments into a narrative on the origins, ancestry, and primitive nature of contemporary Arab and Kabyle society. Prehistoric archaeology thus offered an additional avenue by which French science worked to support the *mission civilisatrice*, once it became official policy in the Third Republic.[134] It helped cement colonial hegemony.[135]

Directed research on this subject was pursued first by Laurent-Charles Féraud, who had resided in Algeria since his teens and served as an interpreter for the general commander of the division of Constantine. In April

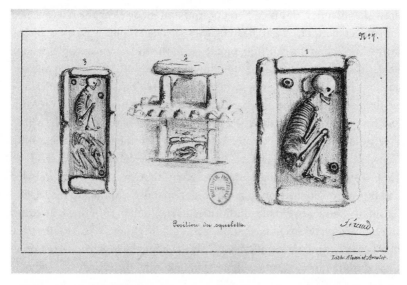

Figure 39. Féraud's sketches of the graves found beneath standing stones at Bou Merzoug. Laurent-Charles Féraud, "Monuments dits celtiques dans la province de Constantine," *Recueil des notices et mémoires de la Société archéologique de la Province de Constantine* (1863). Reproduced by permission of the Bibliothèque nationale de France.

1863, he accompanied the British paleontologist and collector Henry Christy to the springs of Bou-Merzoug.[136] At this location, just 35 kilometers southeast of Constantine, Féraud reported seeing numerous dolmens, cromlechs, menhirs, and tumuli.[137] As similar standing stones were found in France, the men attributed them to the handiwork of the ancient Gauls. With the assistance of several workmen brought along to dig at the site, Féraud and Christy recorded and collected the artifactual and human remains they found, some of which were subsequently donated to the Musée de Constantine.[138]

In the same year, Féraud read a paper on the Gallic standing stones of Bou-Merzoug to the members of the Société archéologique de la province de Constantine, many of whom were fellow interpreters or officers of the Bureaux arabes.[139] Féraud's article on this subject distinguished itself from most contributions to the archaeological society's journal, which focused on ancient Roman monuments and epigraphical evidence.[140] Féraud's claims to the Gallic origin of Algerian prehistoric remains, however, effectively drew the attention of his contemporaries and made clear the relevance of the subject matter to the archaeological society. He contrasted the achievements of these prehistoric inhabitants with the Indigenous people, whom he derided for attributing the standing stones of Bou-Merzoug to ancient pagans (*djouhala*). Using the standing stones as a backdrop, Féraud's discussion commented on the backward and superstitious nature of Arab and Kabyle culture and their fear of vampires and ogres (*el-R'oul*), which they believed inhabited the site.[141] In an essay on the tribes residing near Constantine, published just two years after the humanitarian crisis of 1866–1867, Féraud argued more forcefully that the Arabs and Kabyles had little or no connection to prehistoric remains.[142] Adding to the lack of sensitivity shown by French authorities to the human suffering caused by colonial interventions in the region, Féraud's allegations of the Gallic past of Algeria's standing stones essentially invalidated Indigenous relationships with the monuments of Bou-Merzoug in favor of their new French proprietors.

Féraud's claims to having found Gallic megaliths near Constantine, a conclusion he reiterated more vehemently in an article published in the metropolitan journal *Revue archéologique* in 1864, naturally attracted significant attention from prehistorians.[143] One scholar who read his work closely was Bertrand, who had edited the journal since 1859. Trained at the École française d'Athènes as a classicist, Bertrand had more recently begun to publish on topics stretching from prehistory to Frankish Gaul. Although he hesitated to identify the ancient Gauls as the prehistoric invaders of Algeria, Bertrand attributed the monuments to unnamed dolmen builders, the same people who had occupied France in the Bronze and Iron Age.[144] Namely, he agreed with Féraud that the ancient residents of North Africa had been invaded and dominated by unidentified northern Europeans. Daux, by contrast, who was then engaged in a topographical mission in Tunisia, was skeptical of evidence for a Celtic (or, for that matter, any kind of European) invasion due to the alleged lack of shipbuilding technology among Stone Age populations.[145] In general, however, metropolitan scholars agreed that this external intervention was what made it possible for the Indigenous population of Algeria to undergo a cultural and artistic evolution similar to that which was experienced on the European continent.[146] By then, physical anthropologists like Paul Topinard posited the possibility that the builders of these impressive stone monuments were one and the same as the ancestors of the Kabyles, since many tribes continued to erect stones at cemeteries and use them at their meeting places.[147]

Despite Bertrand's backing and Féraud's election as president of the Société historique algérienne from 1876 to 1878, few outside France accepted the latter's claim to the presence of prehistoric Gauls in Algeria. The fact that similar stone remains were scattered far and wide on the European continent led prehistorians like the Swiss archaeologist Frédéric Troyon to accuse Féraud of unscientific overreach in his thesis.[148] International skepticism also greeted Féraud's transparently subjective claims in favor of French dominance in North Africa. Unlike French classical studies, which were addressed largely to an audience of peers in the metropole, the international nature of prehistoric studies made it more difficult for a French imperialist reading of the monuments to pass muster. Scholarly resistance to Féraud's line of thinking suggested that megaliths could not be as easily and uncritically mapped onto French colonial ideology as Roman remains. Contemporary prehistorians demanded a seemingly more objective view, or at least not one blatantly aimed at advocating France's destiny to rule North Africa.[149]

In Algeria, not only the Société historique algérienne but also the Bureaux arabes offered unwavering backing for Féraud's work on megalithic monuments, which he described as "a new and fecund mine" that would provide evidence for early European migrations to North Africa.[150] This embrace was, no doubt, a response to his interpretation's legitimization of colonial power relations with the Indigenous peoples.[151] By laying claim to evidence for an ancient French presence in the region, Féraud suggested that the armée d'Afrique was simply reviving the colonization of North Africa by Gallic warriors in the distant past. Given Féraud's rapid elevation first to an appointment as the principal interpreter of the division of Constantine (1871), then as the principal interpreter of the governor-general in Algiers (1872), and finally as the French ambassador to Morocco (1877), and the French consul in Tripoli (1878–1884), we can assume that the Ministry of War favored his uncomplicated sentiments (even if they did not directly address the merits of his scholarly approach).[152]

Although echoes of French claims as to the Gallic origins of the Kabyles were still heard in the 1880s and 1890s, the genealogy that alleged partial European ancestry of the Berber peoples triumphed and survived into the mid-twentieth century. Even today, there remains significant uncertainty about even the basic details of Berber ancestry.[153] From the French perspective in the second half of the nineteenth century, however, the Berbers' descent in part from northern Aryans represented an improvement in the relative merit of their place in history vis-à-vis the Arabs. This lineage was a basic tenet of the "Kabyle myth," which was widely embraced by the authorities of the Bureaux arabes during the waning years of the Second Empire and the early decades of the Third Republic.[154] Although most physical anthropologists of the late nineteenth century did not value *métissage* among different races as a positive characteristic of any population, those who promoted assimilationist policies in French Algeria claimed that the Kabyles, as a consequence of this heritage, shared greater affinities with the French than the Arabs. They thus constituted better candidates for integration into European Christian society.[155] For French military officers, especially those of the Bureaux arabes whose purview was oversight of the majority of Muslim inhabitants of Algeria until 1870, prehistoric studies, and particularly those that related to explaining the racial heritage of the Indigenous population of Algeria, contributed to their ideological arsenal.[156] However, prehistoric remains never proved as effective as use of the precedent of ancient Rome to justify French rule in Algeria.

The Tombeau de la Chrétienne: An Imperial Archaeological Venture

In the spring of 1865, in the midst of preparations for the inauguration of the antiquities museum at his château of Saint-Germain-en-Laye, Napoleon III made his second and last visit to Algeria, this time for a period of six weeks. In addition to receiving an update on military, diplomatic, and Indigenous affairs in the three provinces of the territory, the emperor took time to visit several important archaeological sites. On June 2, 1865, he journeyed to Lambaesis. From the small open-air museum that the exiles of 1848 had assembled in the so-called praetorium, the emperor selected a statue of Jupiter to grace the collection of the Louvre.[157] Another site that had an impact on the emperor's thinking was the Tombeau de la Chrétienne (A. Kbeur er Roumia), located between Algiers and Cherchel.[158] Although Napoleon III did not visit it in person, Adrien Berbrugger, director of the Bibliothèque et Musée d'Alger, claimed that the emperor had caught sight of the impressive monument as he crossed the Mitidja plain by carriage. (Owing to the lack of a passable route from the coast, the monument, at least in Berbrugger's recounting of the events, was not on the emperor's agenda.) Intrigued by the mysterious ruins, Napoleon III commissioned Berbrugger and the architect Oscar MacCarthy to investigate the site in detail.[159]

From at least the eighteenth century, the Tombeau de la Chrétienne had been the object of European attention. During their travels in the region, both Thomas Shaw and James Bruce had commented on the mausoleum. Although it had been badly damaged in the early modern period, they identified the pyramid-like structure by reference to a passage recorded by the Spanish geographer Pomponius Mela, who described the Mauretanian royal mausoleum as being located at roughly this location.[160] In the

Figure 40. Antoine Alary's photograph of Napoleon III's visit to Algeria in June 1865. Reproduced by permission of the Bibliothèque nationale de France, Département des estampes et de la photographie.

nineteenth century, French scholars recognized the stone monument as the burial place of Juba II, the Numidian king of Mauretania, and his queen Cleopatra Selena, the daughter of Antony and Cleopatra. Loyal clients to the Roman emperors during Juba II's reign from c. 29 BCE to 20 CE, the monarchs established their capital at Caesarea Julia (F. and A. Cherchel) and built a family mausoleum nearby. However, their dynasty was not long-lived and did not survive Caligula's murder of their son, King Ptolemy, in 40 CE.[161]

Suggesting some inaccuracies in Berbrugger's narrative of Napoleon III's fleeting encounter with the mausoleum and profound interest in the site, Monique Dondin-Payre has argued that it is more likely that the entrepreneurial

Figure 41. The American photographer John Beasley Greene's calotype of the Tombeau de la Chrétienne, taken on January 1, 1856, just three days into Berbrugger's first sponsored exploration of the site. This image captured the site prior to the clearing of much of the fallen stone from the monument. Bibliothèque de l'Institut de France, Folio Z154D, pl. 4. Photograph: Gerard Blot. Reproduced by permission of the Institut de France. © RMN-Grand Palais/Art Resource, NY.

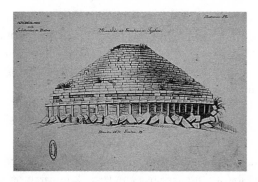

Figure 42. Carbuccia's drawing of Medracen in the military administrative district of Batna in 1850. Jean-Luc Carbuccia, *Archéologie de la subdivision de Batna: Première campagne du 1er novembre 1848 à juillet 1849.* Bibliothèque de l'Institut de France, Ms. 1369B, pl. 19. Photograph: Thierry Le Mage. Reproduced by permission of the Institut de France. © RMN-Grand Palais/Art Resource, NY.

Berbrugger lobbied Napoleon III for financial support for its exploration. Since he had first laid eyes on the ruin in 1835, when he accompanied an expeditionary column led by Governor-General Bertrand Clauzel from Algiers to Cherchel, Berbrugger had been intent on excavating and breaking into the enclosed confines of the Tombeau de la Chrétienne.[162] Over the course of his visit to Algeria in June 1865, the emperor assented to fund Berbrugger's petition to examine the elusive site.[163]

The Tombeau de la Chrétienne, which acquired its French name either because of a carved cross on its exterior or a mistranslation of the Arabic appellation of "Tomb of the Roman Woman," seems to have attracted Berbrugger by its mysterious appearance and origins.[164] His activity at the site was no doubt also a consequence of his competitive nature and resentment of his archaeological colleagues in Constantine, whose region was crowded with a much larger number of Roman monuments than Algiers. It is now thought that the Tombeau de la Chrétienne was likely modeled after a similar (albeit more modest) structure, Medracen, in the administrative district of Batna in the province of Constantine. In 1849–1850, the older site drew the attention of Colonel Jean-Luc Carbuccia, who ordered Captain Collineau, with soldiers from the Foreign Legion, to excavate it while he busied himself with the exploration of Lambaesis.[165] In 1854, the architect F. Becker followed up on the incomplete exploration of Medracen begun by Carbuccia. During the next year, he published a preliminary study of the Numidian monument that highlighted it as an example of the transition from Egyptian to Greek architectural traditions.[166] Although Colonel Foy subsequently published a more impressionistic, meandering article on Medracen in 1856, he did not launch a new excavation of the site.[167]

In the meantime, Count Guyot, director of the interior, visited the Tombeau de la Chrétienne and requested that Minister of War Maréchal Soult provide 5,000 francs so that he might conduct onsite excavations. After this petition was declined, the site remained unexplored while officer-archaeologists and architects undertook research on Medracen.[168] To launch his first excavations at the Tombeau de la Chrétienne in 1855, Berbrugger petitioned Governor-General Randon for funds. In return, he received 500 francs for this purpose; the modest sum meant, however, that Berbrugger could afford to launch only two modest campaigns of roughly two weeks each in December 1855 and March 1856.[169] To unravel the mystery of the monument, he employed a team of approximately fifty Zouaves, a force that in the early 1840s maintained its exotic style of military dress but had become predominantly European rather than Indigenous in composition, as it had been in the 1830s.[170] Berbrugger complained that the men were, in some instances, so young or in such poor health that they were not up to the backbreaking task of moving the heavy stones that impeded access to the monument.[171] By the end of the four-week campaign, they had still not found the entrance to the mausoleum. Berbrugger, however, lacked the financial resources to engage in a more exhaustive study of the intriguing monument.

Evidence of Berbrugger's first archaeological exploration of the Tombeau de la Chrétienne was documented by John Beasley Greene, a young American photographer who had earned renown for creating stills of Egyptian monuments. Drawn to volunteer his skills at the site because of its alleged Egyptian connections, Greene made calotypes of the Tombeau de la Chrétienne. Rare at this time in Algerian archaeology, this photographic technology did not accommodate movement and thus was suitable only for capturing structures and landscapes. However, calotypes were valued because a single negative could create multiple copies.[172] Greene's contribution captured successive phases of the monument's excavation by Berbrugger, which had been damaged both in the early modern period and more recently by the French navy. Unfortunately, Greene's severe illness and demise less than a year afterward, however, meant that the calotypes were never published after their arrival at the Académie des inscriptions et belles-lettres.[173] In subsequent publications, Berbrugger instead relied on daguerreotypes taken by the professional photographer Félix-Jacques Moulin, who had permission from the minister of war to travel to Algeria and create images of the French colony.[174]

A decade later, following his petition to the Napoleon III during his Algerian trip, Berbrugger, in his capacity as inspector general of historical monuments and archaeological museums of Algeria, received an initial allotment of 6,000 francs. In March 1866, the emperor doubled his original investment so that the work at the Tombeau de la Chrétienne could continue.[175] The influx of funding and the emperor's official imprimatur provided Berbrugger with the long awaited means to ease transport to the site and breach the closed structure to determine its contents. Starting in the late summer of 1865, Berbrugger commissioned the building of a road to facilitate access to the ancient monument. The excavation itself, undertaken with the labor of imprisoned French soldiers from the penitentiary in Bab-el-Oued under the direction of Lieutenant Hammer, began on November 5, 1865, and lasted till May 1866.[176] Berbrugger also benefited from the scholarly expertise of the architect Oscar MacCarthy, who joined the undertaking in December 1865 and made scale drawings of the monument.[177]

The stated goals of Berbrugger's excavation of the Tombeau de la Chrétienne were to remove as much of the damaged stone from the structure as possible so that the monument could be studied in its entirety, while leaving the intact stones in their present position. In Berbrugger's estimation, the clearing of damaged stones was necessary to find the best way to penetrate the apparently hollow monument and determine the size and contents of its stone cavity. In addition to the assistance of the chief mining engineer of Algiers, a man named Ville, Clément Purschett, another expert hired for this purpose, employed an artesian probe and other tools to test for possible entrances to the circular structure, which was 63 meters in diameter, 30 meters high, and rested on a square platform. After fourteen attempts, the last of which was on April 28, 1866, workers, laboring with a drill at the site of the thirteenth probe, identified on May 5 what they determined to be an entrance located under the false door on the eastern side.[178] With the help of military explosives to breach the structure, they

Figure 43. Félix-Jacques-Antoine Moulin's photograph of the northern part of the Tombeau de la Chrétienne, featuring the so-called false door and Berbrugger's team of Zouaves, who provided the physical labor necessary to clear away fallen stone from the monument. Bibliothèque nationale de France, Fontainebleau, Réserve OZ-110 (2)-FOL. Reproduced by permission of the Bibliothèque nationale de France.

were finally able to enter the mausoleum on May 15, after seven months of preparatory measures and failed attempts.[179]

Berbrugger reported that he and his men first entered a corridor, which led to a doorway guarded by a sculpted lion and lioness. From there, over the course of several days, they were able to clear debris and proceed up a brief staircase of seven steps to reach the principal gallery, which wound counterclockwise around the base of the circular monument. Berbrugger surmised that this space was used for ancient Egyptian ceremonial purposes. Turning at last to the center of the monument, the hallway passed through a narrower passageway before reaching the main room at the heart of the structure. They believed that this chamber housed the ashes belonging to the royal couple, who, in keeping with contemporary

Roman tradition, had been cremated.[180] Noting that the site had long been avoided by the Kabyles living in the region, a caution that he belittled as their superstitious fear of the ancient monument, Berbrugger condescendingly reported that precautions taken had prevented any of the Indigenous men working at the site from being disturbed by nightmares.[181]

During the course of his excavations, Berbrugger regularly used the *Revue africaine*, the journal which he edited for the Société historique algérienne, the organization of which he was also president, to update fellow scholars on progress at the Tombeau de la Chrétienne.[182] Beyond drawing attention to the royal occupants of the mausoleum, Berbrugger wanted to highlight the fate of the monument following its abandonment in the mid-first century CE. Noting that he and MacCarthy had observed a variety of debris in the cavity of the structure, including skeletal remains and a few vessels with Christian symbolism dating possibly to the Byzantine epoch, Berbrugger hypothesized that the mausoleum had become a hiding place for criminals and Christians in late antiquity. By the time of the Arab invasion, however, Berbrugger believed that the monument was no longer accessible to penetration; overgrown with vegetation and its passage blocked by stones, the original entrance was hidden from sight.[183]

Although Arab historians had little to say about the monument, Berbrugger noted that it had become the subject of at least two strands of Spanish and Arabic folklore. One recounted how Ahmed le Hadjout, after being held captive in Spain, was freed on the condition that he burn a paper covered with arcane characters at the summit of the mausoleum. Having completed this task, Ahmed was amazed to observe a considerable quantity of gold and silver emerge from the monument and depart in the direction of Spain. Although Ahmed was unable to enrich his own family in this fashion, the legend led many to believe that the mausoleum was the repository of untold riches. A second popular story related by Berbrugger involved the story of a local shepherd, who noticed that a black cow from his herd disappeared daily; after secretly following it one evening, the shepherd saw his cow scratch against the wall of the monument, which briefly opened but then closed immediately afterward after it had ambled inside. The next day, the shepherd once again followed the black cow, but this time grabbed it by the tail when it entered the mausoleum so that he might accompany it. As the beast proceeded to give its milk to a baby lying on a golden throne, a figure whom Berbrugger identified as the son of *Halloula*, guardian fairy of the Tombeau de la Chrétienne, the shepherd found himself surrounded by countless riches and took as many items as he could carry before departing with the black cow. It was a journey he was said to have repeated a number of times, each time gathering more treasure, making him wealthier than the most opulent monarchs in the world.[184] Confidence in some quarters regarding the reliability of these legends led Salah Raïs, the pasha of Algiers, to issue orders in 1555 to demolish the stone structure and extract its treasure. This project caused significant damage to the monument despite failing either to penetrate or fully destroy it.[185]

One cannot help but think that Berbrugger, who included an account of the oral traditions associated with the Tombeau de la Chrétienne in his archaeological reports, had himself been drawn to the site for similarly self-aggrandizing reasons. While he underlined the fantastical nature of folkloric traditions attached to the mausoleum and used this opportunity to deride Indigenous superstition, he too had persisted for thirty years in searching for a way into the mausoleum. Although he professed the laudable ideals of safeguarding the parts of the monument that were intact, Berbrugger's methods, including boring at least fourteen access holes into the structure for the artesian probe and laying explosives to breach the structure, were only marginally less destructive than the initiative of the pasha of Algiers in the mid-sixteenth century.[186] When Berbrugger found only bone fragments and scattered artifacts, he even beat the walls of the chambers with a crowbar to determine if there were any additional hollow compartments.[187] In the end, without admitting defeat, Berbrugger made the best of what the site, a colonial Gordian knot, had to offer him. Even if he had come up empty, he had been sponsored by the emperor and could now take credit for having successfully broken into the mysterious Roman-era mausoleum of Juba II and Cleopatra Selena.

Indeed, Berbrugger proved an indefatigable promoter of the Tombeau de la Chrétienne. On May 22, 1866, while a cholera epidemic raged in Algeria and the famine reached devastating proportions among Indigenous inhabitants, Berbrugger welcomed Governor-General Mac-Mahon and his wife, his chief of staff, the Maréchal Niel and his daughter and wife, to tents erected near the royal mausoleum just a week after it had been breached. Berbrugger alleged that such a large number of people arrived at the scene to witness the opening of the enigmatic tomb, both Europeans and Indigenous people, that some were perched on the graded stones of the monument itself. After a tour of the interior of the mausoleum for the most eminent visitors, the governor-general's staff lit flares on the top of the structure as evening came on. Berbrugger recounted: "The effect was more stunning than one had ever hoped and their dim lights, the fantastic reflections on the monument on the spectators at its base, near the entrance of the underground burial place, gave the people and objects a gloomy hue, as if one were transported back eighteen centuries, at the moment when a nocturnal convoy brought some monarch of Mauretania to his final palace."[188] Berbrugger's orchestration of this inaugural ceremony at the Tombeau de la Chrétienne presaged his recognition of a relatively new phenomenon in Algeria: civilian tourism.[189] He prepared for this new development by creating attractive brochures and clearing the grounds of the most pyramid-like structure to grace Algeria.[190]

Just two years before his death at the age of sixty-six, Berbrugger published *Tombeau de la Chrétienne* (1867) for those further afield and unlikely to read the *Revue africaine*. From the sculptor Latour fils of Algiers, he also commissioned two plaster scale models of the Tombeau de la Chrétienne. The first was displayed at Berbrugger's Bibliothèque et Musée d'Alger, and the second was transported to Paris to grace the Algerian pavilion of the Exposition universelle in 1867.[191] Having succeeded in drawing high-level attention to the Tombeau de la Chrétienne, Berbrugger engaged the civic authorities to aid in its promotion. Envisioning the historical and future commercial value of the heretofore neglected monument, they pledged a modest sum of 180 francs per year to subsidize a custodian to guard the grounds and greet visitors who arrived at the mausoleum.[192] Now that the Tombeau de la Chrétienne was more accessible, exotic tales of the now vanquished Roman-era monument could only increase its mystery and attraction among potential European tourists. No doubt, Berbrugger assumed that the humanitarian tragedy unfolding among the Indigenous peoples of Algeria would deter few Europeans from undertaking travel to North Africa.

Epilogue

CLASSICAL ARCHAEOLOGY IN ALGERIA AFTER 1870

Within weeks of the fall of Napoleon III and the creation of the Third Republic, the governance of Algeria shifted from military to civilian footing. On October 24, 1870, the Government-General was moved from the portfolio of the Ministry of War; to that of the Ministry of the Interior, and commanding generals were placed under the authority of the civilian prefects of Algiers, Constantine, and Oran.[1] During the early months of the Third Republic, a half million hectares of tribal lands were earmarked for immediate transfer to French colonists. Civilian settlers seeking greater autonomy for the colony agitated against the new regime, a strategy that paid off not only economically but also politically. Among the metropolitan government's concessions to avert their open rebellion was the allotment of two representatives for each of the Algerian departments in the French Chambre des députés. To satisfy their critics among the European colonist population, authorities also dismantled the once powerful but long resented Bureaux arabes. Local offices overseeing Muslim residents were retained but their activities constricted: they were now subsumed

under the authority of civilian district authorities. Although a Muslim uprising did not break out immediately, it followed shortly thereafter, largely
because of the removal of protections for Indigenous peoples and a general policy shift under the Third Republic. In February 1871, Muhammad
al-Muqrani, the *bash-agha* of much of Grand Kabylia, who had guaranteed debts for his fellow tribesmen during the famine of 1867–1868
and now stood to lose at least a million francs of revenues to the civilian
regime, led a revolt of his followers. Al-Muqrani's actions triggered, in
turn, a larger rebellion of 250 Muslim communities, roughly a third of the
Indigenous population. Many Arab and Kabyle inhabitants led to revolt
were informed by the neo-Sufist order of Rahmaniyya, which attracted a
significant following in Algeria and Tunisia.[2]

Responding to widespread Muslim unrest, the new governor-general of
Algeria, Vice-Admiral Louis de Gueydon, managed to quell the rebellion
only after several months. The severe measures deemed necessary to bring
an end to the Rahmaniyya uprising in mid-August 1871 resulted in the
capture or death of as many as twenty thousand Algerian Arabs and Kabyles. In addition to the destruction of farms and villages that transpired
during the affair, the tribes in Kabylia held responsible for these events
were punished collectively with an indemnity of 36.5 million francs and
the sequestration of their lands.[3] In the end, more than 100,000 hectares
of confiscated lands in the Summam Valley and the region of Sétif and
Constantine were used to resettle roughly ten thousand former inhabitants of Alsace and Lorraine, who had fled the territory annexed by a
newly united Germany and were relocated by the French government to
Algeria. Although the rural resettlement of the formerly urban-based population of refugees ultimately proved unsuccessful, the number of civilian
colonists living outside Algeria's cities and towns came close to doubling
over the course of the next two decades. The European-born population
crested at two hundred thousand in 1898.[4]

With the rapid growth of immigration to the colony, pressure increased
on French authorities to accommodate the new arrivals with land. On
July 26, 1873, metropolitan authorities promulgated the Warnier Law,
a measure that mandated that property holding in Algeria follow French
regulations. Eliminating protections for Indigenous property holders,
whether individual or communal, this legislation further undermined the
longstanding custom of communal property (*arsh*), which had been such an

integral part of the village economy in Algeria but had been eroded by colonial policies of the late 1850s and the 1860s. These severe measures pushed many tribes further onto marginal, often mountainous, terrain and away from the fertile lands they had once occupied.[5] Entire tribes chose exile in Morocco, Tunisia, and Syria rather than remain in French Algeria.[6] Although the opening of the Crédit agricole at the Bank of Algeria in 1872 brought increased metropolitan sponsorship of agricultural projects in Algeria, and the extension of French public works to Algeria resulted in the improvement of transportation infrastructure and public buildings from 1878, these projects mainly benefited European settlers. By contrast, they only marginally ameliorated the day-to-day lives of Arabs and Kabyles.[7]

Ruined financially by the aftermath of the humanitarian catastrophe of 1867–1868 and the harsh penalties exacted by French administrators as punishment for the 1871 revolt, the 3.5 million Muslims then resident in Algeria enjoyed few of the political freedoms extended to other constituencies in the colony by the Third Republic. In October 1870, the Crémieux Decree offered citizenship to the Jewish population of Algeria outside the Sahara.[8] In June 1889, the Naturalization Law granted French citizenship to Europeans of non-French descent living in Algeria. By contrast, the Code de l'indigénat, which was prepared in 1871–1873 but applied first in 1879, cut back sharply on already limited Muslim civil liberties for those unwilling to give up the Islamic faith in exchange for recognition as citizens. Arabs and Kabyles living in Algeria faced severe restrictions on their political rights, juridical status, and freedom of travel, along with the denial of legal procedures if accused of wrongdoing by French civil administrators.[9] The number of Algerians who migrated to France prior to World War I therefore remained extremely small.[10]

In addition, despite the dissipation of the traditional Muslim educational system due to colonial policies and demographic collapse, the Arab and Kabyle population's access to French public schools and adequate health care was severely circumscribed. More than 90 percent of Algerian Muslims lived outside urban centers, the residents of which were overwhelmingly French by the end of the nineteenth century. Consequently, they missed out on the economic advantages enjoyed by the growing population of settlers of European extraction. Instead, Arab and Kabyle rural inhabitants were forced to share-crop or labor for Europeans on lands once possessed by their communities. Others provided lower skill services to the settler economy as domestics and dock workers.[11] The Third Republic thus not only brought no direct resolution of the Indigenous "problem" during the first decades of civilian rule in Algeria, but it also saw the continued worsening of economic and political conditions for Muslims living under French rule in the North African colony.[12]

Professionalization of Archaeology and the Conservation of Roman Monuments in Algeria

As evident from the above-described events, it is not surprising that French authorities did not prioritize the protection of ancient monuments in Algeria. While these issues were not given much attention during the inaugural years of the Third Republic, they were, by contrast, not altogether absent from the developments of this period. In May 1872, the minister of public instruction appointed the architect Edmond Duthoit, who remained resident in metropolitan France, to study the monuments of Algeria.[13] He developed an interest not just in Roman remains but Arab architecture as well.[14] In late 1872, Antoine Héron de Villefosse received authorization from the director of beaux-arts for a mission to Algeria to study Roman inscriptions and antiquities in the region. Embarking on his journey in March 1873, he spent time in Algiers, Cherchel, Tipasa, Constantine, Lambaesis, Djémila (L. Cuiculum), and a number of other locations, taking the time to make detailed observations about inscriptions located both in museums and in situ.[15] Moreover, the foundation of the École française de Rome (March 25, 1873) not long after the unification of Italy also became the source of a small but steady stream of French classical scholars headed to Algeria and the Regency of Tunis with the intention of exploring or excavating the ancient ruins of the region.[16] Greater regularization of the financing of archaeological undertakings, now possible due to the availability of more substantial institutional support, was aided by the creation in 1874 of the Commission des voyages et des missions scientifiques et littéraires at the heart of the Service des voyages et des missions.[17]

However, since metropolitan support for archaeological exploration was not plentiful and priorities remained unfocused, very little changed immediately with respect to antiquities on the ground. Internationally, French treatment of Roman inscriptions and monuments met with severe criticism, which was enumerated most harshly by the German epigrapher Gustav Wilmanns in several posthumously published works.[18] Sent to Algeria and Tunisia in the spring of 1872 by Theodor Mommsen to conduct research for the eighth volume of the *Corpus inscriptionum latinarum (CIL)* dedicated to North Africa (thereby replacing Léon Renier, who resigned from the project in response to the Franco-Prussian War),[19] Wilmanns issued a scathing indictment of the large number of inscriptions the French had destroyed in the two decades since Renier had worked in the region in the early 1850s.[20] Even Héron de Villefosse, whose loyalties were squarely with France, remarked on the striking contrast between the number of ruins that were located in Algeria, and, yet, the complete indifference of French colonists and officers toward their preservation. He noted with chagrin that recently uncovered antiquities rapidly disappeared and could not be located even a short time later.[21] He thus recommended that many of the most precious remains would be better safeguarded by sending them to metropolitan France.[22]

During the visit of Héron de Villefosse to Lambaesis in April 1873, for instance, he reported that the praetorium and its open-air museum had suffered from pillage during the insurrection of 1871; he attributed the damage to the monuments not to local Kabyles but to soldiers from the Bouches-du-Rhône, who had camped two years earlier at this location during the Rahmaniyya uprising. He blamed the servicemen with disrespectfully engraving their names on the statues and breaking those antiquities that were not already sufficiently mutilated. Indeed, following the departure of M. Barnéond, director of the penitentiary of Lambaesis, who had also overseen excavations there in the mid-1860s, no one had taken much interest in the remains of the Third Augustan Legion. Consequently, after the fall of the Second Empire, these monumental ruins lay at the mercy of troops or settlers who passed through the Aurès Mountains.[23] Only in 1880, when their deplorable condition was pointed out to the Ministry of Public Instruction by Émile Boeswillwald, an architect and the general inspector of historical monuments, were conservation measures undertaken at the long abused site.[24] In 1880, a credit of 50,000 francs from metropolitan authorities was directed toward safeguarding monuments in Algeria.[25]

News regarding antiquities did not improve markedly over the next years. In December 1876, Oscar MacCarthy, who directed the Bibliothèque et Musée d'Alger from the time of Adrien Berbrugger's death in 1869, complained of the continuing lack of funding for conserving ancient monuments in Algeria.[26] Similar information was revealed by colonial authorities during the visit of a representative of the archaeological section of the Comité des travaux historiques to Algeria in May 1876; on his arrival, he was confronted with complaints about the lack of sufficient protections for ancient monuments. His report, in which he confirmed the deplorable state of antiquities in Algeria, was sent by Julien-Alexis Courgeon, inspector of the Académie de Paris, to the Ministry of Public Instruction and Beaux-Arts. It set in motion further discussions in the ministry in March 1877.[27] Ultimately it gave teeth to the French decree protecting historical monuments that had been promulgated in 1876.[28] A more powerful antiquities conservation law dated March 30, 1887, reinforced the protections of ancient remains. It applied not just to ancient remains in metropolitan France but had a specific provision, article 16, that made it applicable to monuments and antiquities in Algeria as well.[29] Parallel to these developments, Charles Lavigerie, archbishop of Algiers, created a Diocesan Commission of Archaeology in March 1877 with the objective of protecting ancient monuments and antiquities, both pagan and Christian, discovered in clerical jurisdictions.[30]

With the passage of the 1876 law regulating patrimonial concerns, the minister of public instruction finally took steps toward a more comprehensive assessment of existing needs regarding antiquities across metropolitan France and Algeria. In response to a circular sent in 1876 to learned societies in all the French departments requesting that they collaborate in the publication of an inventory of monuments, authorities in Algiers established a commission in June 1878 intended to identify and catalogue monuments and art objects in the three Algerian departments. Headed by the diocesan architect Théodore-Alexandre Chevalier, the newly created commission included among its members the presidents of the Société des beaux-arts and the Société historique algérienne, in addition to the director of the Bibliothèque et Musée d'Alger, the architect of the government-general, the mufti of Algiers, and other functionaries with relevant expertise.[31] Despite the appointment of this prestigious team, insufficient institutional infrastructure existed to regulate antiquities in the region in a practical manner. The opportunity to create an effective plan for the conservation of monuments and archaeological exploration of Algeria remained unrealized until early in the next decade.[32]

The year 1880 saw the creation of the Service des monuments historiques, headed first by the architect Duthoit. The organization was responsible for overseeing excavations, the restoration and preservation of historical monuments, and the regularization of archaeological collections in local museums in Algeria.[33] It also took the measure of appointing and paying guardians, some former Indigenous soldiers in the armée d'Afrique, at the ruins of Lambaesis, Tombeau de la Chrétienne, Thamugadis, Djémila, and Tébessa.[34] The same year witnessed the foundation of the École supérieure des lettres d'Alger, an institution that not only directed archaeological research but became a meeting point for those engaged in scientific undertakings, including scholars affiliated with the École française de Rome who traveled to North Africa as a part of their studies. The institution's chair of history and antiquities of Africa went first to Émile Masqueray, who had led excavations at the iconic site of Timgad, ancient Thamugadis, in the Aurès Mountains from 1875.[35] From 1890, the École supérieure began to teach its own courses in classical archaeology. These lectures informed the up-and-coming generation of specialists in this area, including most prominently Stéphane Gsell, who became the leading archaeologist in Algeria in the early decades of the twentieth century.[36] Given the ideological orientation of archaeological research in the region over the previous five decades, it is not all that surprising that Masqueray was also the author of *Formation des cités chez les populations sedentaires de l'Algerie* (1886), a work in which he advocated for the Kabyle population's natural affinity (as opposed to that of the Arabs) for assimilation to French rule.[37]

International Competition and Tunisian Antiquities

Despite internal impediments to financing and organizing archaeological activities in Algeria, continuing competition with German and British scholars meant that conservation issues related to antiquities found in the Maghreb could not be entirely ignored by metropolitan authorities. Although French authorities were able to regulate authorization for archaeological undertakings in Algeria, the situation was considerably more complex in the Ottoman Regency of Tunis, where the reigning dey still retained control of antiquities and, with it, a measure of independence in the 1870s. These restrictions notwithstanding, less than a year after his visit to Algeria in spring 1873, Héron de Villefosse received authorization for a mission to Tunis: he was granted 3,000 francs to transport Punic and Roman objects to the Louvre, which arrived in September 1874.[38]

Similarly, following his appointment as dragoman in the French consulate of Tunis in 1872, Évariste-Charles Pricot de Sainte-Marie requested support from the Commission des voyages in 1874 to undertake a study of Punic and neo-Punic inscriptions. This task was meant to supplement Ernest Renan's *Corpus inscriptionum semiticarum* with material from the Maghreb and save face for the French in the international field of epigraphy. One of Pricot de Sainte-Marie's responsibilities was to ship Roman artifacts to the Bibliothèque et Musée d'Alger from Carthage. From the French perspective, Algeria represented a more acceptable repository for these antiquities than the Regency of Tunis, a location over which France did not yet exercise direct hegemony. Pricot de Sainte-Marie also assembled a much larger collection of Carthaginian remains, a total of 2,088 pieces including a number of inscriptions, which were destined for display at the Bibliothèque nationale and the Musée du Louvre. Unfortunately, the weighty cargo was lost at sea in 1875, when the battleship in which it was held, *Le Magenta*, sank in the port of Toulon after a fire ignited the ship's gunpowder magazine. Although some of the epitaphs and bits of statue were salvaged by divers before the ship was dynamited to reopen access to the port, some of *Le Magenta*'s contents were not salvaged until the 1990s.[39]

Competition over antiquities in the Regency of Tunis came not only from other European nation-states but also from Christian clerics. In 1875 and 1877, Charles Lavigerie, the archbishop of Algiers whose religious jurisdiction extended over Tunis, purchased tracts of land on the prominent acropolis of ancient Carthage. His plans included the construction of a chapel in honor of Saint Louis as well as the establishment of a Christian-focused archaeological museum under the authority of the Missionnaires d'Afrique, also known as the White Fathers.[40] With direction provided by Père Alfred-Louis Delattre, a youthful and enthusiastic appointee of

Lavigerie, both clerics envisioned the ruins of the ancient city as not only a showcase for the finds made in the course of Christian excavations in both Tunisia and Algeria but also a pilgrimage destination for devout Christians attracted to the location by the early third-century martyrdoms of Perpetua and Felicity.[41] Following the start of excavations at Carthage's arena in 1880, Delattre offered a number of epitaphs thought to have come from an imperial slave cemetery to the Bibliothèque nationale in Paris, where they were exhibited in the Département des médailles et antiques from some time before 1889.[42]

It is clear that Ottoman authorities saw these actions as a provocation and a signal of the growing French threat to their political and cultural autonomy. Consequently, in 1876, Khereddine Pacha chose to open his own archaeological museum in Tunis, an institution that he intended to be accessible to the public. Undertaken with the support of Delattre, this project was part of the politics of cultural renewal inspired by the European model.[43] While unusual, Khereddine's initiative was nonetheless not the first to be launched by an Ottoman authority in the Regency of Tunis. Khereddine followed in the footsteps of Muhammed, son of the minister Mustapha Khaznadar, who had, in the late 1850s, brought together an important collection of architectural fragments and Latin inscriptions in the garden of the palace of La Manouba.[44] Similar measures by Ottoman authorities had been undertaken even earlier in the Sublime Porte, including the creation of a modest archaeological museum in Istanbul in 1846 and the promulgation of early antiquities protections to guard against European depredations in 1869 and 1874.[45] In the Ottoman capital, the sultan's appointment of Osman Hamdi as the director of the Imperial Museum, and his successful implementation of laws more strictly regulating archaeological excavations and monuments, came shortly afterward in 1884.[46] The Ottomans, using methods similar to those of the French, thereby positioned themselves as active players in the competitive field of archaeological endeavors.

With the French defeat of the Ottoman rulers of the Regency of Tunis and the establishment of the Protectorate of Tunisia in 1881, concern with foreign archaeological competition—including that of the Italians, who had a significant presence in the region—did not cease. With the support of the Commission des voyages, Maurice d'Irisson, count of Hérisson, launched an excavation that spring at a location he identified as the ancient Phoenician trading center of Utica (F. Utique) in northern Tunisia. Although funding for the mission was revoked in late spring because of the count's exaggeration of the achievements of his undertaking, he displayed his collection of artifacts from Utica at the Louvre in the autumn of 1881. However, the antiquities were not well received in metropolitan France. The count's report also became the target of negative scholarly attention due to the large number of transcriptional errors it contained and its alleged plagiarism of earlier published epitaphs from Carthage.[47]

Under the aegis of the French Protectorate of Tunisia, archaeological exploration now shifted from the hands of consuls to military officers and clerics. One notable example was Second-Lieutenant Émile Espérandieu, a recent graduate of the École spéciale militaire de Saint-Cyr, who participated in the French campaign against the Regency of Tunis in 1881. Like his predecessors in Algeria, Espérandieu was inspired by the ruins he encountered in the region, and from 1883 began to publish on archaeological sites in Tunisia. In 1886, when he returned to France as an adjunct instructor at the École militaire d'infanterie de Saint-Maixent, Espérandieu continued his involvement in archaeological study and made a name for himself through his research on Gallo-Roman monuments, including excavations at Alésia.[48] Additional important developments of this period related to antiquities included the commission established in 1885 under the leadership of René du Coudray de la Blanchère, then serving as the minister of public instruction and the beaux-arts. After being appointed the director of antiquities in Tunisia, Coudray de la Blanchère oversaw what would become the twenty-six-volume project *Musées et collections archéologiques de l'Algérie et de la Tunisie* (1890–1928).[49]

The Uneven Legacy of Officer-Led Archaeology in Algeria

As this assessment of Roman archaeology during the first four decades of French rule in the colony of Algeria has demonstrated, the French officer-archaeologists who laid the groundwork for classical excavations in Algeria were motivated by the belief that their military venture was undertaken in the spirit of their ancient Roman forebears. Consequently, "colonial archaeology" of the brand practiced, for the most part, by self-appointed or "incidental" French officer-archaeologists sought to extract the antiquities of the region. Roman monuments, just as Roman history, represented fundamental ideological resources for French military and political conquest of the colony of Algeria and what would become the Protectorate of Tunisia.[50] Although the Académie des inscriptions et belles-lettres and the minister of war set the tone for this undertaking with the long-delayed scholarly expedition of 1839–1842, the archaeological endeavors that followed were far more haphazard and unique in their expression than suggested by this centralized model.[51] Over the next three decades, individual officers, most often on their own initiative, engaged in archaeological endeavors that helped assuage their own doubts about the war of extreme violence that they waged against Muslim civilians. Such activities also fulfilled their vision of the glory of the armée d'Afrique as heir of the Roman legions and offered a means by which civilian settlers could acculturate to the French colony.

As we have seen, although the activities of French officers and civilian-scholars in the period before 1870 were classified as archaeological, their understanding of the material culture in question was largely shaped by a narrative established by classical history and Latin inscriptions. This understanding of the past was reinforced by the increasingly detailed study and cataloguing of the numerous imperial Roman antiquities and monuments encountered by the armée d'Afrique, especially in the province of Constantine. French archaeological activities thus used a symbolism familiar to their scholarly and popular audience and at the same time eased French settlers' transition to and cultivated their pride in their new surroundings.[52] The sense of entitlement they felt in their rule of the territory of Algeria, which was reinforced by reference to the ancient past and the reuse or destruction of many vestiges of the imperial Roman army, set the tone not just for colonial military operations but also for the civilian settlements that followed. Individual officers, most of whom were familiar with the classical past as a consequence of their extensive preparation and training for coveted positions at the École polytechnique or the elite French military schools, handily molded the memory of Rome in the Maghreb to suit contemporary needs. Similar to what had been achieved in Egypt, the ancient past was suitably malleable and could be shaped to accommodate the evolving objectives of French military rule and civilian settlement in Algeria.[53] Although these requirements changed from decade to decade, they almost always faithfully contributed to a narrative that promoted the unquestioned invincibility of Western domination and their historical rights to the territory.

Even if not orchestrated directly by authorities in the metropolitan capital, archaeological undertakings mainly consisted of mapping and drawing remains, transcribing inscriptions, and disengaging monuments from fallen debris. These modest activities nonetheless served the practical and ideological objectives of the conquest and "pacification" of the region. As presented in an informational booklet drawn up by the Service des monuments historiques and reinforced in a similar manual circulated by the Comité des travaux historiques et scientifiques in 1929, anyone could render service to archaeology, even if he was not professionally trained.[54] Officers making topographical maps, forest managers surveying property, mining or bridge engineers reusing ancient Roman infrastructure, or colonial administrators overseeing mixed communities were all potential archaeologists. When encountering previously undocumented antiquities, they could each take the simple step of making photographs, notes, or a drawing to help ensure that all ruins, inscriptions, coins, and sculptures were properly recorded and registered by French authorities.[55] These painstaking efforts to document monuments of the classical Roman past were nonetheless unable to keep up with the level of destruction wreaked first by the armée d'Afrique and then by the civilian settlers who followed.

Like a spider's web or a root system, colonial discourse and the ancient monuments that became an intrinsic part of it during the first forty years of the French conquest became deeply interwoven with the very structure of the administration and the settlement of Algeria.[56] By the start of the Third Republic, this form of knowledge making was so deeply embedded in the life of the young colony that its imprint could no longer be separated from the dictates, cultural mores, and academic research practiced in the region. In works of the 1880s and 1890s, the lines between history and the present became increasingly blurred.[57] Such mores began to change in meaningful ways only with the end of colonialism, when claims to objective knowledge and superiority of method were brought into doubt.[58] With the benefit of hindsight, it is possible to document the all-encompassing nature of a vicious and unforgiving system that turned ancient monuments into fuel that justified the colonialist experiment. In the hands of French military and civilian authorities, historical monuments were not unbiased witnesses of the past. Rather, they were all too frequently manipulated to color contemporary understanding of ancient Rome (and exceptionally even prehistoric North Africa) to confirm the legitimacy of contemporary policy. Awareness of the circularity of this argument reduces the plausibility of triumphal retellings of the development of archaeological methods and institutions as a straightforward history of progress. This critical perspective offers more transparent ways in which to understand the ideological applications of archaeology of the Roman past in French Algeria.

As we have seen, the legacy of European colonial investment of Roman antiquities with meaning specific to "Western civilization" is far from having been forgotten by the citizens of the postcolonial Maghreb.[59] The same is true elsewhere in the former Ottoman Empire and the Middle East.[60] These meanings and values, deeply linked around the Mediterranean and in the Middle East to the trauma of European occupation, color the reception of the interventions of Western museums and UNESCO at endangered archaeological sites around the world.[61] This underacknowledged history, which threatens the movement to conserve and celebrate these very same monuments as part of a shared "world heritage," has met resentment in regions that suffered enormously under the depredations of European imperialism, colonialism, and "encyclopedic" museums. Documenting the early years of classical archaeology and its excesses, helps promote recognition, at the very least, as to why greater sensitivity to the basis for the value and meaning ascribed to ancient sites is an absolute necessity. More must be done to promote archaeological dialogue over decree if there is to be any chance of successfully preserving contested ancient monuments from further disarticulation and destruction.

NOTES

Introduction

1. Daesh is also known as ISIS or the Islamic State.

2. Fiona Rose-Greenland, "ISIS at the Mosul Museum: Material Destruction and Our Moral Economies of the Past," *Perspectives: A Publication of the Theory Section of the American Sociological Association* 37, no. 1 (2015): 18–21.

3. Marcel Bénabou, *La résistance africaine à la romanisation* (Paris: François Maspero, 1975), 9–12.

4. Lynn Meskell, "Archaeology Matters," in *Archaeology under Fire: Nationalism, Politics and Heritage in the Eastern Mediterranean and the Middle East*, ed. Lynn Meskell (London: Routledge, 1998), 1–12; Benjamin Anderson, "An Alternative Discourse: Local Interpreters of Antiquities in the Ottoman Empire," *Journal of Field Archaeology* 40, no. 4 (2015): 450–60.

5. Margarita Díaz-Andreu, *A World History of Nineteenth-Century Archaeology: Nationalism, Colonialism, and the Past* (Oxford: Oxford University Press, 2007), 110–18.

6. Wendy Shaw, *Possessors and Possessed: Museums, Archaeology and the Visualization of History in the Late Ottoman Empire* (Berkeley: University of California Press, 2003); Myriam Bacha, "La constitution d'une notion patrimoniale en Tunisie, XIXe et XXe siècle: Émergence et apport des disciplines de l'archéologie et de l'architecture," in *Chantiers et défis de la recherche sur le Maghreb contemporain*, ed. Pierre-Robert Baduel (Paris: Karthala, 2009), 159–78.

7. Magnus T. Bernhardsson, *Reclaiming a Plundered Past: Archaeology and Nation Building in Modern Iraq* (Austin: University of Texas Press, 2005); Elena T. Corbett, *Competitive*

Archaeology in Jordan: Narrating Identity from the Ottomans to the Hashemites (Austin: University of Texas Press, 2014).

8. Barbara Crossette, "Taliban Explains Buddha Demolition," *New York Times*, March 19, 2001, http://www.nytimes.com/2001/03/19/world/taliban-explains-buddha-demolition.html.

9. United Nations, *United Nations Educational, Scientific and Cultural Organisation Convention Concerning the Protection of the World Cultural and Natural Heritage,* adopted by the General Conference at its seventeenth session, Paris, November 16, 1972.

10. Lynn Meskell, "Gridlock: UNESCO, Global Conflict and Failed Ambitions," *World Archaeology* 47, no. 2 (2015): 225–38.

11. Christina Riggs, "Colonial Visions: Egyptian Antiquities and Contested Histories in the Cairo Museum," *Museum Worlds: Advances in Research* 1, no. 1 (2013): 65–84; Nathan Schlanger, "The Mirror of Perseus: Europe and the Destruction of Archaeological Heritage," *European Journal of Archaeology* 20, no. 1 (2017): 24–26.

12. John H. Merryman, "Two Ways of Thinking about Cultural Property," *American Journal of International Law* 80 (1986): 831–53. This argument, taken to its extreme, may be seen in the sensationalistic Tiffany Jenkins, *Losing Their Marbles: How the Treasures of the Past Ended Up in Museums and Why They Should Stay There* (Oxford: Oxford University Press, 2016).

13. Nadia Abu El-Haj, *Facts on the Ground: Archaeological Practice and Territorial Self-Fashioning in Israeli Society* (Chicago: University of Chicago Press, 2001); Elliott Colla, *Conflicted Antiquities: Egyptology, Egyptomania, Egyptian Modernity* (Durham, NC: Duke University Press, 2007).

14. Edward McAllister, "Silence and Nostalgia: Periodizing the Past in an Algiers Neighborhood," *Der Islam* 91, no. 1 (2014): 135–60.

15. Nacéra Benseddik, "Lambaesis-Lambèse/Tazoult: Grandeur et decadence," in *L'affirmation de l'identité dans l'Algérie antique et medieval: Combats et résistances. Hommage à Kadria Fatima Kadra* (Algiers: Centre national de recherche en archéologie, 2014), 111–19. Thomas le Romanacee, "Algérie: le Tombeau de la Chrétienne en péril," *Le Figaro*, March 17, 2017, http://www.lefigaro.fr/culture/2017/03/17/03004-20170317ARTFIG00010-algerie-le-tombeau-de-la-chretienne-en-peril.php.

16. Clémentine Gutron, *L'archéologie en Tunisie (XIXe–XXe siècle). Jeux généalogiques sur l'Antiquité* (Paris: Karthala, 2010); Corisande Fenwick, "Archaeology and the Search for Authenticity: Colonialist, Nationalist, and Berberist Visions of an Algerian Past," in *TRAC 2007: Proceedings of the 17th Annual Theoretical Roman Archaeology Conference,* ed. Corisande Fenwick, Meredith Wiggins, and Dave Wythe (Oxford: Oxbow, 2008), 75–88.

17. Houcine Jaïdi, "L'archéologie tunisienne au lendemain de la Révolution du 14 janvier 2011: État des lieux, inquiétudes et horizons," in *Pour une histoire de l'archéologie XVIIIe siècle–1945: Hommage de ses collègues et amis à Ève Gran-Aymerich,* ed. Annick Fenet and Natacha Lubtchansky (Bordeaux: Ausonius, 2015), 465–72.

18. Thessa Lageman, "Horror Still Fresh a Year after Tunisia Museum Attack," *Aljazeera,* March 18, 2016, http://www.aljazeera.com/news/2016/03/horror-fresh-year-tunisia-museum-attack-160314115053039.html.

19. Exceedingly influential to this subject has been Patricia Lorcin's "Rome and France in Africa: Recovering Colonial Algeria's Latin Past," *French Historical Studies* 25, no. 2 (2002): 295–329.

20. Yannis Hamilakis, "From Ethics to Politics," in *Archaeology and Capitalism,* ed. Yannis Hamilakis and Philip Duke (Walnut Creek, CA: Left Coast Press, 2007), 15–40.

21. See the interview of M. Pichon by the Commission d'Afrique on January 24, 1834, in *Procès-verbaux et rapports de la Commission d'Afrique instituée par ordonnance du roi*

du 12 décembre 1833 (Paris: Imprimerie royale, 1834); Benjamin Claude Brower, *A Desert Named Peace: The Violence of France's Empire in the Algerian Sahara, 1844–1902* (New York: Columbia University Press, 2009).

22. In this volume, in which I focus on the French exploration of Roman monuments, and thus objects with which the French instinctively self-identified, I have largely skirted current orientalist debates, except with respect to colonial perceptions of the Indigenous peoples of North Africa. Nevertheless, I rely heavily on the guidance offered by Suzanne Marchand's astute observations regarding the necessity of acknowledging antiquarians' individual approaches to their studies and recognizing the variety of motivations that shaped their research and publications; *German Orientalism in the Age of Empire: Religion, Race, and Scholarship* (Princeton, NJ: Princeton University Press, 2009), xvii–xxxiv.

23. This is to be distinguished from the kind of collecting that characterized European exploration and colonialism of previous centuries, which brought a blend of curiosities, natural wonders, and valuables back to the British Isles and the Continent; Chris Gosden, *Anthropology and Archaeology: A Changing Relationship* (Oxford: Routledge, 1999), 15–25.

24. Suzanne Marchand, "The Dialectics of the Antiquities Rush," in *Pour une histoire de l'archéologie*, 191–206.

25. Donald Malcolm Reid, *Whose Pharoahs? Archaeology, Museums, and Egyptian National Identity from Napoleon to World War I* (Berkeley: University of California Press, 2002).

26. Chantal Orgogozo, "Le voyage dans la Basse et la Haute-Egypte," in *Dominique-Vivant Denon: L'oeil de Napoléon, Paris, Musée du Louvre, 20 octobre 1999–17 janvier 2000* (Paris: Réunion des musées nationaux, 1999), 108–15.

27. Nigel Leask, *Curiosity and the Aesthetics of Travel Writing, 1770–1840: From an Antique Land* (Oxford: Oxford University Press, 2002), 116–20.

28. Alain Schnapp, "Préface: L'antiquaire, le Levant et les archéologues," in Gutron, *Archéologie en Tunisie*, 9–13.

29. Edward W. Said, *Culture and Imperialism* (New York: Vintage, 1993), 33–34.

30. For this last reason, the process did not achieve success in France until 1816; Michael Twyman, *Lithography 1800–1850: The Techniques of Drawing on Stone in England and France and Their Application in Works of Topography* (London: Oxford University Press, 1970), 48–57.

31. Anne Godlewska, "Map, Text and Image. The Mentality of Enlightened Conquerors: A New Look at the *Description de l'Égypte*," *Transactions of the Institute of British Geographers* 20, no. 1 (1995): 5–28.

32. Some scholars have sought to play down the centrality of these factors; Bernard Lepetit, "Missions scientifiques et expéditions militaires: Remarques sur leur modalités d'articulation," in *L'invention scientifique de la Méditerranée: Égypte, Morée, Algérie*, ed. Marie-Noëlle Bourguet, Bernard Lepetit, Daniel Nordman, and Maroula Sinarellis (Paris: Éditions de l'École des hautes études en sciences sociales, 1998), 97–116.

33. Michael Heffernan, "'A Dream as Frail as Those of Ancient Time': The Incredible Geographies of Timbuctoo," *Environment and planning D: Society and Space* 19, no. 2 (2001): 203–25.

34. Wendy Doyon, "On Archaeological Labor in Modern Egypt," in *Histories of Egyptology: Interdisciplinary Measures*, ed. William Carruthers (New York: Routledge, 2015), 141–56; Wendy Doyon, "The History of Archaeology through the Eyes of Egyptians," in *Unmasking Ideology: The Vocabulary, Symbols, and Legacy of Imperial and Colonial Archaeology*, ed. Bonnie Effros and Guolong Lai (Los Angeles: Cotsen Institute of Archaeology Press, in press).

35. Timothy Mitchell, *Colonising Egypt* (Cambridge: Cambridge University Press, 1988).

36. Bruce G. Trigger, "Alternative Archaeologies: Nationalist, Colonialist, Imperialist," *Man* n.s. 19, no. 3 (1989): 355–70. Nor is this phenomenon unique to the Mediterranean or Middle Eastern context; Europeans attempted similar actions in China; Justin Jacobs,

"Confronting Indiana Jones: Chinese Nationalism, Historical Imperialism, and the Criminalization of Aurel Stein and the Raiders of Dunhuang, 1899–1944," in *China on the Margins*, ed. Sherman Cochran and Paul G. Pickowicz (Ithaca, NY: Cornell University Press, 2010), 65–90.

37. Timothy C. Champion, "Medieval Archaeology and the Tyranny of the Historical Record," in *From the Baltic to the Black Sea: Studies in Medieval Archaeology*, ed. David Austin and Leslie Alcock (London: Unwin Hyman, 1990), 79–95.

38. Ève Gran-Aymerich, "Épigraphie française et allemande au Maghreb: Entre collaboration et rivalité (1830–1914)," *Mitteilungen des Deutschen archäologischen Instituts, Römische Abteilung* 117 (2011): 567–600; Margarita Díaz-Andreu and Timothy Champion, "Nationalism and Archaeology in Europe: An Introduction," in *Archaeology and Nationalism in Europe*, ed. Margarita Díaz-Andreu and Timothy Champion (London: University College London Press, 1996), 3.

39. Stefan Altekamp, "Modelling Roman North Africa: Advances, Obsessions and Deficiencies of Colonial Archaeology in the Maghreb," in *Under Western Eyes: Approches occidentales de l'archéologie nord-africaine (XIXe–XXe siècle)*, ed. Hédi Dridi and Antonella Mezzolani Andreose (Bologne: BraDypUS, 2016), 19–42; Colla, *Conflicted Antiquities*, 16–19. See also Michael Kunichika, *"Our Native Antiquity": Archaeology and Aesthetics in the Culture of Russian Modernism* (Boston: Academic Studies Press, 2015).

40. Jamil M. Abun-Nasr, *A History of the Maghrib*, 2nd ed. (Cambridge: Cambridge University Press, 1975), 236–38.

41. Jennifer E. Sessions, *By Sword and Plow: France and the Conquest of Algeria* (Ithaca, NY: Cornell University Press, 2011), 19–22.

42. Kamel Kateb, *Européens, "indigènes" et juifs en Algérie (1830–1962): Représentations et réalités des populations* (Paris: Éditions de l'Institut national d'études démographiques, 2001), 9–10.

43. Ibid., 11–14.

44. Cheryl B. Welch, "Colonial Violence and the Rhetoric of Evasion: Tocqueville on Algeria," *Political Theory* 31, no. 2 (2003): 235–64; Sessions, *By Sword and Plow*, 83–94.

45. Patricia Lorcin, *Imperial Identities: Stereotyping, Prejudice, and Race in Colonial Algeria* (London: I. B. Tauris, 1995), 99–102; Osama W. Abi-Mershed, *Apostles of Modernity: Saint-Simonians and the Civilizing Mission in Algeria* (Stanford, CA: Stanford University Press, 2010), 27–33.

46. Hamdan Khodja, *Le Miroir: Aperçu historique et statistique sur la Régence d'Alger*, introduction by Abdelkader Djeghloul (Paris: Sinbad, 1985), 2:155.

47. Nineteenth-century French writers used the term *Kabyle* to refer to Berber populations not just in the region of Kabylia but throughout Algeria; today, Berber identity is widely understood as ethnic, historical, cultural, and linguistic but not racial, as it was then. Firm distinctions between Arabs and Berbers were blurred by the extensive Arabization of the Berber population; Abdelhamid Zouzou, *L'Aurès au temps de la France coloniale: Evolution politique, economique et sociale (1837–1939)* (Algiers: Éditions Distribution Houma, 2001), 1:58–75.

48. Pierre Nora, *Les français d'Algérie* (Paris: René Juillard, 1961), 87–92; Brower, *Desert Named Peace*, 15–18.

49. André Raymond, "Le centre d'Alger en 1830," *Revue de l'Occident musulman et de la Méditerranée* 31, no. 1 (1981): 73–83. On the redesign of cities in this period to make them easier to police, see James C. Scott, *Seeing Like a State: How Certain Schemes to Improve the Human Condition Have Failed* (New Haven: Yale University Press, 1998), 53–63.

50. Ian Haynes, *Blood of the Provinces: The Roman Auxilia and the Making of Provincial Society from Augustus to the Severans* (Oxford: Oxford University Press, 2013), 18–20.

51. Marcel Bénabou, "L'impérialisme et l'Afrique du Nord: Le modèle romain," in *Sciences de l'homme et conquête coloniale: Constitution et usages des sciences humaines en*

Afrique (XIXe–XXe siècles), ed. Daniel Nordman and Jean-Pierre Raison (Paris: Presses de l'École normale supérieure, 1980), 15–22.

52. Díaz-Andreu, *World History*, 6–9.

53. Jennifer E. Sessions, "Why the French Presidential Candidates Are Arguing about Their Colonial History," *The Conversation*, April 11, 2017, http://theconversation.com/why-the-french-presidential-candidates-are-arguing-about-their-colonial-history-75372.

54. A near contemporary example would be French military involvement in the former colony of Saint-Domingue; David Patrick Geggus, "Slavery, War, and Revolution in the Greater Caribbean, 1789–1815," in *A Turbulent Time: The French Revolution and the Greater Caribbean*, ed. David Barry Gaspar and David Patrick Geggus (Bloomington: Indiana University Press, 1997), 1–50.

55. George R. Trumbull IV, *An Empire of Facts: Colonial Power, Cultural Knowledge, and Islam in Algeria, 1870–1914* (Cambridge: Cambridge University Press, 2009), 11–29.

56. "Le nom de Berbers, que dans plusieurs ouvrages on donne aux Kbaïles, n'est point connu dans la régence d'Alger. Il n'est employé que dans la partie de la Barbarie qui touche à l'Egypte." Edmond Pellissier de Reynaud, *Annales algériennes*, new ed. (Paris: Librairie militaire, 1854), 1:4–5.

57. Apuleius, *Apologia*, ed. and trans. Paul Valette, 2nd ed. (Paris: Les Belles Lettres, 2002), 56–57.

58. Homi K. Bhabha, *The Location of Culture* (London: Routledge, 1994), 66.

59. Lauren Benton, *Law and Colonial Cultures: Legal Regimes in World History, 1400–1900* (Cambridge: Cambridge University Press, 2002), 28.

60. Jean-Claude Vatin, *L'Algérie politique: Histoire et société*, Cahiers de la Fondation nationale des sciences politiques 192 (Paris: Armand Colin, 1974), 40–50.

61. Aimé Césaire, *Discourse on Colonialism*, trans. Joan Pinkham (New York: Monthly Review Press, 1972), 40–41.

62. Auguste Pomel, *Des races indigènes d'Algérie et du rôle que leur réservent leurs aptitudes* (Oran: Typographie et lithographie Veuve Dagorn, 1871).

63. Sophie Basch, "Archaeological Travels in Greece and Asia Minor: On the Good Use of Ruins in Nineteenth-Century France," in *Scramble for the Past: A Story of Archaeology in the Ottoman Empire, 1753–1914*, ed. Zainab Bahrani, Zeynep Çelik, and Edhem Eldem (Istanbul: SALT, 2011), 157–79; Suzanne Marchand, *Down from Olympus: Archaeology and Philhellenism in Germany, 1750–1970* (Princeton, NJ: Princeton University Press, 1996); Marchand, *German Orientalism*; Reid, *Whose Pharaohs?*; Colla, *Conflicted Antiquities*.

64. Richard Hingley, *Roman Officers and English Gentlemen: The Imperial Origins of Roman Archaeology* (London: Routledge, 2000); Phiroze Vasunia, "Greater Rome and Greater Britain," in *Classics and Colonialism*, ed. Barbara Goff (London: Gerald Duckworth, 2005), 38–64.

65. Leask, *Curiosity and the Aesthetics*, 16–21.

66. Gustav Wilmanns, *Inscriptiones Africae latinae*, Corpus inscriptionum latinarum 8 (Berlin: Verlag Georg Reimer, 1881), 1:xxiii–xxvii.

67. Christian Windler, *La diplomatie comme expérience de l'autre: Consuls français au Maghreb (1700–1840)* (Geneva: Droz, 2002), 37–42, 153–63.

68. Françoise de Catheu, "Les marbres de Leptis Magna dans les monuments français du XVIIIe siècle," *Bulletin de la Société de l'histoire de l'art français* (1936): 51–74.

69. André Laronde, "Claude Le Maire et l'exportation des marbres de Lepcis Magna," *Bulletin de la Société nationale des antiquaries de France* (1993): 242–55.

70. Hédi Slim, "L'amphithéâtre et le site d'El Jem vus par les voyageurs des siècles derniers," in *La Tunisie mosaïque: Diasporas, cosmopolitisme, archéologies de l'identité* (Toulouse: Presses universitaires du Mirail, 2000), 486–89.

71. Nabila Oulebsir, "From Ruins to Heritage: The Past Perfect and the Idealized Antiquity in North Africa," in *Multiple Antiquities—Multiple Modernities: Ancient Histories in Nineteenth Century European Cultures*, ed. Gábor Klaniczay, Michael Werner, and Ottó Gecser (Frankfurt: Campus, 2011), 337–48; Myriam Bacha, *Patrimoine et monuments en Tunisie* (Rennes: Presses universitaires de Rennes, 2013), 18–20.

72. Leask, *Curiosity and the Aesthetics*, 54–55.

73. Pierre Morizot, "La naissance de l'archéologie romaine en Algérie," in *Histoire et archéologie méditerranéennes sous Napoléon III: Actes du 21e colloque de la Villa Kérylos à Beaulieu-sur-Mer les 8 & 9 octobre 2010*, ed. André Laronde, Pierre Toubert, and Jean Leclant, Cahiers de la Villa 'Kérylos' 22 (Paris: Diffusion de Boccard, 2011), 155–60.

74. Gutron, *Archéologie en Tunisie*, 24; Bacha, *Patrimone et monuments en Tunisie*, 32–41.

75. Stephano Antonio Morcelli, *Africa Christiana*, 3 vols. (Brescia: Ex officina Bettoniana, 1816–1817).

76. Joann Freed, *Bringing Carthage Home: The Excavations of Nathan Davis, 1856–1859* (Oxford: Oxbow Books, 2011), 13–15, 41–43; Jacques Debergh, "Une rencontre improbable dans la Régence de Tunis et ses conséquences fructueuses: Jean Emile Humbert et Camillo Borgia (1815–1816)," in *Du voyage savant aux territoires de l'archéologie: Voyageurs, amateurs et savants à l'origine de l'archéologie moderne*, ed. Manuel Royo et al. (Paris: De Boccard, 2011), 245–48.

77. Assia Djebar, *Vaste est la prison* (Paris: Éditions Albin Michel, 1995), 133–60.

78. Bacha, *Patrimone et monuments en Tunisie*, 21–24.

79. Gran-Aymerich, "Épigraphie française et allemande au Maghreb," 583.

80. Thibaud Serres-Jacquart, "Joseph Vattier de Bourville (1812–1854): Notes sur un explorateur de la Cyrénaïque," *Journal des savants* 2, no. 1 (2001): 393–429.

81. Michael Greenhalgh, *The Military and Colonial Destruction of the Roman Landscape of North Africa, 1830–1900* (Leiden: Brill, 2014), 242–48.

82. Díaz-Andreu, *World History*, 264–65; Gran-Aymerich, "Épigraphie française et allemande au Maghreb," 585–91.

83. Arnauld d'Abbadie, *Douze ans de séjour dans la Haute-Éthiopie (Abyssinie)*, Studi e testi 286 (Vatican City: Biblioteca apostolica Vaticana, 1980), vii–viii, 59–73. I thank Hennig Trupper for directing me to this fascinating source.

84. Nicholas B. Dirks, "Colonial Histories and Native Informants: Biography of an Archive," in *Orientalism and the Postcolonial Predicament: Perspectives on South Asia*, ed. Carol A. Breckenridge and Peter van der Veer (Philadelphia: University of Pennsylvania Press, 1993), 279–313.

85. Général Jourdy, *L'instruction de l'armée française de 1815 à 1902* (Paris: Félix Alcan, 1903), 1–4.

86. William Serman, *Les origines des officiers français, 1848–1870* (Paris: Publications de la Sorbonne, 1979), 35–37.

87. Jourdy, *Instruction de l'armée française*, 1–70.

88. Serman, *Origines des officiers français*, 1–26, 111–30.

89. Frederick B. Artz, *The Development of Technical Education in France, 1500–1850* (Cambridge, MA: MIT Press, 1966), 230–33; *Saint-Cyr: 290 ans d'histoire. Dixième anniversaire de la création par le Général de Gaulle du Collège militaire de Saint-Cyr* (Saint-Cyr: Collège militaire, 1976).

90. Godlewska, "Map, Text and Image," 10–12; Joseph-Daniel Guigniaut, "Notice historique sur la vie et les travaux de Charles-Benoît Hase, membre de l'Académie des inscriptions et belles-lettres," *Mémoires de l'Institut national de France* 27, no. 1 (1877): 247–73.

91. Serman, *Origines des officiers français*, 130–67.

92. Lorcin, "Rome and France in Africa," 327.

93. Artz, *Development of Technical Education*, 234–38; Jean-Pierre Callot, *Histoire de l'École polytechnique* (Paris: Charles Lavauzelle, 1982), 462.

94. Artz, *Development of Technical Education*, 255–56.

95. Ibid., 238–44.

96. Maurice Dumontier, "L'École d'artillerie et du génie de Metz sous l'Empire, la Restauration et la Monarchie de Juillet (1803–1845)," *Le Pays lorrain* 42, no. 3 (1961): 86–89.

97. Maurice Dumontier, "L'École d'application de l'artillerie et du génie à Metz sous la Seconde République et le Second Empire," *Le Pays lorrain* 42, no. 4 (1961): 122–23.

98. Jourdy, *Instruction de l'armée française*, 87–99.

99. Douglas Porch, *The French Foreign Legion: A Complete History of the Legendary Fighting Force* (New York: Harper Collins, 1991), 11–18.

100. Paul Azan, *L'Armée d'Afrique de 1830 à 1852* (Paris: Plon, 1936), 43–50, 61–68.

101. Jennifer E. Sessions, "'Unfortunate Necessities': Violence and Civilization in the Conquest of Algeria," in *France and Its Spaces of War: Experience, Memory, Image*, ed. Patricia M. E. Lorcin and Daniel Brewer (New York: Palgrave Macmillan, 2009), 29–44.

102. Ruth Charlotte-Sophie de Castellane, Comtesse de Beaulaincourt-Marles, ed., *Campagnes d'Afrique 1835–1848: Lettres adressées au Maréchal de Castellane* (Paris: Plon, 1898), 215.

103. Ferdinand-Désiré Quesnoy, *L'armée d'Afrique depuis la conquête d'Alger* (Paris: Furne Jouvet et Cie, 1888), vii–viii.

104. Charles Thoumas, *Les transformations de l'armée française: Essais d'histoire et de critique sur l'état militaire de la France* (Paris: Berger-Levrault et Cie, 1887), 2:632–33.

105. John Reynell Morell, *Algeria: The Topography and History, Political, Social, and Natural of French Africa* (London: Nathaniel Cooke, 1854), 402–3.

106. Paul Rabinow, *French Modern: Norms and Forms of the Social Environment* (Cambridge, MA: MIT Press, 1989).

107. Pierre Berthézène, *Dix-huit mois à Alger* (Montpellier: Chez August Ricard, 1834), 130–31.

108. Jacques Alexandropoulos, "Regards sur l'impérialisme de la Rome antique en Afrique du Nord," in *Idée impérial et impérialisme dans l'Italie fasciste: Journée d'étude organisée par le groupe ERASME le 4 avril 2003 à Toulouse*, ed. Alberto Bianco and Philippe Foro, Collection de l'E.C.R.I.T. 9 (Toulouse: Presses universitaires du Mirail, 2003), 7–19.

109. Jacques Alexandropoulos, "De Louis Bertrand à Pierre Hubac: Images de l'Afrique antique," in *La Tunisie mosaïque*, 457–78.

110. Robert Irwin, *For Lust of Knowing: The Orientalists and Their Enemies* (London: Allen Lane, 2006).

111. Gary Wilder, *The French Imperial Nation State: Negritude and Colonial Humanism between the Two World Wars* (Chicago: University of Chicago Press, 2005), 10.

112. Ta-Nehisi Coates, *Between the World and Me* (New York: Spiegel and Grau, 2015), 99–101.

113. Jan Jansen, "Die Erfindung des Mittelmeerraums im kolonialen Kontext: Die Inszenierungen des 'lateinischen Afrika' beim *Centenaire de l'Algérie française 1930*," in *Der Süden: neue Perspektiven auf eine europäische Geschichtsregion*, ed. Frithjof Benjamin Schenk (Frankfurt: Campus, 2007), 175–205.

114. Myriam Bacha, "Des influences traditionelles et patrimoniales sur les architectures du Maghreb," in *Architectures au Maghreb (XIXe–XXe siècles): Réinvention du patrimoine*, ed. Myriam Bacha (Rennes: IRMC–Presses universitaires François Rabelais, 2011), 11–12; Lewis Pyenson, *Civilizing Mission: Exact Sciences and French Overseas Expansion, 1830–1940* (Baltimore: Johns Hopkins University Press, 1993).

115. Dondin-Payre refers to this phase as "professionalization." Monique Dondin-Payre, "Du voyage à l'archéologie: l'exemple de l'Afrique du Nord," in *Du voyage savant aux territoires de l'archéologie*, 273–90.

116. Jan Jansen, "Inszenierungen des antiken Erbes in 'Französisch-Algerien,'" in *Das große Spiel: Archäeologie und Politik zur Zeit des Kolonialismus (1860–1940)*, ed. Charlotte Trümpler (Cologne: DuMont, 2008), 428–537; Caroline Ford, "The Inheritance of Empire and the Ruins of Rome in French Colonial Algeria," *Past and Present* 226, Suppl. 10 (2015): 57–77.

117. Alice L. Conklin, *In the Museum of Man: Race, Anthropology, and Empire in France, 1850–1950* (Ithaca, NY: Cornell University Press, 2013).

118. Bacha, *Patrimoine et monuments en Tunisie*; Gutron, *Archéologie en Tunisie*.

119. Joann Freed, "Le Père Alfred-Louis Delattre (1850–1932) et les fouilles archéologiques de Carthage," *Histoire, monde et cultures religieuses* 4, no. 8 (2008): 67–100.

120. Gutron, *Archéologie en Tunisie*, 31–32; 137–66; Myriam Bacha, "Un archéologue amateur: Louis Carton (1861–1924) et son project de parc archéologique de Carthage (Tunisie)," in *Initiateurs et entrepreneurs culturels du tourisme (1850–1950)*, ed. Jean-Yves Andrieux and Patrick Harmendy (Rennes: Presses universitaires de Rennes, 2011), 21–33.

121. Jennifer Sessions observes that use of this terminology dates from around 1840; *By Sword and Plow*, 6.

122. Matthew McCarty has argued more forcefully that the French saw themselves not just as the heirs but as the direct or blood descendants of the Romans; "French Archaeology and History in the Colonial Maghreb: Inheritance, Presence, and Absence," in *Unmasking Ideology*.

123. Wilder, *French Imperial Nation-State*, 3–23.

124. Jacques Heurgon, "L'oeuvre archéologique française en Algérie," *Bulletin de l'Association Guillaume Budé* ser. 4, 15, no. 4 (1956), 7.

125. Godlewska, "Map, Text and Image," 5–28.

126. To name just a few of these (in chronological order): Zeynep Çelik, *Urban Forms and Colonial Confrontations: Algiers under French Rule* (Berkeley: University of California Press, 1997); Brower, *Desert Named Peace*; Abi-Mershed, *Apostles of Modernity*; Sessions, *By Sword and Plow*; William Gallois, *A History of Violence in the Early Algerian Colony* (New York: Palgrave Macmillan, 2013).

127. Bénabou, *Résistance africaine*, 9–18; Jacques Frémeaux, "Souvenirs de Rome et présence française au Maghreb: Essai d'investigation," in *Connaissances du Maghreb: Sciences sociales et colonisation*, ed. Jean-Claude Vatin (Paris: CNRS Éditions, 1984), 29–46.

128. Paul-Albert Février, *Approches du Maghreb romain: Pouvoirs, différences et conflits* (Aix-en-Provence: ÉDISUD, 1989), 1:1–92; Clémentine Gutron, "Archéologies maghrébines et relectures de l'histoire: Autour de la patrimonialisation de Paul-Albert Février," *L'année du Maghreb* 10 (2014): 172–76.

129. Lorcin, "Rome and France in Africa, 309–11; Monique Dondin-Payre, *Le Capitaine Delamare: La réussite de l'archéologie romaine au sein de la Commission d'exploration scientifique d'Algérie*, Mémoires de l'Académie des inscriptions et belles-lettres, n. s. 15 (Paris: Imprimerie F. Paillart, 1994); Nabila Oulebsir, *Les usages du patrimoine: Monuments, musées et politique coloniale en Algérie (1830–1930)* (Paris: Éditions de la Maison des sciences de l'homme, 2004); Monique Dondin-Payre, "Un document cartographique inédit sur l'occupation de l'espace dans les Aurès à l'époque romaine," in *L'Africa romana: Atti del X convegno di studio Oristano, 11–13 dicembre 1992*, ed. Attilio Mastino and Paola Ruggeri (Sassari: Editrice Archivio Fotografico Sardo, 1994), 331–46; Gran-Aymerich, "Épigraphie française et allemande au Maghreb," 584–88; Nadia Bayle, "Quelques aspects de l'histoire de l'archéologie au XIXe siècle: L'exemple des publications archéologiques militaires éditées entre 1830 et 1914 en France, en Afrique du Nord et en Indo-Chine," Vol. 1 (unpublished PhD diss., Université de Paris IV–Sorbonne, 1986).

130. Ève Gran-Aymerich, *Naissance de l'archéologie moderne, 1798–1945* (Paris: CNRS Éditions, 1998); Greenhalgh, *Military and Colonial Destruction.*

131. More problematic in terms of its uncritical acceptance of French ideological assessments of the Indigenous population is Michael Greenhalgh, "The New Centurions: French Reliance on the Roman Past during the Conquest of Algeria," *War and Society* 16, no. 1 (1998): 1–28.

132. "Insultes, expropriations militarisés, menaces de mort, condamnations, prison pour les récalcitrants, constituent des épisodes sombres de cette aventure savant évoqués en revanche dans la correspondance personnelle." Gutron, *Archéologie en Tunisie,* 142.

133. William H. C. Frend, *The Archaeology of Early Christianity: A History* (Minneapolis: Fortress Press, 1996), 51–64.

134. Antoinette Burton, "Archive Stories: Gender in the Making of Imperial and Colonial Histories," in *Gender and Empire,* ed. Philippa Levine (Oxford: Oxford University Press, 2007), 281–94.

135. Oulebsir, *Usages du patrimoine,* 5–6.

136. Many recent publications still list these archives as the Centre des archives d'Outre-Mer (CAOM) despite the recent change in name; Élisabeth Rabut, "Le Centre des archives d'Outre-Mer: Premier centre délocalisé des Archives nationales," in *Histoire d'archives: Recueil d'articles offert à Luce Favier par ses collègues et amis* (Paris: Société des amis des Archives de France, 1997), 105–15.

137. Nicholas B. Dirks, "Annals of the Archive: Ethnographic Notes on the Sources of History," in *From the Margins: Historical Anthropology and Its Futures,* ed. Brian Axel (Durham, NC: Duke University Press, 2002), 47–65.

138. Sam Kaplan, "Documenting History, Historicizing Documentation: French Military Officials' Ethnological Reports on Cilicia," *Comparative Studies in Society and History* 44, no. 2 (2002): 344–69.

139. Arrêté of 12 February 1887, Ministre de l'Instruction publique et des beaux-arts, Médiathèque de l'architecture et des monuments historiques, Charenton-le-Pont 81/99/01.

140. Bayle, "Quelques aspects," 47–50.

141. Nadia Bayle, "Armée et archéologie au XIXe siècle: Éléments de recherche sur les travaux archéologiques des officiers français publiés entre 1830 et 1914," *Revue d'archéologie moderne et d'archéologie générale (RAMAGE)* 3 (1985): 219–30.

142. Ann Laura Stoler, *Along the Archival Grain: Epistemic Anxieties and Colonial Common Sense* (Princeton, NJ: Princeton University Press, 2009), 62–64, 253.

143. Bayle, "Quelques aspects," 101–15.

144. Ernest Carette, *Précis historique et archéologique sur Hippone et ses environs* (Paris: Imprimerie Lange Lévy et Compagnie, 1838), 16.

145. Stéphane Gsell, "Introduction," in *Histoire et historiens de l'Algérie,* Collection du centenaire de l'Algérie (1830–1930) 4 (Paris: Félix Alcan, 1931), 1–15; Eugène Albertini, "L'Algérie antique," in *Histoire et historiens de l'Algérie,* 89–109.

146. Heurgon, "L'oeuvre archéologique française en Algérie," 3–26.

147. McCarty, "French Archaeology."

148. Salomon Reinach, "Le vandalisme moderne en Orient," *Revue des deux mondes* 56 (1 March 1883): 132–66.

149. El Bekri, *Descripton de l'Afrique septentrionale,* trans. William Mac Guckin de Slane (Algiers: A. Jourdan, 1913), 93–94.

150. Edrissi, *Description de l'Afrique et de l'Espagne,* trans. Reinhart Pieter Anne Dozy and Michael Jan de Goeje (Leiden: Brill, 1866), 131–33.

151. Slim, "Amphithéâtre," 485–99; M'hamed H. Fantar, "Pionniers de l'archéologie punique," in *La Tunisie mosaïque,* 501–12. Michael Brett, "The Journey of al-Tijāni to Tripoli at the Beginning of the Fourteenth Century AD/Eighth Century AH," *Libyan Studies* 7 (January 1976): 41–51.

152. "Chellah: Rabat, Morocco," Archnet, n.d., https://archnet.org/sites/1744. I thank Ellen Amster for this helpful reference.

153. Alphonse Rousseau, "Voyage du Scheikh El-Tidjani dans la Régence de Tunis pendant les années 706, 707 et 708 de l'Hégire (1306–1309)," *Journal asiatique*, ser. 5, vol. 1 (1853): 124.

154. Franz Rosenthal, trans., *Ibn Khaldûn, an Introduction to History: The Muqaddimah* 3.16, abr. and ed. N. J. Dawood (London: Routledge and Kegan Paul, 1967), 143–46.

155. Edhem Eldem, "From Blissful Indifference to Anguished Concern: Ottoman Perceptions of Antiquities, 1799–1869," in *Scramble for the Past*, 281–329. For the earliest Ottoman legislation protecting antiquities dating to 1869 and 1874, see Demétrius Nicolaïdes, trans., *Législation ottomane ou Recueil des lois, réglements, ordonnances, traités, capitulations et autres documents officiels de l'Empire ottoman* (Istanbul: Bureau du Journal Thraky, 1874), 161–67.

156. Bonnie Effros, "Indigenous Voices at the Margins: Nuancing the History of Colonial Archaeology in Nineteenth-Century Algeria," in *Unmasking Ideology*.

157. Jocelyne Dakhlia, *L'oubli de la cité: La mémoire collective à l'épreuve du lignage dans le Jérid tunisien* (Paris: Éditions la Découverte, 1990), 56–58.

158. "Il est impossible de faire comprendre à celui qui ne l'a pas ressentie lui-même, l'émotion qu'éprouve le voyageur plongé depuis des mois dans la barbarie haineuse de l'Islam lorsque, fatigué de l'indigente architecture arabe, il retrouve le style simple, la belle solidité et l'exécution soignée de ces beaux monuments qui durent comme la marque éternelle du génie latin." Edmond Doutté, *En tribu* (Paris: Paul Geuthner, 1914), 381, 419; Ellen J. Amster, *Medicine and the Saints: Science, Islam, and the Colonial Encounter in Morocco, 1877–1956* (Austin: University of Texas Press, 2013), 68–71.

159. Ahmed Abdesselem, *Les historiens tunisiens des XVIIe, XVIIIe et XIXe siecles: Essai d'histoire culturelle* (Paris: C. Klincksieck, 1973), 474–75.

160. Bonnie Effros, "Museum-Building in Nineteenth-Century Algeria: Colonial Narratives in French Collections of Classical Antiquities," *Journal of the History of Collections* 28, no. 2 (2016): 243–59.

161. Ahmed Saadoui, "Le remploi dans les mosquées ifrîqiyenness aux époques médiévale et moderne," in *Lieux de cultes: Aires votives, temples, églises, mosquées. IXe colloque international sur l'histoire et l'archéologie de l'Afrique du Nord antique et médievale, Tripoli, 19–25 février 2005* (Paris: CNRS Éditions, 2008), 295–304; Michael Greenhalgh, *Marble Past, Monumental Present: Building with Antiquities in the Mediaeval Mediterranean* (Leiden: Brill, 2009), 313–21, 447–68.

162. McAllister, "Science and Nostalgia," 135–60.

163. For instance, see Mahfoud Kaddache, *L'Algérie dans l'antiquité* (Algiers: SNED, 1972).

164. Benseddik, "Lambaesis-Lambèse/Tazoult," 111–19.

Chapter 1. Knowing and Controlling

1. Antoine Denniée, *Précis historique et administratif de la campagne d'Afrique* (Paris: Delaunay, 1830).

2. André Raymond, "The Ottoman Conquest and the Development of the Great Arab Towns," *International Journal of Turkish Studies* 1, no. 1 (1980), 90–91.

3. Hamdan Khodja, *Le Miroir: Aperçu historique et statistique sur la Régence d'Alger*, intro. Abdelkader Djeghloul (Paris: Sinbad, 1985), 15–17.

4. Ibid., 2:162–67.

5. Pierre Berthézène, *Dix-huit mois à Alger* (Montpellier: Chez August Ricard, 1834), 186–87; Peter Dunwoodie, *Writing French Algeria* (Oxford: Clarendon, 1998), 1–10; Khodja, *Miroir*, 2: 202–4.

6. André Raymond, "Le centre d'Alger en 1830," *Revue de l'Occident musulman et de la Méditerranée* 31, no. 1 (1981): 73–83.

7. Miriam Hoexter, *Endowments, Rulers, and Community: Waqf al-Haramayn in Ottoman Algiers* (Leiden: Brill, 1998), 64–67, 145–48.

8. John Ruedy, *Land Policy in Colonial Algeria: The Origins of the Rural Public Domain*, Near Eastern Studies 10 (Berkeley: University of California Press, 1967), 13–22, 69–74.

9. Alexis Belloc, *La télégraphie historique: Depuis les temps les plus reculés jusqu'à nos jours,* 2nd ed. (Paris: Firmin Didot, 1894), 175–78.

10. Jennifer E. Sessions, *By Sword and Plow: France and the Conquest of Algeria* (Ithaca, NY: Cornell University Press, 2011), 29–61.

11. Ann Thomson, *Barbary and Enlightenment: European Attitudes towards the Maghreb in the 18th Century* (Leiden: Brill, 1987), 2–7.

12. Khodja, *Miroir*, 2:206–7; Général Jourdy, *L'instruction de l'armée française de 1815 à 1902* (Paris: Félix Alcan, 1903), 87–92.

13. Ferdinand-Désiré Quesnoy, *L'armée d'Afrique depuis la conquête d'Alger* (Paris: Furne Jouvet et Cie, 1888), 62–63; Nabila Oulebsir, *Les usages du patrimoine: Monuments, musées et politique coloniale en Algérie (1830–1930)* (Paris: Éditions de la Maison des sciences de l'homme, 2004), 87–91.

14. Hoexter, *Endowments, Rulers, and Community*, 15.

15. Perceval Barton Lord, *Algiers, with Notices of the Neighbouring States of Barbary* (London: Whittaker and Co., 1835), 1:147.

16. Adrien-Jacques Follie, *Voyage dans les déserts du Sahara* (Paris: Chez les Directeurs de l'Imprimerie du Cercle social, 1792).

17. See the interview of M. Pichon by the Commission d'Afrique on January 24, 1834, in *Procès-verbaux et rapports de la Commission d'Afrique instituée par ordonnance du roi du 12 décembre 1833* (Paris: Imprimerie royale, 1834); Khodja, *Miroir*, 2: 210–14; Benjamin Claude Brower, *A Desert Named Peace: The Violence of France's Empire in the Algerian Sahara, 1844–1902* (New York: Columbia University Press, 2009), 16–18.

18. Although the themes of French lithography were initially mainly landscapes in metropolitan France, Paul Huet accompanied the expedition to Algeria as a painter in 1830 and used the new technology to illustrate Baron Pierre-Paul Denniée's *Précis historique et administratif de la campagne d'Afrique* (1830). Michael Twyman, *Lithography 1800–1850: The Techniques of Drawing on Stone in England and France and Their Application in Works of Topography* (London: Oxford University Press, 1970), 240–41.

19. Oulebsir, *Usages du patrimoine*, 7–10.

20. Edmond Pellissier de Reynaud, *Annales algériennes*, new ed. (Paris: Librairie militaire, 1854), 1:5.

21. Julia Clancy-Smith, "Exoticism, Erasures, and Absence: The Peopling of Algiers, 1830–1900," in *Walls of Algiers: Narratives of the City through Text and Image*, ed. Zeynep Çelik, Julia Clancy-Smith, and Frances Terpak (Los Angeles: Getty Research Institute, 2009), 19–26.

22. Richard W. Bulliet, *The Camel and the Wheel* (Cambridge, MA: Harvard University Press, 1975), 223–27.

23. Oulebsir, *Usages du patrimoine*, 87–91.

24. Pierre Christian, *L'Afrique française, l'empire de Maroc et les déserts de Sahara* (Paris: A. Barbier, 1846), 130–31.

25. Hamdan Khodja saw this as a direct assault on Islamic institutions; *Miroir*, 2:239–43.

26. Sessions, *By Sword and Plow*, 241–43.

27. Khodja, *Miroir*, 2:237–39.

28. Zeynep Çelik, *Urban Forms and Colonial Confrontations: Algiers under French Rule* (Berkeley: University of California Press, 1997), 21–35; James C. Scott, *Seeing Like a State: How Certain Schemes to Improve the Human Condition Have Failed* (New Haven: Yale University Press, 1998), 53–63.

29. Anne Godlewska, "Map, Text and Image: The Mentality of Enlightened Conquerors: A New Look at the *Description de l'Égypte*," *Transactions of the Institute of British Geographers* 20, no. 1 (1995): 5–28.

30. "As a discourse of race, for instance, modernity is violence that stripped the colonized people of their humanity and relegated them to a space of noncivilization, and of no right and no freedom. While they are there, they become good candidates for colonial genocide in times of conquest and in times of land reform. The discourse of progress makes the natives into children who must be spanked when they misbehave—when they resist or reject colonialism and its violent practices (even then called modernity or civilization)." Abdelmajid Hannoum, *Violent Modernity: France in Algeria* (Cambridge, MA: Harvard University Press, 2010), 9.

31. On the silences in historical narrative, see Michel-Rolph Trouillot, *Silencing the Past: Power and the Production of History* (Boston: Beacon, 1995), 47–53.

32. "Rapport général sur l'occupation des divers points de la Régence, sur l'organisation du gouvernement sur les dépenses de 1834 et 1835," in *Procès-verbaux et rapports*, 402–6.

33. For a fictional yet historically grounded account of the French conquest of Algeria from an Indigenous perspective, the reader should consult Assia Djebar's moving novel *L'Amour, la fantasia* (Paris: Éditions Albin Michel, 1995), first published in 1985.

34. Michael Greenhalgh, *The Military and Colonial Destruction of the Roman Landscape of North Africa, 1830–1900* (Leiden: Brill, 2014), 20–24.

35. Michael J. Heffernan and Keith Sutton, "The Landscape of Colonialism: The Impact of French Colonial Rule on the Algerian Rural Settlement Pattern, 1830–1987," in *Colonialism and Development in the Contemporary World*, ed. Chris Dixon and Michael J. Heffernan (London: Mansell, 1991), 124.

36. Sessions, *By Sword and Plow*, 249–53.

37. See the interview of Sidi Hamdan ben Amin Secca, former agha, on January 20, 1834, in *Procès-verbaux et rapports*, 43–44.

38. Gillian Weiss, *Captives and Corsairs: France and Slavery in the Early Modern Mediterranean* (Stanford, CA: Stanford University Press, 2011), 162–69.

39. Brower, *Desert Named Peace*, 32–33.

40. Greenhalgh, *Military and Colonial Destruction*, 38–47.

41. Brower, *Desert Named Peace*, 15–23.

42. Paul Azan, *L'armée d'Afrique de 1830 à 1852* (Paris: Plon, 1936), 180–84.

43. William Gallois, *A History of Violence in the Early Algerian Colony* (New York: Palgrave Macmillan, 2013), 52–53.

44. *Procès-verbaux et rapports*, 19–21.

45. Ruth Charlotte-Sophie de Castellane, Comtesse de Beaulaincourt-Marles, ed., *Campagnes d'Afrique 1835–1848: Lettres adressées au Maréchal de Castellane* (Paris: Plon, 1898), 38. Original emphasis retained.

46. Berthézène, *Dix-huit mois à Alger*, 193. Original emphasis retained.

47. Osama W. Abi-Mershed, *Apostles of Modernity: Saint-Simonians and the Civilizing Mission in Algeria* (Stanford, CA: Stanford University Press, 2010), 25.

48. On the state of knowledge of the Middle East and Arabic in the late eighteenth century, see Robert Irwin, *For Lust of Knowing: The Orientalists and Their Enemies* (London: Allen Lane, 2006), 134–40.

49. Claude-Antoine Rozet, *Voyage dans la Régence d'Alger ou Description du pays occupé par l'armée française en Afrique* (Paris: Arthus Bertrand, 1833), 3:428.

50. Marcel Emerit, "La lutte entre les généraux et les prêtres aux débuts de l'Algérie française," *Revue africaine* 97, nos. 434–35 (1953): 66–97.

51. Alice L. Conklin, *A Mission to Civilize: The Republican Idea of Empire in France and West Africa, 1895–1930* (Stanford, CA: Stanford University Press, 1997), 14–22. On the contributions of clerics to these activities in the early decades of the conquest, see, for example, the contributions of Abbé Bourgade; Clémentine Gutron, "L'abbé Bourgade (1806–1866), Carthage et l'Orient: De l'antiquaire au publiciste," *Anabases* 2 (2005): 177–91.

52. SHAT 1 H 14-2: Letter dated June 12, 1832, from the duc de Rovigo to Baron d'Uzer, maréchal de camp.

53. Þora Pétursdóttir, "Concrete Matters: Ruins of Modernity and the Things Called Heritage," *Journal of Social Archaeology* 13, no. 1 (2012): 31–53.

54. Greenhalgh, *Military and Colonial Destruction*, 121–25.

55. Jacques Frémeaux, "Souvenirs de Rome et présence française au Maghreb: Essai d'investigation," in *Connaissance du Maghreb: Sciences sociales et colonisation*, ed. Jean-Claude Vatin (Paris: CNRS Éditions, 1984), 30–32.

56. Patricia Lorcin, "Rome and France in Africa: Recovering Colonial Algeria's Latin Past," *French Historical Studies* 25, no. 2 (2002), 296.

57. Monique Dondin-Payre, "L'entrée de l'Algérie antique dans l'espace méditerranéen," in *Enquêtes en Méditerranée: Les expéditions françaises d'Égypte, de Morée et d'Algérie. Actes du colloque Athènes-Napulie, 8–10 juin 1995*, ed. Marie-Noëlle Bourguet et al. (Athens: Institut de recherches néohelléniques, 1999), 186.

58. Jacques Alexandropoulos, "Regards sur l'impérialisme de la Rome antique en Afrique du Nord," in *Idée impérial et impérialisme dans l'Italie fasciste: Journée d'étude organisée par le groupe ERASME le 4 avril 2003 à Toulouse*, ed. Alberto Bianco and Philippe Foro, Collection de l'E.C.R.I.T. 9 (Toulouse: Université de Toulouse-Le Mirail, 2003), 7–19.

59. Michael Greenhalgh, "The New Centurions: French Reliance on the Roman Past during the Conquest of Algeria," *War and Society* 16, no. 1 (1998), 11.

60. Marcel Bénabou, "L'impérialisme et l'Afrique du Nord: Le modèle romain," in *Sciences de l'homme et conquête coloniale: Constitution et usages des sciences humaines en Afrique (XIXe–XXe siècles)*, ed. Daniel Nordman and Jean-Pierre Raison (Paris: Presses de l'École normale supérieure, 1980), 15–22.

61. Eugène Albertini, "L'Algérie antique," in *Histoire et historiens de l'Algérie*, Collection du centenaire de l'Algérie (1830–1930) 4 (Paris: Librairie Alcan, 1931), 102.

62. Berthézène, *Dix-huit mois à Alger*, 33.

63. Although Arabic later became a comparative apparatus for understanding early Aramaic and Hebrew grammar, the linguistic development of the language was not yet well understood in the 1830s. At that time, Arabic was thought to have been fixed over the centuries by Qur'anic usages; Kees Versteegh, *The Arabic Language* (New York: Columbia University Press, 2001), 4–5.

64. Bénabou, "Impérialisme et l'Afrique du Nord," 16.

65. Berthézène, *Dix-huit mois à Alger*, 190–91.

66. Xavier Yacono, "La Régence d'Alger en 1830 d'après l'enquête des Commissions de 1833–1834," *Revue de l'Occident musulman et de la Méditerranée* 2, no. 1 (1966): 229–44; 2, no. 1 (1966): 227–47.

67. Discussion of the twenty-fourth meeting on February 5, 1834, in *Procès-verbaux et rapports*, 199.

68. Mohamed C. Sahli, *Décoloniser l'histoire: Introduction à l'histoire du Maghreb*, Cahiers libres 77 (Paris: François Maspero, 1965), 11–14.

69. Rozet, *Voyage dans la Régence d'Alger* 1:10–11.

70. Albertini, "Algérie antique," 92.

71. Saint-Marc Girardin, "De la domination des Carthaginois et des romaines en Afrique comparée avec la domination française," *Revue des deux mondes* ser. 4, 26 (April–June 1841): 408–9.

72. Eugène Lasserre, trans., *Tite Live, Histoire romaine, Livres XXVII–XXX*, vol. 6 (Paris: Librairie Garnier Frères, 1949), book 30:12–14, 472–83; book 30: 31, 528–31.

73. Sallust, *Bellum Iugurthinum* 6–7, ed. and trans. Alfred Ernout (Paris: Société d'éditions "Les belles lettres," 1960), 135–37; Girardin, "De la domination," 424–33. Jacques Alexandropoulos, "Jugurtha, héros national: jalons sur un itinéraire," *Anabases* 16 (2012): 11–29.

74. Ann McGrath, "Critiquing the Discovery Narrative of Lady Mungo," in *Unmasking Ideology: The Vocabulary, Symbols, and Legacy of Imperial and Colonial Archaeology*, ed. Bonnie Effros and Guolong Lai (Los Angeles: Cotsen Institute of Archaeology Press, in press).

75. Lorcin, "Rome and France in Africa," 296–97.

76. John Zarobell, *Empire of Landscape: Space and Ideology in French Colonial Algeria* (University Park: Pennsylvania State University Press, 2010), 10–26.

77. Nadia Bayle, "Quelques aspects de l'histoire de l'archéologie au XIXe siècle: L'exemple des publications archéologiques militaires éditées entre 1830 et 1914 en France, en Afrique du Nord et en Indo-Chine" (unpublished PhD diss., Université de Paris IV–Sorbonone, 1986), 1:35–38.

78. Irwin, *For Lust of Knowing*, 173–74.

79. Bayle, "Quelques aspects," 1:39–41.

80. Nacéra Benseddik, "L'armée française en Algérie: 'Parfois détruire, souvent construire,'" in *L'Africa romana: Atti de XIII convegno di studio, Djerba, 10–13 dicembre 1998*, ed. Mustapha Khanoussi, Paola Ruggeri, and Cinzia Vismara (Rome: Carocci Editore, 2000), 1:759–96; Greenhalgh, *Military and Colonial Destruction*, 4–5.

81. Bayle, "Quelques aspects," 1:60–62.

82. Ève Gran-Aymerich, *Naissance de l'archéologie moderne, 1798–1945* (Paris: CNRS Éditions, 1998), 78–90.

83. Ève Gran-Aymerich, "L'archéologie française en Grèce: Politique archéologique et politique méditerranéenne 1798–1945," in *Les politiques de l'archéologie du milieu du XIXe à l'orée du XXIe: Colloque organisé par l'École française d'Athènes à l'occasion de la célébration du 150e anniversaire de sa fondation*, ed. Roland Étienne (Athens: École française d'Athènes, 2000), 63–78.

84. Numa Broc, "Les grandes missions scientifiques françaises au XIXe siècle (Morée, Algérie, Mexique) et leurs travaux géographiques," *Revue d'histoire et des sciences* 34, no. 3–4 (1981): 319–31.

85. Jean-Pierre Chaline, *Sociabilité et érudition: Les sociétés savantes en France XIXe–XXe siècles* (Paris: CNRS Éditions, 1998).

86. Bonnie Effros, *Uncovering the Germanic Past: Merovingian Archaeology in France, 1830–1914* (Oxford: Oxford University Press, 2012), 33–47.

87. Xavier Barral I Altet, "Les étapes de la recherche au XIXe siècle et les personnalités," in *Naissance des arts chrétiens: Atlas des monuments paléochrétiens de la France* (Paris: Imprimerie nationale, 1991), 348–49.

88. Laurent Theis, "Guizot et les institutions de mémoire," in *Les lieux de mémoire*, ed. Pierre Nora (Paris: Gallimard, 1986), 2, pt. 2:569–92.

89. Françoise Choay, *The Invention of the Historic Monument*, trans. Lauren M. O'Connell (Cambridge: Cambridge University Press, 2001), 95–99.

90. Chantal Waltisperger, "Regard diachronique sur l'activité des sociétés savantes et leurs publications," in *Patrimoine historique et archéologique de l'Essone*, 2nd ed. (Évry: Association pour le développement de la lecture publique en Essone, 1990), 33; Chaline, *Sociabilité et érudition*, 327–44.

91. Oulebsir, *Usages du patrimoine*, 99–102.

92. Ève Gran-Aymerich, *Dictionnaire biographique d'archéologie 1798–1945* (Paris: CNRS Éditions, 2001), 657–58.

93. Effros, *Uncovering the Germanic Past*, 91–144.

94. Paul Léon, *La vie des monuments français: Destruction, restauration* (Paris: Éditions A. et J. Picard et Cie, 1951), 158–63; Caroline Ford, "The Inheritance of Empire and the Ruins of Rome in French Colonial Algeria," *Past and Present* 226, Suppl. 10 (2015), 62.

95. Salomon Reinach, "La méthode en archéologie," *Revue du mois* 11, no. 3 (1911): 287.

96. Monique Dondin-Payre, "L'archéologie en Algérie à partir de 1830: Une politique patrimoniale?," in *Pour une histoire des politiques du patrimoine*, ed. Philippe Poirrier and Loïc Vadelorge, Travaux et documents 16 (Paris: Comité d'histoire du Ministère de la culture, 2003), 145–70.

97. Jean-Michel Leniaud, "L'état, les sociétés savantes et les associations de défense du patrimoine: L'exceptions françaises," in *Patrimoine et passions identitaires*, ed. Jacques Le Goff (Paris: Arthème Fayard, 1998), 143.

98. Pim den Boer, *History as a Profession: The Study of History in France, 1818–1914*, trans. Arnold J. Pomerans (Princeton, NJ: Princeton University Press, 1988), 66.

99. Françoise Bercé, "Restaurer au XIXe siècle?," in *Nîmes et ses antiquités: Un passé présent: XVIe–XIXe siècle*, ed. Véronique Krings and François Pugnière (Bordeaux: Ausonius Éditions, 2013), 249–50.

100. AD de Calvados, Legs Travers (1941) F 6040: Art. 1er of the Projet des statuts (1839).

101. Bercé, "Restaurer au XIXe siècle?" 254–55.

102. AD de Calvados, Legs Travers (1941) F 6040: Art. 13 of the Projet des statuts (1839).

103. Jean-Michel Leniaud, *Viollet-le-Duc ou les délires du système* (Paris: Éditions Mengès, 1994), 37–38; Jean-Pierre Chaline, "Arcisse de Caumont et les sociétés savantes françaises," in *Arcisse de Caumont (1801–1873): Érudit normand et fondateur de l'archéologie française. Actes du colloque international organisé à Caen du 14 au 16 juin 2001*, ed. Vincent Juhel, Mémoires de la Société des antiquaires de Normandie 40 (Caen: Société des antiquaires de Normandie, 2004), 153.

104. François Guillet, "Arcisse de Caumont, un archéologue provincial," in *Arcisse de Caumont (1801–1873)*, 81–83; Stéphane Gerson, *The Pride of Place: Local Memories and Political Culture in Nineteenth-Century France* (Ithaca, NY: Cornell University Press, 2003), 153.

105. AD de Calvados, Legs Travers (1941) F 6034: Letter from Arcisse de Caumont dated June 1834 accompanying the Règlement constitutif de la Société française pour la conservation et la descriptions des monuments historiques.

106. Patricia Lorcin, *Imperial Identities: Stereotyping, Prejudice and Race in Colonial Algeria* (London: I. B. Tauris, 1995), 99–102.

107. Joseph-Daniel Guigniaut, "Notice historique sur la vie et les travaux de Charles-Benoît Hase, membre de l'Académie des inscriptions et belles-lettres," *Mémoires de l'Institut national de France* 27, no. 1 (1877): 247–73; Alexander von Hase, "Weimar—Paris—St. Petersburg: Karl Benedikt Hase (1780–1864) und sein europäisches Umfeld," *Archiv für Kulturgeschichte* 76, no. 1 (1994): 165–200; Gran-Aymerich, *Naissance de l'archéologie moderne*, 123.

108. Ève Gran-Aymerich and Jürgen von Ungern-Sternberg, *L'antiquité partagée: Correspondances franco-allemandes (1823–1861). Karl Benedikt Hase, Désiré Raoul-Rochette, Karl Otfried Müller, Otto Jahn, Theodor Mommsen*, Mémoires de l'Académie des inscriptions et belles-lettres 47 (Paris: Académie des inscriptions et belles-lettres, 2012), 299n53.

109. AD de la Côte-d'Or 1 J 2447/11: "Séance du 2 mai 1824," in *Procès-Verbaux des Séances de la Commission permanente des Antiquités formée dans le sein de l'Académie des sciences, arts et belles-lettres de Dijon*; Susan A. Crane, *Collecting and Historical Consciousness in Early Nineteenth-Century Germany* (Ithaca, NY: Cornell University Press, 2000), 7–15.

110. Lynn Meskell, "Archaeology Matters," in *Archaeology under Fire: Nationalism, Politics, and Heritage in the Eastern Mediterranean and Middle East* (London: Routledge, 1998), 1–12.

111. Margarita Díaz-Andreu, *A World History of Nineteenth-Century Archaeology: Nationalism, Colonialism, and the Past* (Oxford: Oxford University Press, 2007), 400–405.

112. Jean-Claude Vatin, *L'Algérie politique: Histoire et société*, Cahiers de la Fondation nationale des sciences politiques 192 (Paris: Armand Colin, 1974), 40–50.

113. Frantz Fanon, *The Wretched of the Earth*, trans. Richard Philcox (New York: Grove, 2004), 15.

114. Oulebsir, *Usages du patrimoine*, 7–13.

115. Nadia Bayle, "Armée et archéologie au XIXe siècle: Éléments de recherche sur les travaux archéologiques des officiers français publiés entre 1830 et 1914," *Revue d'archéologie moderne et d'archéologie génerale (RAMAGE)* 3 (1985): 219–21.

116. Adolphe Dureau de la Malle, *Peyssonnel et Desfontaines, Voyages dans les Régences de Tunis et d'Alger* (Paris: Librairie de Gide, 1838), 1:346–56.

117. Berthézène, *Dix-huit mois à Alger*, 130–31.

118. Ann Laura Stoler, *Carnal Knowledge and Imperial Power: Race and the Intimate in Colonial Rule* (Berkeley: University of California Press, 2002), 22–24.

119. ANOM 80 F 1587: Arrêté dated August 24, 1831, from the minister of war to the lieutenant general of Algiers.

120. Ministère de la Guerre, *Collection des actes du gouvernement depuis l'occupation d'Alger jusqu'au 1er octobre 1834* (Paris: Imprimerie royale, 1843), no. 116, 155.

121. "Lazare Costa, l'italien qui découvrit le tophet de Cirta," in *Exposition Internationale "Les Phéniciens en Algérie. Les voies du commerce entre la Méditerranée et l'Afrique Noire,"* Palais de la Culture Moufdi Zakaria-Algeri, 20 janvier–20 février 2011, ed. Lorenza Manfredi and Amel Soltani, http://cherchel-project.isma.cnr.it/index.php?option=com_content&view=article&id=133&Itemid=135&lang=fr.

122. Georges Doublet and Paul Gauckler, *Musée de Constantine*, Musées et collections archéologiques de l'Algérie (Paris: Ernest Leroux, Éditeur, 1892), 5–7. The original catalogue of the collection survives in manuscript form in ANOM 80 F 1587: *Catalogue des objets composant le cabinet d'antiquités de M Lazare Costa à Constantine.*

123. ANOM 80 F 1589: Letter dated June 28, 1839, from the director of the interior in French possessions in North Africa to the minister of war.

124. Raymund F. Wood, "Berbrugger, Founder of Algerian Librarianship," *Journal of Library History* 5, no. 3 (1971): 237–56; Lorcin, "Rome and France in Africa," 309–11; Paul-Albert Février, *Approches du Maghreb romain: Pouvoirs, différences et conflits* (Aix-en-Provence: ÉDISUD, 1989), 1:30.

125. ANOM 80 F 1733: Adrien Berbrugger, *Notes sur la Bibliothèque et sur le Musée d'Alger*, December 10, 1845.

126. Ibid.

127. Ibid.

128. Dondin-Payre, "Archéologie en Algérie," 146–55.

129. ANOM 80 F 1589: Letter dated June 28, 1839, from the director of the interior in Algiers to the minister of war.

130. Ferdinand-Philippe, Duc d'Orléans, *Récits de campagne, 1833–1841*, ed. Comte de Paris and the Duc de Chartres (Paris: Calmann Lévy, 1890), 216–17.

131. ANOM 80 F 1589: Letter dated November 29, 1843, from the minister of war to Governor-General Robert-Thomas Bugeaud.

132. William H. C. Frend, *The Archaeology of Early Christianity: A History* (Minneapolis: Fortress Press, 1996), 55–56; Annie Arnaud-Portelli, "L'exploration archéologique de l'Afrique du Nord des premiers voyageurs au XVIIIe siècle à l'independence des nations

(Maroc, Algérie) d'après les documents publiés," (unpublished PhD diss., Université de Paris IV–Sorbonne, 1991), 2:22.

133. Paul Gauckler, *Musée de Cherchel* (Paris: Ernest Leroux, 1895), 6–7.

134. Ferdinand-Philippe, Duc d'Orléans, *Récits de campagne, 1833–1841*, 426–27.

135. ANOM 80 F 1587: *Rapport sur le projet de démolir l'arc de triomphe de Djémilah et de le transporter en France*, January 9, 1843; Février, *Approches du Maghreb romain*, 38.

136. Archives des Musées Nationaux, Musée du Louvre A4: Mission Delamarre [sic] en Constantine (Algérie), June 19–August 14, 1845; ANOM 80 F 1589: Letter dated July 23, 1853, from the minister of war to the governor-general; Bonnie Effros, "Colliding Empires: French Display of Roman Antiquities Expropriated from Post-Conquest Algeria (1830–1870)," in *Objects of War: The Material Culture of Conflict and Displacement*, ed. Leora Auslander and Tara Zahra (Ithaca, NY: Cornell University Press, in press).

137. Lorcin, "Rome and France in Africa," 300–302; Frémeaux, "Souvenirs de Rome," 32; Stéphane Gsell, "Introduction," in *Histoire et historiens de l'Algérie*, Collection du centenaire de l'Algérie (1830–1930) 4 (Paris: Félix Alcan, 1931), 5.

138. Guigniaut, "Notice historique," 262–63.

139. *Procès-verbaux et rapports*, 3–5.

140. Ibid., 28–44, 110–11.

141. Ibid., 199.

142. Ibid., 201.

143. Jean Leclant, "Préface," in *La Commission d'exploration scientifique d'Algérie: Une héritière méconnue de la Commission d'Égypte*, by Monique Dondin-Payre, Mémoires de l'Académie des inscriptions et belles-lettres, n.s. 14 (Paris: F. Paillart, 1994), 7–10; Février, *Approches du Maghreb romain*, 30.

144. Dondin-Payre, "Entrée de l'Algérie antique," 181–83.

145. Dondin-Payre, *Commission d'exploration scientifique*, 15–23.

146. Greenhalgh, *Military and Colonial Destruction*, 29–32.

147. SHAT 1 H 30-1: Letter dated February 24, 1835, from the minister of war to Governor-General Lieutenant-General Comte d'Erlon; Greenhalgh, "New Centurions," 15.

148. SHAT 1 H 41-3: Ordre du jour of the superior commander of Bougie dated September 20, 1836.

149. Charles A. Walckenaër, "Rapports sur les recherches géographiques, historiques, archéologiques, qu'il convient de continuer ou d'entreprendre dans l'Afrique septentrionale," *Mémoires de l'Institut royal de France: Académie des inscriptions et belles-lettres* 12 (1831–1838), 12:112.

150. ANOM 80 F 1733: Adrien Berbrugger, *Notes sur la Bibliothèque et sur le Musée d'Alger*, December 10, 1845; Wood, "Berbrugger, Founder of Algerian Librarianship," 246.

151. Walckenaër, "Rapports sur les recherches," 112–23.

152. Bernard Lepetit, "Missions scientifiques et expéditions militaires: Remarques sur leurs modalités d'articulation," in *L'invention scientifique de la Méditerranée: Égypte, Morée, Algérie*, ed. Marie-Noëlle Bourguet, Bernard Lepetit, Daniel Nordman, and Maroula Sinarellis (Paris: Éditions de l'École des Hautes Études en Sciences Sociales, 1998), 97–116; Maya Jasanoff, *Edge of Empire: Lives, Culture, and Conquest in the East, 1750–1850* (New York: Knopf, 2005), 124–25.

153. Désiré Raoul-Rochette, "Rapport sur les recherches archéologiques à entreprendre dans la province de Constantine et la Régence d'Alger," *Mémoires de l'Institut royal de France. Académie des inscriptions et belles-lettres* (1831–1838), 12:173.

154. Monique Dondin-Payre, "L'*Exercitus africae* inspiratrice de l'armée française d'Afrique: *Ense et aratro*," *Antiquités africaines* 27 (1991): 143.

155. Dondin-Payre, *Commission d'exploration scientifique*, 25–26.

156. Monique Dondin-Payre, "La mise en place de l'archéologie officielle en Algérie, XIXe–début du XXe," in *Aspects de l'archéologie au XIXème siècle: Actes du colloque international tenu à La Diana à Montbrison les 14 et 15 octobre 1995*, ed. Pierre Jacquet and Robert Périchon, Recueil de mémoires et documents sur Le Forez publiés par la Société de la Diana 28 (Montbrison: La Diana, 2000), 354–55.

157. Frémeaux, "Souvenirs de Rome," 34–42; Abi-Mershed, *Apostles of Modernity*, 37–39.

158. André Raymond, "Les caracteristiques d'une ville arabe "moyenne" au XVIIIe siècle: Le cas de Constantine," *Cahiers de Tunisie* 137–38 (1986): 175–95.

159. For a firsthand description of the two campaigns in November 1836 and September 1837 to take the fortified city of Constantine, see Ernest Watbled, *Souvenirs de l'armée d'Afrique* (Paris: Challamel Aîné, 1877).

160. Dondin-Payre, *Commission d'exploration scientifique*, 28–29.

161. Gallois, *History of Violence*, 59–67.

162. Sessions, *By Sword and Plow*, 148–53.

163. Raymond, "Caracteristiques d'une ville arabe," 193–94.

164. Clémentine Gutron, *L'archéologie en Tunisie (XIXe–XXe siècles): Jeux généalogiques sur l'Antiquité* (Paris: Karthala, 2010), 24–25.

165. Gran-Aymerich, *Naissance de l'archéologie moderne*, 65.

166. Gran-Aymerich, *Dictionnaire biographique d'archéologie*, 639–41.

167. SHAT 1 H 50-1: Letter dated August 31, 1837, from the minister of war to Governor-General Damrémont granting Grenville Temple and Christian Falbe permission to engage in scientific study in French territory.

168. Grenville Temple and Christian Tuxen Falbe, *Relation d'une excursion de Bône à Guelma et à Constantine* (Paris: Société pour l'exploration et les fouilles de l'ancienne Carthage, 1838), vi–xix; Christian Tuxen Falbe, *Recherches sur l'emplacement de Carthage augmentées d'une carte archéologique et topographique* (Paris: Imprimerie royale, 1833–1834); Joann Freed, *Bringing Carthage Home: The Excavations of Nathan Davis, 1856–1859* (Oxford: Oxbow Books, 2011), 15.

169. Azan, *Armée d'Afrique*, 261–62.

170. Michael J. Heffernan, "An Imperial Utopia: French Surveys of North Africa in the Early Colonial Period," in *Maps and Africa: Proceedings of a Colloquium at the University of Aberdeen, April 1993*, ed. Jeffrey C. Stone (Aberdeen: Aberdeen University African Studies Group, 1994), 81–86; Lewis Pyenson, *Civilizing Mission: Exact Sciences and Overseas Expansion, 1830–1940* (Baltimore: Johns Hopkins University Press, 1993), 87–91.

171. On Bory de Saint-Vincent, see Daniel Nordman, "Mission de savants et occupation: L'exploration scientifique de l'Algérie (vers 1840–1860)," in *Vers l'Orient par la Grèce: Avec Nerval et d'autres voyageurs*, ed. Louis Droulia and Vasso Mentzou (Paris: Klincksieck, 1993), 82–83.

172. Greenhalgh, *Military and Colonial Destruction*, 61–62.

173. Archives de l'Institut de France, Archives de l'AIBL E 352: Letter dated August 21, 1839, from the minister of war to Baron Charles Walckenaër, the perpetual secretary of the Académie des inscriptions et belles-lettres; Dondin-Payre, *Commission d'exploration scientifique*, 32–39; Heffernan, "Imperial Utopia," 84–86.

174. Nordman, "Mission de savants et occupation," 84–85

175. Heffernan, "Imperial Utopia," 85–89.

176. Archives de l'Institut de France, Archives de l'AIBL E 361, Correspondances particuliers de 1843: Letter dated January 19, 1843, from Augustin Hardin (?) to Bory de St-Vincent as head of the Commission d'exploration.

177. Gsell, "Introduction," 7–8.

178. Archives de l'Institut de France, Archives de l'AIBL E 359: Letter dated April 30, 1842, from the minister of war to Baron Charles Walckenaër, perpetual secretary of the Académie des inscriptions et belles-lettres; letter dated October 26, 1842, from Jean-Baptiste Bory de St-Vincent to the minister of war.

179. Dondin-Payre, *Commission d'exploration scientifique*, 47–65.

180. Díaz-Andreu, *World History of Nineteenth-Century Archaeology*, 265–67; Frémeaux, "Souvenirs de Rome," 34.

181. Daniel Nordman, "La notion de région dans l'*Exploration scientifique de l'Algérie*. Premiers jalons," in *Enquêtes en Méditerranée*, 141–57.

182. Jehan Desanges, "La commission dite 'de l'Afrique du Nord' au sein du CTHS: Origine, évolution, perspectives," in *Numismatique, langues, écritures et arts du livre, spécificité des arts figurés: Actes du VIIe colloque international sur l'histoire et l'archéologie de l'Afrique du Nord, Nice, 21 au 31 octobre 1996)* (Paris: Éditions du Comité des travaux historiques et scientifiques, 1999), 11–24.

183. Nabila Oulebsir, "Rome ou la Méditerranée? Les relevés d'architecture d'Amable Ravoisié en Algérie, 1840–1842," in *L'invention scientifique de la Méditerranée*, 239–71.

184. Adolphe-Hedwige-Alphonse Delamare, *Exploration scientifique de l'Algérie pendant les années 1840, 1841, 1842, 1843, 1844 et 1845* (Paris: Imprimerie nationale, 1850).

185. Amable Ravoisié, *Exploration scientifique de l'Algérie pendant les années 1840, 1841, 1842*, Beaux-arts, architecture et sculpture, 2 vols. (Paris: Chez Firmin Didot Frères, 1846–1850); Oulebsir, *Usages du patrimoine*, 48–69.

186. Ernest Carette, *Exploration scientifique de l'Algérie pendant les années 1840, 1841, 1842*, Sciences historiques et géographiques 1 (Paris: Imprimerie nationale, 1844); Ernest Carette, *Exploration scientifique de l'Algérie pendant les années 1840, 1841, 1842*, Sciences historiques et géographiques 5 (Paris: Imprimerie nationale, 1848); Ernest Carette, *Exploration scientifique de l'Algérie: Études sur le Kabilie proprement dit*, 2 vols. (Paris: Imprimerie nationale, 1849); Diana K. Davis, *Resurrecting the Granary of Rome: Environmental History and the French Colonial Expansion in North Africa* (Athens: Ohio University Press, 2007), 36–38.

187. It appears that the commission was not informed in advance of Berbrugger's decision to publish his volumes with the publishing house Deshayes; Archives de l'Institut de France, Archives de l'AIBL E359, Correspondance 1842—Commission scientifique de l'Algérie: Letter dated December 29, 1842, from the minister of war to Baron Charles Walckenaër.

188. Adolphe Dureau de la Malle, *Province de Constantine: Recueil de renseignements pour l'expédition ou l'établissement des français dans cette partie de l'Afrique septentrionale* (Paris: Librairie de Gide, 1837); Adrien Berbrugger, *Algérie historique, pittoresque et monumentale ou Recueil de vues, costumes, et portraits faits d'après nature dans les provinces d'Alger, Bône, Constantine et Oran*, 3 vols. (Paris: Chez J. Delehaye, 1843).

189. Edmond Pellissier de Reynaud, *Exploration scientifique de l'Algérie pendant les années 1840, 1841, 1842*, Sciences historiques et géographiques 16 (Paris: Imprimerie impériale, 1853).

190. Adolphe-Hedwige-Alphonse Delamare, "Notes sur quelques villes romaines de l'Algérie," *Revue archéologique* 6, no. 1 (1849): 1–7.

191. Stéphane Gsell, *Exploration scientifique de l'Algérie pendant les années 1840–1845. Archéologie* (Paris: Ernest Léroux, 1912), i–ix; Monique Dondin-Payre, *Le Capitaine Delamare: La réussite de l'archéologie romaine au sein de la Commission d'exploration scientifique d'Algérie*, Mémoires de l'Académie des inscriptions et belles-lettres, n.s. 15 (Paris: Imprimerie F. Paillart, 1994), 9–29.

192. These are documented in Gsell, *Exploration scientifique*.

193. Monique Dondin-Payre, "La production d'images sur l'espace méditerranéen dans la Commission d'exploration scientifique d'Algérie: Les dessins du capitaine Delamare," in *L'invention scientifique de la Méditerranée*, 223–38.

194. Heffernan, "Imperial Utopia," 93–94.

195. Edward W. Said, *Culture and Imperialism* (New York: Vintage, 1993), 78–79.

196. For a comparative case study in the context of North America, see Chip Colwell-Chanthaphonh and J. Brett Hill, "Mapping History: Cartography and the Construction of the San Pedro Valley," *History and Anthropology* 15, no. 2 (2004): 175–200. On the challenges of reviving that voice, see Dipesh Chakrabarty, *Provincializing Europe: Postcolonial Thought and Historical Difference*, new ed. (Princeton, NJ: Princeton University Press, 2008), 102–8.

197. Carette, *Exploration scientifique de l'Algérie* (1844), ix–xviii.

198. Marie-Armand-Pascal d'Azevac, *Esquisse générale de l'Afrique et Afrique ancienne* (Paris: Firmin Didot Frères, 1844), 172–75.

199. Michael Heffernan, "A Paper City: On History, Maps, and Map Collections in Eighteenth- and Nineteenth-Century Paris," *Imago mundi* 66, Suppl. 1 (2014): 5–20; Godlewska, "Map, Text and Image," 5–28.

200. Richard J. A. Talbert, "Carl Müller (1818–1894), S. Jacobs, and the Making of Classical Maps in Paris for John Murray," *Imago mundi* 46 (1994): 144.

201. Greenhalgh, *Military and Colonial Destruction*, 243–45.

202. For this Latin passage alleging that the fertility of Africa sustained Rome, Périer borrowed a suspect phrase from Samuel Bochart's *Geographia sacra seu Phaleg et Canaan* 1 (1707–1712), 490. Bochart, in turn, cited Juvenal, *Satire* 8, but the trail goes cold here.

203. Jean-André-Napoléon Périer, *Exploration scientifique de l'Algérie pendant les années 1840, 1841, 1842*, Sciences médicales 1 (Paris: Imprimerie impériale, 1847), 29–30.

204. Ravoisié, *Expedition scientifique*, 1:iii.

205. Ahmed Koumas and Chéhrazade Nafa, *L'Algérie et son patrimoine: Dessins français du XIXe siècle* (Paris: Monum, Éditions du patrimoine, 2003), 33–43.

206. Greenhalgh, *Military and Colonial Destruction*, 239–41.

207. Michael Greenhalgh, *From the Romans to the Railways: The Fate of Antiquities in Asia Minor* (Leiden: Brill, 2013), 263–80. For the comparison with Greece, see Yannis Hamilakis, "Decolonizing Greek Archaeology: Indigenous Archaeologies, Modernist Archaeology and the Post-Colonial Critique," in *A Singular Authority: Archaeology and Hellenic Identity in Twentieth-Century Greece*, ed. Dimitris Damaskos and Dimitris Plantzos (Athens: Mouseio Benaki, 2008), 273–80.

208. Davis, *Resurrecting the Granary of Rome*; Brent D. Shaw, "Climate, Environment, and History: The Case of Roman North Africa," in *Climate and History: Studies in Past Climates and Their Impact on Man*, ed. T. M. L. Wigley, M. J. Ingram, and G. Farmer (Cambridge: Cambridge University Press, 1981), 379–403.

209. Fanon, *Wretched of the Earth*, 148–52.

210. Zeynep Çelik, "Defining Empire's Patrimony: Late Ottoman Perceptions of Antiquities," in *Scramble for the Past: A Story of Archaeology in the Ottoman Empire, 1753–1914*, ed. Zainab Bahrani, Zeynep Çelik, and Edhem Eldem (Istanbul: SALT, 2011), 443–47.

211. "I hear the storm. They talk to me about progress, about 'achievements,' diseases cured, improved standards of living. *I* am talking about societies drained of their essence, cultures trampled underfoot, institutions undermined, lands confiscated, religions smashed, magnificent artistic creations destroyed, extraordinary *possibilities* wiped out." Aimé Césaire, *Discourse on Colonialism*, trans. Joan Pinkham (New York: Monthly Review Press, 1972), 42–43.

212. Greenhalgh, *From the Romans to the Railways*, 24–27, 283–88.

213. Renier alleged that this account was told to him by Berbrugger. Léon Renier, "Notes d'un voyage archéologique au pied de l'Aurès," *Revue archéologique* 8, no. 2 (1851–1852), 513.

214. Greenhalgh, *Military and Colonial Destruction*, 245–50.

215. Josef W. Konvitz, *Cartography in France 1660–1848: Science, Engineering, and Statecraft* (Chicago: University of Chicago Press, 1987), 134–48.

216. J. Brian Harley, "Maps, Knowledge, and Power," in *The Iconography of Landscape: Essays on the Symbolic Representation, Design, and Use of Past Environments*, ed. Denis Cosgrove and Stephen Daniels (Cambridge: Cambridge University Press, 1988), 277–312.

217. J. Brian Harley, "Deconstructing the Map," *Cartographica* 26, no. 2 (1989): 1–20.

218. Certain aspects of Roman land administration were not well understood by most archaeologists of the 1830s, including centuriation. Greenhalgh, *Military and Colonial Destruction*, 254–57.

Chapter 2. Envisioning the Future

1. Jamil M. Abun-Nasr, *A History of the Maghrib*, 2nd ed. (Cambridge: Cambridge University Press, 1975), 239–45.

2. Alexis Belloc, *La télégraphie historique: Depuis les temps les plus reculés jusqu'à nos jours* 2nd ed. (Paris: Firmin Didot, 1894), 191–92.

3. Jennifer E. Sessions, *By Sword and Plow: France and the Conquest of Algeria* (Ithaca, NY: Cornell University Press, 2011), 177–207.

4. Xavier Marmier, *Lettres sur l'Algérie* (Paris: Arthus Bertrand, 1847), xl.

5. Amédée Desjobert, *L'Algérie en 1844* (Paris: Guillaumin, 1844).

6. Julia Clancy-Smith, "La Femme Arabe: Women and Sexuality in France's North African Empire," in *Women, the Family, and Divorce Laws in Islamic History,* ed. Amira El Azhary Sonbol (Syracuse: Syracuse University Press, 1996), 52–63.

7. Peter Dunwoodie, *Writing French Algeria* (Oxford: Clarendon, 1998), 45–48.

8. Elwood Hartman, *Three Nineteenth-Century French Writers/Artists and the Maghreb: The Literary and Artistic Depictions of North Africa by Théophile Gautier, Eugène Fromentin and Pierre Loti* (Tübingen: Gunter Narr, 1994), 11–13.

9. Cheryl B. Welch, "Colonial Violence and the Rhetoric of Evasion: Tocqueville on Algeria," *Political Theory* 31, no. 2 (2003): 235–64.

10. Jennifer Pitts, ed. and trans, *Writings on Empire and Slavery: Alexis de Tocqueville* (Baltimore: Johns Hopkins University Press, 2001), xix–xxi; Timothy Mitchell, *Colonising Egypt* (Cambridge: Cambridge University Press, 1988), 56–58.

11. Franck Laurent, *Victor Hugo face à la conquête de l'Algérie* (Paris: Maisonneuve et Larose, 2001), 18–22, 47–55.

12. *Procès-verbal de la visite et inspection de la châsse de cristal, contenant les sacrées dépouilles du corps de Saint-Augustin.* Pavia, 12 avril 1842, Archives de la Société des Missionaires d'Afrique (Rome) (A.G.M.Afr.) A16 251; Antoine-Adolphe Dupuch, *Lettre pastorale de Monseigneur l'évêque d'Alger* (Marseille: Marius Olive, 1842); SHAT 1 H 86-2: Letter dated October 21, 1842, from the duc de Dalmatie, minister of war, to the governor-general of Algeria; SHAT 1 M 1317: Capitaine Adjudant-Major Amable Joseph Ardiet, *Mémoire militaire sur la reconnaissance de l'emplacement de l'ancienne ville d'Hippone et ses environs* (1851).

13. Marcel Emerit, "La lutte entre les généraux et les prêtres aux débuts de l'Algérie française," *Revue africaine* 97, nos. 434–35 (1953), 86–87.

14. William H. C. Frend, *The Archaeology of Early Christianity: A History* (Minneapolis: Fortress Press, 1996), 54–56.

15. M. Poujoulat, *Études africaines: Récits et pensées d'un voyageur* (Paris: Comptoir des Imprimeurs-Unis, 1847), 2:128.

16. Antoine Adolphe Dupuch, *Lettre pastorale de Monseigneur l'évêque d'Alger* (Bordeaux: Chez Henry Faye, 1838).

17. Emerit, "Lutte entre les généraux," 66–97.

18. Kyle Francis, "Catholic Missionaries in Colonial Algeria: Faith, Foreigners, and France's Other Civilizing Mission, 1848–1883," *French Historical Studies* 39, no. 4 (2016): 685–715.

19. Antoine-Adolphe Dupuch, *Essai sur l'Algérie chrétienne, romaine et française* (Turin: Imprimerie royale, 1847).

20. Clémentine Gutron, "L'abbé Bourgade (1806–1866), Carthage et l'Orient: De l'antiquaire au publiciste," *Anabases* 2 (2005): 177–91.

21. Ernest Carette, *Précis historique et archéologique sur Hippone et ses environs* (Paris: Lange Lévy et Compagnie, 1838).

22. *Moniteur Universel*, June 6, 1844; Benjamin Claude Brower, *A Desert Named Peace: The Violence of France's Empire in the Algerian Sahara, 1844–1902* (New York: Columbia University Press, 2009), 45.

23. Jan Jansen, *Erobern und Erinnern: Symbolpolitik, öffentlicher Raum und französischer Kolonialismus in Algerien, 1830–1950* (Munich: Oldenbourg, 2013), 30–52.

24. *Moniteur universel*, 1636–37.

25. Amédée Desjobert, *L'Algérie en 1846* (Paris: Guillaumin, 1846), 8–11.

26. Desjobert, *Algérie en 1844*.

27. Ellen J. Amster, *Medicine and the Saints: Science, Islam, and the Colonial Encounter in Morocco, 1877–1956* (Austin: University of Texas Press, 2013), 52–55.

28. Nadia Bayle, "Quelques aspects de l'histoire de l'archéologie au XIXe siècle: L'exemple des publications archéologiques militaires éditées entre 1830 et 1914 en France, en Afrique du Nord et en Indo-Chine," (unpublished PhD diss., Université de Paris IV–Sorbonone, 1986), 1:98–111.

29. Patricia M. Lorcin, "Rome and France in Africa: Recovering Colonial Algeria's Latin Past," *French Historical Studies* 25, no. 2 (2002): 295–329; Patricia Lorcin, *Imperial Identities: Stereotyping, Prejudice and Race in Colonial Algeria* (London: I. B. Tauris, 1995), 21–22.

30. Azéma de Montgravier, *Études historiques pour servir au projet de colonisation d'une partie du territoire de la Province d'Oran* (n. p., May 1846), 73.

31. Ibid., 73.

32. Ibid., 79.

33. Edmond Pellissier de Reynaud. *Annales algériennes*, new ed. (Paris: Librairie militaire, 1854), 3:248; William Gallois, *A History of Violence in the Early Algerian Colony* (New York: Palgrave Macmillan, 2013), 52–53.

34. Olivier Le Cour Grandmaison, "Conquête de l'Algérie: La guerre totale," in *Le massacre, objet d'histoire*, ed. David El Kenz (Paris: Gallimard, 2005), 253–74; Brower, *Desert Named Peace*, 16–17.

35. Djilali Sari, *Le désastre démographique* (Algiers: Société nationale d'Édition et Diffusion, 1982), 129–202; Yvonne Turin, "La crise de campagnes algériennes en 1868, d'après l'enquête de la même année," *Revue d'histoire et de civilisation du Maghreb* 13 (January 1976): 79–86.

36. Dawson Borrer, *Narrative of a Campaign against the Kabaïles of Algeria* (London: Longman, Brown, Green, and Longmans, 1848), 100–115.

37. Gallois, *History of Violence*, 4–5. I thank Yücel Yanikdağ for his helpful explanation of the distinction between *ghaza* and *razzia*.

38. In the modern French edition of Tacitus's *Annals*, the raids launched by Tacfarinas are translated as "razzias": Henri Goellzer, ed. and trans., *Tacite Annales livres I–III* (Paris:

Société d'Édition "Les belles lettres," 1965), 1:3.20, 131. This is not true, however, of some earlier editions and translations of the same passage, which referred to the same activity more generically; Auguste Materne, ed. and trans., *Les auteurs latins: Tacite, troisième livre des Annales* (Paris: L. Hachette, 1853), 3.20, 45.

39. Paul Azan, *L'armée d'Afrique de 1830 à 1852* (Paris: Plon, 1936), 334–41.

40. Borrer, *Narrative of a Campaign*, 245–46.

41. The conditions in ancient North Africa were probably much more similar to those that prevailed in the nineteenth century than the French claimed; Brent D. Shaw, "Climate, Environment, and History: The Case of Roman North Africa," in *Climate and History: Studies in Past Climates and Their Impact on Man*, ed. T. M. L. Wigley, M. J. Ingram, and G. Farmer (Cambridge: Cambridge University Press, 1981), 379–403.

42. Michel-Rolph Trouillot, *Silencing the Past: Power and the Production of History* (Boston: Beacon, 1995), 47–53.

43. Diana K. Davis, "Eco-Governance in French Algeria: Environmental History, Policy, and Colonial Administration," *Proceedings of the Western Society for French History* 32 (2004): 328–45.

44. Jennifer E. Sessions, "'Unfortunate Necessities': Violence and Civilization in the Conquest of Algeria," in *France and Its Spaces of War: Experience, Memory, Image*, ed. Patricia M. E. Lorcin and Daniel Brewer (New York: Palgrave Macmillan, 2009), 29–44.

45. "P. Christian (1811–1872): pseudonym individuel," Bibliothèque Nationale de France: Data.bnf.fr, last updated July 2, 2017, http://data.bnf.fr/12327453/p__christian/#author. other_forms.

46. Pierre Christian, *L'Afrique française, l'empire de Maroc et les déserts de Sahara* (Paris: A. Barbier, 1846), 66–68.

47. Yannis Hamilakis, *The Nation and Its Ruins: Antiquity, Archaeology, and the National Imagination in Greece* (Oxford: Oxford University Press, 2007), 102.

48. Pierre Berthézène, *Dix-huit mois à Alger* (Montpellier: Chez August Ricard, 1834), 33.

49. André Joubin, ed., *Correspondance générale de Eugène Delacroix*, vol. 1: *1804–1837* (Paris: Librairie Plon, 1936), 318–19, 327.

50. Stéphane Gsell, "Introduction," in *Histoire et historiens de l'Algérie*. Collection du centenaire de l'Algérie (1830–1930) 4 (Paris: Félix Alcan, 1931), 4.

51. *Lettres du Maréchal de Saint-Arnaud* (Paris: Michel Lévy Frères, 1855), 1:170.

52. Denis Roussel, trans., *Polybe, Histoire* (Paris: Gallimard, 2003), 36.4:1313–14.

53. Eugène Lasserre, trans., *Tite Live, Histoire romaine, Livres XXVII–XXX* (Paris: Librairie Garnier Frères, 1949), 6:30.12–14, 472–83.

54. Marcel Bénabou, " L'impérialisme et l'Afrique du Nord: le modèle romain," in *Sciences de l'homme et conquête coloniale: Constitution et usages des sciences humaines en Afrique (XIXe–XXe siècles)*, ed. Daniel Nordman and Jean-Pierre Raison (Paris: Presses de l'École normale supérieure, 1980), 15–22.

55. George R. Trumbull IV, *An Empire of Facts: Colonial Power, Cultural Knowledge, and Islam in Algeria, 1870–1914* (Cambridge: Cambridge University Press, 2009), 148–49.

56. SHAT 8 Yd 3356: Ministère de la Guerre, État des services de M. Cler, Jean-Joseph-Gustave.

57. Jean-Joseph-Gustave Cler, *Reminiscences of an Officer of Zouaves* (New York: D. Appleton and Co., 1860), 97–101.

58. Ruth Charlotte-Sophie de Castellane, Comtesse de Beaulaincourt-Marles, ed., *Campagnes d'Afrique 1835–1848: Lettres adressées au Maréchal de Castellane* (Paris: Plon, 1898), 286.

59. Lorcin, *Imperial Identities*, 114–18.

60. Pam Hirsch, *Barbara Leigh Smith Bodichon, 1827–1891: Feminist, Artist and Rebel* (London: Chatto and Windus, 1998), 122–25.

61. Bonnie Effros, "Berber Genealogy and the Politics of Prehistoric Archaeology and Craniology in French Algeria (1860s to 1880s)," *British Journal of History of Science* 50, no. 1 (2017): 61–81, doi:10.1017/S0007087417000024.

62. Paul Gaffarel, *L'Algérie: Histoire, conquête et colonisation* (Paris: Firmin-Didot et Cie, 1883), 268–69.

63. SHAT 1 M 1316: Aléxis Robardey, *Mémoire descriptive et militaire* (August 10, 1845).

64. Henri Leclercq, "Orléansville," in *Dictionnaire d'archéologie chrétienne et de liturgie*, ed. Fernand Cabrol and Henri Leclercq (Paris: Letouzey et Ané, 1936), 12, pt. 2:2719–35; Frend, *Archaeology of Early Christianity*, 58.

65. Letter dated December 20, 1844, from Saint-Arnaud to his brother Adolphe, in *Lettres du Maréchal de Saint-Arnaud*, 2:5.

66. Musée de l'armée, Ms. M 737: Mémoires et papiers du général Desvaux, vol. 3, journal entry dated June 1, 1842.

67. John Ruedy, *Land Policy in Colonial Algeria: The Origins of the Rural Public Domain*, Near Eastern Studies 10 (Berkeley: University of California Press, 1967), 25.

68. He wrote this letter from the city of Algiers on March 27, 1844: Léon Blondel, *Aperçus sur l'état actuel de l'Algérie, Lettres d'un voyageur à son frère* (Algiers: Imprimerie du Gouvernement, 1844), 4.

69. SHAT 7 Yd 1208: Admission certificate from the governor of the École impériale polytechnique dated September 29, 1812.

70. SHAT 7 Yd 1208: Letter dated January 28, 1830, from Franciade Fleurus Duvivier to the minister of war.

71. SHAT 7 Yd 1208: Letter dated February 17, 1830, from the Ministry of War to Franciade Fleurus Duvivier.

72. SHAT 7 Yd 1208: Letter dated January 23, 1831, from the lieutenant colonel, chef d'état major de la division d'occupation, to Franciade Fleurus Duvivier.

73. Patricia Lorcin, "Imperialism, Colonial Identity, and Race in Algeria, 1830–1870: The Role of the French Medical Corps," *Isis* 90, no. 4 (1999): 653–79.

74. SHAT 7 Yd 1208: Letter dated April 22, 1835, from the armée d'Afrique to Franciade Fleurus Duvivier granting him six months of requested leave for convalescence.

75. For the former, see Berthézène, *Dix-huit mois à Alger*, 264–65.

76. SHAT 7 Yd 1208: Report by M. de Tinan, squadron chief of the general staff, dated June 7, 1833.

77. Eugène Daumas and Paul Dieudonné Fabar, *La Grande Kabylie: Études historiques* (Paris: L. Hachette, 1847), 100.

78. Osama W. Abi-Mershed, *Apostles of Modernity: Saint-Simonians and the Civilizing Mission in Algeria* (Stanford, CA: Stanford University Press, 2010), 76–77.

79. SHAT 7 Yd 1208: Various documents related to Duvivier's career dated 1837 to 1841.

80. Franciade Fleurus Duvivier, *Recherches et notes sur la portion de l'Algérie au sud de Guelma depuis la frontière de Tunis jusqu'au Mont Aurèss compris* (Paris: L. Vassal et Cie, 1841), 66.

81. SHAT 7 Yd 1208: The duc de Dalmatie accepted Duvivier's request with regret in a letter dated February 5, 1841.

82. Ibid.

83. Ibid.

84. SHAT 7 Yd 1208: Duvivier's letter of recognition addressed to the minister of war was dated May 12, 1848; C. Mullié, *Biographie des célébrités militaires des armées de terre et mer de 1789 à 1850* (Paris: Chez Poignavant et Cie, 1851), 1:486.

85. SHAT 7 Yd 1208: Extract of the Summary report of the Inspection générale de 1838, 24e Rég. D'Infantrie de ligne, dated July 6, 1839.

86. SHAT 7 Yd 1208: Letter dated March 23, 1837, from the head of the division in Bône to the minister of war.

87. SHAT 1 H 43-3: Duvivier's handwritten *Plan du camp de Guelma* and related inscriptional finds dated December 31, 1836.

88. Michael Greenhalgh, *The Military and Colonial Destruction of the Roman Landscape of North Africa, 1830–1900* (Leiden: Brill, 2014), 137–41.

89. Ibid., 139–40.

90. Monique Dondin-Payre, "La mise en place de l'archéologie officielle en Algérie, XIXe–début du XXe," in *Aspects de l'archéologie française au XIXème siècle: Actes du colloque international tenu à La Diana à Montbrison les 14 et 15 octobre 1995*, ed. Pierre Jacquet and Robert Périchon, Recueil de mémoires et documents sur Le Forez publiés par la Société de la Diana 28 (Montbrison: La Diana, 2000), 353–54.

91. SHAT 1 H 48-3: Document dated June 1, 1837, titled "Camp de Ghelma 1837."

92. Archives des musées nationaux, Musée du Louvre A4: Mission Delamarre [sic] en Constantine (Algérie), June 19–August 14, 1845.

93. SHAT 6 Yd 39.

94. Michael Greenhalgh, *Constantinople to Córdoba: Dismantling Ancient Architecture in the East, North Africa, and Islamic Spain* (Leiden: Brill, 2012), 407.

95. Greenhalgh, *Military and Colonial Destruction*, 127–28.

96. SHAT 1 H 74-1: Governor-General Valée's report to the duc of Dalmatie, minister of war dated January 5, 1841.

97. Adolphe Dureau de la Malle, *Peyssonnel et Desfontaines, Voyages dans les Régences de Tunis et d'Alger 1* (Paris: Gide, 1838); Adolphe Dureau de la Malle, *Province de Constantine: Recueil de renseignements pour l'expédition ou l'établissement des français dans cette partie de l'Afrique septentrionale* (Paris: Gide, 1837).

98. Duvivier, *Recherches et notes*, 1.

99. SHAT 7 Yd 1208: Receipts dated September 23 and 25, 1841, from Vassal et Cie and Lithographie de N. Gratia.

100. Franciade Fleurus Duvivier, *Les inscriptions phéniciennes, puniques, numidiques, expliquées par une méthode incontestable* (Paris: J. Dumaine, Neveu et Succ. de G. Laguioni, 1846), 1–16.

101. SHAT 7 Yd 1208: Letter dated February 1, 1846, from the minister of war to Duvivier.

102. Franciade Fleurus Duvivier, *Solution de la question de l'Algérie* (Paris: Imprimerie et librairie militaire de Gaultier-Laguionie, 1841), 41–48.

103. Ibid., 139–41, 285.

104. Duvivier, *Recherches et notes*, 57–61.

105. Franciade Fleurus Duvivier, *Algérie: Quatorze observations sur le dernier mémoire du Général Bugeaud* (Paris: H.-L. Delloye, 1842), 132.

106. Antony Thrall Sullivan, *Thomas-Robert Bugeaud: France and Algeria, 1874–1849. Politics, Power, and the Good Society* (Hamden, CT: Archon Books, 1983), 17–26.

107. Barnett Singer and John Langdon, *Cultured Force: Makers and Defenders of the French Colonial Empire* (Madison: University of Wisconsin Press, 2004), 61–64.

108. Richard A. Roughton, "Economic Motives and French Imperialism: The 1837 Tafna Treaty as a Case Study," *Historian* 47, no. 3 (1985): 360–81; Singer and Langdon, *Cultured Force*, 65–66.

109. Thomas-Robert Bugeaud, *Quelques réflexions sur trois questions fondamentales de notre établissement en Algérie* (Algiers: A. Besancenez, 1846), 15; SHAT 1 M 882: General Rivet, *Histoire du gouvernement du Maréchal Bugeaud de 1841 à 1847*, chaps. 1, 2–4.

110. Sullivan, *Thomas-Robert Bugeaud*, 61–73.

111. SHAT 1 M 1319: Letter dated August 25, 1843 from Thomas-Robert Bugeaud to General Pelet, general director of the ordnance depot.

112. Sallust, *Bellum Iugurthinum*, ed. and trans. Alfred Ernout (Paris: Société d'Édition "Les belles lettres," 1960), 6–7: 135–37; Montgravier, *Études historiques*, 81. Jacques Alex-andropoulos, "Jugurtha, héros national: jalons sur un itinéraire," *Anabases* 16 (2012): 11–29.

113. Thomas-Robert Bugeaud, *Histoire de l'Algérie française* (Paris: Henri Morel et Cie, 1850), 1:34–35.

114. SHAT 1 H 92-1: Letter dated October 10, 1843, from Governor-General Bugeaud to the minister of war.

115. Bugeaud, *Histoire de l'Algérie française* 2:75.

116. *Bulletin officiel des actes du gouvernement*, vol. 4 (Algiers: Imprimerie du gouverne-ment, 1844), no. 167, 13; no. 173, 64–65.

117. Philip Brebner, "The Impact of Thomas-Robert Bugeaud and the Decree of 9 June 1844 on the Development of Constantine, Algeria," *Revue de l'Occident musulman et de la Méditerranée* 38 (1984): 5–14.

118. Charles Marcotte de Quivières, *Deux ans en Afrique* (Paris: Librairie nouvelle, 1855), 24.

119. Nabila Oulebsir, *Les usages du patrimoine: Monuments, musées et politique colo-niale en Algérie (1830–1930)* (Paris: Éditions de la Maison des sciences de l'homme, 2004), 95–97.

120. Jack Blaine Ridley, "Marshal Bugeaud, the July Monarchy and the Question of Al-geria, 1841–1847: A Study in Civil-Military Relations" (unpublished PhD diss., University of Oklahoma, 1970), 13–15.

121. John Reynell Morell, *Algeria: The Topography and History, Political, Social, and Natural of French Africa* (London: Nathaniel Cooke, 1854), 389.

122. Charles Thoumas, *Les transformations de l'armée française: Essais d'histoire et de critique sur l'état militaire de la France* (Paris: Berger-Levrault et Cie, 1887), 2:630–32.

123. SHAT 1 H 76-1: Letter from Baraguey d'Hilliers to Maréchal de Dieu Soult, minis-ter of war, dated June 18, 1841.

124. SHAT 1 M 1317: L. H. Bartel, *Études sur l'histoire de la ville de Bougie* (July 1847), unpublished manuscript.

125. Castellane, *Campagnes d'Afrique 1835–1848*, 247.

126. SHAT 7 Yd 1256: Letter from the governor-general to the minister of war dated No-vember 23, 1849, on the topic of General Émile Herbillon's use of excessive force at the siege of Zaatcha in October 1849.

127. Sullivan, *Thomas-Robert Bugeaud*, 77–99; Singer and Langdon, *Cultured Force*, 61–69.

128. Louis-Charles-Pierre, Comte de Castellane, *Souvenirs of Military Life in Algeria*, trans. Margaret Josephine Lovett (London: Remington and Co., 1886), 1:110.

129. *Lettres du Maréchal de Saint-Arnaud*, 1:381.

130. Brent D. Shaw, *Bringing in the Sheaves: Economy and Metaphor in the Roman World* (Toronto: University of Toronto Press, 2013), 3–47.

131. Brower, *Desert Named Peace*, 1–112.

132. Pierre Pluchon, *Toussaint Louverture: Un révolutionnaire noir d'Ancien Régime* (Paris: Fayard, 1989), 476–92; Bernard Foubert, "Les volontaires nationaux de l'Aube et de la Seine-Inférieure à Saint-Domingue (octobre 1792–janvier 1793)," *Bulletin de la Société d'histoire de la Guadeloupe* 51, no. 1 (1982): 3–54; David Patrick Geggus, "Slavery, War, and Revolution in the Greater Caribbean, 1789–1815," in *A Turbulent Time: The French Revolution and the Greater Caribbean*, ed. David Barry Gaspar and David Patrick Geggus (Bloomington: Indiana University Press, 1997), 22–25. On the experience of the Foreign Legion in Spain during the mid-1830s, see Douglas Porch, *The French Foreign Legion: A Complete History of the Legendary Fighting Force* (New York: HarperCollins, 1991), 21–49.

133. Castellane, *Campagnes d'Afrique 1835–1848*, 245, 253–54.

134. Bugeaud, *Quelques réflexions*, 21.

135. Pitts, *Writings on Empire and Slavery*, 59–116.

136. SHAT 6 Yd 52.

137. William Gallois, "Dahra and the History of Violence in Early Colonial Algeria," in *The French Colonial Mind: Violence, Military Encounters, and Colonialism*, ed. Martin Thomas (Lincoln: University of Nebraska Press, 2011), 2:3–25.

138. *Lettres du Maréchal de Saint-Arnaud*, 2:28–31.

139. Castellane, *Campagnes d'Afrique 1835–1848*, 215.

140. Letter of Captain Cler to General Castellane dated November 20, 1832; Castellane, *Campagnes d'Afrique 1835–1848*, 275.

141. Castellane, *Campagnes d'Afrique 1835–1848*, 275; Thoumas, *Les transformations de l'armée française*, 632–33.

142. Jennifer E. Sessions, "Colonizing Revolutionary Politics: Algeria and the French Revolution of 1848," *French Politics, Culture and Society* 33, no. 1 (2015): 77–79; Morell, *Algeria*, 402–3.

143. Sullivan, *Thomas-Robert Bugeaud*, 134–39; Singer and Langdon, *Cultured Force*, 80–83.

144. Duvivier, *Algérie*, 1–8.

145. Bugeaud, *Histoire de l'Algérie française*, 1:14.

146. Diana K. Davis, *Resurrecting the Granary of Rome: Environmental History and French Colonial Expansion in North Africa* (Athens: Ohio University Press, 2007), 5–13, 38.

147. Desjobert, *Algérie en 1844*, 50.

148. Jehan Desanges, ed. and trans., *Pline l'Ancien, Histoire naturelle livre V, 1–46* (Paris: Société d'Édition "Les belles lettres," 1980), 5.1–5, 46–64.

149. Maria Antonia Garcés, ed., *An Early Modern Dialogue with Islam: Antonio de Sosa's 'Topography of Algiers' (1612)*, trans. Diana de Armas Wilson (Notre Dame, IN: University of Notre Dame Press, 2011), 98.

150. Henri Goellzer, ed. and trans., *Tacite, Annales livres IV–XII* (Paris: Société d'Édition "Les belles lettres," 1966), 2:4.23–25, 189–91.

151. Bugeaud, *Histoire de l'Algérie française*, 1:38–39.

152. Saint-Marc Girardin, "De la domination des Carthaginois et des romaines en Afrique comparée avec la domination française," *Revue des deux mondes*, ser. 4, 26 (April–June 1841): 434–38.

153. Bugeaud, *Histoire de l'Algérie française* 1:40–44.

154. Ibid., 1:48, 72.

155. Ibid., 1:344.

156. Duvivier, *Algérie*, 69–74.

157. Sullivan, *Thomas-Robert Bugeaud*, 99–106.

158. Frantz Fanon, *The Wretched of the Earth*, trans. Richard Philcox (New York: Grove Press, 2004), 42–43.

159. *Lettres du Maréchal de Saint-Arnaud,* 1:247.

160. For an introduction to the value of this collection of letters sent to the Maréchal de Castellane, see Brower, *Desert Named Peace,* 47–49.

161. Castellane, *Campagnes d'Afrique 1835–1848,* 221.

162. Ernest Watbled, *Souvenirs de l'armée d'Afrique* (Paris: Challamel Ainé, 1877).

163. Castellane, *Campagnes d'Afrique 1835–1848,* 274–77.

164. Général Jourdy, *L'instruction de l'armée française de 1815 à 1902* (Paris: Félix Alcan, 1903), esp. 67–102; Maurice Dumontier, "L'École d'artillerie et du génie de Metz sous l'Empire, la Restauration et la Monarchie de Juillet (1803–1845)," *Pays lorrain* 42, no. 3 (1961): 86–102; Maurice Dumontier, "L'École d'application de l'artillerie et du génie à Metz sous la Seconde République et le Second Empire," *Pays lorrain* 42, no. 4 (1961): 122–35.

165. Morell, *Algeria,* 388.

166. Hugo wrote against the torture of French soldiers imprisoned in Algerian military prisons, taking up the case of a prisoner named Dubois de Gennes; Laurent, *Victor Hugo,* 49–54.

167. Poujoulat, *Études africaines* 1: 76.

168. Sessions, "'Unfortunate Necessities,'" 29–44.

169. In the *Gallic Wars*, one finds a mix of tactics resembling the razzia, with the destruction of homes and crops of the enemy (4.38), collection of booty (6.35), and laying waste to the dominions of enemies (8.24–25), and acts of greater moderation, such as Julius Caesar's claim that he did not allow his troops to plunder (8.3–4); Julius Caesar, *The Gallic War*, ed. and trans. Henry J. Edwards, Loeb Classical Library 72 (Cambridge, MA: Harvard University Press, 1917). In contrast, Michel Rambaud argues that this representation is misleading: not only did Caesar seek to elevate his own place in the narrative but his testimony was also inconsistent and thus not fully transparent about the violence of his military undertakings; *L'art de la déformation historique dans les commentaires de César,* rev. ed. (Paris: Société d'Édition "Les belles lettres," 1966), 245–47. I thank Michael Kulikowski for his insight on this point.

170. Pellissier de Reynaud, *Annales algériennes* 3:247–50.

171. Michael J. Heffernan and Keith Sutton, "The Landscape of Colonialism: The Impact of French Colonial Rule on the Algerian Rural Settlement Pattern, 1830–1987," in *Colonialism and Development in the Contemporary World,* ed. Chris Dixon and Michael J. Heffernan (London: Mansell, 1991), 126–27.

172. For criticism of agricultural settlement in Algeria, see Joly's contribution to the Chambre des députés on June 5, 1844, in *Moniteur universel,* 1636–37.

173. Blondel, *Aperçus sur l'état actuel,* 13–19.

174. Sessions, *By Sword and Plow,* 232–40.

175. Pellissier de Reynaud, *Annales algériennes* 3:262–66.

176. Thomas-Robert Bugeaud, *De la colonisation de l'Algérie* (Paris: A. Guyot, 1847), 33–34; Bugeaud, *Histoire de l'Algérie française,* 2:239–49; Duvivier, *Algérie,* 14–16; Garcés, *Early Modern Dialogue with Islam,* 96–97.

177. Bugeaud, *De la colonisation de l'Algérie,* 35–42.

178. Ibid., 45–50, 56, 65.

179. Bugeaud, *Histoire de l'Algérie française,* 1:47–49.

180. Duvivier, *Algérie,* 17–18.

181. Brebner, "Impact of Thomas-Robert Bugeaud."

182. Jacques Frémeaux, *Les bureaux arabes dans l'Algérie de la conquête* (Paris: Éditions Denoël, 1993), 33–34.

183. SHAT 1 M 882: General Rivet, *Histoire du gouvernement du Maréchal Bugeaud de 1841 à 1847*, chap. 12, 230–33.

184. Bugeaud, *Quelques réflexions*, 19–21.

185. Castellane, *Campagnes d'Afrique 1835–1848*, 311.

186. In recounting on October 13, 1837, the assault on Constantine, Leroy de Saint-Arnaud suggested that it would be a very long time until the Indigenous people forgot what had occurred in its aftermath; *Lettres du Maréchal de Saint-Arnaud*, 1:122.

187. Poujoulat, *Études africaines* 1:111.

188. Raymund F. Wood, "Berbrugger, Forgotten Founder of Algerian Librarianship," *Journal of Library History* 5, no. 3 (1970): 237–56.

189. ANOM 80 F 1733: Adrien Berbrugger, *Notes sur la Bibliothèque et sur le Musée d'Alger*, December 10, 1845.

190. Castellane, *Campagnes d'Afrique 1835–1848*, 221.

191. Ibid., 307–8.

192. Michael J. Heffernan, "The Parisian Poor and the Colonization of Algeria during the Second Republic," *French History* 3, no. 4 (1989): 377–403.

193. Morell, *Algeria*, 402–3; Sullivan, *Thomas-Robert Bugeaud*, 142–44.

194. Sessions, "Colonizing Revolutionary Politics," 77.

195. SHAT 1 M 1314: Edmond Pellissier de Reynaud, *Mémoire sur la géographie ancienne de l'Algérie* (1843).

196. SHAT 1 M 1314: Pellissier de Reynaud, *Mémoire sur la géographie ancienne*.

197. Greenhalgh, *Military and Colonial Destruction*. See also Greenhalgh, *Constantinople to Córdoba*, 397–419.

198. Poujoulat, *Études africaines*, 1:34.

199. Michael J. Heffernan, "An Imperial Utopia: French Surveys of North Africa in the Early Colonial Period," in *Maps and Africa: Proceedings of a Colloquium at the University of Aberdeen, April 1993*, ed. Jeffrey C. Stone (Aberdeen: Aberdeen University, African Studies Group, 1994), 84.

200. Jacques Frémeaux, "Souvenirs de Rome et présence française au Maghreb: Essai d'investigation," in *Connaissances du Maghreb: Sciences sociales et colonisation*, ed. Jean-Claude Vatin (Paris: CNRS Éditions, 1984), 29–46.

201. Catherine Rigambert, *Le droit de l'archéologie française* (Paris: Picard, 1996), 20–21.

202. Bonnie Effros, *Uncovering the Germanic Past: Merovingian Archaeology in France, 1830–1914* (Oxford: Oxford University Press, 2012), 17–23.

203. Nacéra Benseddik, "L'armée français en Algérie: 'Parfois détruire, souvent construire,'" in *L'Africa romana: Atti del XIII convegno di studio, Djerba, 10–13 dicembre 1998*, ed. Mustapha Khanoussi, Paola Ruggeri, and Cinzia Vismara (Rome: Carocci editore, 2000), 1:759–96.

204. Greenhalgh, *Military and Colonial Destruction*, 145–50.

205. Adolphe-Hedwige-Alphonse Delamare, "Étude sur Stora, port de Philippeville (l'ancienne Rusicade)," *Mémoires de la Société impériale des antiquaires de France* 24 (1859): 155–57, 172.

206. Michael Greenhalgh, "The New Centurions: French Reliance on the Roman Past during the Conquest of Algeria," *War and Society* 16, no. 1 (1998), 12–13.

207. Annie Arnaud-Portelli, "L'exploration archéologique de l'Afrique du Nord des premiers voyageurs au XVIIIe siècle à l'indépendance des nations (Maroc, Algérie) d'après les documents publiés," 3 vols. (unpublished PhD diss., Université de Paris IV–Sorbonne, 1991), 2:18, 58–59. Poujoulat, *Études africaines*, 1:306.

208. Poujoulat, *Études africaines*, 1:237.

209. Oulebsir, *Usages du patrimoine*, 18–22, 54–56, 94–102.

210. ANOM 80 F 1589: Letter dated November 29, 1843, from the minister of war to Governor-General Thomas-Robert Bugeaud.

211. *Bulletin officiel des actes du gouvernement*, no. 166, circulaire n. 3, 9.

212. ANOM 80 F 1589: Letter dated February 6, 1844 from the minister of war to Governor-General Thomas-Robert Bugeaud.

213. *Bulletin officiel des actes du gouvernement*, no. 173, circulaire n. 15, 61–65.

214. ANOM 80 F 1589: Letter dated April 6, 1844, from the minister of war to Governor-General Thomas-Robert Bugeaud.

215. Ève Gran-Aymerich, *Dictionnaire biographique d'archéologie 1798–1945* (Paris: CNRS Éditions, 2001), 657–58.

216. Françoise Bercé, "Restaurer au XIXe siècle?," in *Nîmes et ses antiquités: Un passé présent, XVIe–XIXe siècle,* ed. Véronique Krings and François Pugnière (Bordeaux: Ausonius Éditions, 2013), 249–50.

217. ANOM 80 F 1589: Letter dated November 29, 1843, from the minister of war to Governor-General Thomas-Robert Bugeaud.

218. Charles Texier, "Extrait d'un aperçu statistique des monuments de l'Algérie," *Revue archéologique* 3, no. 2 (1846–1847): 724–35.

219. ANOM ALG GGA N2: Letter dated January 19, 1848, from Charles Texier to the minister of war.

220. Médiathèque de l'architecture et des monuments historiques, Charenton-le-Pont: 80/1/119, Carton 1: Letter dated June 23, 1847, from Charles Texier to the minister of the interior.

221. ANOM ALG GGA N3: "Note à l'appui du rapport fait au Ministre concernant l'inspection générale des bâtiments civils en Algérie pendant la campagne 1850–1851."

222. Monique Dondin-Payre, "L'*Exercitus africae* inspiratrice de l'armée française d'Afrique: *Ense et aratro*," *Antiquités africaines* 27, no. 1 (1991): 141–49.

223. M. de Blinière, "Antiquités de la ville de Cherchel (Algérie)," *Revue archéologique* 5, no. 1 (1848): 345–46.

224. Greenhalgh, *Military and Colonial Destruction*.

Chapter 3. The View from Ancient Lambaesis

1. Ève Gran-Aymerich and Jürgen von Ungern-Sternberg, *L'Antiquité partagé: Correspondances franco-allemandes (1823–1861)*, Mémoires de l'Académie des inscriptions et belles-lettres 47 (Paris: AIBL, 2012), 22–25; Ahmed Koumas and Chéhrazade Nafa, *L'Algérie et son patrimoine: Dessins français du XIXe siècle* (Paris: Monum, Éditions du patrimoine, 2003), 33.

2. ANOM FM 5 80 1595: Report by Karl Benedikt Hase, member of the Académie des inscriptions et belles-lettres, dated September 27, 1844.

3. Ibid.

4. Annie Arnaud-Portelli, "L'exploration archéologique de l'Afrique du Nord des premiers voyageurs au XVIIIe siècle à l'indépendance des nations (Maroc, Algérie) d'après les documents publiés" (PhD diss., Université de Paris IV-Sorbonne, Histoire de l'art et archéologie, 1991), 2:101–2.

5. René Cagnat, *L'armée romaine d'Afrique et l'occupation militaire de l'Afrique sous les empereurs* (Paris: Imprimerie nationale, 1892), 501–46.

6. Yann Le Bohec, *La Troisième légion auguste* (Paris: CNRS Éditions, 1989), 407–24.

7. Ibid., 407; Michel Janon, "Recherches à Lambèse," *Antiquités africaines* 7, no. 1 (1973): 193–95.

8. Janon, "Recherches à Lambèse," 197–220.

9. David J. Mattingly, *Tripolitania* (London: B. T. Batsford, 1995), 271.

10. William H. C. Frend, *From Dogma to History: How Our Understanding of the Early Church Developed* (London: SCM Press, 2003), 21.

11. Yvette Duval, *Lambèse chrétienne: La gloire et l'oubli de la Numidie romaine à l'Ifrîqiya* (Paris: Institut d'études augustiniennes, 1995), 104.

12. Ève Gran-Aymerich, *Dictionnaire biographique d'archéologie, 1798–1945* (Paris: CNRS Éditions, 2001), 576–78.

13. Nabila Oulebsir, *Les usages du patrimoine: Monuments, musées et politique coloniale en Algérie (1830–1930)* (Paris: Éditions de la Maison des sciences de l'homme, 2004), 205–11. The late date of its excavation pushes Thamugadis largely beyond the scope of the present book.

14. Although the mountainous region of the Aurès did not form part of what the French referred to as Grande Kabylie or Petite Kabylie, travelers of the eighteenth century and military and civilian authorities of the nineteenth century referred to Berber inhabitants of the Aurès Mountains with this nomenclature. Alain Mahé, *Histoire de la Grande Kabylie XIXe–XXe siècles: Anthropologie historique du lien social dans les communautés villageoises* (Saint Denis: Éditions Bouchene, 2001), 15–21; 154–55; Ann Thomson, *Barbary and Enlightenment: European Attitudes towards the Maghreb in the 18th Century* (Leiden: Brill, 1987), 107.

15. For a detailed list of travelers to the region who worked on inscriptions, see Gustav Wilmanns, *Inscriptiones Africae latinae*, Corpus inscriptionum latinarum 8 (Berlin: Georg Reimer, 1881), 1:xxiii–xxxii.

16. Adolphe Dureau de la Malle, *Peyssonnel et Desfontaines: Voyages dans les régences de Tunis et d'Alger* 1 (Paris: Gide, 1838), 346–56; Adolphe Dureau de la Malle, *Province de Constantine: Recueil de renseignements pour l'expédition ou l'établissement des français dans cette partie de l'Afrique septentrionale* (Paris: Gide, 1837), 209–11.

17. Stephanie Moser, "Making Expert Knowledge through the Image: Connections between Antiquarian and Early Modern Scientific Illustration," *Isis* 105, no. 1 (2014): 58–99; Lorraine Daston and Peter Galison, "The Image of Objectivity," *Representations*, no. 40 (1992): 81–128; Londa Scheibinger, "Skeletons in the Closet: The First Illustrations of the Female Skeleton in Eighteenth-Century Anatomy," *Representations*, no. 14 (1986): 42–82.

18. In actuality, a variety of tribes grazed their flocks seasonally near Lambaesis, including the Ouled Fedhala and the 'Achèches. Abdelhamid Zouzou, *L'Aurès au temps de la France colonial: Evolution politique, economique et sociale (1837–1939)* (Algiers: Éditions Distribution HOUMA, 2001), 1:98–99.

19. Ibid., 60–61. Jean Morizot, *L'Aurès ou le mythe de la montagne rebelle* (Paris: L'Harmattan, 1991), 118.

20. Dureau de la Malle, *Peyssonnel et Desfontaines*, 1:346–49.

21. Thomas Shaw, *Travels or Observations Relating to Several Parts of Barbary and the Levant* (Oxford: Theatre, 1738), 117–18.

22. Nabila Oulebsir, "From Ruins to Heritage: The Past Perfect and the Idealized Antiquity in North Africa," in *Multiple Antiquities—Multiple Modernities: Ancient Histories in Nineteenth Century European Cultures*, ed. Gábor Klaniczay, Michael Werner, and Ottó Gecser (Frankfurt: Campus, 2011), 337–39.

23. Italicized sections are found highlighted in the original: Shaw, *Travels or Observations Relating to Several Parts of Barbary*, 120.

24. Yves Modéran has suggested a more positive relationship between Romans and the Indigenous people of the Aurès, whom he sees as continuators and not destroyers of Roman

North Africa: *Les Maures et l'Afrique romaine (IVe–VIIe siecle)*, Bibliothèque des Écoles françaises d'Athènes et de Rome 340 (Rome: École française de Rome, 2003), 383–415.

25. James Bruce, *Travels Between the Years 1765 and 1773, through Part of Africa, Syria, Egypt, and Arabia into Abyssinia* (London: Albion, 1812), 27–28.

26. Thomson, *Barbary and Enlightenment*, 107–12.

27. Duval, *Lambèse chrétienne*, 116–18.

28. Nigel Leask, *Curiosity and the Aesthetics of Travel Writing, 1770–1840: 'From an Antique Land'* (Oxford: Oxford University Press, 2002), 64–73; Oulebsir, "From Ruins to Heritage," 332–48.

29. Bruce, *Travels Between the Years 1765 and 1773*, 27–28.

30. Christopher Charles Parslow, *Rediscovering Antiquity: Karl Weber and the Excavation of Herculaneum, Pompeii, and Stabiae* (Cambridge: Cambridge University Press, 1995).

31. Leask, *Curiosity and the Aesthetics*, 112–15.

32. From Constantine, one could take the train to Batna (on the Biskra line) and a carriage, offered twice daily, for the last leg to Lambaesis. René Cagnat, *Lambèse*, Guides en Algérie (Paris: Ernest Leroux, 1893), 29–30.

33. Franciade Fleurus Duvivier, *Recherches et notes sur la portion de l'Algérie au sud de Guelma depuis la frontière de Tunis jusqu'au Mont Aurèss compris* (Paris: L. Vassal et Cie, 1841), 48–56.

34. Dureau de la Malle, *Peyssonnel et Desfontaines*, 1:vii.

35. Ibid.

36. Antony Thrall Sullivan, *Thomas-Robert Bugeaud: France and Algeria, 1784–1849. Politics, Power, and the Good Society* (Hamden, CT: Archon Books, 1983), 72–76.

37. William Gallois, *A History of Violence in the Early Algerian Colony* (New York: Palgrave Macmillan, 2013).

38. SHAT 6 Yd 52: For the correspondence, see Baraguey d'Hillier's career dossier.

39. Morizot, *Aurès ou le mythe*, 129–34.

40. Abdelmajid Hannoum, *Violent Modernity: France in Algeria* (Cambridge, MA: Harvard University Press, 2010), 32–33.

41. A French inquest suggested that there were roughly 3,500 inhabitants of Biskra in the mid-1840s. Zouzou, *Aurès au temps de la France colonial*, 111–14.

42. Benjamin Claude Brower, *A Desert Named Peace: The Violence of France's Empire in the Algerian Sahara, 1844–1902* (New York: Columbia University Press, 2009), 37–41.

43. Zouzou, *Aurès au temps de la France coloniale*, 184–88; 439–44.

44. ANOM 80 F 1586: Letter from the minister of war dated September 24, 1850, permitting Léon Renier to travel to Lambaesis to copy inscriptions.

45. Adolphe-Hedwige-Alphonse Delamare, "Notice sur Lambaesa ville de la province de Constantine avec l'indication des principaux monuments qui se trouvent dans cette ville," *Revue archéologique* 4, no. 2 (1847–1848): 449–53; Oulebsir, *Usages du patrimoine*, 163.

46. Monique Dondin-Payre, "La production d'images sur l'espace méditerranéen dans la Commission d'exploration scientifique d'Algérie: Les dessins du capitaine Delamare," in *L'invention scientifique de la Méditerranée: Égypte, Morée, Algérie*, ed. Marie-Noëlle Bourguet et al. (Paris: Éditions de l'École des Hautes Études en Sciences Sociales, 1998), 223–28.

47. ANÒM F 80 1595: On the working conditions of the site, see Delamare's letter to the minister of war in September 1853.

48. Monique Dondin-Payre, "L'éxercitus africae inspiratrice de l'armée française d'Afrique: *Ense et aratro*," *Antiquités africaines* 27, no. 1 (1991): 141–49; Monique Dondin-Payre, *Le Capitaine Delamare: La réussite de l'archéologie romaine au sein de la Commission d'exploration scientifique d'Algérie*, Mémoires de l'Académie des inscriptions et belles-lettres, n.s. 15 (Paris: F. Paillart, 1994).

49. Patricia Lorcin, "Imperialism, Colonial Identity, and Race in Algeria, 1830–1870: The Role of the French Medical Corps," *Isis* 90, no. 4 (1999): 653–79. For the definition of Ziban used here, see Charles Bocher, "Le siége de Zaatcha: Souvenirs de l'expédition dans les Ziban en 1849," *Revue des deux mondes* (April 1, 1851): 71.

50. Jean Guyon, *Voyage d'Alger aux Ziban l'ancienne Zebe* (Algiers: Imprimerie du gouvernement, 1852), 113.

51. Frederick N. Bohrer, *Orientalism and Visual Culture: Imagining Mesopotamia in Nineteenth-Century France* (Cambridge: Cambridge University Press, 2003); Elena D. Corbett, *Competitive Archaeology in Jordan: Narrating Identity from the Ottomans to the Hashemites* (Austin: University of Texas Press, 2014).

52. Osama W. Abi-Mershed, *Apostles of Modernity: Saint-Simonians and the Civilizing Mission in Algeria* (Stanford, CA: Stanford University Press, 2010), 13–14; 84–86.

53. Guyon, *Voyage d'Alger*, 114.

54. Ibid., 140–41.

55. Edouard Lapène, "Tableau historique, moral et politique sur les Kabyles," *Mémoires de l'Académie nationale de Metz* 27 (1845–1846): 227–87. First published in 1838 as part of Lapene's widely cited *Dix-huit mois à Bougie*, the text was reissued at the time of the first major assault on Kabylia. Patricia Lorcin, *Imperial Identities: Stereotyping, Prejudice and Race in Colonial Algeria* (London: I. B. Tauris, 1995), 301–7.

56. On the deep connections between the work of officer-archaeologists and ethnologists and the myth of the Kabyle in the nineteenth century, see Lorcin, *Imperial Identities,* 114–35.

57. Dawson Borrer, *Narrative of a Campaign against the Kabaïles of Algeria* (London: Longman, Brown, Green, and Longmans, 1848), 366–68.

58. Ibid., 366–68.

59. Ibid., 368–69.

60. Ibid., 369.

61. SHAT 1 M 1317: Champion de Nansouty and Duzun, *Mémoire sur Bathna et Lambaesa avec les recherches historiques* (Batna, August 15, 1847).

62. ANOM ALG GGA N2: Letter dated January 19, 1848, from Charles Texier to the minister of war.

63. Charles Texier, "Praetorium de Lambaesa," *Revue archéologique 5*, no. 2 (1848–1849): 417–18.

64. Fanny Colonna, "La carte Carbuccia au 1:100.000e de la subdivision de Batna, ou le violon d'Ingres du 2e régiment de la Légion étrangère (vers 1850)," in *L'invention scientifique de la Méditerranée*, 60–61.

65. SHAT 8 Yd 3268: Surviving correspondence in Carbuccia's military dossier is largely positive but contains some criticisms of his conduct.

66. Claude Collot, *Les institutions de l'Algérie durant la période coloniale (1830–1962)* (Paris: Éditions du CNRS, 1987), 8.

67. Bibliothèque de l'Institut de France, Ms. 1369B: Jean-Luc Carbuccia, Archéologie de la Subdivision de Batna.

68. Noël Duval and Michel Janon, "Le dossier des églises d'Hr Guesseria: Redécouverte du rapport Carbuccia (1849) et de l'aquarelle originale de la mosaïque. Une fouille partielle en 1908?" *Mélanges de l'École française de Rome: Antiquité* 97, no. 2 (1985): 1079–112; William H. C. Frend, *The Archaeology of Early Christianity: A History* (Minneapolis: Fortress Press, 1996), 59.

69. Bibliothèque de l'Institut de France, Ms. 1369B: Jean-Luc Carbuccia, Archéologie de la Subdivision de Batna.

70. Monique Dondin-Payre, "Réussites et déboires d'une oeuvre archéologique unique: Le Colonel Carbuccia au nord de l'Aurès (1848–1850)," *Antiquités africaines* 32, no. 1 (1996): 145–48.

71. Colonna, "Carte Carbuccia au 1:100.000e," 53–54. For the details of these military expeditions, see Raoul de Lartigue, *Monographie de l'Aurès* (Constantine: Marle Audrino, 1904), 225–30.

72. Bibliothèque de l'Institut de France, Ms. 1369B: Jean-Luc Carbuccia, Archéologie de la Subdivision de Batna.

73. Ibid.

74. Ibid.

75. Gran-Aymerich, *Dictionnaire biographique d'archéologie*, 365.

76. Edme-François Jomard, "Séance du 11 avril 1851: Rapport sur les travaux archéologiques du Colonel Carbuccia," *Mémoires de l'Institut national de France: Académie des inscriptions et belles-lettres* 18, no. 1 (1855): 161–70.

77. For a fuller picture of the French Foreign Legion during this period, see Douglas Porch, *The French Foreign Legion: A Complete History of the Legendary Fighting Force* (New York: Harper Collins, 1991), 84–116.

78. Carbuccia did not specify the punishment in his archaeological report, but his accusation against Muslims for hating Christians has a very ominous tone. Bibliothèque de l'Institut de France, Ms. 1369B: Jean-Luc Carbuccia, Archéologie de la Subdivision de Batna.

79. Le Bohec, *Troisième légion auguste*, 134.

80. Bibliothèque de l'Institut de France, Ms. 1369B: Jean-Luc Carbuccia, Archéologie de la Subdivision de Batna.

81. Léon Renier, "Notice sur le tombeau de T. Flavius Maximus," *Revue archéologique* 7, no. 1 (1850): 186–87.

82. In 1983, the contentious colonial monument was destroyed, but authorities were unable to identify and apprehend the perpetrators. Nacéra Benseddik, "L'Armée français en Algérie: 'Parfois détruire, souvent construire,'" in *L'Africa romana: Atti del XIII convegno di studio, Djerba, 10–13 dicembre 1998*, ed. Mustapha Khanoussi, Paola Ruggeri, and Cinzia Vismara (Rome: Carocci editore, 2000), 1:796; Nacéra Benseddik, "Lambaesis-Lambèse/Tazoult: Grandeur et décadences," in *L'affirmation de l'identité dans l'Algérie antique et médiévale: Combats et résistances. Hommage à Kadria Fatima Kadra*, ed. Sabah Ferdi (Algiers: Centre national de recherche en archéologie, 2014), 216.

83. Brower, *Desert Named Peace*, 81–83; Porch, *French Foreign Legion*, 97–116.

84. For an eyewitness French account of the campaign in Zaatcha and its background, see Bocher, "Le siége de Zaatcha," 70–101.

85. Bibliothèque de l'Institut de France, Ms. 1369A and B: Jean-Luc Carbuccia, Archéologie de la subdivision de Batna, includes an unpublished manuscript and supplementary unbound documentation.

86. Bibliothèque de l'Institut de France Ms. 1935 (and Ms. 7453, a more complete version): Jean-Luc Carbuccia, *Carte archéologique de la subdivision de Batna*; Monique Dondin-Payre, "Un document cartographique inédit sur l'occupation de l'espace dans les Aurès à l'époque romaine," in *L'Africa romana: Atti del X convegno di studio Oristano, 11–13 dicembre 1992*, ed. Attilio Mastino and Paola Ruggeri (Sassari: Editrice Archivio Fotografico Sardo, 1994), 331–46.

87. SHAT 8 Yd 3268: The citation for Carbuccia's appointment to the Legion of Honor, awarded on December 2, 1850, by Louis Napoleon Bonaparte, recognized his twenty-five years of service, nineteen campaigns, and two wounds. His archaeological contributions cannot have failed to register with the future emperor, who was an impassioned Roman historian.

88. ANOM 80 F 1733: Letter dated November 17, 1858, from Léon Renier to Napoleon III, cited in Dondin-Payre, "Document cartographique," 337–38.

89. "Correspondance officielle concernant les missions et les entreprise scientifiques," *Mémoires de l'Institut impérial de France: Académie des inscriptions et belles-lettres* 18, no. 1 (1849–1852): 166.

90. ANOM 80 F 1587: Report to the minister of war dated May 7, 1851; Dondin-Payre, "Réussites et déboires," 148–65; Dondin-Payre, "Document cartographique," 338–39, 344.

91. ANOM 80 F 1587: Report to the minister of war dated May 7, 1851.

92. Bibliothèque de l'Institut de France, Ms 1369B: Letter of October 14, 1853, from the director of the military depot in the Ministry of War to Jean-Luc Carbuccia.

93. SHAT 8 Yd 3268.

94. Bibliothèque de l'Institut de France, Ms. 1369B: Jean-Luc Carbuccia, Archéologie de la Subdivision de Batna.

95. Colonna, "Carte Carbuccia au 1:100.000e," 53–70.

96. Benseddik, "Armée française en Algérie," 790–92.

97. John Reynell Morell, *Algeria: The Topography and History, Political, Social, and Natural of French Africa* (London: Nathaniel Cooke, 1854), 370.

98. This was not the sole example of the appropriation of ancient materials for military constructions at Lambaesis; Carbuccia cited his choice of the location of the command post at Barrika on the basis of its access to the river and the availability of cut stones from ruins. Bibliothèque de l'Institut de France, Ms. 1369B: Jean-Luc Carbuccia, Archéologie de la Subdivision de Batna; Monique Dondin-Payre, "De la Gaule romaine à l'Africa: À la recherche d'un héritage commun," in *Camille Jullian, l'histoire de la Gaule et le nationalisme français: Actes du colloque organisé à Lyon le 6 décembre 1988* (Lyons: Société des amis de Jacob Spon, 1991), 44–45.

99. Michael Greenhalgh, *The Military and Colonial Construction of the Roman Landscape of North Africa, 1830–1900* (Leiden: Brill, 2014), 280–84; Janon, "Recherches à Lambèse," 194.

100. L. Leclère, "Lettre à M. le Commandant de la Mare sur les ruines de Lambesa (Algérie)," *Revue archéologique* 7, no. 1 (1850): 123–25.

101. Charles Bocher, "Prise de Narah: Souvenirs d'une expédition dans le Djebel-Aurès," *Revue des deux mondes* (15 June 1857): 861.

102. Ibid., 855–74.

103. *Lettres du Maréchal de Saint-Arnaud* (Paris: Michel Lévy Frères, 1855), 2:260–63; Louis de Charbonnières, *Une grande figure, Saint-Arnaud, maréchal de France* (Paris: Nouvelles Éditions Latines, 1960), 87–90.

104. *Lettres du Maréchal de Saint-Arnaud*, 2:263.

105. Bibliothèque de l'Institut de France Ms 1369B: Jean-Luc Carbuccia, *Description des ruines situées sur la route suivie par la colonne du Général de St Arnaud dans les Nemënchas et dans l'Aurèss.*

106. Bibliothèque de l'Institut de France, Ms. 1369B: Jean-Luc Carbuccia, Archéologie de la Subdivision de Batna.

107. Bocher, "Prise de Narah," 874.

108. Charbonnières, *Grande figure*, 88–89.

109. Gallois, *History of Violence*, 115–17; Jennifer E. Sessions, *By Sword and Plow: France and the Conquest of Algeria* (Ithaca, NY: Cornell University Press, 2011), 6.

110. Greenhalgh, *Military and Colonial Destruction*, 280–84. The use of Lambaesis in this fashion was part of a larger decision to make Algeria a warehouse for political undesirables. Julia Clancy-Smith, *Mediterraneans: North Africa and Europe in an Age of Migration, c. 1800–1900* (Berkeley: University of California Press, 2011), 94–95.

111. Jennifer E. Sessions, "Colonizing Revolutionary Politics: Algeria and the French Revolution of 1848," *French Politics, Culture, and Society* 33, no. 1 (2015): 76.

112. Allyson Jaye Delnore, "Empire by Example? Deportees in France and Algeria and the Re-Making of a Modern Empire, 1846–1854," *French Politics, Culture, and Society* 33, no. 1 (2015): 33–54.

113. On the necessity of seeing the colonial undertaking as part of the republican enterprise, see Gary Wilder, *The French Imperial Nation-State: Negritude and Colonial Humanism between the Two World Wars* (Chicago: University of Chicago Press, 2005).

114. Louis-José Barbançon, "Les transportés de 1848 (statistiques, analyse, commentaires)," *Criminocorpus*, http://criminocorpus.revues.org/48.

115. Bibliothèque de l'Arsenal, Paris, Ms. 15462: Jean Terson, *Mémoires d'un ancien apôtre Saint-Simonien*, part 4, chap. 2.

116. *Lettres du Maréchal de Saint-Arnaud*, 2:246–47.

117. Morell, *Algeria*, 370.

118. Louis Hincker, "Archive d'une 'Afrique fantôme,'" *L'Homme* 195–96, nos. 3–4 (2010): 312–14, 330n20.

119. Delnore, "Empire by Example?," 43–45.

120. Bibliothèque de l'Arsenal, Paris, Ms. 15462: Terson, *Mémoires d'un ancien apôtre Saint-Simonien*, part 3, chaps. 19, 30; part 4, chaps. 2, 7.

121. Barbançon, "Transportés de 1848."

122. Bibliothèque de l'Arsenal, Paris, Ms. 15462: Terson, *Mémoires d'un ancien apôtre Saint-Simonien*, part 4, chaps. 7, 40.

123. Barbançon, "Transportés de 1848."

124. Jacques-Eugène Leiris, *Jadis* (Paris: Forbis, 1990), 99–102.

125. Bibliothèque littéraire Jacques Doucet, Paris, Ms. 45138: Letter dated April 18, 1852, from Jacques-Eugène Leiris to his sister Anaïs Labey; Hincker, "Archive d'une 'Afrique fantôme,'" 31.

126. Leiris did not compose these memoirs until March 1888. Leiris, *Jadis*, 93–94.

127. Barbançon, "Transportés de 1848."

128. Bibliothèque littéraire Jacques Doucet, Paris, Ms. 45138: Letter dated March 20, 1850, from Jacques-Eugène Leiris to his sister Anaïs and her husband Adolphe Labey.

129. Bibliothèque de l'Arsenal, Paris, Ms. 15462: Terson, *Mémoires d'un ancien apôtre Saint-Simonien*, part 4, chaps. 12, 13; Marcel Emerit, "Les mémoires de Terson déporté de 1848," *Revue africaine* 91 (1947): 235–53.

130. On Desvaux, see Marcel Émerit, "Une source pour l'histoire du Second Empire: Les souvenirs du général Desvaux," *Revue d'histoire moderne et contemporaine* 21, no. 1 (1974): 27–32. For his career dossier, see SHAT 7 Yd 1363.

131. Musée de l'Armée, Paris, Ms. 737, vol. 4. For Desvaux's activities, see SHAT 7 Yd 1363.

132. Bibliothèque de l'Arsenal, Paris, Ms. 15462: Terson, *Mémoires d'un ancien apôtre Saint-Simonien*. part 4, chap. 13; Emerit, "Mémoires de Terson," 235–53. References to these works are also scattered throughout Desvaux's diary during the years 1841–1843. Musée de l'Armée, Paris, Ms 737, vol. 3.

133. Louis-Charles-Pierre, Comte de Castellane, *Souvenirs of Military Life in Algeria*, trans. Margaret Josephine Lovett (London: Remington and Co., 1886), 1:211–12.

134. ANOM 80 F 1587: Cahiers des transportés de juin 1848 à Lambèse.

135. ANOM 80 F 1587: Jean Terson, *Notice sur les ruines de Lambèse*, in the Cahiers des transportés de juin 1848 à Lambèse.

136. Emerit, "Mémoires de Terson," 249–50.

137. These remarks were made with respect not to Lambaesis but to other ruins that the prisoners were permitted to explore during their long journey to the Aurès Mountains. Hincker, "Archive d'une 'Afrique fantôme,'" 319–20, 328. Leiris wrote only briefly of his participation in the excavations at Lambaesis in *Jadis*, 104.

138. Brief references to the excursion are in Desvaux's journal for November 30 and December 1, 1852. Musée de l'armée, Paris, Ms. 737, vol. 8.

139. Bibliothèque de l'Institut de France, Ms. 1369B: Jean-Luc Carbuccia, Archéologie de la Subdivision de Batna.

140. ANOM 80 F 1587: Thuillier Pellotier, *Travaux archéologiques des transportés de 1848* (dated December 20, 1852), in the Cahiers des transportés de juin 1848 à Lambèse;

Marcel Emerit, "Un curé de l'Aude ateint du mal du siècle: Jean Terson," in *Actes du 102e Congrès national des Sociétés savantes, Limoges 1977*, Section d'histoire moderne et contemporaine 1 (Paris: Bibliothèque nationale, 1978), 351–60.

141. ANOM 80 F 1587: Pellotier, *Travaux archéologiques des transportés de 1848*.

142. Ibid.; Oulebsir, *Usages du patrimoine*, 91–93; Musée de l'armée (Paris), Ms. 737, vol. 8: Desvaux commented briefly on the museum on November 25 and 30, 1852, including mention of the return of relevant monuments. The provenance of many of these finds was undocumented. Arnaud-Portelli, *L'exploration archéologique de l'Afrique du Nord*, 108–9.

143. Beury, "Note sur les ruines de Lambèse en 1852," *Recueil des notices et mémoires de la Société archéologique de la province de Constantine*, ser. 3, 7 (1893): 95–103.

144. Only sixty-eight of the prisoners of 1848 sent to Lambaesis opted to stay in Algeria after the amnesty of 1859. Delnore, "Empire by Example?," 45.

145. Bibliothèque de l'Arsenal, Paris, Ms. 15462: Terson, *Mémoires d'un ancien apôtre Saint-Simonien*. part 4, chap. 13; Daniel Fabre, ed., *Jean Terson: Mémoires d'un apôtre saint-simonien* (Carcassonne: Édition Fédération Audoise des Oeuvres Laïques, 1979), 48.

146. ANOM 80 F 1588: Letter of March 12, 1853, from the minister of war to the commander of Lambaesis.

147. ANOM 80 F 1588: A letter of September 13, 1854, informed the minister of war that M. Becker, one of those interned who had also published on Medracen had died after illness at Lambaesis.

148. Fernand Rude, ed., *Bagnes d'Afrique: Trois transportés en Algérie après le coup d'état du 2 décembre 1851* (Paris: François Maspero, 1981), 72.

149. Bibliothèque littéraire Jacques Doucet, Ms. 45138: Letter dated August 28, 1853, from Jacques-Eugène Leiris to his brother-in-law Adolphe Labey.

150. Rude, *Bagnes d'Afrique*, 80–84.

151. A. Moll, "Note sur des fouilles faites à Lambèse, aux sources d'Aïn-Drinn et d'Aïn-Boubennana," *Annuaire de la Société archéologique de la province de Constantine* (1856–1857): 157–62. A. Moll, "Quelques inscriptions trouvées à Lambèse dans le courant de 1857," *Annuaire de la Société archéologique de la province de Constantine* (1856–1857): 163–69.

152. Franck Laurent, *Victor Hugo face à la conquête de l'Algérie* (Paris: Maisonneuve et Larose, 2001), 91–99.

153. Victor Hugo, "Pauline Roland," in *Bagnes d'Afrique*, 211–14.

154. Rude, *Bagnes d'Afrique*, 17–27.

155. Laurent, *Victor Hugo face à la conquête*, 55–77.

156. Archives des Musées nationaux, Musée du Louvre A4: October 24–25, 1865.

157. René Pillorget, "Les deux voyages de Napoléon III en Algérie (1860 et 1865)," *Revue du Souvenir Napoléonien* 363 (February 1989): 30–36. I thank Matt Delvaux for pointing out the relevance of this issue to the concept of "key terrain" in military terrain analysis.

158. M. Barnéond, "Rapport adressé à M. le préfet sur les recherches exécutées à Lambèse en 1865," *Recueil des notices et mémoires de la Société archéologique de la province de Constantine* (1866): 239–61.

159. AN Pierrefittes F 17 2920: Letter dated April 17, 1873, from Antoine Héron de Villefosse to Léon Renier.

160. Marcel Bénabou, "L'impérialisme et l'Afrique du Nord: Le modèle romain," in *Sciences de l'homme et conquête coloniale: Constitution et usages des sciences humaines en Afrique (XIXe–XXe siècles)*, ed. Daniel Nordman and Jean-Pierre Raison (Paris: Presses de l'École normale supérieure, 1980), 15–22.

161. Michel-Rolph Trouillot, *Silencing the Past: Power and the Production of History* (Boston: Beacon, 1995), 70–107.

162. Nicholas B. Dirks, "Annals of the Archive: Ethnographic Notes on the Sources of History," in *From the Margins: Historical Anthropology and Its Futures*, ed. Brian Keith Axel (Durham, NC: Duke University Press, 2002), 63.

163. Frantz Fanon, *The Wretched of the Earth*, trans. Richard Philcox (New York: Grove Press, 2004), 148–52.

164. Monique Dondin-Payre, *La Commission d'exploration scientifique d'Algérie: Une héritière méconnue de la Commission d'Égypte*, Mémoires de l'Académie des inscriptions et belles-lettres, n.s. 14 (Paris: F. Paillart, 1994), 16.

165. Monique Dondin-Payre, "Du voyage à l'archéologie: L'exemple de l'Afrique du Nord," in *Du voyage savant aux territoires de l'archéologie: Voyageurs, amateurs et savants à l'origine de l'archéologie moderne*, ed. Manuel Royo, Martine Denoyelle, Emmanuelle Hindy, Timothy Champion, and David Louyot (Paris: De Boccard, 2011), 278–80.

166. Claude-Antoine Rozet, *Voyage dans la Régence d'Alger ou Description du pays occupé par l'armée française en Afrique* (Paris: Arthus Bertrand, Libraire-Éditeur, 1833), 3:182–83.

167. Ahmed Saadoui, "Le remploi dans les mosquées ifrîqiyennes aux époques médiévale et moderne," in *Lieux de cultes: Aires votives, temples, églises, mosquées. IXe colloque international sur l'histoire et l'archéologie de l'Afrique du Nord antique et médiévale, Tripoli, 19–25 février 2005* (Paris: CNRS Éditions, 2008), 295–304; Michael Greenhalgh, *Marble Past, Monumental Present: Building with Antiquities in the Mediaeval Mediterranean* (Leiden: Brill, 2009), 313–21, 447–68.

168. Auguste Cherbonneau, "Constantine et ses antiquités," *Annuaire de la Société archéologique de la province de Constantine* (1853): 112.

169. James Malarkey, "The Dramatic Structure of Scientific Discovery in Colonial Algeria: A Critique of the Journal of the 'Société archéologique de Constantine' (1853–1876)," in *Connaissances du Maghreb: Sciences sociales et colonisation*, ed. Jean-Claude Vatin (Paris: CNRS Éditions, 1984), 144–52.

170. Oscar MacCarthy, "*Algeria romana*: Recherches sur l'occupation et la colonisation de l'Algérie par les romains," *Revue africaine* 1, no. 5 (1857): 364.

171. Léon Renier, "Notes d'un voyage archéologique au pied de l'Aurès," *Revue archéologique* 8, no. 2 (1852): 513.

172. Charles Diehl, "Les découvertes de l'archéologie française en Algérie et en Tunisie," *Revue internationale de l'enseignement* 24 (1892): 97–130.

173. Yannis Hamilakis, "Indigenous Archaeologies in Ottoman Greece," in *Scramble for the Past: A Story of Archaeology in the Ottoman Empire, 1753–1914*, ed. Zainab Bahrani, Zeynep Çelik, and Edhem Eldem (Istanbul: SALT, 2011), 49–69.

174. Elliot Colla, *Conflicted Antiquities: Egyptology, Egyptomania, Egyptian Modernity* (Durham, NC: Duke University Press, 2007), 10–20, 121–26; Asher Kaufman, "The Formation of an Identity in Lebanon in 1920," *Middle Eastern Studies* 37, no. 1 (2001): 173–94; Corbett, *Competitive Archaeology in Jordan*.

175. Jean-Louis Huot, "L'archéologie dans le monde musulman," in *L'avenir du passé: Modernité de l'archéologie*, ed. Jean-Paul Demoule and Bernard Stiegler (Paris: La Découverte, 2008), 183–95.

176. Trouillot, *Silencing the Past*, 22–30.

177. Ernest Carette, *Exploration scientifique de l'Algérie pendant les années 1840, 1841, 1842*, Sciences historiques et géographiques 1 (Paris: Imprimerie nationale, 1844), 33.

178. Duvivier, *Recherches et notes sur la portion de l'Algérie au sud de Guelma*, 1–2.

179. Ibid., 2.

180. Guyon, *Voyage d'Alger*, 113–14.

181. It is difficult to determine from this passage whether this name, a variant on the name of the Prophet, was meant to refer generically to Muslims or if it specifically referred to Sharif Muhammed ben-Abdellah, known widely as Bou-Maza, who called for holy war against the French in 1845. *Lettres du Maréchal de Saint-Arnaud*, 2:16, 27; M. Poujoulat, *Études africaines: Récits et pensées d'un voyageur* (Paris: Comptoir des Imprimeurs-Unis, 1847), 2:119; Paul Azan, *L'Armée d'Afrique de 1830 à 1852* (Paris: Plon, 1936), 383, 411–12.

182. ANOM 80 F 1587: Terson, *Notice sur les ruines de Lambèse*.

183. Morizot, *Aurès ou le mythe*, 118.

184. Julia Clancy-Smith, *Rebel and Saint: Muslim Notables, Populist Protest, Colonial Encounters (Algeria and Tunisia, 1800–1904)* (Berkeley: University of California Press, 1994), 218–25; Zouzou, *Aurès au temps de la France coloniale*, 157–58.

185. See, for instance, the account of Louis-Guillaume Follie, who was briefly made a slave after the ship he was sailing on foundered on the coast of Morocco in 1784: *Voyages dans les déserts d'Afrique* (Paris: Directeurs de l'Imprimerie du Cercle sociale, 1792).

186. ANOM 80 F 1587: Pellotier, *Travaux archéologiques des transportés*.

187. *Lettres du Maréchal de Saint-Arnaud*, 2:272.

188. Triptolemus was thought by the ancient Greeks to be the son of Celeus, king of Eleusis, and a favorite of Ceres. He was credited with inventing the plow and settled agriculture. Joseph Thomas, *The Universal Dictionary of Biography and Mythology*, reprint ed. (New York: Cosimo, 2009), 4:2150.

189. Emerit, "Mémoires de Terson," 249–50.

Chapter 4. Institutionalizing Algerian Archaeology

1. "Les Romains se sont perpétués en Afrique; la race créole française, née sur place et fille des premiers immigrants, commence elle-même a y faire souche." Gustave Boissière, *Esquisse d'une histoire de la conquête et de l'administration romaines dans le nord de l'Afrique et particulièrement dans la province de Numidie* (Paris: Hachette et Cie, 1878), 81.

2. Osama W. Abi-Mershed, *Apostles of Modernity: Saint-Simonians and the Civilizing Mission in Algeria* (Stanford, CA: Stanford University Press, 2010), 119–20.

3. SHAT 1 M 1314: Monsieur de Colomb, head of the 2nd Battalion of the Foreign Legion, "Les oasis du Sahara et les routes qui y conduisent, 1e partie," December 1859.

4. Michael J. Heffernan, "The Parisian Poor and the Colonization of Algeria during the Second Republic," *French History* 3, no. 4 (1989): 377–403.

5. Jennifer E. Sessions, *By Sword and Plow: France and the Conquest of Algeria* (Ithaca, NY: Cornell University Press, 2011), 317–18.

6. Joseph Bard, *L'Algérie en 1854: Itinéraire général de Tunis à Tanger* (Paris: L. Maison, 1854), 66–73.

7. Michael Greenhalgh, *The Military and Colonial Destruction of the Roman Landscape of North Africa, 1830–1900* (Leiden: Brill, 2014), 197–201.

8. John Reynell Morell, *Algeria: The Topography and History, Political, Social, and Natural, of French Algeria* (London: Nathaniel Cooke, 1854), 354.

9. Julia Clancy-Smith, "Exoticism, Erasures, and Absence: The Peopling of Algiers, 1830–1900," in *Walls of Algiers: Narratives of the City through Text and Image*, ed. Zeynep Çelik, Julia Clancy-Smith, and Frances Terpak (Los Angeles: Getty Research Institute, 2009), 19–24.

10. Julia A. Clancy-Smith, *Mediterraneans: North Africa and Europe in an Age of Migration, c. 1800–1900* (Berkeley: University of California Press, 2011), 90–91, 148.

11. On the close links between colonial law's cultural distinctions and control of property, see Lauren Benton, *Law and Colonial Cultures: Legal Regimes in World History, 1400–1900* (Cambridge: Cambridge University Press, 2002), 10–11, 22–24.

12. "In receiving these and other statements of French writers about the Arabs, it is necessary to observe great caution, as it is in the interest of the conquerors to represent their victims in the most odious light possible, in order to justify their own injustice and cruelty." Morell, *Algeria*, 303.

13. Bard, *L'Algérie en 1854*, 3.

14. Morell, *Algeria*, 110; Timothy Mitchell, *Colonising Egypt* (Cambridge: Cambridge University Press, 1988).

15. Jacques Frémeaux, *Les bureaux arabes dans l'Algérie de la conquête* (Paris: Éditions Denoël, 1993), 35–38.

16. Abi Mershed, *Apostles of Modernity*, 96–126.

17. Michael J. Heffernan and Keith Sutton, "The Landscape of Colonialism: The Impact of French Colonial Rule on the Algerian Rural Settlement Pattern, 1830–1987," in *Colonialism and Development in the Contemporary World*, ed. Chris Dixon and Michael J. Heffernan (New York: Mansell, 1991), 121–23, 127.

18. John Ruedy, *Land Policy in Colonial Algeria: The Origins of the Rural Public Domain*, Near Eastern Studies 10 (Berkeley: University of California Press, 1967), 30–32.

19. Abi-Mershed, *Apostles of Modernity*, 121–24, 163–64.

20. Ruedy, *Land Policy*, 87–89, 99.

21. Jamil M. Abun-Nasr, *A History of the Maghrib*, 2nd ed. (Cambridge: Cambridge University Press, 1975), 249–50.

22. Annie Rey-Goldzeiguer, *Le royaume arabe: la politique algérienne de Napoléon III, 1861–1870* (Algiers: Société nationale d'édition et de diffusion, 1977), 70–71.

23. Heffernan and Sutton, "Landscape of Colonialism," 130; David Prochaska, *Making Algeria French: Colonialism in Bône, 1870–1920* (Cambridge: Cambridge University Press, 1990), 17–23.

24. Sessions, *By Sword and Plow*, 232, 318–19.

25. E. Pellissier de Reynaud, *Annales algériennes*, new ed. (Paris: Librairie militaire, 1854), 3:247–77.

26. Amable Ravoisié, *Exploration scientifique de l'Algérie pendant les années 1840, 1841, 1842* (Paris: Chez Firmin Didot Frères, 1846–1850), 1:iii.

27. Bard, *Algérie en 1854*, 115–16.

28. Ibid., 36–37, 148.

29. "Découvertes et nouvelles," *Revue archéologique* 5, no. 2 (1848–1849): 500–505.

30. Charles Diehl, "Les découvertes de l'archéologie française en Algérie et en Tunisie," *Revue internationale de l'enseignement* 24 (1892): 105–9.

31. Charles Nozeran, "De l'opportunité de faire exécuter des fouilles à Cherchel," *L'Algérie nouvelle: Journal politique quotidien* 1, no. 7 (1858).

32. Adrien Berbrugger, "L'Afrique septentrionale après le partage du monde romain en Empire d'Orient et Empire d'Occident," *Revue africaine* 1, no. 2 (1856): 82.

33. ANOM 80 F 1587: Oscar MacCarthy, *De l'occupation romaine dans la subdivision de Tlemsen*, September 5, 1851.

34. Oscar MacCarthy, "*Algeria romana*: Recherches sur l'occupation et la colonisation de l'Algérie par les romains," *Revue africaine* 1, no. 2 (1856): 88–91.

35. David Prochaska, "Fire on the Mountain: Resisting Colonialism in Algeria," in *Banditry, Rebellion, and Social Protest in Africa*, ed. Donald Crummey (London: James Currey, 1986), 229–52; Caroline Ford, "Culture and Conservation in France and Her Colonies 1840–1940," *Past and Present*, no. 183 (2004): 173–98.

36. Diana K. Davis, "Eco-Governance in French Algeria: Environmental History, Policy, and Colonial Administration," *Proceedings of the Western Society for French History* 32

(2004): 328–45; Michael J. Heffernan, "The Desert in French Orientalist Painting during the Nineteenth Century," *Landscape Research* 16, no. 2 (1991): 37–42.

37. Diana K. Davis, *Resurrecting the Granary of Rome: Environmental History and French Colonial Expansion in North Africa* (Athens: Ohio University Press, 2007), 58, 85–89.

38. Brent D. Shaw, "Climate, Environment, and History: The Case of Roman North Africa," in *Climate and History: Studies in Past Climates and Their Impact on Man*, ed. T. M. L. Wigley, M. J. Ingram, and G. Farmer (Cambridge: Cambridge University Press, 1981), 379–403; Jean-Louis Ballais, "Conquests and Land Degradation in the Eastern Maghreb during Classical Antiquity and the Middle Ages," in *The Archaeology of Drylands: Living at the Margin*, ed. Graeme Barker and David Gilbertson (London: Routledge, 2000), 125–36.

39. Myriam Bacha, *Patrimoine et monuments en Tunisie* (Rennes: Presses universitaires de Rennes, 2013), 42.

40. Ève and Jean Gran-Aymerich, "La création des Écoles françaises d'Athènes, Rome et Madrid," in *Les débuts des sciences de l'homme*, ed. Bernard-Pierre Lécuyer and Benjamin Matalon, Communications 56 (Paris: Seuil, 1992), 175–87.

41. Ève Gran-Aymerich, *Naissance de l'archéologie moderne, 1798–1945* (Paris: CNRS Éditions, 1998), 146–47.

42. Frederick N. Bohrer, *Orientalism and Visual Culture: Imagining Mesopotamia in Nineteenth-Century Europe* (Cambridge: Cambridge University Press, 2003), 63–76; Nicolas Grimal, "Mariette Pacha," in *Histoire et archéologie méditerranéennes sous Napoléon III: Actes du 21e colloque de la Villa Kérylos à Beaulieu-sur-Mer les 8 & 9 octobre 2010*, ed. André Laronde, Pierre Toubert, and Jean Leclant, Cahiers de la Villa 'Kérylos' 22 (Paris: Diffusion de Boccard, 2011), 179–92.

43. Wendy Doyon, "The History of Archaeology through the Eyes of Egyptians," in *Unmasking Ideology: The Vocabulary, Symbols, and Legacy of Imperial and Colonial Archaeology*, ed. Bonnie Effros and Guolong Lai (Los Angeles: Cotsen Institute of Archaeology Press, in press).

44. Edmund Richardson, "Of Doubtful Antiquity: Fighting for the Past in the Crimean War," in *From Plunder to Preservation: Britain and the Heritage of Empire, c. 1800–1940*, ed. Astrid Swenson and Peter Mandler, Proceedings of the British Academy 187 (Oxford: Oxford University Press, 2013), 31–48.

45. Ève Gran-Aymerich, "Épigraphie française et allemande au Maghreb: Entre collaboration et rivalité (1830–1914)," *Mitteilungen des Deutschen archäologischen Instituts, Römische Abteilung* 117 (2011): 583–84; Thibaud Serres-Jacquart, "Joseph Vattier de Bourville (1812–1854): Notes sur un explorateur de la Cyrénaïque," *Journal des savants* 2, no. 1 (2001): 393–429.

46. Dorothy M. Thorn, *The Four Seasons of Cyrene: The Excavation and Exploration in 1861 of Lieutenants R. Murdoch Smith, R. E., and Edwin A. Porcher, R. N.* (Rome: "L'Erma" di Bretschneider, 2007).

47. Joann Freed, *Bringing Carthage Home: The Excavations of Nathan Davis, 1856–1859* (Oxford: Oxbow Books, 2011), 15–16.

48. Christophe Chandezon, "Ernest Beulé (1826–1874): Archéologie classique, histoire romaine et vie politique sous Napoléon III," in *L'hellénisme, d'une rive à l'autre de la Méditerranée: Mélanges offerts à André Laronde* (Paris: De Boccard, 2012), 36–38. Myriam Bacha notes that in actual fact, the excavations of Beulé were secretly financed by the French state (*Patrimoine et monuments*, 43–45).

49. Gran-Aymerich, "Épigraphie française et allemande," 567–79.

50. Nadia Bayle, "Quelques aspects de l'histoire de l'archéologie au XIXe siècle: l'exemple des publications archéologiques militaires éditées entre 1830 et 1914 en France, en Afrique du Nord et en Indo-Chine" (PhD diss., Université de Paris-Sorbonne [Paris IV], 1986), 1:183–87.

51. Ernest Desjardins, "Léon Renier," in *Mélanges Renier*, Bibliothèque de l'École des hautes études, sciences philologiques et historiques 73 (Paris: F. Vieweg, 1887), vi–vii.

52. *Lettres du Maréchal de Saint-Arnaud* (Paris: Michel Lévy Frères, 1855), 2:262–63; Louis de Charbonnières, *Une grande figure, Saint-Arnaud, maréchal de France* (Paris: Nouvelles Editions Latines, 1960), 88; Léon Renier, "Lettre au ministre pour demander une mission à Lambèse," *Archives des missions scientifiques et littéraires* 2 (1851): 57–62.

53. Ève Gran-Aymerich, "Theodor Mommsen (1817–1903) et ses correspondants français: La 'fabrique' internationale de la science," *Journal des savants* 1, no. 1 (2008): 177–229; Gran-Aymerich, *Naissance de l'archéologie moderne*, 154.

54. Gran-Aymerich, *Naissance de l'archéologie moderne*, 68.

55. ANOM 80 F 1586: Letter dated September 24, 1850, from the minister of war to the governor-general.

56. Léon Renier, "Notes d'un voyage archéologique au pied de l'Aurès," *Revue archéologique* 8, no. 2 (1851–1852): 512.

57. ANOM 80 F 1595: Letter dated December 21, 1850, from Commandant Adolphe Delamare to the minister of war asking for permission to extend his stay in Lambaesis.

58. Léon Renier, "Premier rapport de M. Renier, en mission dans la province de Constantine pour la recherche des monuments épigraphiques," *Archives des missions scientifiques et littéraires* 2 (1851): 169–86.

59. Desjardins, "Léon Renier," vi–vii.

60. Léon Renier, "Troisième rapport de M. Renier, en mission dans la province de Constantine pour la recherche des monuments épigraphiques," *Archives des missions scientifiques et littéraires* 2 (1851): 435–57; Léon Renier, "Quatrième rapport de M. Renier, en mission dans la province de Constantine pour la recherche des monuments épigraphiques," *Archives des missions scientifiques et littéraires* 2 (1851): 473–83; Annie Arnaud-Portelli, "L'exploration archéologique de l'Afrique du Nord des premiers voyageurs au XVIIIe siècle à l'indépendance des nations (Maroc, Algérie) d'après les documents publiés" (PhD diss., Université de Paris IV-Sorbonne, 1991), 2:103–9.

61. In this work, each inscription is accompanied by a notice signifying who transcribed the material. A sizeable number of officers beyond Renier's guide Delamare contributed to the undertaking.

62. Greenhalgh, *Military and Colonial Destruction*, 227–36.

63. Ian Haynes, *Blood of the Provinces: The Roman Auxilia and the Making of Provincial Society from Augustus to the Severans* (Oxford: Oxford University Press, 2013), 124–25.

64. Mounir Bouchenaki, "L'oeuvre des épigraphistes français en Algérie: La Numidie et la Maurétanie Césarienne," in *Un siècle d'épigraphie classique: Aspects de l'oeuvre des savants français dans les pays du bassin méditerranéen de 1888 à nos jours. Actes du colloque international du centenaire de 'L'année epigraphique,' Paris, 19–21 octobre 1988* (Paris: Presses universitaires de France, 1991), 53–69.

65. Paul-Albert Février, *Approches du Maghreb romain: Pouvoirs, différences et conflits* (Aix-en-Provence: ÉDISUD, 1989), 1:34–37.

66. Renier, "Notes d'un voyage archéologique," 513.

67. Gran Aymerich, "Theodor Mommsen," 216–17.

68. Gran-Aymerich, "Épigraphie française et allemande," 580–81; Gran Aymerich, "Theodor Mommsen," 197–99.

69. Desjardins, "Léon Renier," viii–x.

70. Ève Gran-Aymerich, "Karl Benedikt Hase (1780–1864) et Désiré Raoul-Rochette (1789–1854) d'après leur correspondance: Deux médiateurs culturels entre France et Allemagne à la Bibliothèque nationale (1801–1864)," in *S'écrire et écrire sur l'antiquité: L'apport des correspondances à l'histoire des travaux scientifiques*, ed. Corinne Bonnet and Véronique Krings (Grenoble: Éditions Jérôme Millon, 2008), 83–103.

71. Gran-Aymerich, "Theodor Mommsen," 197–99.

72. Gustav Wilmanns, "Étude sur le camp et la ville de Lambèse," *Bulletin trimestriel des antiquités africaines* 1 (1882): 186–87; Greenhalgh, *Military and Colonial Destruction*, 220–25.

73. Gustav Wilmanns, *Inscriptiones Africae latinae*, in Corpus inscriptionum latinarum 8 (Berlin: Georg Reimer, 1881), 1:xxix–xxxii; Gran-Aymerich, "Épigraphie française et allemande," 580–85.

74. It is of interest that the passage quoted did not use *Franj* (Arabic), *Frenk* (Ottoman), or *Frangi* (Persian), which referred to foreigners and Europeans, including the French. In a core Ottoman context, *Rum* typically meant Byzantine or Greek. I thank Yüçel Yanikdağ for sharing this observation.

75. Renier, "Notes d'un voyage archéologique," 513.

76. For the argument that the French claimed biological descent from the ancient Romans, see Matthew M. McCarty, "French Archaeology and History in the Colonial Maghreb: Inheritance, Presence, and Absence," in *Unmasking Ideology: The Vocabulary, Symbols and Legacy of Imperial and Colonial Archaeology*, ed. Bonnie Effros and Guolong Lai (Los Angeles: Cotsen Institute of Archaeology Press, in press).

77. The aspect of the "Kabyle myth" that claimed that the Berbers were descended from ancient Christians and only superficially converted to Islam gained increasing force among Europeans in subsequent decades. Patricia Lorcin, *Imperial Identities: Stereotyping, Prejudice and Race in Colonial Algeria* (London: I. B. Tauris, 1995), 118–35.

78. Greenhalgh, *Military and Colonial Destruction*, 217–20.

79. Léon Renier, *Instructions pour la recherche des antiquités en Algérie* (Paris: L. Hachette et Cie, 1859), 15.

80. Nicholas Ridout, *Passionate Amateurs: Theatre, Communism, and Love* (Ann Arbor: University of Michigan Press, 2013), 78.

81. Renier, *Instructions pour la recherche*, 1–15.

82. Nabila Oulebsir, *Les usages du patrimoine: Monuments, musées et politique coloniale en Algérie (1830–1930)* (Paris: Éditions de la Maison des sciences de l'homme, 2004), 75–93; Clémentine Gutron, *L'archéologie en Tunisie (XIXe–XXe siècles): Jeux généalogiques sur l'Antiquité* (Paris: Karthala, 2010), 137–66.

83. Bayle, "Quelques aspects de l'histoire," 1:146–54.

84. For similar issues in areas of Asia Minor distant from the coast, see Michael Greenhalgh, *From the Romans to the Railways: The Fate of Antiquities in Asia Minor* (Leiden: Brill, 2013), 352–54.

85. Février, *Approches du Maghreb romain*, 38.

86. Léon Renier, "Deuxième rapport de M. Renier, en mission dans la province de Constantine pour la recherche des monuments épigraphiques," *Archives des missions scientifiques et littéraires* 2 (1851): 217–22.

87. Oulebsir, *Usages du patrimoine*, 103–4.

88. On inscriptions held at the Cabinet des médailles at the Bibliothèque nationale, including those from Carthage but not Algeria, see Felicity Bodenstein, "L'histoire du Cabinet des médailles et antiques de la Bibliothèque nationale (1819–1924): Un cabinet pour l'érudition à l'âge des musées" (PhD diss., Université de Paris-Sorbonne, 2015), 1:330–39.

89. ANOM 80 F 1587: Colonel Creuly, "Rapport sur les collections archéologiques existantes dans la province de Constantine, territoire militaire, et sur les mesures prises ou à prendre pour leur conservation," January 24, 1854.

90. ANOM 80 F 1587: A series of letters sent by the minister of war, the minister of public instruction, the minister of the interior, and various military authorities between July 1851 and April 1852.

91. I have roughly translated this title from references to "La Tribune de la Schola des Optiones de la Légion III d'Auguste." Archives des Musées nationaux, Musée du Louvre A4:

Letter dated September 10, 1851, to the director of national museums from the minister of the interior, Division of Beaux Arts. The epitaph was reportedly found by Renier in Batna.

92. ANOM 80 F 1587: Report of Chief of the Engineering Brigade Foy to the governor-general on July 20, 1851; Renier, "Notes d'un voyage archéologique," 512–13.

93. ANOM 80 F 1587: Creuly, "Rapport sur les collections archéologiques," January 24, 1854.

94. Archives des musées nationaux, Musée du Louvre A4: August 21, 1874.

95. ANOM FM 5 80 1595: Report by Karl Benedikt Hase, member of the Académie des inscriptions et belles-lettres, dated September 27, 1844.

96. ANOM 80 F 1589: Letter dated November 29, 1843, from the minister of war to Governor-General Thomas-Robert Bugeaud.

97. Oulebsir, Usages du patrimoine, 99–102.

98. Ève Gran-Aymerich, Dictionnaire biographique d'archéologie 1798–1945 (Paris: CNRS Éditions, 2001), 657–58.

99. ANOM ALG GGA N3: "Note à l'appui du rapport fait au Ministre concernant l'inspection générale des bâtiments civils en Algérie pendant la campagne 1850–1851."

100. Barnett Singer and John Langdon, Cultured Force: Makers and Defenders of the French Colonial Empire (Madison: University of Wisconsin Press, 2004), 65–69.

101. Jacques Frémeaux, "Souvenirs de Rome et présence française au Maghreb: Essai d'investigation," in Connaissances du Maghreb: Sciences sociales et colonisation, ed. Jean-Claude Vatin (Paris: CNRS Éditions, 1984), 33–34.

102. Adrien Berbrugger, "Origines de la Société historique algérienne," Revue africaine 6 (1862): 218–21.

103. Graham Robb, The Discovery of France: A Historical Geography from the Revolution to the First World War (New York: W. W. Norton, 2007), 306–7.

104. Jean-Pierre Chaline, Sociabilité et érudition: Les sociétés savantes en France, XIXe et XXe siècles (Paris: Comité des travaux historiques et scientifiques, 1998).

105. Marquis de Castellane, "Discours lu à la Société archéologique dans sa séance du 16 juillet 1831," Mémoires de la Société archéologique du Midi de la France (1832–1833), 1:viii.

106. Caroline Barrera, Les sociétés savantes de Toulouse au XIXe siècle (1797–1865) (Paris: Éditions du Comité des travaux historiques et scientifiques, 2003), 64–68, 101–17, 232.

107. SHAT 1 H 9-3: Letter dated October 3, 1831, from Alexandre du Mège to the aide-de-camp of General Pierre Berthézène; Bonnie Effros, "Colliding Empires: French Display of Roman Antiquities Expropriated from Post-Conquest Algeria (1830–1870)," in Objects of War: The Material Culture of Conflict and Displacement, ed. Leora Auslander and Tara Zahra (Ithaca, NY: Cornell University Press, 2018).

108. Bonnie Effros, Uncovering the Germanic Past: Merovingian Archaeology in France, 1830–1914 (Oxford: Oxford University Press, 2012), 35–47, 59–87.

109. Donald Malcolm Reid, Whose Pharaohs? Archaeology, Museums, and Egyptian National Identity from Napoleon to World War I (Berkeley: University of California Press, 2002), 48–49.

110. Adrien Berbrugger, Bibliothèque-Musée d'Alger: Livret explicatif des collections diverses de ces deux établissements (Algiers: Imprimerie Bastiede, 1861), 13.

111. Arnaud-Portelli, Exploration archéologique de l'Afrique du Nord, 2:22.

112. Février, Approches du Maghreb romain, 45.

113. Adrien Berbrugger, "Introduction," Revue africaine 1, no. 1 (1856): 7; Berbrugger, Bibliothèque-Musée d'Alger, 15.

114. Lorcin, Imperial Identities, 114–15; Gran-Aymerich, Naissance de l'archéologie moderne, 46–62.

115. Nozeran, "De l'opportunité."

116. Abi-Mershed, *Apostles of Modernity*, 13–14.

117. Ernest Watbled, *Souvenirs de l'armée d'Afrique* (Paris: Challamel Aîné, 1877).

118. AN de Pierrefitte F 17 17213: Statuts de la Société archéologique de la province de Constantine (1852).

119. ANOM 80 F 1587: Creuly, "Rapport sur les collections archéologiques," January 24, 1854.

120. James Malarkey, "The Dramatic Structure of Scientific Discovery in Colonial Algeria: A Critique of the Journal of the 'Société archéologique de Constantine' (1853–1876)," in *Connaissances du Maghreb*, 144; Ernest Mercier, "Nécrologie: Auguste Cherbonneau," *Recueil des notices et mémoires de la Société archéologique de la province de Constantine*, 3e ser., no. 1 (1882): 413–18.

121. Auguste Cherbonneau, "Constantine et ses antiquités," *Annuaire de la Société archéologique de la province de Constantine* (1853): 108–9.

122. SHAT 8 Yd 3378: "Rapport particulier de M. Casimir Cruely, colonel du génie, directeur des fortifications" (October 8, 1854); Lorcin, *Imperial Identities*, 115.

123. ANOM 80 F 1587: Colonel Creuly, "Rapport sur les collections archéologiques existantes dans la province de Constantine, territoire militaire, et sur les mesures prises ou à prendre pour leur conservation," January 24, 1854.

124. "Coup-d'oeil sur les antiquités de la province de Constantine," *Annuaire de la Société archéologique de la province de Constantine* (1853): 15.

125. Georges Doublet and Paul Gauckler, *Musée de Constantine*, Musées et collections archéologiques de l'Algérie (Paris: Ernest Leroux, 1892), 5–7; Oulebsir, *Usages du patrimoine*, 106–7.

126. SHAT 8 Yd 3378: Letter dated May 26, 1859, from the minister of public instruction to the minister of war.

127. Malarkey, "Dramatic Structure," 139–40.

128. AN Pierrefitte F 17 17213: Letter from the president of the Société archéologique de Constantine to the minister of public instruction dated October 26, 1858.

129. AN Pierrefitte F 17 17213: "Statuts de la Société archéologique de Constantine" (1852); Oulebsir, *Usages du patrimoine*, 104–5.

130. Diehl, "Découvertes de l'archéologie," 100–102.

131. Malarkey, "Dramatic Structure," 140–53.

132. Prochaska, *Making Algeria French*, 214; Victoria Thompson, "'I Went Pale with Pleasure': The Body, Sexuality, and National Identity among French Travelers to Algiers in the Nineteenth Century," in *Algeria and France, 1800–2000: Identity-Memory-Nostalgia*, ed. Patricia M. E. Lorcin (Syracuse: Syracuse University Press, 2006), 18–32.

133. Chip Colwell-Chanthaphonh and J. Brett Hill, "Mapping History: Cartography and the Construction of the San Pedro Valley," *History and Anthropology* 15, no. 2 (2004): 175–200.

134. AN Pierrefitte 17 F 17213: Société historique algérienne, correspondence dated to October 8, 1883.

135. Oran gained its own scholarly society only in 1878 with the creation of the Société de géographie et d'archéologie de la province d'Oran. Lorcin, *Imperial Identities*, 140.

136. Raymund F. Wood, "Berbrugger, Founder of Algerian Librarianship," *Journal of Library History* 5, no. 3 (1971): 237–56; Patricia Lorcin, "Rome and France in Africa: Recovering Colonial Algeria's Latin Past," *French Historical Studies* 25, no. 2 (2002): 309–11.

137. SHAT 7 Yd 1526: Career dossier of Estève-Laurent Boissonnet dated May 28, 1890; Lorcin, *Imperial Identities*, 115–19.

138. Berbrugger, "Introduction," 3–4.

139. ANOM 80 F 1586: Letter from Adrien Berbrugger on behalf of the emergent Société historique algérienne to Governor-General Randon dated March 18, 1856.

140. Oulebsir, *Usages du patrimoine*, 105–8.

141. Adrien Berbrugger, "Société historique algérienne: Rapport sur la situation et celle de la *Revue africaine* depuis le 7 avril 1856," *Revue africaine* 1, no. 5 (1857): 329–34.

142. ANOM 80 F 1588: Letter dated October 30, 1851, from the prefect of Algiers to the minister of war following the discovery of a large number of Roman coins in Médéah in the province of Algiers; ANOM 80 F 1587: Letter dated March 26, 1853, from J. Nicole to the chief architect in the Office of Civilian Structures in Oran on the discovery of the remains of a Roman house.

143. Berbrugger, "Afrique septentrionale," 82.

144. Monique Dondin-Payre, "L'archéologie en Algérie à partir de 1830: Une politique patrimoniale?," in *Pour une histoire des politiques du patrimoine*, ed. Philippe Poirrier and Loïc Vadelorge, Travaux et documents 16 (Paris: Comité d'histoire du Ministère de la Culture, 2003), 145–70.

145. Berbrugger, "Afrique septentrionale," 87.

146. Sessions, *By Sword and Plow*, 231–61.

147. Oulebsir, *Usages du patrimoine*, 7–13.

148. Margarita Díaz-Andreu, *A World History of Nineteenth-Century Archaeology: Nationalism, Colonialism, and the Past* (Oxford: Oxford University Press, 2007), 265–68.

149. Bonnie Effros, "Museum-Building in Nineteenth-Century Algeria: Colonial Narratives in French Collections of Classical Antiquities," *Journal of the History of Collections* 28, no. 2 (2016): 243–59.

150. ANOM 80 F 1588: Letter dated July 7, 1853, from the prefect of Constantine to the minister of war.

151. ANOM 80 F 1587: Letter dated April 5, 1854, from the prefect of Constantine to the governor-general of Algeria.

152. Reid, *Whose Pharaohs?*, 54–58.

153. ANOM 80 F 1588: Letter dated January 13, 1854, from the prefect of Algiers to the governor-general; ANOM 80 F 1589: Letter dated March 14, 1854, from the governor-general to the minister of war.

154. ANOM 80 F 1588 : Creuly, "Rapport sur les collections archéologiques."

155. "Lazare Costa, l'italien qui découvrit le tophet de Cirta," in *Exposition Internationale "Les Phéniciens en Algérie: Les voies du commerce entre la Méditerranée et l'Afrique Noire", Palais de la Culture Moufdi Zakaria-Algeri, 20 janvier–20 février 2011*, ed. Lorenza Manfredi and Amel Soltani, http://cherchel-projet.isma.cnr.it/index.php?option=com_content&view=article&id=133&Itemid=135&lang=fr.

156. ANOM 80 F 1587: Letter dated May 27, 1856, from the prefect of Constantine to the governor-general.

157. Doublet and Gauckler, *Musée de Constantine*, 7–15.

158. "Seance du vendredi 18 avril 1879," *Revue des Sociétés savantes de la France et de l'étranger* 7, no. 1 (1880): 484.

159. Doublet and Gauckler, *Musée de Constantine*, 13–15.

160. AN Pierrefittes F 17 2920: Letter dated March 27, 1873, from Antoine Héron de Villefosse to Léon Renier.

161. Doublet and Gauckler, *Musée de Constantine*, 8–9.

162. ANOM 80 F 1587, Cahiers des transportés de juin 1848 à Lambèse: Thuillier Pellotier, "Travaux archéologiques des transportés de 1848" (dated December 20, 1852).

163. Arnaud-Portelli, *L'exploration archéologique de l'Afrique du Nord*, 2:108–9.

164. AN Pierrefittes F 17 2920: Letter dated April 17, 1873, from Antoine Héron de Villefosse to Léon Renier.

165. Archives des musées nationaux, Musée du Louvre A4: August 21, 1874.

166. ANOM 80 F 1733: Adrien Berbrugger, "Notes sur la Bibliothèque et sur le Musée d'Alger" (dated December 10, 1845).

167. AN Pierrefitte F 17 3510/1: Bibliothèque nationale d'Alger. "Inspection générale" (dated June 30, 1870); Lorcin, "Rome and France," 309–11; Oulebsir, *Usages du patrimoine*, 108–9.

168. Wood, "Berbrugger," 237–56.

169. Berbrugger, *Bibliothèque-Musée d'Alger*, 18–23 ; ANOM 80 F 1733 : Berbrugger, "Notes sur la Bibliothèque."

170. John Zarobell, *Empire of Landscape: Space and Ideology in French Colonial Algeria* (University Park: Pennsylvania State University Press, 2010), 71–73.

171. Oulebsir, *Usages du patrimoine*, 110; Effros, *Uncovering the Germanic Past*, 237–63.

172. ANOM 80 F 1733 : Berbrugger, "Notes sur la Bibliothèque."

173. ANOM 80 F 1586: Letter dated August 16, 1852, from the minister of war to the governor-general.

174. Clémentine Gutron, "L'abbé Bourgade (1806–1866), Carthage et l'Orient: De l'antiquaire au publiciste," *Anabases* 2 (2005): 178–82.

175. AN Pierrefitte F 17 2975: Antoine Héron de Villefosse, "Rapport sur une mission archéologique en Algérie" (dated November 1, 1873).

176. Archives des Musées nationaux, Musée du Louvre A4: Letter dated June 14, 1845, from the duc de Dalmatie to King Louis-Philippe and letter dated June 19, 1845, from the duc de Dalmatie to the comte de Montalivet, general director of the civil list.

177. Stéphane Gsell, *Exploration scientifique de l'Algérie pendant les années 1840–1845: Archéologie* (Paris: Ernest Leroux, 1912), i–ix.

178. Archives des Musées nationaux, Musée du Louvre A4: Letters dated July 15, August 1, and August 30, 1845, from the duc de Dalmatie to the comte de Montalivet, general director of the civil list; dispatch by de Lagau, consul in Tunis, of mosaics from Carthage, dated February 25, 1845.

179. *Bulletin officiel des actes du gouvernement*, vol. 4 (Algiers: Imprimerie du gouvernement, 1844), 181–85, no. 209, circulaire n. 32; Maya Jasanoff, *Edge of Empire: Lives, Culture, and Conquest in the East, 1750–1850* (New York: Knopf, 2005), 278–86.

180. Mitchell, *Colonising Egypt*, 1–33; Effros, "Colliding Empires," in press.

181. Ahmed Koumas and Chéhrazade Nafa, *L'Algérie et son patrimoine: Dessins français du XIXe siècle* (Paris: Monum, Éditions du patrimoine, 2003), 49.

182. Adrien de Longpérier, "À M. A. Leleux, éditeur de la *Revue archéologique*," *Revue archéologique* 5, no. 2 (1848–1849): 570–71.

183. Archives des Musées nationaux, Musée du Louvre A4: Letter dated April 25, 1851, from M. Royer to the inspector general; Archives des Musées nationaux, Musée du Louvre A4: Correspondence from November 27, 1850, and December 15, 1851, between Adrien de Longpérier, curator of antiquities at the Louvre, the general director of beaux-arts, and the general director of national museums; Archives des Musées nationaux, Musée du Louvre A8: Letters dated from September 18, 1856, to June 3, 1857, between the director general of imperial museums, Adrien de Longpérier, and M. Lalaaisse, who wrote on behalf of the architect M. Rattier; Archives des Musées nationaux, Musée du Louvre A4: Letter dated February 2, 1856, from the minister of the imperial household to M. Pfeiffer, general agent of transport and war, and letter dated March 12, 1856, from the general director of imperial museums to the minister of foreign affairs.

184. ANOM 80 F 1589: Letter dated July 23, 1853, from the minister of war to the governor-general. For more on the Musée algérien, see Effros, "Colliding Empires," in press.

185. ANOM 80 F 1589: Correspondence dated from July 3, 1855, to February 27, 1856, involving the minister of war, the governor-general, and Adrien Berbrugger.

186. A Roman boat found during the dredging of the ancient port disintegrated almost as quickly as it dried. "Bateau romain découvert à Cherchell," *Revue archéologique* 1, no. 2 (1844–1845): 696.

187. M. de Blinière, "Antiquités de la ville de Cherchel (Algérie)," *Revue archéologique* 5, no. 1 (1848): 344–47.

188. *Bulletin officiel des actes du gouvernement*, vol. 4, no. 173, Circulaire n. 15: "Monumens anciens et objets d'antiquité de M. le Gouverneur-Général à MM. les chefs des divers services, touchant les dispositions à prendre pour la conservation des monumens et des restes d'antiquité" (March 23, 1844).

189. Arnaud-Portelli, "Exploration archéologique," 2:237–39; Blinière, "Antiquités de la ville," 347–50.

190. Paul Gauckler, *Musée de Cherchel* (Paris: Ernest Leroux, 1895), 5–7.

191. ANOM 80 F 1589: Letter dated November 15, 1854, from the governor-general to the minister of war.

192. ANOM 80 F 1589: Letter dated October 19, 1854, from the minister of war to the governor-general of Algeria. More detailed information about Berbrugger's charge was contained in a circular from the governor-general to the prefects on November 15, 1854.

193. Février, *Approches du Maghreb romain*, 46.

194. Médiathèque de l'architecture et des monuments historiques, Charenton-le-Pont 81/99/01: Arrêté from Napoleon III dated January 13, 1862.

195. ANOM 80 F 1587: Letter from the minister of war to the governor-general of Algeria dated November 28, 1851.

196. On the Napoleonic Civil code, see http://www.legifrance.gouv.fr/affichCodeArticle.do?cidTexte=LEGITEXT000006070721&idArticle=LEGIARTI000006430628&dateTexte=20100727.

197. ANOM 80 F 1588: Letter from the governor-general of Algeria to the minister of war dated March 14, 1854.

198. ANOM 80 F 1589: Letter of November 17, 1854, from the governor-general to Adrien Berbrugger.

199. ANOM 80 F 1587: Letter of January 13, 1854, from the prefect of Algiers to the governor-general.

200. ANOM 80 F 1587: Letter dated October 12, 1853, from the commander of the subdivision of Orléansville to the governor-general; ANOM 80 F 1587: Letter dated January 9, 1858, from Adrien Berbrugger to Governor-General Randon regarding the transport of a Roman marble tomb from Dellys to the Musée d'Alger.

201. Édouard Pommier, "Naissance des musées de province," in *Les lieux de mémoire*, ed. Pierre Nora (Paris: Gallimard, 1986), 2, pt. 2:472–75; Bette W. Oliver, *From Royal to National: The Louvre Museum and the Bibliothèque nationale* (Lanham, MD: Rowman and Littlefield, 2007), 21–22.

202. Gauckler, *Musée de Cherchel*, 5–8.

203. ANOM 80 F 1587: Letter dated August 21, 1856, from the prefect of Algiers to the governor-general.

204. AN Pierrefitte F 17 2975: Héron de Villefosse, "Rapport sur une mission archéologique en Algérie."

205. "Chronique: Province d'Alger. Cherchel," *Revue africaine* 1 (1856): 54–56.

206. ANOM 80 F 1587: Joint letter dated December 2, 1856, sent by the inhabitants of Cherchel to the governor-general; Nozeran, "De l'opportunité."

207. Pierre Morizot, "La naissance de l'archéologie romaine en Algérie," in *Histoire et archéologie*, 168–70; Gauckler, *Musée de Cherchel*, 9.

208. AN Pierrefitte F 17 2975: Héron de Villefosse, "Rapport sur une mission archéologique en Algérie."

209. Gauckler, *Musée de Cherchel*, 9, 83–84.

210. Alphonse Delamare, "Étude sur Stora, port de Philippeville (l'ancienne Rusicade)," *Mémoires de la Société impériale des antiquaries de France* 24 (1859): 132–89.

211. Zarobell, *Empire of Landscape*, 104–20.

212. Joseph Roger, *Catalogue du Musée archéologique de Philippeville (Algérie)* (Philippeville: Imprimerie Chevalier et Luth, 1860), 3–17.

213. Stéphane Gsell, *Musée de Philippeville* (Paris: Ernest Leroux, 1898), 10–11.

214. ANOM 80 F 1733: Letter dated November 11, 1867, from the minister of the imperial household to the minister of war.

5. Cartography and Field Archaeology during the Second Empire

1. Alain Mahé, *Histoire de la Grande Kabylie XIXe–XXe siècles: Anthropologie historique du lien social dans les communautés villageoises* (Saint Denis: Éditions Bouchene, 2001), 165–66.

2. Annie Rey-Goldzeiguer, *Le royaume arabe: La politique algérienne de Napoléon III, 1861–1870* (Algiers: Société nationale d'édition et de diffusion, 1977), 69–71; David Prochaska, *Making Algeria French: Colonialism in Bône, 1870–1920* (Cambridge: Cambridge University Press, 1990), 8–11.

3. Michael J. Heffernan and Keith Sutton, "The Landscape of Colonialism: The Impact of French Colonial Rule on the Algerian Rural Settlement Pattern, 1830–1987," in *Colonialism and Development in the Contemporary World*, ed. Chris Dixon and Michael J. Heffernan (New York: Mansell, 1991), 130.

4. Osama Abi-Mershed, *Apostles of Modernity: Saint-Simonians and the Civilizing Mission in Algeria* (Stanford, CA: Stanford University Press, 2010), 164–66.

5. John Ruedy, *Land Policy in Colonial Algeria: The Origins of the Rural Public Domain*, Near Eastern Studies 10 (Berkeley: University of California Press, 1967), 87–92.

6. Olivier Le Cour Grandmaison, "Conquête de l'Algérie: La guerre totale," in *Le massacre, objet d'histoire*, ed. David El Kenz (Paris: Gallimard, 2005), 264–65.

7. *Le centenaire de Saint-Cyr, 1808–1908* (Paris: Berger-Levrault et Cie, 1908), 85.

8. Jacques Frémeaux, *Les bureaux arabes dans l'Algérie de la conquête* (Paris: Éditions Denoël, 1993), 38–45.

9. Heffernan and Sutton, "Landscape of Colonialism," 131–32.

10. Claude Collot, *Les institutions de l'Algérie durant la période coloniale (1830–1962)* (Paris: CNRS Éditions, 1987), 8–9.

11. Jamil M. Abun-Nasr, *A History of the Maghrib*, 2nd ed. (Cambridge: Cambridge University Press, 1975), 251–54; Abi-Mershed, *Apostles of Modernity*, 174–99.

12. *Centenaire de Saint-Cyr*, 86–87.

13. Abi-Mershed, *Apostles of Modernity*, 182.

14. René de Saint-Félix, ed., *Le voyage de S. M. l'Empereur Napoléon III en Algérie et la régence de S. M. l'Impératrice, mai–juin 1865* (Paris: E. Pick, 1865), 107–8.

15. Rey-Goldzeiguer, *Royaume arabe*, 73–74; Abdelhamid Zouzou, *L'Aurès au temps de la France coloniale: Évolution politique, économique et sociale (1837–1939)* 1 (Algiers: Éditions Distribution HOUMA, 2001), 483–84.

16. George R. Trumbull IV, *An Empire of Facts: Colonial Power, Cultural Knowledge, and Islam in Algeria, 1870–1914* (Cambridge: Cambridge University Press, 2009), 4–5.

17. Jennifer E. Sessions, *By Sword and Plow: France and the Conquest of Algeria* (Ithaca, NY: Cornell University Press, 2011), 317–19.

18. Frémeaux, *Bureaux arabes*, 249–59.

19. Between 1865 and 1915, Patrick Weil calculates that only 2,396 Algerian Muslims successfully became French. Most of them were military men, civil servants, or Catholic converts. Patrick Weil, *How to Be French: Nationality in the Making Since 1789*, trans. Catherine Porter (Durham, NC: Duke University Press, 2008), 219.

20. Kamel Kateb, *Européens, "indigènes," et juifs en Algérie (1830–1962): Représentations et réalités des populations*, Cahier 145 (Paris: Éditions de l'Institut national d'études démographiques, 2001), 47; Benjamin Claude Brower, *A Desert Named Peace: The Violence of France's Empire in the Algerian Sahara, 1844–1902* (New York: Columbia University Press, 2009), 4–6.

21. Auguste Pomel, *Des races indigènes d'Algérie et du rôle que leur réservent leurs aptitudes* (Oran: Veuve Dagorn, 1871), 31.

22. Bertrand Taithe, "Humanitarianism and Colonialism: Religious Responses to the Algerian Drought and Famine of 1866–1870," in *Natural Disasters, Cultural Responses: Case Studies toward a Global Environmental History*, ed. Christof Mauch and Christian Pfister (Lanham, MD: Lexington, 2009), 137–44.

23. William Gallois, *A History of Violence in the Early Algerian Colony* (New York: Palgrave Macmillan, 2013), 149–71; Grandmaison, "Conquête de l'Algérie," 253–74.

24. Zouzou, *Aurès*, 447–55.

25. Brent Shaw, "Climate, Environment, and History: The Case of Roman North Africa," in *Climate and History: Studies in Past Climates and Their Impact on Man*, ed. T. M. L. Wigley, M. J. Ingram, and G. Farmer (Cambridge: Cambridge University Press, 1981), 390–91; Zouzou, *Aurès*, 479–501.

26. Djilali Sari, *Le désastre démographique* (Algiers: Société nationale d'Édition et Diffusion, 1982), 171–91. A near parallel to this policy was the British export of grain and other foodstuffs from Ireland during the great famine of the late 1840s. Christine Kinealy, *This Great Calamity: The Irish Famine* (Dublin: Gill and Macmillan, 1994).

27. Frémeaux, *Bureaux arabes*, 77–111, 191–227.

28. Sari, *Désastre démographique*, 129–65, 217–21; Kateb, *Européens, "indigènes,"* 58–68.

29. Pomel, *Des races indigènes d'Algérie*, 65–66.

30. Taithe, "Humanitarianism and Colonialism," 144–53.

31. Joann Freed, "Le Père Alfred-Louis Delattre (1850–1932) et les fouilles archéologiques de Carthage," *Histoire, monde et cultures religieuses* 4, no. 8 (2008): 67–100; Jan Jansen, "Karthago und die Pères blancs," in *Das große Spiel: Archäeologie und Politik zur Zeit des Kolonialismus (1860–1940), Ruhr-Museum, Weltkulturerbe Zollverein, Essen, 11. Februar–13. Juni 2010*, ed. Charlotte Trümpler (Cologne: DuMont, 2008), 538–49.

32. Karima Direche-Slimani, *Chrétiens de Kabylie (1873–1954): Une action missionaire dans l'Algérie colonial* (Saint-Denis: Éditions Bouchene, 2004), 9–10, 24–26. Indigenous Christian populations in North Africa had disappeared between the eleventh and thirteenth centuries. Christian Windler, *La diplomatie comme experience de l'autre: Consuls français au Maghreb (1700–1840)* (Geneva: Droz, 2002), 25.

33. Clémentine Gutron, "L'abbé Bourgade (1806–1866), Carthage et l'Orient: De l'antiquaire au publiciste," *Anabases* 2 (2005): 177–91.

34. Ugo Colonna, "La compagnie de Jésus en Algérie (1840–1880): L'exemple de la mission de Kabylie (1863–1880)," *Monde arabe Maghreb Machrek* 135 (January–March 1992): 68–78.

35. "L'affaire du marabout Si-Sadoq-be-Hadj, ce nouveau Jabdas qui vient de soulever une partie des montagnes de l'Aurès, au nom de la foi musulmane, m'a privé du plaisir de prendre une plus large part aux travaux de la Société." Payen, "Inscriptions inédites de la subdivision de Batna," *Annuaire de la Société archéologique de la province de Constantine* 4 (1858–1859): 87.

36. Numa-Denis Fustel de Coulanges, *La cité antique* (Paris: Hachette, 1927), 2.

37. Numa-Denis Fustel de Coulanges, "De la manière d'écrire l'histoire en France et en Allemagne depuis cinquante ans," *Revue des deux mondes* 42 (September 1, 1872): 246–47; Bonnie Effros, "The Germanic Invasions and the Academic Politics of National Identity in Late Nineteenth-Century France," in *Gebrauch und Missbrauch des Mittelalters, 19.–21. Jahrhundert/Uses and Abuses of the Middle Ages, 19th–21st Century/Usages et mésuages du Moyen Age du XIXe au XXIe siècle,* ed. János Bak, Jörg Jarnut, Pierre Monnet, and Bernd Schneidmüller, MittelalterStudien 17 (Munich: Wilhelm Fink, 2009), 81–94.

38. Auguste Cherbonneau, "Rapport sur les fouilles du Krenag (Tiddis et Calda): Inscriptions romaines inédites," *Recueils des notices et mémoires de la Société archéologique de la province de Constantine* (1863): 213.

39. Nabila Oulebsir, "From Ruins to Heritage: The Past Perfect and the Idealized Antiquity in North Africa," in *Multiple Antiquities—Multiple Modernities: Ancient Histories in Nineteenth Century European Cultures,* ed. Gábor Klaniczay, Michael Werner, and Ottó Gecser (Frankfurt: Campus, 2011), 361–62.

40. Josef W. Konvitz, *Cartography in France 1660–1848: Science, Engineering, and Statecraft* (Chicago: University of Chicago Press, 1987).

41. Patricia Lorcin, *Imperial Identities: Stereotyping, Prejudice and Race in Colonial Algeria* (London: I. B. Tauris, 1995), 147–48.

42. Interest in mapmaking was certainly not limited to the French. The start of the Ordnance Survey in Great Britain dated to the period of the French Revolution, when the British began to map their most vulnerable coasts. For more on this topic, see https://www.ordnancesurvey.co.uk/about/overview/history.html.

43. Michael J. Heffernan, "An Imperial Utopia: French Surveys of North Africa in the Early Colonial Period," in *Maps and Africa: Proceedings of a Colloquium at the University of Aberdeen, April 1993,* ed. Jeffrey C. Stone (Aberdeen: Aberdeen University African Studies Group, 1994), 80–107.

44. Ernest Carette, *Exploration scientifique de l'Algérie pendant les années 1840, 1841, 1842,* Sciences historiques et géographiques 1 (Paris: Imprimerie nationale, 1844), iv–v.

45. Michael Greenhalgh, *The Military and Colonial Destruction of the Roman Landscape of North Africa, 1830–1900* (Leiden: Brill, 2014), 248–50.

46. Brower, *Desert Named Peace,* 69–70.

47. Ernest Carette, *Exploration scientifique de l'Algérie pendant les années 1840, 1841, 1842,* Sciences historiques et géographiques 5 (Paris: Imprimerie nationale, 1848); Diana K. Davis, *Resurrecting the Granary of Rome: Environmental History and French Colonial Expansion in North Africa* (Athens: Ohio University Press, 2007), 36–38.

48. Greenhalgh, *Military and Colonial Destruction,* 250–54.

49. Claude-Antoine Rozet and Ernest Carette, *Algérie* (Paris: Firmin Didot, 1850).

50. Frédéric Lacroix, "Colonisation et administration romaines dans l'Afrique septentrionale," *Revue africaine* 41 (1863): 363–83, 415–32; Patricia Lorcin, "Rome and France in Africa: Recovering Colonial Algeria's Latin Past," *French Historical Studies* 25, no. 2 (2002): 308–9.

51. Jacques Frémeaux, "Souvenirs de Rome et présence française au Maghreb: Essai d'investigation," in *Connaissances du Maghreb: Sciences sociales et colonisation,* ed. Jean-Claude Vatin (Paris: CNRS Éditions, 1984), 33–34.

52. Ernest Carette, *Précis historique et archéologique sur Hippone et ses environs* (Paris: Lange Lévy et Cie, 1838). Ancient Roman mile markers were a critical component of Arab cartographic practice just as his own. See Carette, *Exploration scientifique de l'Algérie* 1:lv–lxiii.

53. Charles de Vigneral, *Ruines romaines de l'Algérie, subdivision de Bône, cercle de Guelma* (Paris: J. Claye, 1867); Charles de Vigneral, *Ruines romaines de l'Algérie, Kabylie du Djurdjura* (Paris: J. Claye, 1868).

54. Adolphe Daux, *Recherches sur l'origine et l'emplacement des emporia phéniciens dans le Zeugis et le Byzacium (Afrique septentrionale) faites par ordre de l'Empereur* (Paris: Imprimerie impériale, 1869), 1–15.

55. Myriam Bacha, *Patrimoine et monuments en Tunisie* (Rennes: Presses universitaires de Rennes, 2013), 46.

56. Daux, *Recherches sur l'origine*, 17–19; Lorcin, *Imperial Identities*, 115–16.

57. Paul-Albert Février, *Approches du Maghreb romain: Pouvoirs, différences et conflits* (Aix-en-Provence: ÉDISUD, 1989), 1:54.

58. Alain Schnapp, "L'archéologie en France et en Europe au temps de Napoléon III," *Bulletin de la Société historique de Compiègne* 37 (2001): 23–24.

59. Catherine Granger, *L'empereur et les arts: La liste civile de Napoléon III*, Mémoires et documents de l'École des chartes 79 (Paris: École des chartes, 2005), 7–8, 59.

60. Napoléon III, *Histoire de Jules César*, 3 vols. (Paris: Henri Plon, 1865), 1:vi; Marie-Laure Berdeaux-Le Brazidec, "Aperçu des fouilles et des missions archéologiques sous le Second Empire," *Bulletin de la Société historique de Compiègne* 37 (2001): 153–56.

61. Anne Vatan, "Le camp de Châlons et les fouilles de l'empereur," *Bulletin de la Société historique de Compiègne* 37 (2001): 83–92.

62. Marie-Laure Berdeaux-Le Brazidec, "Napoléon III, le camp de Châlons et l'archéologie en Champagne," *La vie en Champagne* 30 (April–June 2002): 40–43.

63. "The Commission de Topographie des Gaules," http://passes-present.eu/en/themes-research/active-knowledge-past/commission-de-topographie-des-gaules-1858-1879-371; Berdeaux-Le Brazidec, "Aperçu des fouilles," 157–59.

64. Alexandre Bertrand, "Les voies romaines en Gaule: Résumé du travail de la Commission de topographie des Gaules," *Revue archéologique* n.s. 7 (January–June 1863): 406–12.

65. Berdeaux-Le Brazidec, "Aperçu des fouilles," 159–67.

66. Ève Gran-Aymerich, *Naissance de l'archéologie moderne, 1798–1945* (Paris: CNRS Éditions, 1998), 149–50; Pim den Boer, *History as a Profession: The Study of History in France, 1818–1914*, trans. A. J. Pomerans (Princeton, NJ: Princeton University Press, 1998), 80–84; Steven L. Dyson, *In Pursuit of Ancient Pasts: A History of Classical Archaeology in the Nineteenth and Twentieth Centuries* (New Haven: Yale University Press, 2006), 58–59.

67. Letter dated October 1, 1861, from the duc de Malakoff to Napoleon III. The request was for 15,000 francs. Médiathèque d'architecture et des monuments historiques, Charenton-le-Pont 81/99/01 Carton 4, Dossier 85.

68. Cherbonneau, "Rapport sur les fouilles du Krenag," 170–81.

69. SHAT 8 Yd 3378: "Rapport particulier de M. Casimir Cruely, Colonel du génie, Directeur des fortifications" (October 8, 1854).

70. SHAT 8 Yd 3378: Letter dated May 26, 1859, from the minister of public instruction to the minister of war.

71. Casimir Creuly, "Carte de la Gaule: Examen des observations auxquelles elle a donné lieu (part 6)," *Revue archéologique* n.s. 8 (July–December 1863): 400–401; *Commission de la Topographie des Gaules.*

72. Casimir Creuly, "Carte de la Gaule (part 1)," 388.

73. Casimir Creuly, "Carte de la Gaule: Examen des observations auxquelles elle a donné lieu (part 4)," *Revue archéologique* n.s. 8 (July–December 1863): 254–55.

74. In March 1861, Creuly and Bertrand traveled for such purposes and explored the banks of the Sambre and Meuse to understand some of the military positions described by Caesar. Creuly, "Carte de la Gaule (part 1)," 391; Berdeaux-Le Brazidec, "Aperçu des fouilles," 160.

75. Jean Leclant, "Allocation d'ouverture," in *Histoire et archéologie méditerranéennes sous Napoléon III: Actes du 21e colloque de la Villa Kérylos à Beaulieu-sur-Mer les 8 & 9 octobre 2010*, ed. André Laronde, Pierre Toubert, and Jean Leclant, Cahiers de la Villa 'Kérylos' 22 (Paris: Diffusion de Boccard, 2011), vii–xii.

76. The duc d'Aumale wrote under the pseudonym V. de Mars in favor of Alise: "Alésia: Étude sur la séptième campagne de César en Gaule," *Revue des deux mondes* (May 1, 1858): 64–146. See also Joël Le Gall, *Alésia: Archéologie et histoire*, new ed. (Paris: Fayard, 1980), 38–39; and Michel Reddé, *Alésia: L'archéologie face à l'imaginaire* (Paris: Éditions Errance, 2003), 76–81.

77. Raymond de Coynart, "L'Alésia de César laissée à sa place: Lettre à M. J. Quicherat," *Le spectateur militaire* 2e ser., 20 (1857): 70–113, but esp. 88–89 on this point.

78. Lieutenant-Colonel Sarette, "Démonstration militaire du problem d'Alésia," *Mémoires de la Société d'émulation du Doubs*, 4e ser., 2 (1866): 11–69.

79. Indeed, Quicherat was one of the first to lecture on archaeology in France. From 1847, he offered a course on medieval Christian archaeology at the École du Louvre. Marc Smith, "Jules Quicherat," in *L'École nationale des chartes: Histoire de l'École depuis 1821*, ed. Yves-Marie Bercé, Olivier Guyotjeannin, and Marc Smith (Thionville: Gerard Klopp, 1997), 149–50.

80. Joël Le Gall, "Nouveaux apercus sur les fouilles d'Alésia sous le Second Empire," *Comptes rendus des séances de l'Académie des inscriptions et belles-lettres* 105, no. 1 (1961): 73.

81. AD de la Côte-d'Or, 29 T 3a: Letters dated February 14, 1862, and March 29, 1862; Granger, *L'empereur et les arts*, 355.

82. Le Gall, *Alésia*, 42–43.

83. Le Gall, "Nouveaux apercus," 75.

84. Many of these remained forgotten until they were rediscovered in the 1950s. Jacques Harmand, "Les travaux de la Commission de la topographie des Gaules autour d'Alésia et l'album inédit conservé au Musée des antiquités nationales," *Comptes rendus des séances de l'Académie des inscriptions et belles-lettres* 104, no. 1 (1960): 107–15.

85. Bibliothèque de l'Institut de France, Ms. 2655, Pièce 5: Letter dated April 28, 1862, from Casimir Creuly to Alfred Maury on the ongoing excavations at Alésia; Nadia Bayle, "Contribution des officiers français à l'étude archéologique du site d'Alésia," *Revue historique des armées* 167 (1987): 6–18; Reddé, *Alésia*, 83–98.

86. Casimir Creuly, "Carte de la Gaule: Examen des observations auxquelles elle a donné lieu (part 7)," *Revue archéologique* n.s. 8 (July–December 1863): 501, 508.

87. A budget of 8,000 francs was allotted by the emperor for this purpose. AD de la Côte-d'Or, 33 T 15: Letter dated September 16, 1861, and addressed to the prefect of the Côte-d'Or.

88. SHAT 4 Yf 76381: "Eugène-Georges-Henri-Céleste Stoffel, État des services" (August 6, 1872).

89. Bibliothèque de la Service de l'armée de terre à Vincennes, Ms. 66174: Willi Schädler, "Les Barons Stoffel" 1 (1979), 1:53–57, 61–62.

90. SHAT 4 Yf 76381: "Stoffel, État des services."

91. Le Gall, "Nouveaux apercus," 75–76; Le Gall, *Alésia*, 64–71.

92. Harmand, "Travaux de la Commission," 113.

93. Salomon Reinach, "Nécrologie: Le Colonel Stoffel," *Revue archéologique* ser. 3, 17 (January–June 1907): 329–32.

94. Michel Reddé, "Les fouilles du Second Empire autour d'Alésia: À la lumière des recherches récentes," *Bulletin de la Société historique de Compiègne* 37 (2001): 93–116.

95. Ibid., 99–101.

96. Bayle, "Contribution des officiers français," 7–8.

97. Vincent Guichard, "Les recherches archéologiques à Gergovie sous le Second Empire: Quelques notes historiographiques," *Bulletin de la Société historique de Compiègne* 37 (2001): 117–26.

98. Françoise Paquelot and Vincent Guichard, eds., *Sur les traces de César: Enquête archéologique sur les sites de la guerre des Gaules* (Glux-en-Glenne: Musée de Bibracte, 2002), 7. Presumably these were agricultural laborers as had been used by the commission since no specific mention of soldiers was made in contemporary sources.

99. Kurt Böhner, "Die archäologische Erforschung der 'Teufelsmauer': Zum 100-jährigen Bestehen der Reichs-Limes-Kommission," *Nürnberger Blätter zur Archäologie* 9 (1992–1993): 63–76.

100. Dondin-Payre, "Napoléon III," 195.

101. Émile Masqueray, "Rapport à M. le Général Chanzy, Gouverneur-Général de l'Algérie sur la mission dans le sud de la province de Constantine: Thamgad," *Revue africaine* (1876): 164–72.

102. Wendy Doyon, "On Archaeological Labor in Modern Egypt," in *Histories of Egyptology: Interdisciplinary Measures*, ed. William Carruthers (New York: Routledge, 2015), 141–56.

103. Granger, *Empereur et les arts*, 355.

104. Marcel Emerit, *Madame Cornu et Napoléon III d'après les lettres de l'empereur et d'autres documents inédits* (Paris: Les Presses Modernes, 1937), 17–25.

105. Bonnie Effros, "'Elle pensait comme un homme et sentait comme une femme': Hortense Lacroix Cornu (1809–1875) and the Musée des antiquités nationales de Saint-Germain-en-Laye," *Journal of the History of Collections* 24, no. 1 (2012): 25–43; Granger, *Empereur et les arts*, 114.

106. Maxime du Camp, *Souvenirs d'un demi-siècle: Au temps de Louis-Philippe et de Napoléon III, 1830–1870* 1 (Paris: Hachette, 1949), 172–75; Ernest Renan, "Madame Hortense Cornu," in his *Feuilles détachées faisant suite aux souvenirs d'enfance et de jeunesse* (Paris: Calmann Lévy, 1982), 302–21.

107. Maurice Gasnier, ed., *Ernest Renan-Hortense Cornu: Correspondance 1856–1861 (Mission en Phénicie)* (Brest: Centre d'étude des correspondances, 1994), nos. 30, 36, 40, 92–94, 104–6, 112.

108. Bibliothèque de l'Institut de France, Ms. 2650: Alfred Maury, "Souvenirs d'un homme de lettres" 4:232–33; Ève Gran-Aymerich, "Le Musée Napoléon III au Palais de l'industrie, miroir de la politique archéologique du Second Empire," *Bulletin de la Société historique de Compiègne* 37 (2001): 29–47.

109. Jean Pommier, ed., *Un témoignage sur E. Renan: Les "Souvenirs" de L. F. A. Maury* (Paris: Éditions A.-G. Nizet, 1971), 27–28.

110. Alexandre Bertrand and Casimir Creuly, trans., *Commentaires de Jules César: Guerre des Gaules* (Paris: Didier et Cie., 1865).

111. Maury, *Souvenirs d'un homme de lettres* 4:2; Victor Duruy, *Notes et souvenirs (1811–1894)* (Paris: Hachette et Cie, 1901), 1:108–10.

112. One of Froehner's tasks was to correct the emperor's Latin errors. La Comtesse de Rohan-Chabot, ed., *Souvenirs de Froehner* (Nogent-le-Rotrou: Imprimerie de Daupeley-Gouverneur, 1931), 4–15; Michèle Bouron and Christiane Lyon-Caen, "202bis: Histoire de Jules César," in *Vercingétorix et Alésia: Saint-Germain-en-Laye. Musée des Antiquités nationales 29 mars–18 juillet 1994* (Paris: Réunion des Musées nationaux, 1994), 239.

113. Elisabeth Rabeisen, "Les hommes de l'empereur ou les pionniers des Antiquités nationales," in *Vercingétorix et Alésia*, 240–43; Marie-Laure Berdeaux-Le Brazidec, "L'archéologie au service de l'empereur," in *Prosper Mérimée au temps de Napoléon III: Actes du colloque organisé au Musée national du château de Compiègne le 18 octobre 2003* (Paris: Éditions de la Réunion des musées nationaux, 2008), 75–90; Den Boer, *History as a Profession*, 80–84; Gran-Aymerich, *Naissance de l'archéologie moderne*, 142; Du Camp, *Souvenirs* 1:139–40.

114. One of the few in this period to propose a far more negative image of the Roman emperors was Ernest Beulé, who composed four volumes on the emperors of the Principate between 1867 and 1870. He wisely omitted discussion of Julius Caesar from his publication. Christophe Chandezon, "Ernest Beulé (1826–1874): Archéologie classique, histoire romaine et vie politique sous Napoléon III," in *L'hellénisme, d'une rive à l'autre de la Méditerranée: Mélanges offerts à André Laronde* (Paris: De Boccard, 2012), 42–44.

115. MAN Archives, Carton 2: "Précis-verbaux de la Commission consultative pour l'organisation du Musée gallo-romain de Saint-Germain," dated from April 1, 1865 to January 8, 1866; Hélène Chew, "Les échanges archéologiques internationaux au XIXe siècle: L'exemple d'Alexandre Bertrand et du musée des Antiquités nationales," in *Les dépôts de l'État au XIXe siècle: Politiques patrimoniales et destins d'oeuvres (Colloque du 8 décembre 2007)* (Paris: Ministère de la culture et de la communication, 2008), 125–37.

116. Granger, *Empereur et les arts*, 358–62.

117. BNF Ms. Fr. N.A. 1066, Letter I.24: Letter dated February 20, 1842, from Louis-Napoleon to Hortense Cornu; Napoléon-Louis Bonaparte, *Études sur le passé et l'avenir de l'artillerie* (Paris: J. Dumaine, 1846), xii.

118. Hélène Chew, "Les machines de guerre de Verchère de Reffye et l'expérimentation archéologique sous le Second Empire," *Bulletin de la Société historique de Compiègne* 37 (2001): 211–24.

119. Auguste Verchère de Reffye, "Les armes d'Alise," *Revue archéologique* 10 (1864): 337–49. Bayle, "Contribution des officiers francais," 14–15.

120. Chew, "Machines de guerre," 224–31.

121. MAN Archives, Carton 2: Rapport de la Commission consultative pour l'organisation du Musée de Saint-Germain, undated.

122. Patricia Larrouy, "Le Musée de Saint-Germain sous la Troisième République," *Bulletin archéologique du Comité des travaux historiques et scientifiques* 28 (2001): 26–27; Bonnie Effros, *Uncovering the Germanic Past: Merovingian Archaeology in France, 1830–1914* (Oxford: Oxford University Press, 2012), 272–73.

123. A. Moll, "Mémoire historique et archéologique sur Tébessa (Théveste) et ses environs," *Annuaire de la Société de la province de Constantine* (1858–1859): 26–86.

124. Commandant Sériziat, "La basilique de Tébessa," *Recueil des notices et mémoires de la Société de la province de Constantine* 12 (1868): 473–77.

125. Commandant Clarinval, "Rapport sur les fouilles faites à la basilique de Tébessa pendant l'année 1870," *Recueil des notices et mémoires de la Société de la province de Constantine* 14 (1870): 605–11.

126. William H. C. Frend, *The Archaeology of Early Christianity: A History* (Minneapolis: Fortress Press, 1996), 60–62.

127. Claude-Antoine Rozet, *Voyage dans la Régence d'Alger ou Description du pays occupé par l'armée française en Afrique* (Paris: Arthus Bertrand, 1833), 1:11.

128. Gran-Aymerich, *Naissance de l'archéologie moderne*, 150–52.

129. Gabriel Camps, *Aux origines de la Berbérie: Monuments et rites funéraires protohistoriques* (Paris: Arts et métiers graphiques, 1961), 13–14.

130. Lorcin, *Imperial Identities*, 116–20; Frémeaux, *Bureaux arabes*, 46–48.

131. Frémeaux, *Bureaux arabes*, 51–53.

132. Zouzou, *Aurès*, 355.

133. Ann Laura Stoler, *Along the Archival Grain: Epistemic Anxieties and Colonial Common Sense* (Princeton, NJ: Princeton University Press, 2009), 1–22; Frémeaux, *Bureaux arabes*, 56–67.

134. Alice L. Conklin, *A Mission to Civilize: The Republican Idea of Empire in France and West Africa, 1895–1930* (Stanford, CA: Stanford University Press, 1997).

135. Gary Wilder, *The French Imperial Nation-State: Negritude and Colonial Humanism between the Two World Wars* (Chicago: University of Chicago Press, 2005).

136. For a more detailed account of these events, and their implications for craniological studies in the 1870s and 1880s, see Bonnie Effros, "Berber Genealogy and the Politics of Prehistoric Archaeology and Craniology in French Algeria (1860s to 1880s)," *British Journal of the History of Science* 50, no. 1 (2017): 61–81, doi:10.1017/S0007087417000024.

137. For Féraud's biography, see Nora Lafi, "Biographie de Laurent-Charles Féraud: Une passion coloniale," in *Laurent-Charles Féraud: Peintre et témoin de la conquête de l'Algérie*, ed. Bernard Merlin (Saint-Rémy-en-l'Eau: Éditions Monelle Hayot, 2010), 103–8; and L. Paysant, "Un président de la Société historique algérienne," *Revue africaine* 55 (1911): 5–15.

138. Laurent-Charles Féraud, "Monuments dits celtiques dans la province de Constantine," *Recueil des notices et mémoires de la Société archéologique de la Province de Constantine* 1 (1863): 214–34.

139. Laurent-Charles Féraud, *Les interprètes de l'armée d'Afrique (Archives du corps)* (Algiers: A. Jourdan, 1876), 141–43.

140. James Malarkey, "The Dramatic Structure of Scientific Discovery in Colonial Algeria: A Critique of the Journal of the 'Société archéologique de Constantine' (1853–1876)," in *Connaissances du Maghreb*, 153.

141. Féraud, "Monuments dits celtiques," 229–30.

142. Laurent-Charles Féraud, "Notes historiques sur les tribus de la province de Constantine," *Recueil des notes et mémoires de la Société archéologique de la province de Constantine* 13 (1869): 1–68.

143. Laurent-Charles Féraud, "Recherches sur les monuments dits celtiques de la province de Constantine," *Revue archéologique* n.s. 11 (January–June 1865): 202–17.

144. Alexandre Bertrand, "Monuments dits celtiques dans la province de Constantine," *Revue archéologique*, n.s. 8 (July–December 1863): 519–30.

145. Daux, *Recherches sur l'origine*, 26–37.

146. M. Laumonier, "Essai sur l'histoire ethnologique des races préhistoriques de la France," *Bulletin de la Société des antiquaires de l'Ouest* 4 (1879): 540–41.

147. Paul Topinard, "Instructions particulières," in *Instructions sur l'anthropologie de l'Algérie*, ed. Léon Faidherbe (Paris: A. Hennuyer, 1874), 50–51.

148. Frédéric Troyon, "Lettre à M. A. Bertrand sur l'attitude repliée dans les sépultures antiques," *Revue archéologique* n.s. 9 (January–June 1864): 289–99.

149. Laurent-Charles Féraud, *Exposition universelle de Paris en 1878: Algérie. Archéologie et histoire* (Algiers: Adolphe Jourdan, 1878), 18.

150. Féraud, "Recherches sur les monuments," 217.

151. Trumbull, *Empire of Facts*, 11–17.

152. Lafi, "Biographie," 104–6.

153. Michael Brett and Elizabeth Fentress, *The Berbers* (Oxford: Blackwell, 1996), 14–17.

154. Lorcin, *Imperial Identities*, 118–19.

155. Paul Topinard, "De la race indigène, ou race berbère, en Algérie," *Revue d'anthropologie* 3 (1874): 491–98.

156. Abi-Mershed, *Apostles of Modernity*, 199–204.

157. Archives des Musées nationaux, Musée du Louvre A4: October 24–25, 1865.

158. Ahmed Koumas and Chéhrazade Nafa, *L'Algérie et son patrimoine: Dessins français du XIXe siècle* (Paris: Monum, Éditions du patrimoine, 2003), 152.

159. Adrien Berbrugger, "Le Tombeau de la Chrétienne, première partie," *Revue africaine* 11 (1867): 1–3.

160. Adrien Berbrugger, "Le Tombeau de la Chrétienne d'après Shaw et Bruce," *Revue africaine* 10 (1866): 441–50.

161. Berbrugger, "Tombeau de la Chrétienne, première partie," 11–28.

162. Adrien Berbrugger, "Le Tombeau de la Chrétienne, 2e article," *Revue africaine* 11 (1867): 97–112; Dondin-Payre, "Napoléon III," 201–10.

163. Monique Dondin-Payre, "L'Académie des inscriptions et belles-lettres et la photographie: Les fouilles du Tombeau de la chrétienne au XIXe siècle," *Comptes-rendus des séances de l'Académie des inscriptions et belles-lettres* 147, no. 3 (2003): 1139–40.

164. Monique Dondin-Payre, "Le premier reportage photographique archéologique en Afrique du Nord: Les fouilles du Tombeau de la Chrétienne en 1855–56," in *L'Africa romana XIV: Atti del XIV convegno di studio, Sassari, 7–10 dicembre 2000*, ed. Mustapha Khanoussi, Paola Ruggeri, and Cinzia Vismara (Rome: Carocci, 2002), 2119–21.

165. Berbrugger, "Tombeau de la Chrétienne, première partie," 19–22.

166. Becker died later the same year in Batna. F. Becker, "Essai sur le Madr'asen," *Annuaire de la Société archéologique de la province de Constantine* (1854–1855): 108–18.

167. Colonel Foy, "Notice archéologique sur Madrazen," *Annuaire de la Société archéologique de la province de Constantine* (1856–1857): 58–69; Gabrielle Camps, "Nouvelles observations sur l'architecture et l'âge du Medracen, mausolée royal de Numidie," *Comptes-rendus des séances de l'Académie des inscriptions et belles-lettres* 117, no. 3 (1973): 470–71, 473–76.

168. Adrien Berbrugger, *Le Tombeau de la Chrétienne: Mausolée des rois mauritaniens de la dernière dynastie* (Algiers: Bastide, 1867), 55–56.

169. Adrien Berbrugger, "Exploration du Tombeau de la Chrétienne," *Revue africaine* 1 (1856): 31–38.

170. Jean-Joseph-Gustav Cler, *Reminiscences of an Officer of the Zouaves* (New York: D. Appleton and Co., 1860), 3–4.

171. Monique Dondin-Payre, "Une étape méconnue de l'histoire du Tombeau de la Chrétienne: Les premières fouilles (1855–1856)," in *Ubique amici: Mélanges offerts à Jean-Marie Lassère*, ed. Christine Hamdoune (Montpellier: Université Paul-Valéry, CERCAM, 2001), 87–99.

172. Léon Renier, *Instructions pour la recherche des antiquités en Algérie* (Paris: L. Hachette et Cie, 1859), 11.

173. Calotypes were also used by Victor Place to document Assyrian excavations at Khorsabad from 1852 to 1855. Those by Greene that survive are today preserved at the Bibliothèque de l'Institut de France with associated correspondence from Berbrugger to the Académie des inscriptions et belles-lettres. Dondin-Payre, "Premier reportage photographique archéologique," 2120–46.

174. Dondin-Payre, "Académie des inscriptions," 1139–57.

175. Adrien Berbrugger, "Tombeau de la Chrétienne," *Revue africaine* 9 (1865): 240; Adrien Berbrugger, "Travaux du Tombeau de la Chrétienne," *Revue africaine* 10 (1866): 137–39.

176. One of these men, named Morel, died at the site in April 1866. Adrien Berbrugger, "Tombeau de la Chrétienne, deuxième partie: Travaux d'exploration du monument et résultats obtenus," *Revue africaine* 11 (1867): 205–6.

177. Adrien Berbrugger, "Chronique," *Revue africaine* 9 (1865): 475–76; Adrien Berbrugger, "Tombeau de la Chrétienne," *Revue africaine* 10 (1866): 161; Monique Dondin-Payre, "Napoléon III et l'archéologie algérienne," *Bulletin de la Société historique de Compiègne* 37 (2001): 198, 201–10.

178. Marcel Christofle, *Le Tombeau de la Chrétienne* (Paris: Arts et métiers graphiques, 1951), 39–40.

179. Berbrugger, *Tombeau de la Chrétienne*, 68–71.

180. Ibid., 71–93.

181. Adrien Berbrugger, "Exploration du Tombeau de la Chrétienne," *Revue africaine* 10 (1866): 208–20.

182. Raymund F. Wood, "Berbrugger, Forgotten Founder of Algerian Librarianship," *Journal of Library History* 5, no. 3 (1970): 249–51.

183. Berbrugger, "Tombeau de la Chrétienne, première partie," 29–31.

184. Berbrugger, *Tombeau de la Chrétienne*, 31–33.

185. Berbrugger, "Tombeau de la Chrétienne, première partie," 31–40.

186. On the condition of the monument in the early to mid-nineteenth century and the restoration work that followed, see Christofle, *Tombeau de la Chrétienne*. For a somewhat more recent publication on the state of the monument, see Mounir Bouchenaki, *Le mausolée royal de Maurétanie*, trans. Abdelhamid Hadjiat (Algiers: Direction des affaires culturelles, 1970).

187. Berbrugger, "Tombeau de la Chrétienne, deuxième partie: Travaux," 177–98.

188. Berbrugger, "Tombeau de la Chrétienne, deuxième partie: Travaux," 199.

189. The development of more formal nodes of tourism in the Maghreb lay another thirty years in the future. Myriam Bacha, "Patrimoine et tourisme en Tunisie au début du Protectorat: Interactions et dépendances," in *Le tourisme dans l'empire français: Politiques, pratiques et imaginaires (XIXe–XXe siècles). Un outil de la domination coloniale?* (Paris: Publications de la Société française d'histoire d'outre-mer, 2009), 155–63.

190. Berbrugger, "Tombeau de la Chrétienne, deuxième partie: Travaux," 199–200.

191. Berbrugger, "Travaux du Tombeau de la Chrétienne," 137–39; Adrien Berbrugger, "Le Tombeau de la Chrétienne," *Revue africaine* 10 (1866): 471. Adrien Berbrugger, "Modèle de Tombeau de la Chrétienne," *Revue africaine* 12 (1868): 404–5.

192. Adrien Berbrugger, "L'archéologie au Conseil général: Tombeau de la Chrétienne," *Revue africaine* 10 (1866): 393–95.

Epilogue

1. Osama W. Abi-Mershed, *Apostles of Modernity: Saint-Simonians and the Civilizing Mission in Algeria* (Stanford, CA: Stanford University Press, 2010), 199–201; Claude Collot, *Les institutions de l'Algérie durant la période coloniale (1830–1962)* (Paris: CNRS Éditions, 1987), 10–11.

2. Jamil M. Abun-Nasr, *A History of the Maghrib*, 2nd ed. (Cambridge: Cambridge University Press, 1975), 253–55.

3. Abi-Mershed, *Apostles of Modernity*, 202–3.

4. Abu-Nasr, *History of the Maghrib*, 255–56.

5. Michael J. Heffernan and Keith Sutton, "The Landscape of Colonialism: The Impact of French Colonial Rule on the Algerian Rural Settlement Pattern, 1830–1987," in *Colonialism and Development in the Contemporary World*, ed. Chris Dixon and Michael J. Heffernan (New York: Mansell, 1991), 132–33; Peter Dunwoodie, *Writing French Algeria* (Oxford: Clarendon, 1998), 17–18; Collot, *Institutions de l'Algérie*, 10.

6. Very few native Algerians, by contrast, emigrated from Algeria to France in the 1870s and 1880s. Alain Gillette and Abdelmalek Sayad, *L'immigration algérienne en France,* 2nd ed. (Paris: Entente, 1984), 31, 39–41.

7. Patricia Lorcin, *Imperial Identities: Stereotyping, Prejudice and Race in Colonial Algeria* (London: I. B. Tauris, 1995), 7–9.

8. Sarah Abrevaya Stein, *Saharan Jews and the Fate of French Algeria* (Chicago: University of Chicago Press, 2014).

9. Pierre Nora, *Les français d'Algérie* (Paris: René Julliard, 1961), 92–93; Abi-Mershed, *Apostles of Modernity*, 204–5.

10. Amelia H. Lyons, *The Civilizing Mission in the Metropole: Algerian Families and the French Welfare State during Decolonization* (Stanford, CA: Stanford University Press, 2013), 22–24.

11. David Prochaska, *Making Algeria French: Colonialism in Bône, 1870–1920* (Cambridge: Cambridge University Press, 1990), 1–25; Abu-Nasr, *History of the Maghrib*, 256–58.

12. Lorcin, *Imperial Identities*, 8–10, 167–72.

13. ANOM F 80 1733: Letter dated May 15, 1872, from the minister of public instruction to the minister of the interior.

14. Médiathèque de l'architecture et des monuments historiques, Charenton-le-Pont 80/1/119 Carton 1: Edmond Duthoit, "Rapport sur les monuments historiques de l'Algérie: Architecture musulmane dans la province d'Oran" (1875).

15. AN Pierrefitte 17 F 2920: Letters dated March 24 and 27, 1873, from Antoine Héron de Villefosse to the director of beaux-arts. Héron de Villefosse would later take a mission to Tunisia (1874) and a second one to Algeria (1877).

16. Ève and Jean Gran-Aymerich, "La création des Écoles française d'Athènes, Rome et Madrid," in *Les débuts des sciences de l'homme*, ed. Bernard-Pierre Lécuyer and Benjamin Matalon, Communications 56 (Paris: Seuil, 1992), 175–87.

17. Myriam Bacha, "La création des institutions patrimoniales de Tunisie: oeuvre des savants de l'Académie des inscriptions et belles-lettres et des fonctionnaires du ministère de l'instruction publique et des beaux-arts," *Livraisons d'histoire de l'architecture* 12, no. 2 (2006): 123–34; Myriam Bacha, *Patrimoine et monuments en Tunisie* (Rennes: Presses universitaires de Rennes, 2013), 42.

18. Ève Gran-Aymerich, "Épigraphie française et allemande au Maghreb: Entre collaboration et rivalité (1830–1914)," *Mitteilungen des Deutschen archäologischen Instituts, Römische Abteilung* 117 (2011): 585–87.

19. Ève Gran-Aymerich, "Theodor Mommsen (1817–1903) et ses correspondants français: La 'fabrique' internationale de la science," *Journal des savants* 1, no. 1 (2008): 197–99.

20. Gustav Wilmanns, "Étude sur le camp et la ville de Lambèse," *Bulletin trimestriel des antiquités africaines* 1 (1882): 185–200. Gustav Wilmanns, *Inscriptiones africae latinae*, in Corpus inscriptionum latinarum (Berlin: Apud Georgium Reimerum, 1881), 8, part 1:xv–xxxii.

21. AN Pierrefitte 17 F 2920: Letter dated March 24, 1873, from Antoine Héron de Villefosse to the director of beaux-arts.

22. AN Pierrefitte 17 F 2975: Letter dated November 1, 1873, from Antoine Héron de Villefosse to the minister of public instruction.

23. AN Pierrefitte 17 F 2920: Letter dated April 17, 1873, from Antoine Héron de Villefosse to Léon Renier.

24. Médiathèque de l'architecture et des monuments historiques, Charenton-le-Pont 81/99/01, Carton 4, Dossier 96: Letter dated August 7, 1880; Nabila Oulebsir, *Les usages du patrimoine: Monuments, musées et politique coloniale en Algérie (1830–1930)* (Paris: Éditions de la Maison des sciences de l'homme, 2004), 325.

25. Médiathèque de l'architecture et des monuments historiques, Charenton-le-Pont 80/1/119 Carton 1: "Note sur la repartition et l'emploi de crédit des 50.000 francs, ouvert sur l'exercises de 1880 pour la conservation des Monuments historiques en Algérie" (December 8, 1879).

26. ANOM 60 S 1: Letter dated December 3, 1876, from Oscar MacCarthy to the governor-general of Algeria. It was accompanied by the report "Note sur l'importance des antiquités de l'Algérie et sur l'intérêt que nous avons à les conserver."

27. AN Pierrefitte F 17 2828: Letter dated March 1, 1877, from the head of the archaeological division of the Comité des travaux historiques to the director of beaux-arts of the Ministry of Public Instruction, and letter dated March 13, 1877, from the director of beaux-arts to the president of the Commission du projet de loi pour la conservation des monuments historiques.

28. Médiathèque de l'architecture et des monuments historiques, Charenton-le-Pont 81/99/01: Arrêté of February 12, 1887, from the Ministry of Public Instruction.

29. Théophile Ducrocq, *La loi du 30 mars 1887 et les décrets du 3 janvier 1889 sur la conservation des monuments et objets mobiliers présentant un intérêt national au point de vue de l'histoire ou de l'art* (Paris: Alphonse Picard, 1889), 51.

30. Archives de la Société des Missionaires d'Afrique (A.G.M.Afr.) B4-1: "Lettre circulaire de Monseigneur l'archevêque d'Alger au clergé de son diocèse relativement aux recherches archéologiques recommandés par le Concile Provincial d'Alger et Ordonnance portant création d'une commission diocésaine d'archéologie" (March 19, 1877).

31. Ahmed Koumas and Chéhrazade Nafa, *L'Algérie et son patrimoine: Dessins français du XIXe siècle* (Paris: Monum, Éditions du patrimoine, 2003), 69.

32. Paul-Albert Février, *Approches du Maghreb romain: Pouvoirs, différences et conflits* 1 (Aix-en-Provnce: ÉDISUD, 1989), 54.

33. Oulebsir, *Usages du patrimoine*, 180–81; Margarita Díaz-Andreu, *A World History of Nineteenth-Century Archaeology: Nationalism, Colonialism, and the Past* (Oxford: Oxford University Press, 2007), 270.

34. Médiathèque de l'architecture et des monuments historiques, Charenton-le-Pont 80/1/121 Carton 3: Personnel files for guardians of Lambaesis, Tombeau de la Chrétienne, Thamugadis, Djémila, and Tébessa during the 1880s, 1890s, and early 1900s.

35. Émile Masqueray, "Rapport à M. le Général Chanzy, gouverneur-général de l'Algérie sur la mission dans le sud de la province de Constantine: Thamgad," *Revue africaine* 20 (1876): 164–72.

36. Février, *Approches du Maghreb romaine*, 54.

37. Lorcin, *Imperial Identities*, 189–92.

38. AN Pierrefitte 17 F 2975: Letter dated March 19, 1874, from the minister of public instruction to Antoine Héron de Villefosse.

39. Of the 1,400 or so artifacts salvaged, only about 102 of the pieces, roughly 5 percent, were relatively intact. Bacha, *Patrimoine et monuments*, 46–48.

40. Myriam Bacha, "La constitution d'une notion patrimoniale en Tunisie, XIXe et XXe siècle: Émergence et apport des disciplines de l'archéologie et de l'architecture," in *Chantiers et défis de la recherche sur le Maghreb contemporain*, ed. Pierre-Robert Baduel (Paris: Karthala, 2009), 159–78; William H. C. Frend, *The Archaeology of Early Christianity: A History* (Minneapolis: Fortress Press, 1996), 69–72.

41. A.G.M.Afr B.3/631-1: Letter dated December 27, 1875, from Alfred-Louis Delattre at Saint Louis de Carthage to Archbishop Charles Lavigerie in Algiers.

42. *Notice sommaire des principaux monuments dans le Département des médailles et antiques de la Bibliothèque nationale* (Paris: Imprimerie nationale, 1889), 5.

43. Joann Freed, "Le père Alfred-Louis Delattre (1850–1932) et les fouillles archéologiques de Carthage," *Histoire, monde et cultures religieuses* 4, no. 8 (2008): 71–73; Jan Jansen, "Karthago und die Pères Blancs," in *Das große Spiel: Archäeologie und Politik zur Zeit des Kolonialismus (1860–1940)*, ed. Charlotte Trümpler (Cologne: DuMont, 2008), 538–49; Bacha, *Patrimoine et monuments*, 52–53.

44. Clémentine Gutron, *L'archéologie en Tunisie (XIXe–XXe siècles): Jeux généalogiques sur l'Antiquité* (Paris: Karthala, 2010), 32.

45. Zainab Bahrani, Zeynep Çelik and Edhem Eldem, "Introduction: Archaeology and Empire," in *Scramble for the Past: A Story of Archaeology in the Ottoman Empire, 1753–1914*, ed. Zainab Bahrani, Zeynep Çelik and Edhem Eldem (Istanbul: SALT, 2011), 13.

46. Wendy Shaw, "From Mausoleum to Museum: Resurrecting Antiquity for Ottoman Modernity," in *Scramble for the Past*, 423–41.

47. François Baratte, "Une curieuse expédition archéologique en Tunisie: La mission Hérisson," *La revue du Louvre et des musées de France* 21, no. 1 (1971): 335–46; Bacha, *Patrimoine et monuments*, 50–51.

48. Charles Picard, "Éloge funèbre de M. Émile Espérandieu, membre libre de l'Académie," *Comptes-rendus des séances de l'Académie des inscriptions et belles-lettres* 83, no. 2 (1939): 161–72.

49. Février, *Approches du Maghreb romaine*, 55.

50. Bruce G. Trigger, "Alternative Archaeologies: Nationalist, Colonialist, Imperialist," *Man* n.s. 19 (1989): 355–70.

51. Marcel Bénabou, "L'impérialisme et l'Afrique du Nord: Le modèle romain," in *Sciences de l'homme et conquête coloniale: Constitution et usages des sciences humaines en Afrique (XIXe–XXe siècles)*, ed. Daniel Nordman and Jean-Pierre Raison (Paris: Presses de l'École normale supérieure, 1980), 15–22.

52. Stefan Altekamp, "Modelling Roman North Africa: Advances, Obsessions and Deficiencies of Colonial Archaeology in the Maghreb," in *Under Western Eyes: Approches occidentales de l'archéologie nord-africaine (XIXe–XXe siècle)*, ed. Hédi Dridi and Antonella Mezzolani Andreose (Bologne: BraDypUS, 2016), 19–42.

53. Elliott Colla, *Conflicted Antiquities: Egyptology, Egypomania, Egyptian Modernity* (Durham, NC: Duke University Press, 2007), 16–19.

54. *Instructions pour la conduite des fouilles archéologiques en Algérie* (Algiers: Typographie Adolphe Jourdan, 1901).

55. Salomon Reinach et al., *Recherches des antiquités dans le nord de l'Afrique: Conseils aux archéologues et voyageurs* (Paris: Ernest Leroux, 1929), 1–34.

56. Díaz-Andreu, *World History of Nineteenth-Century Archaeology*, 6–9.

57. René Cagnat, *L'armée romaine d'Afrique et l'occupation militaire de l'Afrique sous les empereurs* (Paris: Imprimerie nationale, 1892).

58. Chris Gosden, *Anthropology and Archaeology: A Changing Relationship* (New York: Routledge, 1999), 58–61.

59. Nacéra Benseddik, "Lambaesis-Lambèse/Tazoult. Grandeur et décadence," in *L'affirmation de l'identité dans l'Algérie antique et médiévale: Combats et résistances. Hommage à Kadria Fatima Kadra* (Algiers: Centre national de recherche en archéologie, 2014), 111–19; Corisande Fenwick, "Archaeology and the Search for Authenticity: Colonialist, Nationalist, and Berberist Visions of an Algerian Past," in *TRAC 2007: Proceedings of the 17th Annual Theoretical Roman Archaeology Conference*, ed. Corisande Fenwick, Meredith Wiggins, and Dave Wythe (Oxford: Oxbow, 2008), 75–88; Gutron, *Archéologie en Tunisie (XIXe–XXe siècles)*.

60. Nadia Abu El-Haj, *Facts on the Ground: Archaeological Practice and Territorial Self-Fashioning in Israeli Society* (Chicago: University of Chicago Press, 2001); Talinn Grigor, "'They Have Not Changed in 2,500 Years': Art, Archaeology, and Modernity in Iran," in *Unmasking Ideology: The Vocabulary, Symbols, and Legacy of Imperial and Colonial Archaeology*, ed. Bonnie Effros and Guolong Lai (Los Angeles: Cotsen Institute of Archaeology Press, in press).

61. Lynn Meskell, "Gridlock: UNESCO, Global Conflict and Failed Ambitions," *World Archaeology* 47, no. 2 (2015): 225–38.

BIBLIOGRAPHY

Archival Sources

Archives de la Société des Missionaires d'Afrique (A.G.M.Afr.), Rome — A16 251; B3/631-1; B4-1

Archives de l'Institut de France, Paris: Archives de l'Académie des inscriptions et belles-lettres (AIBL) — E 352; E 359; E 361

Archives départementales (AD) de Calvados, Caen, France: Legs Travers (1941) — F 6034; F 6040

Archives départementales (AD) de la Côte-d'Or, Dijon, France — 1 J 2447/11; 29 T 3a; 33 T 15

Archives des Musées Nationaux, Musée du Louvre, Paris (recently transferred to the Archives nationales de France (Pierrefittes) and reclassified) — Séries A4; A8

Archives nationales (AN) de Pierrefitte, Pierrefitte-sur-Seine cedex, France — F 17 2828; F 17 2920; F 17 2975; F 17 3510/1; F 17 17213

Archives nationales d'Outre-Mer (ANOM), Aix-en-Provence, France	ALG GGA N2; ALG GGA N3; FM 5 80 1595; 60 S 1; 80 F 1586; 80 F 1587; 80 F 1588; 80 F 1589; 80 F 1595; 80 F 1733
Bibliothèque de l'Arsenal, Paris	Ms. 15462
Bibliothèque de la Service de l'armée de terre à Vincennes, Vicennes, France	Ms. 66174
Bibliothèque de l'Institut de France, Paris	Ms. 1369A and B; Ms. 1935; Ms. 2650; Ms. 2655; Ms. 7453, Ms. Folio Z154D
Bibliothèque littéraire Jacques Doucet, Paris	Ms. 45138
Bibliothèque nationale de France (BNF), Paris	Ms. Fr. N.A. 1066
Médiathèque de l'architecture et des monuments historiques, Charenton-le-Pont, France	80/1/119; 80/1/121; 81/99/01
Musée d'archéologie nationale (MAN): Archives, Saint-Germain-en-Laye, France	Carton 2
Musée de l'armée, Paris	Ms. M 737
Services historiques de l'armée de Vincennes (SHAT), Vincennes, France	1 H 9-3; 1 H 14-2; 1 H 30-1; 1 H 41-3; 1 H 43-3; 1 H 48-3; 1 H 50-1; 1 H 74-1; 1 H 76-1; 1 H 86-2; 1 H 92-1; 1 M 8821; 1 M 1314; 1 M 1316; 1 M 1317; 1 M 1319; 4 Yf 76381; 6 Yd 39; 6 Yd 52; 7 Yd 1208; 7 Yd 1256; 7 Yd 1363; 7 Yd 1526; 8 Yd 3268; 8 Yd 3356; 8 Yd 3378

Primary Printed Sources

Apuleius. *Apologia*. Edited and translated by Paul Valette. 2nd ed. Paris: Les Belles Lettres, 2002.

Azan, Paul. *L'Armée d'Afrique de 1830 à 1852*. Paris: Plon, 1936.

Bard, Joseph. *L'Algérie en 1854: Itinéraire général de Tunis à Tanger*. Paris: L. Maison, 1854.

Barnéond, M. "Rapport adressé à M. le préfet sur les recherches exécutées à Lambèse en 1865." *Recueil des notices et mémoires de la Société archéologique de la province de Constantine* 10 (1866): 239–61.

"Bateau romain découvert à Cherchell." *Revue archéologique* 1, no. 2 (1844–1845): 696.

Becker, F. "Essai sur le Madr'asen." *Annuaire de la Société archéologique de la province de Constantine* 2 (1854–1855): 108–18.

Belloc, Alexis. *La télégraphie historique: Depuis les temps les plus reculés jusqu'à nos jours*. 2nd ed. Paris: Firmin Didot, 1894.

Berbrugger, Adrien. "L'Afrique septentrionale après le partage du monde romain en Empire d'Orient et Empire d'Occident." *Revue africaine* 1, no. 2 (1856): 81–88.

——. *Algérie historique, pittoresque et monumentale ou Recueil de vues, costumes, et portraits faits d'après nature dans les provinces d'Alger, Bône, Constantine et Oran.* 3 vols. Paris: Chez J. Delehaye, 1843.

——. "L'archéologie au Conseil général: Tombeau de la Chrétienne." *Revue africaine* 10 (1866): 393–95.

——. *Bibliothèque-Musée d'Alger : Livret explicatif des collections diverses de ces deux établissements.* Algiers : Imprimerie Bastiede, 1861.

——. "Chronique." *Revue africaine* 9 (1865): 475–76.

——. "Exploration du Tombeau de la Chrétienne." *Revue africaine* 1 (1856): 31–38.

——. "Exploration du Tombeau de la Chrétienne." *Revue africaine* 10 (1866): 208–20.

——. "Introduction." *Revue africaine* 1, no. 1 (1856): 3–11.

——. "Modèle de Tombeau de la Chrétienne." *Revue africaine* 12 (1868): 404–5.

——. "Origines de la Société historique algérienne." *Revue africaine* 6 (1862): 218–21.

——. "Tombeau de la Chrétienne." *Revue africaine* 9 (1865): 240; 10 (1866): 161.

——. "Le Tombeau de la Chrétienne." *Revue africaine* 10 (1866): 471.

——. "Le Tombeau de la Chrétienne d'après Shaw et Bruce." *Revue africaine* 10 (1866): 441–50.

——. "Le Tombeau de la Chrétienne, 2e article." *Revue africaine* 11 (1867): 97–112.

——. "Tombeau de la Chrétienne, deuxième partie: Travaux d'exploration du monument et résultats obtenus." *Revue africaine* 11 (1867): 177–206.

——. *Le Tombeau de la Chrétienne: Mausolée des rois mauritaniens de la dernière dynastie.* Algiers: Bastide, 1867.

——. "Le Tombeau de la Chrétienne, première partie." *Revue africaine* 11 (1867): 5–48.

——. "Travaux du Tombeau de la Chrétienne." *Revue africaine* 10 (1866): 137–39.

Berthézène, Pierre. *Dix-huit mois à Alger.* Montpellier: Chez August Ricard, 1834.

Bertrand, Alexandre. "Monuments dits celtiques dans la province de Constantine." *Revue archéologique*, n.s. 8 (1863): 519–30.

——. "Les voies romaines en Gaule: Résumé du travail de la Commission de topographie des Gaules." *Revue archéologique* n.s. 7 (1863): 406–12.

Bertrand, Alexandre, and Casimir Creuly, trans. *Commentaires de Jules César: Guerre des Gaules.* Paris: Didier et Cie, 1865.

Beury, M. "Note sur les ruines de Lambèse en 1852." *Recueil des notices et mémoires de la Société archéologique de la province de Constantine* ser. 3, 7 (1893): 95–103.

Blinière, M., de. "Antiquités de la ville de Cherchel (Algérie)." *Revue archéologique* 5, no. 1 (1848): 344–52.

Blondel, Léon. *Aperçus sur l'état actuel de l'Algérie: Lettres d'un voyageur à son frère.* Algiers: Imprimerie du gouvernement, 1844.

Bocher, Charles. "Prise de Narah: Souvenirs d'une expédition dans le Djebel-Aurès." *Revue des deux mondes* (June 15, 1857): 855–74.

——. "Le siége de Zaatcha: Souvenirs de l'expédition dans les Ziban en 1849." *Revue des deux mondes* (April 1, 1851): 70–101.

Boissière, Gustave. *Esquisse d'une histoire de la conquête et de l'administration romaines dans le nord de l'Afrique et particulièrement dans la province de Numidie.* Paris: Hachette et Cie, 1878.

Bonaparte, Napoléon-Louis. *Études sur le passé et l'avenir de l'artillerie*. Paris: J. Dumaine, 1846.

Borrer, Dawson. *Narrative of a Campaign against the Kabaïles of Algeria*. London: Longman, Brown, Green, and Longmans, 1848.

Bruce, James. *Travels between the Years 1765 and 1773, through Part of Africa, Syria, Egypt, and Arabia into Abyssinia*. London: Albion, 1812.

Bugeaud, Thomas-Robert. *De la colonisation de l'Algérie*. Paris: A. Guyot, 1847.

——. *Histoire de l'Algérie française*. 2 vols. Paris: Henri Morel et Cie, 1850.

——. *Quelques réflexions sur trois questions fondamentales de notre établissement en Algérie*. Algiers: A. Besancenez, 1846.

Bulletin officiel des actes du gouvernement. Vol. 4. Algiers: Imprimerie du gouvernement, 1844.

Cagnat, René. *L'armée romaine d'Afrique et l'occupation militaire de l'Afrique sous les empereurs*. Paris: Imprimerie nationale, 1892.

——. *Lambèse*. Guides en Algérie. Paris: Ernest Leroux, 1893.

Camp, Maxime du. *Souvenirs d'un demi-siècle: Au temps de Louis-Philippe et de Napoléon III, 1830–1870*. Vol. 1. Paris: Hachette, 1949.

Carette, Ernest. *Exploration scientifique de l'Algérie: Études sur le Kabilie proprement dit*. 2 vols. Paris: Imprimerie nationale, 1849.

——. *Exploration scientifique de l'Algérie pendant les années 1840, 1841, 1842. Sciences historiques et géographiques 1*. Paris: Imprimerie nationale, 1844.

——. *Exploration scientifique de l'Algérie pendant les années 1840, 1841, 1842. Sciences historiques et géographiques 5*. Paris: Imprimerie nationale, 1848.

——. *Précis historique et archéologique sur Hippone et ses environs*. Paris: Imprimerie Lange Lévy et Compagnie, 1838.

Castellane, Louis-Charles-Pierre, Comte de, *Souvenirs of Military Life in Algeria*. Vol. 1. Translated by Margaret Josephine Lovett. London: Remington and Co., 1886.

Castellane, Marquis de. "Discours lu à la Société archéologique dans sa séance du 16 juillet 1831." *Mémoires de la Société archéologique du Midi de la France* 1 (1832–1833): iii–ix.

Castellane, Ruth Charlotte-Sophie de, Comtesse de Beaulaincourt-Marles, ed. *Campagnes d'Afrique 1835–1848: Lettres adressées au Maréchal de Castellane*. Paris: Librairie Plon, 1898.

Cherbonneau, Auguste. "Constantine et ses antiquités." *Annuaire de la Société archéologique de la province de Constantine* 1 (1853): 102–36.

——. "Rapport sur les fouilles du Krenag (Tiddis et Calda): Inscriptions romaines inédites." *Recueils des notices et mémoires de la Société archéologique de la province de Constantine* (1863):170–213.

Christian, Pierre. *L'Afrique française, l'empire de Maroc et les déserts de Sahara*. Paris: A. Barbier, 1846.

"Chronique: Province d'Alger. Cherchel." *Revue africaine* 1 (1856): 54–56.

Clarinval, Commandant. "Rapport sur les fouilles faites à la basilique de Tébessa pendant l'année 1870." *Recueil des notices et mémoires de la Société de la province de Constantine* 14 (1870): 605–11.

Cler, Jean-Joseph-Gustave. *Reminiscences of an Officer of Zouaves*. New York, D. Appleton and Co., 1860.

"Correspondance officielle concernant les missions et les entreprises scientifiques." *Mémoires de l'Institut impérial de France: Académie des inscriptions et belles-lettres* 18, no. 1 (1849–1852): 97–272.

"Coup-d'oeil sur les antiquités de la province de Constantine." *Annuaire de la Société archéologique de la province de Constantine* 1 (1853): 13–19.

Coynart, Raymond de. "L'Alésia de César laissée à sa place: Lettre à M. J. Quicherat." *Spectateur militaire* ser. 2, 20 (1857): 70–113.

Creuly, Casimir. "Carte de la Gaule: Examen des observations auxquelles elle a donné lieu (part 1)." *Revue archéologique* n.s. 7 (1863): 383–96.

———. "Carte de la Gaule: Examen des observations auxquelles elle a donné lieu (part 4)." *Revue archéologique* n.s. 8 (1863): 253–63.

———. "Carte de la Gaule: Examen des observations auxquelles elle a donné lieu (part 6)." *Revue archéologique* n.s. 8 (1863): 387–401.

———. "Carte de la Gaule: Examen des observations auxquelles elle a donné lieu (part 7)." *Revue archéologique* n.s. 8 (1863): 496–518.

d'Abbadie, Arnauld. *Douze ans de séjour dans la Haute-Éthiopie (Abyssinie)*. Studi e testi 286. Vatican City: Biblioteca apostolica Vaticana, 1980.

Daumas, Eugène, and Paul Dieudonné Fabar. *La Grande Kabylie: Études historiques*. Paris: L. Hachette, 1847.

Daux, Adolphe. *Recherches sur l'origine et l'emplacement des emporia phéniciens dans le Zeugis et le Byzacium (Afrique septentrionale) faites par ordre de l'Empereur*. Paris: Imprimerie impériale, 1869.

d'Azevac, Marie-Armand-Pascal. *Esquisse générale de l'Afrique et Afrique ancienne*. Paris: Firmin Didot Frères, 1844.

"Découvertes et nouvelles." *Revue archéologique* 5, no. 2 (1848–1849): 500–505.

Delamare, Adolphe-Hedwige-Alphonse. "Étude sur Stora, port de Philippeville (l'ancienne Rusicade)." *Mémoires de la Société impériale des antiquaires de France* 24 (1859): 132–89.

———. *Exploration scientifique de l'Algérie pendant les années 1840, 1841, 1842, 1843, 1844 et 1845*. Paris: Imprimerie nationale, 1850.

———. "Notes sur quelques villes romaines de l'Algérie." *Revue archéologique* 6, no. 1 (1849): 1–22.

———. "Notice sur Lambaesa ville de la province de Constantine avec l'indication des principaux monuments qui se trouvent dans cette ville." *Revue archéologique* 4, no. 2 (1847–1848): 449–53.

Denniée, Antoine. *Précis historique et administratif de la campagne d'Afrique*. Paris: Delaunay, 1830.

Desjardins, Ernest. "Léon Renier." In *Mélanges Renier*, i–xxi. Bibliotheque de l'École des hautes études, sciences philologiques et historiques 73. Paris: F. Vieweg, 1887.

Desjobert, Amédée. *L'Algérie en 1844*. Paris: Guillaumin, 1844.

———. *L'Algérie en 1846*. Paris: Guillaumin, 1846.

Diehl, Charles. "Les découvertes de l'archéologie française en Algérie et en Tunisie." *Revue internationale de l'enseignement* 24 (1892): 97–130.

Doublet, Georges, and Paul Gauckler. *Musée de Constantine*. Musées et collections archéologiques de l'Algérie. Paris: Ernest Leroux, 1892.

Ducrocq, Théophile. *La loi du 30 mars 1887 et les décrets du 3 janvier 1889 sur la conservation des monuments et objets mobiliers présentant un intérêt national au point de vue de l'histoire ou de l'art.* Paris: Alphonse Picard, 1889.

Dupuch, Antoine-Adolphe. *Essai sur l'Algérie chrétienne, romaine et française.* Turin: Imprimerie royale, 1847.

——. *Lettre pastorale de Monseigneur l'évêque d'Alger.* Bordeaux: Chez Henry Faye, 1838.

——. *Lettre pastorale de Monseigneur l'évêque d'Alger.* Marseille: Marius Olive, 1842.

Dureau de la Malle, Adolphe. *Peyssonnel et Desfontaines: Voyages dans les Régences de Tunis et d'Alger.* Vol. 1. Paris: Gide, 1838.

——. *Province de Constantine: Recueil de renseignements pour l'expédition ou l'établissement des français dans cette partie de l'Afrique septentrionale.* Paris: Gide, 1837.

Duruy, Victor. *Notes et souvenirs (1811–1894).* Vol. 1. Paris: Hachette et Cie, 1901.

Duvivier, Franciade Fleurus. *Algérie: Quatorze observations sur le dernier mémoire du Général Bugeaud.* Paris: H.-L. Delloye, 1842.

——. *Les inscriptions phéniciennes, puniques, numidiques, expliquées par une méthode incontestable.* Paris: J. Dumaine, 1846.

——. *Recherches et notes sur la portion de l'Algérie au sud de Guelma depuis la frontière de Tunis jusqu'au Mont Aurèss compris.* Paris: L. Vassal et Cie, 1841.

——. *Solution de la question de l'Algérie.* Paris: Imprimerie et librairie militaire de Gaultier-Laguionie, 1841.

Edrissi. *Description de l'Afrique et de l'Espagne*, translated by Reinhart Pieter Anne Dozy and Michael Jan de Goeje. Leiden: Brill, 1866.

El Bekri. *Description de l'Afrique septentrionale*, translated by William Mac Guckin de Slane. Algiers: A. Jourdan, 1913.

Fabre, Daniel, ed. *Jean Terson: Mémoires d'un apôtre saint-simonien.* Carcassonne: Édition Fédération Audoise des Oeuvres Laïques, 1979.

Falbe, Christian Tuxen. *Recherches sur l'emplacement de Carthage augmentées d'une carte archéologique et topographique.* Paris: Imprimerie royale, 1833–1834.

Féraud, Laurent-Charles. *Exposition universelle de Paris en 1878: Algérie. Archéologie et histoire.* Algiers: Adolphe Jourdan, 1878.

——. *Les interprètes de l'armée d'Afrique (Archives du corps).* Algiers: A. Jourdan, 1876.

——. "Monuments dits celtiques dans la province de Constantine." *Recueil des notices et mémoires de la Société archéologique de la province de Constantine* 1 (1863): 214–34.

——. "Notes historiques sur les tribus de la province de Constantine." *Recueil des notes et mémoires de la Société archéologique de la province de Constantine* 13 (1869): 1–68.

——. "Recherches sur les monuments dits celtiques de la province de Constantine." *Revue archéologique* n.s. 11 (1865): 202–17.

Ferdinand-Philippe, Duc d'Orléans. *Récits de campagne, 1833–1841*, edited by the Comte de Paris and the Duc de Chartres. Paris: Calmann Lévy, 1890.

Follie, Adrien-Jacques. *Voyage dans les déserts du Sahara*. Paris: Chez les Directeurs de l'Imprimerie du Cercle social, 1792.

Foy, Colonel. "Notice archéologique sur Madrazen." *Annuaire de la Société archéologique de la province de Constantine* 3 (1856–1857): 58–69.

Fustel de Coulanges, Numa-Denis. *La cité antique*. Paris: Hachette, 1927.

——. "De la manière d'écrire l'histoire en France et en Allemagne depuis cinquante ans." *Revue des deux mondes* 42 (1872): 241–51.

Gaffarel, Paul. *L'Algérie: Histoire, conquête et colonisation*. Paris: Firmin-Didot et Cie, 1883.

Garcés, Maria Antonia, ed. *An Early Modern Dialogue with Islam: Antonio des Sosa's "Topography of Algiers" (1612)*. Translated by Diana de Armas Wilson. Notre Dame, IN: University of Notre Dame Press, 2011.

Gasnier, Maurice, ed. *Ernest Renan-Hortense Cornu: Correspondance 1856–1861 (Mission en Phénicie)*. Brest: Centre d'étude des correspondances, 1994.

Gauckler, Paul. *Musée de Cherchel*. Paris: Ernest Leroux, 1895.

Girardin, Saint-Marc. "De la domination des Carthaginois et des romaines en Afrique comparée avec la domination française." *Revue des deux mondes* ser. 4, 26 (April–June 1841): 408–45.

Gsell, Stéphane. *Musée de Philippeville*. Paris: Ernest Leroux, 1898.

Guigniaut, Joseph-Daniel. "Notice historique sur la vie et les travaux de Charles-Benoît Hase, *membre* de l'Académie des inscriptions et belles-lettres." *Mémoires de l'Institut national de France* 27 (1877): 247–73.

Guyon, Jean. *Voyage d'Alger aux Ziban l'ancienne Zebe*. Algiers: Imprimerie du gouvernement, 1852.

Instructions pour la conduite des fouilles archéologiques en Algérie. Algiers: Adolphe Jourdan, 1901.

Jomard, Edme-François. "Séance du 11 avril 1851: Rapport sur les travaux archéologiques du colonel Carbuccia." *Mémoires de l'Institut national de France: Académie des inscriptions et belles-lettres* 18, no. 1 (1855): 161–70.

Joubin, André, ed. *Correspondance générale de Eugène Delacroix*. Vol. 1: *1804–1837*. Paris: Plon, 1936.

Julius Caesar, *The Gallic War*. Edited and translated by Henry J. Edwards. Loeb Classical Library 72. Cambridge, MA: Harvard University Press, 1917.

Khodja, Hamdan. *Le Miroir: Aperçu historique et statistique sur la Régence d'Alger*. Introduction by Abdelkader Djeghloul. Paris: Sinbad, 1985.

Lacroix, Frédéric. "Colonisation et administration romanes dans l'Afrique septentrionale." *Revue africaine* 41 (1863): 363–83, 415–32.

Lapène, Edouard. "Tableau historique, moral et politique sur les Kabyles." *Mémoires de l'Académie nationale de Metz* 27 (1845–1846): 227–87.

Lartigue, Raoul de. *Monographie de l'Aurès*. Constantine: Marle Audrino, 1904.

Laumonier, M. "Essai sur l'histoire ethnologique des races préhistoriques de la France." *Bulletin de la Société des antiquaries de l'Ouest* 4 (1879): 519–50.

Leclère, L. "Lettre à M. le Commandant de la Mare sur les ruines de Lambesa (Algérie)." *Revue archéologique* 7, no. 1 (1850): 123–25.

Leiris, Jacques-Eugène. *Jadis*. Paris: Forbis, 1990.

Leroux, Alexandre. *L'Algérie illustrée*. 2 vols. Algiers: A. Leroux, 1888–92.

Lettres du Maréchal de Saint-Arnaud. 2 vols. Paris: Michel Lévy Frères, 1855.

Livy, *Histoire romaine, Livres XXVII–XXX*. Edited and translated by Eugène Lasserre. Vol. 6. Paris: Garnier Frères, 1949.

Longpérier, Adrien de. "À M. A. Leleux, éditeur de la *Revue archéologique*." *Revue archéologique* 5, no. 2 (1848–1849): 570–71.

Lord, Perceval Barton. *Algiers, with Notices of the Neighbouring States of Barbary*. Vol. 1. London: Whittaker and Co., 1835.

MacCarthy, Oscar. "*Algeria romana*: Recherches sur l'occupation et la colonisation de l'Algérie par les romains." *Revue africaine* 1, no. 2 (1856): 88–113; no. 5 (1857): 364–69.

Marcotte de Quivières, Charles. *Deux ans en Afrique*. Paris: Librairie nouvelle, 1855.

Marmier, Xavier. *Lettres sur l'Algérie*. Paris: Arthus Bertrand, 1847.

Mars, V. de. "Alésia: Étude sur la séptième campagne de César en Gaule." *Revue des deux mondes* (1858): 64–146.

Masqueray, Émile. "Rapport à M. le Général Chanzy, gouverneur-général de l'Algérie sur la mission dans le sud de la province de Constantine: Thamgad." *Revue africaine* 20 (1876): 164–72.

Materne, Auguste, ed. and trans. *Les auteurs latins: Tacite, troisième livre des Annales*. Paris: L. Hachette, 1853.

Mercier, Ernest. "Nécrologie: Auguste Cherbonneau." *Recueil des notices et mémoires de la Société archéologique de la province de Constantine* ser. 3, 1 (1882): 413–18.

Ministère de la Guerre. *Collection des actes du gouvernement depuis l'occupation d'Alger jusqu'au 1er octobre 1834*. Paris: Imprimerie royale, 1843.

Moll, A. "Mémoire historique et archéologique sur Tébessa (Théveste) et ses environs." *Annuaire de la Société archéologique de la province de Constantine* 4 (1858–1859): 26–86.

———. "Note sur des fouilles faites à Lambèse, aux sources d'Aïn-Drinn et d'Aïn-Boubennana." *Annuaire de la Société archéologique de la province de Constantine* 3 (1856–1857): 157–62.

———. "Quelques inscriptions trouvées à Lambèse dans le courant de 1857." *Annuaire de la Société archéologique de la province de Constantine* 3 (1856–1857): 163–69.

Moniteur universel, June 6, 1844.

Montgravier, Azéma de. *Études historiques pour servir au projet de colonisation d'une partie du territoire de la Province d'Oran*. May 1846.

Morcelli, Stephano Antonio. *Africa Christiana*, 3 vols. Brescia: Ex officina Bettoniana, 1816–1817.

Morell, John Reynell. *Algeria: The Topography and History, Political, Social, and Natural of French Africa*. London: Nathaniel Cooke, 1854.

Mullié, C. *Biographie des célébrités militaires des armées de terre et mer de 1789 à 1850*. Vol. 1. Paris: Chez Poignavant et Cie, 1851.

Napoléon III. *Histoire de Jules César*. Vol. 1. Paris: Henri Plon, 1865.

Nicolaïdes, Demétrius, trans. *Législation ottomane ou Recueil des lois, réglements, ordonnances, traités, capitulations et autres documents officiels de l'Empire ottoman*. Istanbul: Bureau du Journal Thraky, 1874.

Notice sommaire des principaux monuments dans le Département des médailles et antiques de la Bibliothèque nationale. Paris: Imprimerie nationale, 1889.

Nozeran, Charles. "De l'opportunité de faire exécuter des fouilles à Cherchel." *L'Algérie nouvelle: Journal politique quotidien* 1, no. 7 (1858).

Payen. "Inscriptions inédites de la subdivision de Batna." *Annuaire de la Société archéologique de la province de Constantine* 4 (1858–1859): 87–103.

Pellissier de Reynaud, Edmond. *Annales algériennes*. New ed. 3 vols. Paris: Librairie militaire, 1854.

——. *Exploration scientifique de l'Algérie pendant les années 1840, 1841, 1842*. Sciences historiques et géographiques 16. Paris: Imprimerie impériale, 1853.

Périer, Jean-André-Napoléon. *Exploration scientifique de l'Algérie pendant les années 1840, 1841, 1842*. Sciences médicales 1. Paris: Imprimerie impériale, 1847.

Pitts, Jennifer, ed. and trans. *Writings on Empire and Slavery: Alexis de Tocqueville*. Baltimore: Johns Hopkins University Press, 2001.

Pliny the Elder, *Histoire naturelle livre V, 1–46*. Edited and translated by Jehan Desanges. Paris: Société d'Édition "Les belles lettres," 1980.

Polybius, *Histoire*. Translated by Denis Roussel. Paris: Gallimard, 2003.

Pomel, Auguste. *Des races indigènes d'Algérie et du rôle que leur réservent leurs aptitudes*. Oran: Veuve Dagorn, 1871.

Pommier, Jean, ed. *Un témoignage sur E. Renan: Les 'Souvenirs' de L. F. A. Maury*. Paris: Éditions A.-G. Nizet, 1971.

Poujoulat, M. *Études africaines: Récits et pensées d'un voyageur*. Vol. 2. Paris: Comptoir des imprimeurs-unis, 1847.

Procès-verbaux et rapports de la Commission d'Afrique instituée par ordonnance du roi du 12 décembre 1833. Paris: Imprimerie royale, 1834.

Quesnoy, Ferdinand-Désiré. *L'armée d'Afrique depuis la conquête d'Alger*. Paris: Furne Jouvet et Cie, 1888.

Raoul-Rochette, Désiré. "Rapport sur les recherches archéologiques à entreprendre dans la province de Constantine et la Régence d'Alger." *Mémoires de l'Institut royal de France: Académie des inscriptions et belles-lettres* 12 (1831–1838): 135–81.

Ravoisié, Amable. *Exploration scientifique de l'Algérie pendant les années 1840, 1841, 1842*. Beaux-arts, architecture et sculpture. 2 vols. Paris: Chez Firmin Didot Frères, 1846–1850.

Reinach, Salomon. "La méthode en archéologie." *Revue du mois* 11, no. 3 (1911): 279–92.

——. "Le vandalisme moderne en Orient." *Revue des deux mondes* 56 (1 March 1883): 132–66.

Reinach, Salomon, Renée Cagnat, Henri Saladin, Général Derrécagaix, and Philippe Berger. *Recherches des antiquités dans le nord de l'Afrique: Conseils aux archéologues et voyageurs*. Paris: Ernest Leroux, 1929.

Renan, Ernest. "Madame Hortense Cornu." In *Feuilles détachées faisant suite aux souvenirs d'enfance et de jeunesse*, 302–21. Paris: Calmann Lévy, 1982.

Renier, Léon. "Deuxième rapport de M. Renier, en mission dans la province de Constantine pour la recherche des monuments épigraphiques." *Archives des missions scientifiques et littéraires* 2 (1851): 217–22.

——. *Instructions pour la recherche des antiquités en Algérie*. Paris: L. Hachette et Cie, 1859.

———. "Lettre au ministre pour demander une mission à Lambèse." *Archives des missions scientifiques et littéraires* 2 (1851): 57–62.

———. "Notes d'un voyage archéologique au pied de l'Aurès." *Revue archéologique* 8, no. 2 (1851–1852): 492–513.

———. "Notice sur le tombeau de T. Flavius Maximus." *Revue archéologique* 7, no. 1 (1850): 186–87.

———. "Premier rapport de M. Renier, en mission dans la province de Constantine pour la recherche des monuments épigraphiques." *Archives des missions scientifiques et littéraires* 2 (1851): 169–86.

———. "Quatrième rapport de M. Renier, en mission dans la province de Constantine pour la recherche des monuments épigraphiques." *Archives des missions scientifiques et littéraires* 2 (1851): 473–83.

———. "Troisième rapport de M. Renier, en mission dans la province de Constantine pour la recherche des monuments épigraphiques." *Archives des missions scientifiques et littéraires* 2 (1851): 435–57.

Roger, Joseph. *Catalogue du Musée archéologique de Philippeville (Algérie)*. Philippeville: Chevalier et Luth, 1860.

Rosenthal, Franz, trans. *Ibn Khaldûn, an Introduction to History: The Muqaddimah*. Abridged and edited by N. J. Dawood. London: Routledge and Kegan Paul, 1967.

Rousseau, Alphonse. "Voyage du Scheikh El-Tidjani dans la Régence de Tunis pendant les années 706, 707 et 708 de l'Hégire (1306–1309)." *Journal asiatique* ser. 5, 1 (1853): 101–68.

Rozet, Claude-Antoine. *Voyage dans la Régence d'Alger ou Description du pays occupé par l'armée française en Afrique*. 3 vols. Paris: Arthus Bertrand, 1833.

Rozet, Claude-Antoine, and Ernest Carette. *Algérie*. Paris: Firmin Didot, 1850.

Rude, Fernand, ed. *Bagnes d'Afrique: Trois transportés en Algérie après le coup d'état du 2 décembre 1851*. Paris: François Maspero, 1981.

Saint-Félix, René de, ed. *Le voyage de S. M. l'Empereur Napoléon III en Algérie et la régence de S. M. l'Impératrice, mai–juin 1865*. Paris: E. Pick, 1865.

Sallust. *Bellum Iugurthinum*. Edited and translated by Alfred Ernout. Paris: Société d'éditions "Les belles lettres," 1960.

Sarette, Lieutenant-Colonel. "Démonstration militaire du problem d'Alésia." *Mémoires de la Société d'émulation du Doubs* ser. 4, 2 (1866): 11–69.

"Seance du vendredi 18 avril 1879." *Revue des sociétés savantes de la France et de l'étranger* 7, no. 1 (1880): 482–90.

Sériziat, Commandant. "La basilique de Tébessa." *Recueil des notices et mémoires de la Société de la province de Constantine* 12 (1868): 473–77.

Shaw, Thomas. *Travels or Observations Relating to Several Parts of Barbary and the Levant*. Oxford: Theatre, 1738.

Tacitus, *Annales livres I–III*. Edited and translated by Henri Goellzer. Vol. 1. Paris: Société d'Édition "Les belles lettres," 1965.

———, *Annales livres IV–XII*. Edited and translated by Henri Goellzer. Vol. 2. Paris: Société d'Édition "Les belles lettres," 1966.

Temple, Grenville, and Christian Tuxen Falbe. *Relation d'une excursion de Bône à Guelma et à Constantine*. Paris: Société pour l'exploration et les fouilles de l'ancienne Carthage, 1838.

Texier, Charles. "Extrait d'un aperçu statistique des monuments de l'Algérie." *Revue archéologique* 3, no. 2 (1846–1847): 724–35.

——. "Praetorium de Lambaesa." *Revue archéologique* 5, no. 2 (1848–1849): 417–18.

Thoumas, Charles. *Les transformations de l'armée française: Essais d'histoire et de critique sur l'état militaire de la France*. Vol. 2. Paris: Berger-Levrault et Cie, 1887.

Topinard, Paul. "De la race indigène, ou race berbère, en Algérie." *Revue d'anthropologie* 3 (1874): 491–98.

——. "Instructions particulières." In *Instructions sur l'anthropologie de l'Algérie*, edited by Léon Faidherbe, 13–58. Paris: A. Hennuyer, 1874.

Troyon, Frédéric. "Lettre à M. A. Bertrand sur l'attitude repliée dans les sépultures antiques." *Revue archéologique* n.s. 9 (1864): 289–99.

Verchère de Reffye, Auguste. "Les armes d'Alise." *Revue archéologique* 10 (1864): 337–49.

Vigneral, Charles de. *Ruines romaines de l'Algérie, Kabylie du Djurdjura*. Paris: J. Claye, 1868.

——. *Ruines romaines de l'Algérie, subdivision de Bône, cercle de Guelma*. Paris: J. Claye, 1867.

Walckenaër, Charles A. "Rapports sur les recherches géographiques, historiques, archéologiques, qu'il convient de continuer ou d'entreprendre dans l'Afrique septentrionale." *Mémoires de l'Institut royal de France: Académie des inscriptions et belles-lettres* 12 (1831–1838): 98–134.

Watbled, Ernest. *Souvenirs de l'armée d'Afrique*. Paris: Challamel Ainé, 1877.

Wilmanns, Gustav. "Étude sur le camp et la ville de Lambèse." *Bulletin trimestriel des antiquités africaines* 1 (1882): 185–200.

——. *Inscriptiones Africae latinae*. Vol. 1. Corpus inscriptionum latinarum 8. Berlin: Georg Reimer, 1881.

Secondary Sources

Abdesselem, Ahmed. *Les historiens tunisiens des XVIIe, XVIIIe et XIXe siècles: Essai d'histoire culturelle*. Paris: C. Klincksieck, 1973.

Abi-Mershed, Osama W. *Apostles of Modernity: Saint-Simonians and the Civilizing Mission in Algeria*. Stanford, CA: Stanford University Press, 2010.

Abu El-Haj, Nadia. *Facts on the Ground: Archaeological Practice and Territorial Self-Fashioning in Israeli Society*. Chicago: University of Chicago Press, 2001.

Abun-Nasr, Jamil M. *A History of the Maghrib*. 2nd ed. Cambridge: Cambridge University Press, 1975.

Albertini, Eugène. "L'Algérie antique." In *Histoire et historiens de l'Algérie*, 89–109. Collection du centenaire de l'Algérie (1830–1930) 4. Paris: Félix Alcan, 1931.

Alexandropoulos, Jacques. "De Louis Bertrand à Pierre Hubac: Images de l'Afrique antique." In *La Tunisie mosaïque: Diasporas, cosmopolitisme, archéologies de l'identité*, 457–78. Toulouse: Presses universitaires du Mirail, 2000.

——. "Jugurtha, héros national: jalons sur un itinéraire." *Anabases* 16 (2012): 11–29.

——. "Regards sur l'impérialisme de la Rome antique en Afrique du Nord." In *Idée impérial et impérialisme dans l'Italie fasciste: Journée d'étude organisée par le groupe ERASME le 4 avril 2003 à Toulouse,* edited by Alberto Bianco and Philippe Foro, 7–19. Collection de l'E.C.R.I.T. 9. Toulouse: Presses universitaires du Mirail, 2003.

Altekamp, Stefan. "Modelling Roman North Africa: Advances, Obsessions and Deficiencies of Colonial Archaeology in the Maghreb." In *Under Western Eyes: Approches occidentales de l'archéologie nord-africaine (XIXe–XXe siècle),* edited by Hédi Dridi and Antonella Mezzolani Andreose, 19–42. Bologne: BraDypUS, 2016.

Amster, Ellen J. *Medicine and the Saints: Science, Islam, and the Colonial Encounter in Morocco, 1877–1956.* Austin: University of Texas Press, 2013.

Anderson, Benjamin. "An Alternative Discourse: Local Interpreters of Antiquities in the Ottoman Empire." *Journal of Field Archaeology* 40, no. 4 (2015): 450–60.

Arnaud-Portelli, Annie. "L'exploration archéologique de l'Afrique du Nord des premiers voyageurs au XVIIIe siècle à l'indépendance des nations (Maroc, Algérie) d'après les documents publiés." 3 vols. PhD diss., Université de Paris IV-Sorbonne, 1991.

Artz, Frederick B. *The Development of Technical Education in France, 1500–1850.* Cambridge, MA: MIT Press, 1966.

Azan, Paul. *L'armée d'Afrique de 1830 à 1852.* Paris: Plon, 1936.

Bacha, Myriam. "Un archéologue amateur: Louis Carton (1861–1924) et son project de parc archéologique de Carthage (Tunisie)." In *Initiateurs et entrepreneurs culturels du tourisme (1850–1950),* edited by Jean-Yves Andrieux and Patrick Harmendy, 21–33. Rennes: Presses universitaires de Rennes, 2011.

——. "La constitution d'une notion patrimoniale en Tunisie, XIXe et XXe siècle: Émergence et apport des disciplines de l'archéologie et de l'architecture." In *Chantiers et défis de la recherche sur le Maghreb contemporain,* edited by Pierre-Robert Baduel, 159–78. Paris: Karthala, 2009.

——. "La création des institutions patrimoniales de Tunisie: Oeuvre des savants de l'Académie des inscriptions et belles-lettres et des fonctionnaires du Ministère de l'instruction publique et des beaux-arts." *Livraisons d'histoire de l'architecture* 12, no. 2 (2006): 123–34.

——. "Des influences traditionelles et patrimoniales sur les architectures du Maghreb." In *Architectures au Maghreb (XIXe–XXe siècles): Réinvention du patrimoine,* edited by Myriam Bacha, 4–16. Rennes: IRMC—Presses universitaires François Rabelais, 2011.

——. *Patrimoine et monuments en Tunisie.* Rennes: Presses universitaires de Rennes, 2013.

——. "Patrimoine et tourisme en Tunisie au début du Protectorat: Interactions et dépendances." In *Le tourisme dans l'empire français: Politiques, pratiques et imaginaires (XIXe–XXe siècles). Un outil de la domination coloniale?,* 155–63. Paris: Publications de la Société française d'histoire d'outre-mer, 2009.

Bahrani, Zainab, Çelik, Zeynep, and Edhem Eldem. "Introduction: Archaeology and Empire." In *Scramble for the Past: A Story of Archaeology in the Ottoman Empire, 1753–1914,* edited by Zainab Bahrani, Zeynep Çelik, and Edhem Eldem, 13–44. Istanbul: SALT, 2011.

Ballais, Jean-Louis. "Conquests and Land Degradation in the Eastern Maghreb during Classical Antiquity and the Middle Ages." In *The Archaeology of Drylands: Living at the Margin,* edited by Graeme Barker and David Gilbertson, 125–36. London: Routledge, 2000.

Baratte, François. "Une curieuse expédition archéologique en Tunisie: La mission Hérisson." *Revue du Louvre et des musées de France* 21, no. 1 (1971): 335–46.

Barbançon, Louis-José. "Les transportés de 1848 (statistiques, analyse, commentaires)." *Criminocorpus,* January 1, 2008. http://criminocorpus.revues.org/48.

Barral I Altet, Xavier. "Les étapes de la recherche au XIXe siècle et les personnalités." In *Naissance des arts chrétiens: Atlas des monuments paléochrétiens de la France,* 346–67. Paris: Imprimerie nationale, 1991.

Barrera, Caroline. *Les sociétés savantes de Toulouse au XIXe siècle (1797–1865).* Paris: Éditions du Comité des travaux historiques et scientifiques, 2003.

Basch, Sophie. "Archaeological Travels in Greece and Asia Minor: On the Good Use of Ruins in Nineteenth-Century France." In *Scramble for the Past: A Story of Archaeology in the Ottoman Empire, 1753–1914,* edited by Zainab Bahrani, Zeynep Çelik, and Edhem Eldem, 157–79. Istanbul: SALT, 2011.

Bayle, Nadia. "Armée et archéologie au XIXe siècle: Éléments de recherche sur les travaux archéologiques des officiers français publiés entre 1830 et 1914." *Revue d'archéologie moderne et d'archéologie générale (RAMAGE)* 3 (1985): 219–30.

———. "Contribution des officiers français à l'étude archéologique du site d'Alésia." *Revue historique des armées* 167 (1987): 6–18.

———. "Quelques aspects de l'histoire de l'archéologie au XIXe siècle: L'exemple des publications archéologiques militaires éditées entre 1830 et 1914 en France, en Afrique du Nord et en Indo-Chine." Vol. 1. PhD diss., Université de Paris IV-Sorbonne, 1986.

Bénabou, Marcel. "L'impérialisme et l'Afrique du Nord: Le modèle romain." In *Sciences de l'homme et conquête coloniale: Constitution et usages des sciences humaines en Afrique (XIXe–XXe siècles),* edited by Daniel Nordman and Jean-Pierre Raison, 15–22. Paris: Presses de l'École normale supérieure, 1980.

———. *La résistance africaine à la romanisation.* Paris: François Maspero, 1975.

Benseddik, Nacéra. "L'armée française en Algérie: 'Parfois détruire, souvent construire.'" In *L'Africa romana: Atti di XIII convegno di studio, Djerba, 10–13 dicembre 1998,* edited by Mustapha Khanoussi, Paola Ruggeri, and Cinzia Vismara, 1:759–96. Rome: Carocci Editore, 2000.

———. "Lambaesis-Lambèse/Tazoult. Grandeur et décadence." In *L'affirmation de l'identité dans l'Algérie antique et médiévale: Combats et résistances. Hommage à Kadria Fatima Kadra,* 111–19. Algiers: Centre national de recherche en archéologie, 2014.

Benton, Lauren. *Law and Colonial Cultures: Legal Regimes in World History, 1400–1900.* Cambridge: Cambridge University Press, 2002.

Bercé, Françoise. "Restaurer au XIXe siècle?" In *Nîmes et ses antiquités: Un passé présent, XVIe–XIXe siècle,* edited by Véronique Krings and François Pugnière, 249–66. Bordeaux: Ausonius Éditions, 2013.

Berdeaux-Le Brazidec, Marie-Laure. "Aperçu des fouilles et des missions archéologiques sous le Second Empire." *Bulletin de la Société historique de Compiègne* 37 (2001): 153–74.

——. "L'archéologie au service de l'empereur." In *Prosper Mérimée au temps de Napoléon III: Actes du colloque organisé au Musée national du château de Compiègne le 18 octobre 2003*, 75–90. Paris: Éditions de la Réunion des musées nationaux, 2008.

——. "Napoléon III, le camp de Châlons et l'archéologie en Champagne." *Vie en Champagne* 30 (2002): 40–43.

Bernhardsson, Magnus T. *Reclaiming a Plundered Past: Archaeology and Nation Building in Modern Iraq*. Austin: University of Texas Press, 2005.

Bhabha, Homi K. *The Location of Culture*. London: Routledge, 1994.

Bodenstein, Felicity. "L'histoire du Cabinet des médailles et antiques de la Bibliothèque nationale (1819–1924): Un cabinet pour l'érudition à l'âge des musées." Vol. 1. PhD diss., Université de Paris-Sorbonne, 2015.

Boer, Pim den. *History as a Profession: The Study of History in France, 1818–1914*. Translated by Arnold J. Pomerans. Princeton, NJ: Princeton University Press, 1988.

Böhner, Kurt. "Die archäologische Erforschung der 'Teufelsmauer': Zum 100-jährigen Bestehen der Reichs-Limes-Kommission." *Nürnberger Blätter zur Archäologie* 9 (1992–1993): 63–76.

Bohrer, Frederick N. *Orientalism and Visual Culture: Imagining Mesopotamia in Nineteenth-Century France*. Cambridge: Cambridge University Press, 2003.

Bouchenaki, Mounir. *Le mausolée royal de Maurétanie*. Translated by Abdelhamid Hadjiat. Algiers: Direction des affaires culturelles, 1970.

——. "L'oeuvre des épigraphistes français en Algérie: La Numidie et la Maurétanie Césarienne." In *Un siècle d'épigraphie classique: Aspects de l'oeuvre des savants français dans les pays du bassin méditerranéen de 1888 à nos jours. Actes du colloque international du centenaire de "L'année epigraphique," Paris, 19–21 octobre 1988*, 53–69. Paris: Presses universitaires de France, 1991.

Bouron, Michèle, and Christiane Lyon-Caen. "202bis: Histoire de Jules César." In *Vercingétorix et Alésia: Saint-Germain-en-Laye. Musée des Antiquités nationales 29 mars–18 juillet 1994*, 239. Paris: Réunion des Musées nationaux, 1994.

Brebner, Philip. "The Impact of Thomas-Robert Bugeaud and the Decree of 9 June 1844 on the Development of Constantine, Algeria." *Revue de l'Occident musulman et de la Méditerranée* 38 (1984): 5–14.

Brett, Michael. "The Journey of al-Tijāni to Tripoli at the Beginning of the Fourteenth Century AD/Eighth Century AH." *Libyan Studies* 7 (1976): 41–51.

Brett, Michael, and Elizabeth Fentress. *The Berbers*. Oxford: Blackwell, 1996.

Broc, Numa. "Les grandes missions scientifiques françaises au XIXe siècle (Morée, Algérie, Mexique) et leurs travaux géographiques." *Revue d'histoire et des sciences* 34, nos. 3–4 (1981): 319–31.

Brower, Benjamin Claude. *A Desert Named Peace: The Violence of France's Empire in the Algerian Sahara, 1844–1902*. New York: Columbia University Press, 2009.

Bulliet, Richard W. *The Camel and the Wheel*. Cambridge, MA: Harvard University Press, 1975.

Burton, Antoinette. "Archive Stories: Gender in the Making of Imperial and Colonial Histories." In *Gender and Empire*, edited by Philippa Levine, 281–94. Oxford: Oxford University Press, 2007.

Callot, Jean-Pierre. *Histoire de l'École polytechnique.* Paris: Charles Lavauzelle, 1982.

Camps, Gabriel. *Aux origines de la Berbérie: Monuments et rites funéraires protohistoriques.* Paris: Arts et métiers graphiques, 1961.

——. "Nouvelles observations sur l'architecture et l'âge du Medracen, mausolée royal de Numidie." *Comptes-rendus des séances de l'Académie des inscriptions et belleslettres* 117, no. 3 (1973): 470–517.

Catheu, Françoise de. "Les marbres de Leptis Magna dans les monuments français du XVIIIe siècle." *Bulletin de la Société de l'histoire de l'art français* (1936): 51–74.

Çelik, Zeynep. "Defining Empire's Patrimony: Late Ottoman Perceptions of Antiquities." In *Scramble for the Past: A Story of Archaeology in the Ottoman Empire, 1753–1914*, edited by Zainab Bahrani, Zeynep Çelik, and Edhem Eldem, 443–77. Istanbul: SALT, 2011.

——. *Urban Forms and Colonial Confrontations: Algiers under French Rule.* Berkeley: University of California Press, 1997.

Le centenaire de Saint-Cyr, 1808–1908. Paris: Berger-Levrault et Cie, 1908.

Césaire, Aimé. *Discourse on Colonialism.* Translated by Joan Pinkham. New York: Monthly Review Press, 1972.

Chakrabarty, Dipesh. *Provincializing Europe: Postcolonial Thought and Historical Difference.* New ed. Princeton, NJ: Princeton University Press, 2008.

Chaline, Jean-Pierre. "Arcisse de Caumont et les sociétés savantes françaises." In *Arcisse de Caumont (1801–1873): Érudit normand et fondateur de l'archéologie française. Actes du colloque international organisé à Caen du 14 au 16 juin 2001*, edited by Vincent Juhel, 147–54. Mémoires de la Société des antiquaires de Normandie 40. Caen: Société des antiquaires de Normandie, 2004.

——. *Sociabilité et érudition: Les sociétés savantes en France XIXe–XXe siècles.* Paris: CNRS Éditions, 1998.

Champion, Timothy C. "Medieval Archaeology and the Tyranny of the Historical Record." In *From the Baltic to the Black Sea: Studies in Medieval Archaeology*, edited by David Austin and Leslie Alcock, 79–95. London: Unwin Hyman, 1990.

Chandezon, Christophe. "Ernest Beulé (1826–1874): Archéologie classique, histoire romaine et vie politique sous Napoléon III." In *L'hellénisme, d'une rive à l'autre de la Méditerranée: Mélanges offerts à André Laronde*, 29–55. Paris: De Boccard, 2012.

Charbonnières, Louis de. *Une grande figure: Saint-Arnaud, maréchal de France.* Paris: Nouvelles Éditions Latines, 1960.

Chew, Hélène. "Les échanges archéologiques internationaux au XIXe siècle: L'exemple d'Alexandre Bertrand et du musée des Antiquités nationales." In *Les dépôts de l'État au XIXe siècle: Politiques patrimoniales et destins d'oeuvres (Colloque du 8 décembre 2007)*, 125–37. Paris: Ministère de la culture et de la communication, 2008.

——. "Les machines de guerre de Verchère de Reffye et l'expérimentation archéologique sous le Second Empire." *Bulletin de la Société historique de Compiègne* 37 (2001): 211–38.

Choay, Françoise. *The Invention of the Historic Monument.* Translated by Lauren M. O'Connell. Cambridge: Cambridge University Press, 2001.

Christofle, Marcel. *Le Tombeau de la Chrétienne.* Paris: Arts et métiers graphiques, 1951.

Clancy-Smith, Julia. "Exoticism, Erasures, and Absence: The Peopling of Algiers, 1830–1900." In *Walls of Algiers: Narratives of the City through Text and Image,* edited by Zeynep Çelik, Julia Clancy-Smith, and Frances Terpak, 19–61. Los Angeles: Getty Research Institute, 2009.

———. "La Femme Arabe: Women and Sexuality in France's North African Empire." In *Women, the Family, and Divorce Laws in Islamic History,* edited by Amira El Azhary Sonbol, 52–63. Syracuse: Syracuse University Press, 1996.

———. *Mediterraneans: North Africa and Europe in an Age of Migration, c. 1800–1900.* Berkeley: University of California Press, 2011.

———. *Rebel and Saint: Muslim Notables, Populist Protest, Colonial Encounters (Algeria and Tunisia, 1800–1904).* Berkeley: University of California Press, 1994.

Coates, Ta-Nehisi. *Between the World and Me.* New York: Spiegel and Grau, 2015.

Colla, Elliot. *Conflicted Antiquities: Egyptology, Egyptomania, Egyptian Modernity.* Durham, NC: Duke University Press, 2007.

Collot, Claude. *Les institutions de l'Algérie durant la période coloniale (1830–1962).* Paris: CNRS Éditions, 1987.

Colonna, Fanny. "La carte Carbuccia au 1:100.000e de la subdivision de Batna, ou le violon d'Ingres du 2e régiment de la Légion étrangère (vers 1850)." In *L'invention scientifique de la Méditerranée: Égypte, Morée, Algérie,* edited by Marie-Noëlle Bourguet, Bernard Lepetit, Daniel Nordman, and Maroula Sinarellis, 53–70. Paris: Éditions de l'École des hautes études en sciences sociales, 1998.

Colonna, Ugo. "La compagnie de Jésus en Algérie (1840–1880): L'exemple de la mission de Kabylie (1863–1880)." *Monde arabe Maghreb Machrek* 135 (1992): 68–78.

Colwell-Chanthaphonh, Chip, and J. Brett Hill. "Mapping History: Cartography and the Construction of the San Pedro Valley." *History and Anthropology* 15, no. 2 (2004): 175–200.

"The Commission de Topographie des Gaules." Les Passés dans le Présent, n.d. http://passes-present.eu/en/themes-research/active-knowledge-past/commission-de-topographie-des-gaules-1858-1879-371.

Conklin, Alice L. *In the Museum of Man: Race, Anthropology, and Empire in France, 1850–1950.* Ithaca, NY: Cornell University Press, 2013.

———. *A Mission to Civilize: The Republican Idea of Empire in France and West Africa, 1895–1930.* Stanford, CA: Stanford University Press, 1997.

Corbett, Elena T. *Competitive Archaeology in Jordan: Narrating Identity from the Ottomans to the Hashemites.* Austin: University of Texas Press, 2014.

Crane, Susan A. *Collecting and Historical Consciousness in Early Nineteenth-Century Germany.* Ithaca, NY: Cornell University Press, 2000.

Crossette, Barbara. "Taliban Explains Buddha Demolition." *New York Times,* March 19, 2001. http://www.nytimes.com/2001/03/19/world/taliban-explains-buddha-demolition.html.

Dakhlia, Jocelyne. *L'oubli de la cité: La mémoire collective à l'épreuve du lignage dans le Jérid tunisien.* Paris: Éditions la Découverte, 1990.

Daston, Lorraine, and Peter Galison. "The Image of Objectivity." *Representations* 40 (1992): 81–128.

Davis, Diana K. "Eco-Governance in French Algeria: Environmental History, Policy, and Colonial Administration." *Proceedings of the Western Society for French History* 32 (2004): 328–45.

———. *Resurrecting the Granary of Rome: Environmental History and French Colonial Expansion in North Africa*. Athens: Ohio University Press, 2007.

Debergh, Jacques. "Une rencontre improbable dans la Régence de Tunis et ses conséquences fructueuses: Jean Emile Humbert et Camillo Borgia (1815–1816)." In *Du voyage savant aux territoires de l'archéologie: Voyageurs, amateurs et savants à l'origine de l'archéologie moderne*, edited by Manuel Royo, Martine Denoyelle, Emmanuelle Hindy, Timothy Champion, and David Louyot, 245–48. Paris: De Boccard, 2011.

Delnore, Allyson Jaye. "Empire by Example? Deportees in France and Algeria and the Re-Making of a Modern Empire, 1846–1854." *French Politics, Culture and Society* 33, no. 1 (2015): 33–54.

Desanges, Jehan. "La commission dite 'de l'Afrique du Nord' au sein du CTHS: Origine, évolution, perspectives." In *Numismatique, langues, écritures et arts du livre, spécificité des arts figurés: Actes du VIIe colloque international sur l'histoire et l'archéologie de l'Afrique du Nord, Nice, 21 au 31 octobre 1996)*, 11–24. Paris: Éditions du Comité des travaux historiques et scientifiques, 1999.

Díaz-Andreu, Margarita. *A World History of Nineteenth-Century Archaeology: Nationalism, Colonialism, and the Past*. Oxford: Oxford University Press, 2007.

Díaz-Andreu, Margarita, and Timothy Champion. "Nationalism and Archaeology in Europe: An Introduction." In *Archaeology and Nationalism in Europe*, edited by Margarita Díaz-Andreu and Timothy Champion, 1–23. London: University College London Press, 1996.

Direche-Slimani, Karima. *Chrétiens de Kabylie (1873–1954): Une action missionaire dans l'Algérie coloniale*. Saint-Denis: Éditions Bouchene, 2004.

Dirks, Nicholas B. "Annals of the Archive: Ethnographic Notes on the Sources of History." In *From the Margins: Historical Anthropology and Its Futures*, edited by Brian Axel, 47–65. Durham, NC: Duke University Press, 2002.

———. "Colonial Histories and Native Informants: Biography of an Archive." In *Orientalism and the Postcolonial Predicament: Perspectives on South Asia*, edited by Carol A. Breckenridge and Peter van der Veer, 279–313. Philadelphia: University of Pennsylvania Press, 1993.

Djebar, Assia. *L'Amour, la fantasia*. Paris: Éditions Albin Michel, 1995.

———. *Vaste est la prison*. Paris: Éditions Albin Michel, 1995.

Dondin-Payre, Monique. "L'Académie des inscriptions et belles-lettres et la photographie: Les fouilles du Tombeau de la chrétienne au XIXe siècle." *Comptes-rendus des séances de l'Académie des inscriptions et belles-lettres* 147, no. 3 (2003): 1139–57.

———. "L'árcheologie en Algérie à partir de 1830: Une politique patrimoniale?" In *Pour une histoire des politiques du patrimoine*, edited by Philippe Poirrier and Loïc Vadelorge, 145–70. Travaux et documents 16. Paris: Comité d'histoire du Ministère de la culture, 2003.

——. *Le Capitaine Delamare: La réussite de l'archéologie romaine au sein de la Commission d'exploration scientifique d'Algérie.* Mémoires de l'Académie des inscriptions et belles-lettres, n.s. 15. Paris: F. Paillart, 1994.

——. *La Commission d'exploration scientifique d'Algérie: Une héritière méconnue de la Commission d'Égypte.* Mémoires de l'Académie des inscriptions et belles-lettres, n.s. 14. Paris: F. Paillart, 1994.

——. "De la Gaule romaine à l'Africa: À la recherche d'un héritage commun." In *Camille Jullian, l'histoire de la Gaule et le nationalisme français: Actes du colloque organisé à Lyon le 6 décembre 1988*, 39–49. Lyons: Société des amis de Jacob Spon, 1991.

——. "Un document cartographique inédit sur l'occupation de l'espace dans les Aurès à l'époque romaine." In *L'Africa romana: Atti del X convegno di studio, Oristano, 11–13 dicembre 1992*, edited by Attilio Mastino and Paola Ruggeri, 331–46. Sassari: Editrice Archivio Fotografico Sardo, 1994.

——. "Du voyage à l'archéologie: L'exemple de l'Afrique du Nord." In *Du voyage savant aux territoires de l'archéologie. Voyageurs, amateurs et savants à l'origine de l'archéologie moderne*, edited by Manuel Royo, Martine Denoyelle, Emmanuelle Hindy, Timothy Champion, and David Louyot, 273–90. Paris: De Boccard, 2011.

——. "L'entrée de l'Algérie antique dans l'espace méditerranéen." In *Enquêtes en Méditerranée: Les expéditions françaises d'Égypte, de Morée et d'Algérie. Actes du colloque Athènes-Napulie, 8–10 juin 1995*, edited by Marie-Noëlle Bourguet, Daniel Nordman, Vassilis Panayotopoulos, and Maroula Sinarellis, 179–91. Athens: Institut de recherches néohelléniques, 1999.

——. "Une étape méconnue de l'histoire du Tombeau de la Chrétienne: Les premières fouilles (1855–1856)." In *Ubique amici: Mélanges offerts à Jean-Marie Lassère*, edited by Christine Hamdoune, 87–99. Montpellier: Université Paul-Valéry, CERCAM, 2001.

——. "L'*Exercitus africae* inspiratrice de l'armée française d'Afrique: *Ense et aratro.*" *Antiquités africaines* 27, no. 1 (1991): 141–49.

——. "La mise en place de l'archéologie officielle en Algérie, XIXe–début du XXe." In *Aspects de l'archéologie au XIXème siècle; Actes du colloque international tenu à La Diana à Montbrison les 14 et 15 octobre 1995*, edited by Pierre Jacquet and Robert Périchon, 351–400. Recueil de mémoires et documents sur Le Forez publiés par la Société de la Diana 28. Montbrison: La Diana, 2000.

——. "Napoléon III et l'archéologie algérienne." *Bulletin de la Société historique de Compiègne* 37 (2001): 193–210.

——. "Le premier reportage photographique archéologique en Afrique du Nord: Les fouilles du Tombeau de la Chrétienne en 1855–56." In *L'Africa romana XIV: Atti del XIV convegno di studio, Sassari, 7–10 dicembre 2000*, edited by Mustapha Khanoussi, Paola Ruggeri, and Cinzia Vismara, 2119–21. Rome: Carocci, 2002.

——. "La production d'images sur l'espace méditerranéen dans la Commission d'exploration scientifique d'Algérie: Les dessins du capitaine Delamare." In *L'invention scientifique de la Méditerranée: Égypte, Morée, Algérie*, edited by Marie-Noëlle Bourguet, Bernard Lepetit, Daniel Nordman, and Maroula Sinarellis, 223–38. Paris: Éditions de l'École des hautes études en sciences sociales, 1998.

——. "Réussites et déboires d'une oeuvre archéologique unique: Le Colonel Carbuccia au nord de l'Aurès (1848–1850)." *Antiquités africaines* 32, no. 1 (1996): 145–74.

Doutté, Edmond. *En tribu*. Paris: Paul Geuthner, 1914.

Doyon, Wendy. "The History of Archaeology through the Eyes of Egyptians." In *Unmasking Ideology: The Vocabulary, Symbols, and Legacy of Imperial and Colonial Archaeology*, edited by Bonnie Effros and Guolong Lai. Los Angeles: Cotsen Institute of Archaeology Press, in press.

——. "On Archaeological Labor in Modern Egypt." In *Histories of Egyptology: Interdisciplinary Measures*, edited by William Carruthers, 141–56. New York: Routledge, 2015.

Dumontier, Maurice. "L'École d'application de l'artillerie et du génie à Metz sous la Seconde République et le Second Empire." *Pays lorrain* 42, no. 4 (1961): 122–35.

——. "L'École d'artillerie et du génie de Metz sous l'Empire, la Restauration et la Monarchie de Juillet (1803–1845)." *Pays lorrain* 42, no. 3 (1961): 86–102.

Dunwoodie, Peter. *Writing French Algeria*. Oxford: Clarendon, 1998.

Duval, Noël, and Michel Janon. "Le dossier des églises d'Hr Guesseria: Redécouverte du rapport Carbuccia (1849) et de l'aquarelle originale de la mosaïque. Une fouille partielle en 1908?" *Mélanges de l'École française de Rome: Antiquité* 97, no. 2 (1985): 1079–112.

Duval, Yvette. *Lambèse chrétienne: La gloire et l'oubli de la Numidie romaine à l'Ifrîqiya*. Paris: Institut d'études augustiniennes, 1995.

Dyson, Steven L. *In Pursuit of Ancient Pasts: A History of Classical Archaeology in the Nineteenth and Twentieth Centuries*. New Haven: Yale University Press, 2006.

Effros, Bonnie. "Berber Genealogy and the Politics of Prehistoric Archaeology and Craniology in French Algeria (1860s–1880s)." *British Journal for the History of Science* 50, no. 1 (2017): 61–81. doi:10.1017/S0007087417000024.

——. "Colliding Empires: French Display of Roman Antiquities Expropriated from Postconquest Algeria (1830–1870)." In *Objects of War: The Material Culture of Conflict and Displacement*, edited by Leora Auslander and Tara Zahra. Ithaca, NY: Cornell University Press, 2018, 50–77.

——. "'Elle pensait comme un homme et sentait comme une femme': Hortense Lacroix Cornu (1809–1875) and the Musée des antiquités nationales de Saint-Germain-en-Laye." *Journal of the History of Collections* 24, no. 1 (2012): 25–43.

——. "The Germanic Invasions and the Academic Politics of National Identity in Late Nineteenth-Century France." In *Gebrauch und Missbrauch des Mittelalters, 19.–21. Jahrhundert/Uses and Abuses of the Middle Ages, 19th–21st Century/Usages et mésuages du Moyen Age du XIXe au XXIe siècle*, edited by János Bak, Jörg Jarnut, Pierre Monnet, and Bernd Schneidmüller, 81–94. MittelalterStudien 17. Munich: Wilhelm Fink, 2009.

——. "Indigenous Voices at the Margins: Nuancing the History of Colonial Archaeology in Nineteenth-Century Algeria." In *Unmasking Ideology: The Vocabulary, Symbols, and Legacy of Imperial and Colonial Archaeology*, edited by Bonnie Effros and Guolong Lai. Los Angeles: Cotsen Institute of Archaeology Press, in press.

——. "Museum-Building in Nineteenth-Century Algeria: Colonial Narratives in French Collections of Classical Antiquities." *Journal of the History of Collections* 28, no. 2 (2016): 243–59.

——. *Uncovering the Germanic Past: Merovingian Archaeology in France, 1830–1914.* Oxford: Oxford University Press, 2012.

Eldem, Edhem. "From Blissful Indifference to Anguished Concern: Ottoman Perceptions of Antiquities, 1799–1869." In *Scramble for the Past: A Story of Archaeology in the Ottoman Empire, 1753–1914,* edited by Zainab Bahrani, Zeynep Çelik, and Edhem Eldem, 281–329. Istanbul: SALT, 2011.

Emerit, Marcel. "Un curé de l'Aude ateint du mal du siècle: Jean Terson." In *Actes du 102e Congrès national des Sociétés savantes, Limoges 1977,* 351–60. Section d'histoire moderne et contemporaine 1. Paris: Bibliothèque nationale, 1978.

——. "La lutte entre les généraux et les prêtres aux débuts de l'Algérie française." *Revue africaine* 97, nos. 434–435 (1953): 66–97.

——. *Madame Cornu et Napoléon III d'après les lettres de l'empereur et d'autres documents inédits.* Paris: Les Presses Modernes, 1937.

——. "Les mémoires de Terson déporté de 1848." *Revue africaine* 91 (1947): 235–53.

——. "Une source pour l'histoire du Second Empire: Les souvenirs du général Desvaux." *Revue d'histoire moderne et contemporaine* 21, no. 1 (1974): 27–32.

Fanon, Frantz. *The Wretched of the Earth.* Translated by Richard Philcox. New York: Grove Press, 2004.

Fantar, M'hamed H. "Pionniers de l'archéologie punique." In *La Tunisie mosaïque: Diasporas, cosmopolitisme, archéologies de l'identité,* 501–12. Toulouse: Presses universitaires du Mirail, 2000.

Fenwick, Corisande. "Archaeology and the Search for Authenticity: Colonialist, Nationalist, and Berberist Visions of an Algerian Past." In *TRAC 2007: Proceedings of the 17th Annual Theoretical Roman Archaeology Conference,* edited by Corisande Fenwick, Meredith Wiggins, and Dave Wythe, 75–88. Oxford: Oxbow Books, 2008.

Février, Paul-Albert. *Approches du Maghreb romain: Pouvoirs, différences et conflits.* Vol. 1. Aix-en-Provence: ÉDISUD, 1989.

Ford, Caroline. "Culture and Conservation in France and Her Colonies 1840–1940." *Past and Present* 183 (2004): 173–98.

——. "The Inheritance of Empire and the Ruins of Rome in French Colonial Algeria." *Past and Present* 226, Suppl. 10 (2015): 57–77.

Foubert, Bernard. "Les volontaires nationaux de l'Aube et de la Seine-Inférieure à Saint-Domingue (octobre 1792–janvier 1793)." *Bulletin de la Société d'histoire de la Guadeloupe* 51, no. 1 (1982): 3–54.

Francis, Kyle. "Catholic Missionaries in Colonial Algeria: Faith, Foreigners, and France's Other Civilizing Mission, 1848–1883." *French Historical Studies* 39, no. 4 (2016): 685–715.

Freed, Joann. *Bringing Carthage Home: The Excavations of Nathan Davis, 1856–1859.* Oxford: Oxbow Books, 2011.

——. "Le Père Alfred-Louis Delattre (1850–1932) et les fouilles archéologiques de Carthage." *Histoire, monde et cultures religieuses* 4, no. 8 (2008): 67–100.

Frémeaux, Jacques. *Les bureaux arabes dans l'Algérie de la conquête.* Paris: Éditions Denoël, 1993.

——. "Souvenirs de Rome et présence française au Maghreb: Essai d'investigation." In *Connaissances du Maghreb: Sciences sociales et colonisation,* edited by Jean-Claude Vatin, 29–46. Paris: CNRS Éditions, 1984.

Frend, William H. C. *The Archaeology of Early Christianity: A History*. Minneapolis: Fortress Press, 1996.

——. *From Dogma to History: How Our Understanding of the Early Church Developed*. London: SCM Press, 2003.

Gallois, William. "Dahra and the History of Violence in Early Colonial Algeria." In *The French Colonial Mind*, Vol. 2: *Violence, Military Encounters, and Colonialism*, edited by Martin Thomas, 3–25. Lincoln: University of Nebraska Press, 2011.

——. *A History of Violence in the Early Algerian Colony*. New York: Palgrave Macmillan, 2013.

Geggus, David Patrick. "Slavery, War, and Revolution in the Greater Caribbean, 1789–1815." In *A Turbulent Time: The French Revolution and the Greater Caribbean*, edited by David Barry Gaspar and David Patrick Geggus, 1–50. Bloomington: Indiana University Press, 1997.

Gerson, Stéphane. *The Pride of Place: Local Memories and Political Culture in Nineteenth-Century France*. Ithaca, NY: Cornell University Press, 2003.

Gillette, Alain, and Abdelmalek Sayad. *L'immigration algérienne en France*. 2nd ed. Paris: Éditions Entente, 1984.

Godlewska, Anne. "Map, Text and Image: The Mentality of Enlightened Conquerors. A New Look at the *Description de l'Égypte*." *Transactions of the Institute of British Geographers* 20, no. 1 (1995): 5–28.

Gosden, Chris. *Anthropology and Archaeology: A Changing Relationship*. Oxford: Routledge, 1999.

Gran-Aymerich, Ève. "L'archéologie française en Grèce: Politique archéologique et politique méditerranéenne 1798–1945." In *Les politiques de l'archéologie du milieu du XIXe à l'orée du XXIe: Colloque organisé par l'École française d'Athènes à l'occasion de la célébration du 150e anniversaire de sa fondation*, edited by Roland Étienne, 63–78. Athens: École française d'Athènes, 2000.

——. *Dictionnaire biographique d'archéologie, 1798–1945*. Paris: CNRS Éditions, 2001.

——. "Épigraphie française et allemande au Maghreb: Entre collaboration et rivalité (1830–1914)." *Mitteilungen des Deutschen archäologischen Instituts, Römische Abteilung* 117 (2011): 567–600.

——. "Karl Benedikt Hase (1780–1864) et Désiré Raoul-Rochette (1789–1854) d'après leur correspondance: Deux médiateurs culturels entre France et Allemagne à la Bibliothèque nationale (1801–1864)." In *S'écrire et écrire sur l'antiquité: L'apport des correspondances à l'histoire des travaux scientifiques*, edited by Corinne Bonnet and Véronique Krings, 83–103. Grenoble: Éditions Jérôme Millon, 2008.

——. "Le Musée Napoléon III au Palais de l'industrie, miroir de la politique archéologique du Second Empire." *Bulletin de la Société historique de Compiègne* 37 (2001): 29–47.

——. *Naissance de l'archéologie moderne, 1798–1945*. Paris: CNRS Éditions, 1998.

——. "Theodor Mommsen (1817–1903) et ses correspondants français: La 'fabrique' internationale de la science." *Journal des savants* 1, no. 1 (2008): 177–229.

Gran-Aymerich, Ève, and Jean Gran-Aymerich. "La création des Écoles françaises d'Athènes, Rome et Madrid." In *Les débuts des sciences de l'homme*, edited by Bernard-Pierre Lécuyer and Benjamin Matalon, 175–87. Communications 56. Paris: Seuil, 1992.

Gran-Aymerich, Ève, and Jürgen von Ungern-Sternberg. *L'antiquité partagée: Correspondances franco-allemandes (1823–1861)*. *Karl Benedikt Hase, Désiré Raoul-Rochette, Karl Otfried Müller, Otto Jahn, Theodor Mommsen*. Mémoires de l'Académie des inscriptions et belles-lettres 47. Paris: Académie des inscriptions et belles-lettres, 2012.

Granger, Catherine. *L'empereur et les arts: La liste civile de Napoléon III*. Mémoires et documents de l'École des chartes 79. Paris: École des chartes, 2005.

Greenhalgh, Michael. *Constantinople to Córdoba: Dismantling Ancient Architecture in the East, North Africa, and Islamic Spain*. Leiden: Brill, 2012.

——. *From the Romans to the Railways: The Fate of Antiquities in Asia Minor*. Leiden: Brill, 2013.

——. *Marble Past, Monumental Present: Building with Antiquities in the Mediaeval Mediterranean*. Leiden: Brill, 2009.

——. *The Military and Colonial Destruction of the Roman Landscape of North Africa, 1830–1900*. Leiden: Brill, 2014.

——. "The New Centurions: French Reliance on the Roman Past during the Conquest of Algeria." *War and Society* 16, no. 1 (1998): 1–28.

Grigor, Talinn. "'They Have Not Changed in 2,500 Years': Art, Archaeology, and Modernity in Iran." In *Unmasking Ideology: The Vocabulary, Symbols, and Legacy of Imperial and Colonial Archaeology*, edited by Bonnie Effros and Guolong Lai. Los Angeles: Cotsen Institute of Archaeology Press, in press.

Grimal, Nicolas. "Mariette Pacha." In *Histoire et archéologie méditerranéennes sous Napoléon III: Actes du 21e colloque de la Villa Kérylos à Beaulieu-sur-Mer les 8 & 9 octobre 2010*, edited by André Laronde, Pierre Toubert, and Jean Leclant, 179–92. Cahiers de la Villa 'Kérylos' 22. Paris: Diffusion de Boccard, 2011.

Gsell, Stéphane. *Exploration scientifique de l'Algérie pendant les années 1840–1845: Archéologie*. Paris: Ernest Leroux, 1912.

——. "Introduction." In *Histoire et historiens de l'Algérie*, 1–15. Collection du centenaire de l'Algérie (1830–1930) 4. Paris: Félix Alcan, 1931.

Guichard, Vincent. "Les recherches archéologiques à Gergovie sous le Second Empire: Quelques notes historiographiques." *Bulletin de la Société historique de Compiègne* 37 (2001): 117–26.

Guigniaut, Joseph-Daniel. "Notice historique sur la vie et les travaux de Charles-Benoît Hase, membre de l'Académie des inscriptions et belles-lettres." *Mémoires de l'Institut national de France* 27, no. 1 (1877): 247–73.

Guillet, François. "Arcisse de Caumont, un archéologue provincial." In *Arcisse de Caumont (1801–1873): Érudit normand et fondateur de l'archéologie française. Actes du colloque international organisé à Caen du 14 au 16 juin 2001*, edited by Vincent Juhel, 81–93. Mémoires de la Société des antiquaires de Normandie 40. Caen: Société des antiquaires de Normandie, 2004.

Gutron, Clémentine. "L'abbé Bourgade (1806–1866), Carthage et l'Orient: De l'antiquaire au publiciste." *Anabases* 2 (2005): 177–91.

——. *L'archéologie en Tunisie (XIXe–XXe siècle): Jeux généalogiques sur l'Antiquité*. Paris: Karthala, 2010.

——. "Archéologies maghrébines et relectures de l'histoire: Autour de la patrimonialisation de Paul-Albert Février." *L'année du Maghreb* 10 (2014): 163–80.

Hamilakis, Yannis. "Decolonizing Greek Archaeology: Indigenous Archaeologies, Modernist Archaeology and the Post-Colonial Critique." In *A Singular Authority: Archaeology and Hellenic Identity in Twentieth-Century Greece*, edited by Dimitris Damaskos and Dimitris Plantzos, 273–84. Athens: Mouseio Benaki, 2008.

———. "From Ethics to Politics." In *Archaeology and Capitalism*, edited by Yannis Hamilakis and Philip Duke, 15–40. Walnut Creek, CA: Left Coast Press, 2007.

———. "Indigenous Archaeologies in Ottoman Greece." In *Scramble for the Past: A Story of Archaeology in the Ottoman Empire, 1753–1914*, edited by Zainab Bahrani, Zeynep Çelik, and Edhem Eldem, 49–69. Istanbul: SALT, 2011.

———. *The Nation and Its Ruins: Antiquity, Archaeology, and the National Imagination in Greece*. Oxford: Oxford University Press, 2007.

Hannoum, Abdelmajid. *Violent Modernity: France in Algeria*. Cambridge, MA: Harvard University Press, 2010.

Harley, J. Brian. "Deconstructing the Map." *Cartographica* 26, no. 2 (1989): 1–20.

———. "Maps, Knowledge, and Power." In *The Iconography of Landscape: Essays on the Symbolic Representation, Design, and Use of Past Environments*, edited by Denis Cosgrove and Stephen Daniels, 277–312. Cambridge: Cambridge University Press, 1988.

Harmand, Jacques. "Les travaux de la Commission de topographie des Gaules autour d'Alésia et l'album inédit conservé au Musée des antiquités nationales." *Comptes rendus des séances de l'Académie des inscriptions et belles-lettres* 104, no. 1 (1960): 107–15.

Hartman, Elwood. *Three Nineteenth-Century French Writers/Artists and the Maghreb: The Literary and Artistic Depictions of North Africa by Théophile Gautier, Eugène Fromentin and Pierre Loti*. Tübingen: Gunter Narr, 1994.

Hase, Alexander von. "Weimar–Paris–St. Petersburg: Karl Benedikt Hase (1780–1864) und sein europäisches Umfeld." *Archiv für Kulturgeschichte* 76, no. 1 (1994): 165–200.

Haynes, Ian. *Blood of the Provinces: The Roman Auxilia and the Making of a Provincial Society from Augustus to the Severans*. Oxford: Oxford University Press, 2013.

Heffernan, Michael J. "The Desert in French Orientalist Painting during the Nineteenth Century." *Landscape Research* 16, no. 2 (1991): 37–42.

———. "'A Dream as Frail as Those of Ancient Time': The Incredible Geographies of Timbuctoo." *Environment and Planning D: Society and Space* 19, no. 2 (2001): 203–25.

———. "An Imperial Utopia: French Surveys of North Africa in the Early Colonial Period." In *Maps and Africa: Proceedings of a Colloquium at the University of Aberdeen, April 1993*, edited by Jeffrey C. Stone, 80–107. Aberdeen: Aberdeen University African Studies Group, 1994.

———. "A Paper City: On History, Maps, and Map Collections in Eighteenth- and Nineteenth-Century Paris." *Imago mundi* 66, Suppl. 1 (2014): 5–20.

———. "The Parisian Poor and the Colonization of Algeria during the Second Republic." *French History* 3, no. 4 (1989): 377–403.

Heffernan, Michael J., and Keith Sutton. "The Landscape of Colonialism: The Impact of French Colonial Rule on the Algerian Rural Settlement Pattern, 1830–1987." In

Colonialism and Development in the Contemporary World, edited by Chris Dixon and Michael J. Heffernan, 121–52. London: Mansell, 1991.

Heurgon, Jacques. "L'oeuvre archéologique française en Algérie." *Bulletin de l'Association Guillaume Budé* ser. 4, 15, no. 4 (1956): 3–26.

Hincker, Louis. "Archive d'une 'Afrique fantôme.'" *L'Homme* 195–196, nos. 3–4 (2010): 307–32.

Hingley, Richard. *Roman Officers and English Gentlemen: The Imperial Origins of Roman Archaeology.* London: Routledge, 2000.

Hirsch, Pam. *Barbara Leigh Smith Bodichon, 1827–1891: Feminist, Artist and Rebel.* London: Chatto and Windus, 1998.

Hoexter, Miriam. *Endowments, Rulers, and Community: Waqf al-Haramayn in Ottoman Algiers.* Leiden: Brill, 1998.

Huot, Jean-Louis. "L'archéologie dans le monde musulman." In *L'avenir du passé: Modernité de l'archéologie*, edited by Jean-Paul Demoule and Bernard Stiegler, 183–95. Paris: La Découverte, 2008.

Irwin, Robert. *For Lust of Knowing: The Orientalists and Their Enemies.* London: Allen Lane, 2006.

Jacobs, Justin. "Confronting Indiana Jones: Chinese Nationalism, Historical Imperialism, and the Criminalization of Aurel Stein and the Raiders of Dunhuang, 1899–1944." In *China on the Margins*, edited by Sherman Cochran and Paul G. Pickowicz, 65–90. Ithaca, NY: Cornell University Press, 2010.

Jaïdi, Houcine. "L'archéologie tunisienne au lendemain de la Révolution du 14 janvier 2011: État des lieux, inquiétudes et horizons." In *Pour une histoire de l'archéologie XVIIIe siècle–1945: Hommage de ses collègues et amis à Ève Gran-Aymerich*, edited by Annick Fenet and Natacha Lubtchansky, 465–72. Bordeaux: Ausonius, 2015.

Janon, Michel. "Recherches à Lambèse." *Antiquités africaines* 7, no. 1 (1973): 193–220.

Jansen, Jan. "Die Erfindung des Mittelmeerraums im kolonialen Kontext: Die Inszenierungen des 'lateinischen Afrika' beim *Centenaire de l'Algérie française 1930*." In *Der Süden: Neue Perspektiven auf eine europäische Geschichtsregion*, edited by Frithjof Benjamin Schenk, 175–205. Frankfurt: Campus, 2007.

——. *Erobern und Erinnern: Symbolpolitik, öffentlicher Raum und französischer Kolonialismus in Algerien, 1830–1950.* Munich: Oldenbourg, 2013.

——. "Inszenierungen des antiken Erbes in 'Französisch-Algerien.'" In *Das große Spiel: Archäologie und Politik zur Zeit des Kolonialismus (1860–1940), Ruhr-Museum, Weltkulturerbe Zollverein, Essen, 11. Februar–13. Juni 2010*, edited by Charlotte Trümpler, 528–37. Cologne: DuMont, 2008.

——. "Karthago und die Pères blancs." In *Das große Spiel: Archäologie und Politik zur Zeit des Kolonialismus (1860–1940), Ruhr-Museum, Weltkulturerbe Zollverein, Essen, 11. Februar–13. Juni 2010*, edited by Charlotte Trümpler, 538–49. Cologne: DuMont, 2008.

Jasanoff, Maya. *Edge of Empire: Lives, Culture, and Conquest in the East, 1750–1850.* New York: Knopf, 2005.

Jenkins, Tiffany. *Losing Their Marbles: How the Treasures of the Past Ended Up in Museums and Why They Should Stay There.* Oxford: Oxford University Press, 2016.

Jourdy, Général. *L'instruction de l'armée française de 1815 à 1902.* Paris: Félix Alcan, 1903.

Kaddache, Mahfoud. *L'Algérie dans l'antiquité*. Algiers: SNED, 1972.

Kaplan, Sam. "Documenting History, Historicizing Documentation: French Military Officials' Ethnological Reports on Cilicia." *Comparative Studies in Society and History* 44, no. 2 (2002): 344–69.

Kateb, Kamel. *Européens, "indigènes" et juifs en Algérie (1830–1962): Représentations et réalités des populations*. Cahier 145. Paris: Éditions de l'Institut national d'études démographiques, 2001.

Kaufman, Asher. "The Formation of an Identity in Lebanon in 1920." *Middle Eastern Studies* 37, no. 1 (2001): 173–94.

Kinealy, Christine. *This Great Calamity: The Irish Famine*. Dublin: Gill and Macmillan, 1994.

Konvitz, Josef W. *Cartography in France 1660–1848: Science, Engineering, and Statecraft*. Chicago: University of Chicago Press, 1987.

Koumas, Ahmed, and Chéhrazade Nafa. *L'Algérie et son patrimoine: Dessins français du XIXe siècle*. Paris: Monum, Éditions du patrimoine, 2003.

Kunichika, Michael. *"Our Native Antiquity": Archaeology and Aesthetics in the Culture of Russian Modernism*. Boston: Academic Studies Press, 2015.

Lafi, Nora. "Biographie de Laurent-Charles Féraud: Une passion coloniale." In *Laurent-Charles Féraud: Peintre et témoin de la conquête de l'Algérie*, edited by Bernard Merlin, 103–8. Saint-Rémy-en-l'Eau: Éditions Monelle Hayot, 2010.

Lageman, Thessa. "Horror Still Fresh a Year after Tunisia Museum Attack." *Aljazeera*, March 18, 2016. http://www.aljazeera.com/news/2016/03/horror-fresh-year-tunisia-museum-attack-160314115053039.html.

Laronde, André. "Claude Le Maire et l'exportation des marbres de Lepcis Magna." *Bulletin de la Société nationale des antiquaries de France* (1993): 242–55.

Larrouy, Patricia. "Le Musée de Saint-Germain sous la Troisième République." *Bulletin archéologique du Comité des travaux historiques et scientifiques* 28 (2001): 25–43.

Laurent, Franck. *Victor Hugo face à la conquête de l'Algérie*. Paris: Maisonneuve et Larose, 2001.

"Lazare Costa, l'italien qui découvrit le tophet de Cirta." In *Exposition Internationale "Les Phéniciens en Algérie: Les voies du commerce entre la Méditerranée et l'Afrique Noire" Palais de la Culture Moufdi Zakaria-Algeri, 20 janvier–20 février 2011*, edited by Lorenza Manfredi and Amel Soltani. http://cherchel-project.isma.cnr.it/index.php?option=com_content&view=article&id=133&Itemid=135&lang=fr.

Leask, Nigel. *Curiosity and the Aesthetics of Travel Writing, 1770–1840: From an Antique Land*. Oxford: Oxford University Press, 2002.

Le Bohec, Yann. *La Troisième légion auguste*. Paris: CNRS Éditions, 1989.

Leclant, Jean. "Allocation d'ouverture." In *Histoire et archéologie méditerranéennes sous Napoléon III: Actes du 21e colloque de la Villa Kérylos à Beaulieu-sur-Mer les 8 & 9 octobre 2010*, edited by André Laronde, Pierre Toubert, and Jean Leclant, vii–xii. Cahiers de la Villa 'Kérylos' 22. Paris: Diffusion de Boccard, 2011.

———. "Préface." In *La Commission d'exploration scientifique d'Algérie: Une héritière méconnue de la Commission d'Égypte*, edited by Monique Dondin-Payre, 7–10. Mémoires de l'Académie des inscriptions et belles-lettres, n.s. 14. Paris: F. Paillart, 1994.

Leclercq, Henri. "Orléansville." In *Dictionnaire d'archéologie chrétienne et de liturgie*, Vol. 12, pt. 2, edited by Fernand Cabrol and Henri Leclercq, 2719–35. Paris: Letouzey et Ané, 1936.

Le Cour Grandmaison, Olivier. "Conquête de l'Algérie: La guerre totale." In *Le massacre, objet d'histoire*, edited by David El Kenz, 253–74. Paris: Gallimard, 2005.

Le Gall, Joël. *Alésia: Archéologie et histoire*. New ed. Paris: Fayard, 1980.

——. "Nouveaux apercus sur les fouilles d'Alésia sous le Second Empire." *Comptes rendus des séances de l'Académie des inscriptions et belles-lettres* 105, no. 1 (1961): 73–79.

Leniaud, Jean-Michel. "L'état, les sociétés savantes et les associations de défense du patrimoine: L'exceptions françaises." In *Patrimoine et passions identitaires*, edited by Jacques Le Goff, 137–54. Paris: Arthème Fayard, 1998.

——. *Viollet-le-Duc ou les délires du système*. Paris: Éditions Mengès, 1994.

Léon, Paul. *La vie des monuments français: Destruction, restauration*. Paris: Éditions A. et J. Picard et Cie, 1951.

Lepetit, Bernard. "Missions scientifiques et expéditions militaires: Remarques sur leur modalités d'articulation." In *L'invention scientifique de la Méditerranée: Égypte, Morée, Algérie*, edited by Marie-Noëlle Bourguet, Bernard Lepetit, Daniel Nordman, and Maroula Sinarellis, 97–116. Paris: Éditions de l'École des hautes études en sciences sociales, 1998.

Le Romanacee, Thomas. "Algérie: le Tombeau de la Chrétienne en péril." *Le Figaro*, March 17, 2017, http://www.lefigaro.fr/culture/2017/03/17/03004-20170317ARTFIG 00010-algerie-le-tombeau-de-la-chretienne-en-peril.php.

Lorcin, Patricia. *Imperial Identities: Sterotyping, Prejudice and Race in Colonial Algeria*. London: I. B. Tauris, 1995.

——. "Imperialism, Colonial Identity, and Race in Algeria, 1830–1870: The Role of the French Medical Corps." *Isis* 90, no. 4 (1999): 653–79.

——. "Rome and France in Africa: Recovering Colonial Algeria's Latin Past." *French Historical Studies* 25, no. 2 (2002): 295–329.

Lyons, Amelia H. *The Civilizing Mission in the Metropole: Algerian Families and the French Welfare State during Decolonization*. Stanford, CA: Stanford University Press, 2013.

Mahé, Alain. *Histoire de la Grande Kabylie XIXe–XXe siècles: Anthropologie historique du lien social dans les communautés villageoises*. Saint Denis: Éditions Bouchene, 2001.

Malarkey, James. "The Dramatic Structure of Scientific Discovery in Colonial Algeria; A Critique of the Journal of the 'Société archéologique de Constantine' (1853–1876)." In *Connaissances du Maghreb: Sciences sociales et colonisation*, edited by Jean-Claude Vatin, 137–60. Paris: CNRS Éditions, 1984.

Marchand, Suzanne L. "The Dialectics of the Antiquities Rush." In *Pour une histoire de l'archéologie XVIIIe siècle–1945: Hommage de ses collègues et amis à Ève Gran-Aymerich*, edited by Annick Fenet and Natacha Lubtchansky, 191–206. Bordeaux: Ausonius, 2015.

——. *Down from Olympus: Archaeology and Philhellenism in Germany, 1750–1970*. Princeton, NJ: Princeton University Press, 1996.

——. *German Orientalism in the Age of Empire: Religion, Race, and Scholarship*. Cambridge: Cambridge University Press, 2009.

Mattingly, David J. *Tripolitania*. London: B. T. Batsford, 1995.

McAllister, Edward. "Silence and Nostalgia: Periodizing the Past in an Algiers Neighborhood." *Der Islam* 91, no. 1 (2014): 135–60.

McCarty, Matthew. "French Archaeology and History in the Colonial Maghreb: Inheritance, Presence, and Absence." In *Unmasking Ideology: The Vocabulary, Symbols, and Legacy of Imperial and Colonial Archaeology*, edited by Bonnie Effros and Guolong Lai. Los Angeles: Cotsen Institute of Archaeology Press, in press.

McGrath, Ann. "Critiquing the Discovery Narrative of Lady Mungo." In *Unmasking Ideology: The Vocabulary, Symbols, and Legacy of Imperial and Colonial Archaeology*, edited by Bonnie Effros and Guolong Lai. Los Angeles: Cotsen Institute of Archaeology Press, in press.

Merryman, John H. "Two Ways of Thinking about Cultural Property." *American Journal of International Law* 80 (1986): 831–53.

Meskell, Lynn. "Archaeology Matters." In *Archaeology under Fire: Nationalism, Politics, and Heritage in the Eastern Mediterranean and Middle East*, edited by Lynn Meskell, 1–12. London: Routledge, 1998.

———. "Gridlock: UNESCO, Global Conflict, and Failed Ambitions." *World Archaeology* 47, no. 2 (2015): 225–38.

Mitchell, Timothy. *Colonising Egypt*. Cambridge: Cambridge University Press, 1988.

Modéran, Yves. *Les Maures et l'Afrique romaine (IVe–VIIe siecle)*. Bibliothèque des Écoles françaises d'Athènes et de Rome 340. Rome: École française de Rome, 2003.

Morizot, Jean. *L'Aurès ou le mythe de la montagne rebelle*. Paris: L'Harmattan, 1991.

Morizot, Pierre. "La naissance de l'archéologie romaine en Algérie." In *Histoire et archéologie méditerranéennes sous Napoléon III: Actes du 21e colloque de la Villa Kérylos à Beaulieu-sur-Mer les 8 & 9 octobre 2010*, edited by André Laronde, Pierre Toubert, and Jean Leclant, 155–77. Cahiers de la Villa 'Kérylos' 22. Paris: Diffusion de Boccard, 2011.

Moser, Stephanie. "Making Expert Knowledge through the Image: Connections between Antiquarian and Early Modern Scientific Illustration." *Isis* 105, no. 1 (2014): 58–99.

Nora, Pierre. *Les français d'Algérie*. Paris: René Julliard, 1961.

Nordman, Daniel. "Mission de savants et occupation: L'exploration scientifique de l'Algérie (vers 1840–1860)." In *Vers l'Orient par la Grèce: Avec Nerval et d'autres voyageurs*, edited by Louis Droulia and Vasso Mentzou, 81–89. Paris: Klincksieck, 1993.

———. "La notion de région dans l'*Exploration scientifique de l'Algérie*. Premiers jalons," In *Enquêtes en Méditerranée: Les expéditions françaises d'Égypte, de Morée et d'Algérie. Actes du colloque Athènes-Napulie, 8–10 juin 1995*, edited by Marie-Noëlle Bourguet, Daniel Nordman, Vassilis Panayotopoulos, and Maroula Sinarellis, 141–57. Athens: Institut de recherches néohelléniques, 1999.

Oliver, Bette W. *From Royal to National: The Louvre Museum and the Bibliothèque Nationale*. Lanham, MD: Rowman and Littlefield, 2007.

Orgogozo, Chantal. "Le voyage dans la Basse et la Haute-Egypte." In *Dominique-Vivant Denon: L'oeil de Napoléon, Paris, musée du Louvre, 20 octobre 1999–17 janvier 2000*, 108–15. Paris: Réunion des musées nationaux, 1999.

Oulebsir, Nabila. "From Ruins to Heritage: The Past Perfect and the Idealized Antiquity in North Africa." In *Multiple Antiquities—Multiple Modernities: Ancient Histories in Nineteenth Century European Cultures*, edited by Gábor Klaniczay, Michael Werner, and Ottó Gecser, 335–64. Frankfurt: Campus, 2011.

——. "Rome ou la Méditerranée? Les relevés d'architecture d'Amable Ravoisié en Algérie, 1840–1842." In *L'invention scientifique de la Méditerranée: Égypte, Morée, Algérie*, edited by Marie-Noëlle Bourguet, Bernard Lepetit, Daniel Nordman, and Maroula Sinarellis, 239–71. Paris: Éditions de l'École des hautes études en sciences sociales, 1998.

——. *Les usages du patrimoine: Monuments, musées et politique coloniale en Algérie (1830–1930)*. Paris: Éditions de la Maison des sciences de l'homme, 2004.

Paquelot, Françoise, and Vincent Guichard, eds. *Sur les traces de César: Enquête archéologique sur les sites de la guerre des Gaules*. Glux-en-Glenne: Musée de Bibracte, 2002.

Parslow, Christopher Charles. *Rediscovering Antiquity: Karl Weber and the Excavation of Herculaneum, Pompeii, and Stabiae*. Cambridge: Cambridge University Press, 1995.

Paysant, L. "Un président de la Société historique algérienne." *Revue africaine 55* (1911): 5–15.

"P. Christian (1811–1872): Pseudonym individuel." Bibliothèque Nationale de France: Data.bnf.fr. Last updated July 2, 2017. http://data.bnf.fr/12327453/p__christian/#author. other_forms.

Pétursdóttir, Þora. "Concrete Matters: Ruins of Modernity and the Things Called Heritage." *Journal of Social Archaeology* 13, no. 1 (2012): 31–53.

Picard, Charles. "Éloge funèbre de M. Émile Espérandieu, membre libre de l'Académie." *Comptes-rendus des séances de l'Académie des inscriptions et belles-lettres* 83, no. 2 (1939): 161–72.

Pillorget, René. "Les deux voyages de Napoléon III en Algérie (1860 et 1865)." *Revue du Souvenir Napoléonien* 363 (1989): 30–36.

Pluchon, Pierre. *Toussaint Louverture: Un révolutionnaire noir d'Ancien Régime*. Paris: Fayard, 1989.

Pommier, Édouard. "Naissance des musées de province." In *Les lieux de mémoire*, Vol. 2, pt. 2, edited by Pierre Nora, 451–95. Paris: Gallimard, 1986.

Porch, Douglas. *The French Foreign Legion: A Complete History of the Legendary Fighting Force*. New York: Harper Collins, 1991.

Prochaska, David. "Fire on the Mountain: Resisting Colonialism in Algeria." In *Banditry, Rebellion, and Social Protest in Africa*, edited by Donald Crummey, 229–52. London: James Currey, 1986.

——. *Making Algeria French: Colonialism in Bône, 1870–1920*. Cambridge: Cambridge University Press, 1990.

Pyenson, Lewis. *Civilizing Mission: Exact Sciences and French Overseas Expansion, 1830–1940*. Baltimore: Johns Hopkins University Press, 1993.

Rabeisen, Elisabeth. "Les hommes de l'empereur ou les pionniers des Antiquités nationales." In *Vercingétorix et Alésia: Saint-Germain-en-Laye. Musée des Antiquités nationales 29 mars–18 juillet 1994*, 240–43. Paris: Réunion des Musées nationaux, 1994.

Rabinow, Paul. *French Modern: Norms and Forms of the Social Environment*. Cambridge, MA: MIT Press, 1989.

Rabut, Élisabeth. "Le Centre des archives d'Outre-Mer: Premier centre délocalisé des Archives nationales." In *Histoire d'archives: Recueil d'articles offert à Luce Favier par ses collègues et amis*, 105–15. Paris: Société des amis des Archives de France, 1997.

Rambaud, Michel. *L'art de la déformation historique dans les commentaires de César.* Rev. ed. Paris: Société d'Édition "Les belles lettres," 1966.

Raymond, André. "Les caracteristiques d'une ville arabe 'moyenne' au XVIIIe siècle: Le cas de Constantine." *Cahiers de Tunisie* 137–38 (1986): 175–95.

———. "Le centre d'Alger en 1830." *Revue de l'Occident musulman et de la Méditerranée* 31, no. 1 (1981): 73–83.

———. "The Ottoman Conquest and the Development of the Great Arab Towns." *International Journal of Turkish Studies* 1, no. 1 (1980): 84–101.

Reddé, Michel. *Alésia: L'archéologie face à l'imaginaire.* Paris: Éditions Errance, 2003.

———. "Les fouilles du Second Empire autour d'Alésia: À la lumière des recherches récentes." *Bulletin de la Société historique de Compiègne* 37 (2001): 93–116.

Reid, Donald Malcolm. *Whose Pharoahs? Archaeology, Museums, and Egyptian National Identity from Napoleon to World War I.* Berkeley: University of California Press, 2002.

Reinach, Salomon. "Nécrologie: Le Colonel Stoffel." *Revue archéologique* ser. 3, 17 (1907): 329–32.

Rey-Goldzeiguer, Annie. *Le royaume arabe: La politique algérienne de Napoléon III, 1861–1870.* Algiers: Société nationale d'édition et de diffusion, 1977.

Richardson, Edmund. "Of Doubtful Antiquity: Fighting for the Past in the Crimean War." In *From Plunder to Preservation: Britain and the Heritage of Empire, c. 1800–1940*, edited by Astrid Swenson and Peter Mandler, 31–48. Proceedings of the British Academy 187. Oxford: Oxford University Press, 2013.

Ridley, Jack Blaine. "Marshal Bugeaud, the July Monarchy and the Question of Algeria, 1841–1847: A Study in Civil-Military Relations." PhD diss., University of Oklahoma, 1970.

Ridout, Nicholas. *Passionate Amateurs: Theatre, Communism, and Love.* Ann Arbor: University of Michigan Press, 2013.

Rigambert, Catherine. *Le droit de l'archéologie française.* Paris: Picard, 1996.

Riggs, Christina. "Colonial Visions: Egyptian Antiquities and Contested Histories in the Cairo Museum." *Museum Worlds: Advances in Research* 1, no. 1 (2013): 65–84.

Robb, Graham. *The Discovery of France: A Historical Geography from the Revolution to the First World War.* New York: W. W. Norton, 2007.

Rohan-Chabot, La Comtesse de, ed. *Souvenirs de Froehner.* Nogent-le-Rotrou: Imprimerie de Daupeley-Gouverneur, 1931.

Rose-Greenland, Fiona. "ISIS at the Mosul Museum: Material Destruction and Our Moral Economies of the Past." *Perspectives: A Publication of the Theory Section of the American Sociological Association* 37, no. 1 (2015): 18–21.

Roughton, Richard A. "Economic Motives and French Imperialism: The 1837 Tafna Treaty as a Case Study." *Historian* 47, no. 3 (1985): 360–81.

Ruedy, John. *Land Policy in Colonial Algeria: The Origins of the Rural Public Domain.* Near Eastern Studies 10. Berkeley: University of California Press, 1967.

Saadoui, Ahmed. "Le remploi dans les mosquées ifrîqiyennes aux époques médiévale et moderne." In *Lieux de cultes: Aires votives, temples, églises, mosquées. IXe colloque international sur l'histoire et l'archéologie de l'Afrique du Nord antique et médiévale, Tripoli, 19–25 février 2005*, 295–304. Paris: CNRS Éditions, 2008.

Sahli, Mohamed C. *Décoloniser l'histoire: Introduction à l'histoire du Maghreb*. Cahiers libres 77. Paris: François Maspero, 1965.

Said, Edward W. *Culture and Imperialism*. New York: Vintage, 1993.

Saint-Cyr: 290 ans d'histoire. Dixième aniversaire de la création par le Général de Gaulle du Collège militaire de Saint-Cyr. Saint-Cyr: Collège militaire, 1976.

Sari, Djilali. *Le désastre démographique*. Algiers: Société nationale d'Édition et Diffusion, 1982.

Scheibinger, Londa. "Skeletons in the Closet: The First Illustrations of the Female Skeleton in Eighteenth-Century Anatomy." *Representations* 14 (1986): 42–82.

Schlanger, Nathan. "The Mirror of Perseus: Europe and the Destruction of Archaeological Heritage." *European Journal of Archaeology* 20, no. 1 (2017): 24–26.

Schnapp, Alain. "L'archéologie en France et en Europe au temps de Napoléon III." *Bulletin de la Société historique de Compiègne* 37 (2001): 15–28.

———. "Préface: L'antiquaire, le Levant et les archéologues." In *L'archéologie en Tunisie (XIXe–XXe siècle): Jeux généalogiques sur l'Antiquité*, by Clémentine Gutron, 9–13. Paris: Karthala, 2010.

Scott, James C. *Seeing Like a State: How Certain Schemes to Improve the Human Condition Have Failed*. New Haven: Yale University Press, 1998.

Serman, William. *Les origines des officiers français, 1848–1870*. Paris: Publications de la Sorbonne, 1979.

Serres-Jacquart, Thibaud. "Joseph Vattier de Bourville (1812–1854): Notes sur un explorateur de la Cyrénaïque." *Journal des savants* 2, no. 1 (2001): 393–429.

Sessions, Jennifer E. *By Sword and Plow: France and the Conquest of Algeria*. Ithaca, NY: Cornell University Press, 2011.

———. "Colonizing Revolutionary Politics: Algeria and the French Revolution of 1848." *French Politics, Culture, and Society* 33, no. 1 (2015): 75–100.

———. "'Unfortunate Necessities': Violence and Civilization in the Conquest of Algeria." In *France and Its Spaces of War: Experience, Memory, Image*, edited by Patricia M. E. Lorcin and Daniel Brewer, 29–44. New York: Palgrave Macmillan, 2009.

———. "Why the French Presidential Candidates Are Arguing about Their Colonial History." *The Conversation*. April 11, 2017. http://theconversation.com/why-the-french-presidential-candidates-are-arguing-about-their-colonial-history-75372.

Shaw, Brent D. *Bringing in the Sheaves: Economy and Metaphor in the Roman World*. Toronto: University of Toronto Press, 2013.

———. "Climate, Environment, and History: The Case of Roman North Africa." In *Climate and History: Studies in Past Climates and Their Impact on Man*, edited by T. M. L. Wigley, M. J. Ingram, and G. Farmer, 379–403. Cambridge: Cambridge University Press, 1981.

Shaw, Wendy. "From Mausoleum to Museum: Resurrecting Antiquity for Ottoman Modernity." In *Scramble for the Past: A Story of Archaeology in the Ottoman Empire, 1753–1914*, edited by Zainab Bahrani, Zeynep Çelik, and Edhem Eldem, 423–41. Istanbul: SALT, 2011.

———. *Possessors and Possessed: Museums, Archaeology, and the Visualization of History in the Late Ottoman Empire*. Berkeley: University of California Press, 2003.

Singer, Barnett, and John Langdon. *Cultured Force: Makers and Defenders of the French Colonial Empire.* Madison: University of Wisconsin Press, 2004.

Slim, Hédi. "L'amphithéâtre et le site d'El Jem vus par les voyageurs des siècles derniers." In *La Tunisie mosaïque: Diasporas, cosmopolitisme, archéologies de l'identité,* 485–99. Toulouse: Presses universitaires du Mirail, 2000.

Smith, Marc. "Jules Quicherat." In *L'École nationale des chartes: Histoire de l'École depuis 1821,* edited by Yves-Marie Bercé, Olivier Guyotjeannin, and Marc Smith, 149–50. Thionville: Gerard Klopp, 1997.

Stein, Sarah Abrevaya. *Saharan Jews and the Fate of French Algeria.* Chicago: University of Chicago Press, 2014.

Stoler, Ann Laura. *Along the Archival Grain: Epistemic Anxieties and Colonial Common Sense.* Princeton, NJ: Princeton University Press, 2009.

———. *Carnal Knowledge and Imperial Power: Race and the Intimate in Colonial Rule.* Berkeley: University of California Press, 2002.

Sullivan, Antony Thrall. *Thomas-Robert Bugeaud: France and Algeria, 1874–1849. Politics, Power and the Good Society.* Hamden, CT: Archon Books, 1983.

Taithe, Bertrand. "Humanitarianism and Colonialism: Religious Responses to the Algerian Drought and Famine of 1866–1870." In *Natural Disasters, Cultural Responses: Case Studies toward a Global Environmental History,* edited by Christof Mauch and Christian Pfister, 137–65. Lanham, MD: Lexington Books, 2009.

Talbert, Richard J. A. "Carl Müller (1818–1894), S. Jacobs, and the Making of Classical Maps in Paris for John Murray." *Imago mundi* 46 (1994): 128–50.

Theis, Laurent. "Guizot et les institutions de mémoire." In *Les lieux de mémoire,* Vol. 2, pt. 2, edited by Pierre Nora, 569–92. Paris: Gallimard, 1986.

Thomas, Joseph. *The Universal Dictionary of Biography and Mythology.* Vol. 4. Reprint ed. New York: Cosimo, 2009.

Thompson, Victoria. "'I Went Pale with Pleasure': The Body, Sexuality, and National Identity among French Travelers to Algiers in the Nineteenth Century." In *Algeria and France 1800–2000: Identity-Memory-Nostalgia,* edited by Patricia M. E. Lorcin, 18–32. Syracuse: Syracuse University Press, 2006.

Thomson, Ann. *Barbary and Enlightenment: European Attitudes towards the Maghreb in the 18th Century.* Leiden: Brill, 1987.

Thorn, Dorothy M. *The Four Seasons of Cyrene: The Excavation and Explorations in 1861 of Lieutenants R. Murdoch Smith, R. E. and Edwin A. Porcher, R. N.* Rome: "L'Erma" di Bretschneider, 2007.

Trigger, Bruce G. "Alternative Archaeologies: Nationalist, Colonialist, Imperialist." *Man* n.s. 19, no. 3 (1989): 355–70.

Trouillot, Michel-Rolph. *Silencing the Past: Power and the Production of History.* Boston: Beacon, 1995.

Trumbull, George R., IV. *An Empire of Facts: Colonial Power, Cultural Knowledge, and Islam in Algeria, 1870–1914.* Cambridge: Cambridge University Press, 2009.

Turin, Yvonne. "La crise de campagnes algériennes en 1868, d'après l'enquête de la même année." *Revue d'histoire et de civilisation du Maghreb* 13 (January 1976): 79–86.

Twyman, Michael. *Lithography 1800–1850: The Techniques of Drawing on Stone in England and France and Their Application in Works of Topography.* London: Oxford University Press, 1970.

United Nations. *United Nations Educational, Scientific and Cultural Organisation Convention Concerning the Protection of the World Cultural and Natural Heritage.* Adopted by the General Conference at its seventeenth session, Paris, November 16, 1972.

Vasunia, Phiroze. "Greater Rome and Greater Britain." In *Classics and Colonialism,* edited by Barbara Goff, 38–64. London: Gerald Duckworth, 2005.

Vatan, Anne. "Le camp de Châlons et les fouilles de l'empereur." *Bulletin de la Société historique de Compiègne* 37 (2001): 83–92.

Vatin, Jean-Claude. *L'Algérie politique: Histoire et société.* Cahiers de la Fondation nationale des sciences politiques 192. Paris: Armand Colin, 1974.

Versteegh, Kees. *The Arabic Language.* New York: Columbia University Press, 2001.

Waltisperger, Chantal. "Regard diachronique sur l'activité des sociétés savantes et leurs publications." In *Patrimoine historique et archéologique de l'Essone,* 2nd ed., 33–38. Évry: Association pour le développement de la lecture publique en Essone, 1990.

Weil, Patrick. *How to Be French: Nationality in the Making since 1789.* Translated by Catherine Porter. Durham, NC: Duke University Press, 2008.

Weiss, Gillian. *Captives and Corsairs: France and Slavery in the Early Modern Mediterranean.* Stanford, CA: Stanford University Press, 2011.

Welch, Cheryl B. "Colonial Violence and the Rhetoric of Evasion: Tocqueville on Algeria." *Political Theory* 31, no. 2 (2003): 235–64.

Wilder, Gary. *The French Imperial Nation-State: Negritude and Colonial Humanism between the Two World Wars.* Chicago: University of Chicago Press, 2005.

Windler, Christian. *La diplomatie comme expérience de l'autre: Consuls français au Maghreb (1700–1840).* Geneva: Droz, 2002.

Wood, Raymund F. "Berbrugger, Founder of Algerian Librarianship." *Journal of Library History* 5, no. 3 (1971): 237–56.

Yacono, Xavier. "La Régence d'Alger en 1830 d'après l'enquête des Commissions de 1833–1834." *Revue de l'Occident musulman et de la Méditerranée* 1, no. 1 (1966): 229–44; 2, no. 1 (1966): 227–47.

Zarobell, John. *Empire of Landscape: Space and Ideology in French Colonial Algeria.* University Park: Pennsylvania State University Press, 2010.

Zouzou, Abdelhamid. *L'Aurès au temps de la France coloniale: Évolution politique, économique et sociale (1837–1939).* Vol. 1. Algiers: Éditions Distribution Houma, 2001.

INDEX

Note: Page numbers in *italics* indicate illustrations